15.22

Philosophy of the Buddha
The Heart of Confucius
Tao Teh King by Lao Tzu
Bhagavad Gita: The Wisdom of Krishna
Yoga: Union with the Ultimate
Yoga for Business Executives
Types of Intuition
Polarity, Dialectic, and Organicity
Philosophy, an Introduction
What Makes Acts Right?
Logic for Beginners
Directory of American Philosophers

The World's
Living Religions

Archie J. Bahm

SOUTHERN ILLINOIS UNIVERSITY PRESS
Carbondale and Edwardsville

FEFFER & SIMONS, INC.
London and Amsterdam

Dedication: To Hubert G. Alexander

COPYRIGHT © 1964 *by* Archie J. Bahm
All rights reserved
Reprinted by arrangement with Archie J. Bahm
Arcturus Books edition October 1971
This edition printed by offset lithography
  in the United States of America
International Standard Book Number 0–8093–0529–1

contents

Errata

Page 53, line 22:	*For* century *read* millennium
Page 156, line 31:	*For Bah-Kua read* Yin-Yang symbol or Tao symbol
Page 157, line 15:	*For Bah-Kua read* Yin-Yang symbol or Tao symbol
Page 159, line 3:	*For* ☰ *read* ☰
Page 159, line 4:	*For* ☰ *read* ☰
Page 169, line 9:	*For* Khing *read* King
Page 207, line 22:	*For* then *read* than
Page 319, line 33:	*For* limitation *read* limitations

Introduction

Chapter 1 What is Religion?

A new trend in religious thinking augurs arrival of a new dimension in religious outlook. Interest in comparing religions is as old as their first contacts. But what was once a slow trickle of books on comparative religion has grown to a steady stream. Increase in quantity does not, by itself, constitute a difference in kind or dimension. But the concern felt by adherents of one religion in formulating their attitudes toward other religions, previously more often regarded as optional and dealt with casually, has developed a sense of urgency. The natural tendency of each religious tradition to judge itself superior and self-sufficient, even when recognizing the need for coexistence, has warranted relative complacency. But increasingly, Christians, for example, realize that they now engage in "an encounter," something they can no longer run away from if they choose.

The growing number of calls that I receive to speak about Oriental religions to church groups is evidence of a deep need. The study of other religions has ceased to be merely a matter of personal curiosity; it is becoming a standard feature of instruction, in which each religion has a vested interest. The widening spread of awareness of the existence of such vested interests in studying religions comparatively is part of the new dimension indicated here. We may not yet be ready for still another dimension characterized by concern for ways of amalgamating. The few who dream of practical progress in such a dimension must be judged as out of step and living before their time. Today's problems consist in a growing need for dealing with ways of coexisting interactively. Yesterday's problem—how to secure "religious freedom" and mutual "religious toleration"—has been largely solved in many places. But the need for attaining relatively passive accommodation now gives way to concern about how to deal with a more dynamic situation, in which persons inspired by different religions interact in intricate and intimate ways. The adjustment problems of highly specialized and increasingly interdependent persons guided by differing religions intensify the urgency for greater sympathetic insight into other religions. This forced cooperation and competition of differing religious ideals produces a natural demand for insights that can be relied upon. Proponents of each religion must now be able to justify to adherents their own evaluations of other religions in ways that they can regard as fair and objectively defensible. Growing awareness that each religion has an interest in not running away from this challenge characterizes our new dimension in religious thinking.

Consequently, each religious and sectarian group that has become alive to its situation either already has prepared or is now busily engaged in preparing a book on comparative religions. The example with which I happen to be most familiar is a volume, *Our Religion and Our Neighbors,* developed under the auspices of the Union of American Hebrew Congregations by Rabbis M. G. Miller and S. D. Schwartzmann. An experimental edition, not for general circulation, was submitted to interested parties for critical examination. The difficult task of pleasing both conservative and liberal, broad and narrow, and scholarly and popular preferences in the production of such a volume is certainly unenviable. But I wish to focus attention upon a particular predicament. The publication of such a work involves both value and danger.

Each group, though it might wish to keep its devotees comfortably isolated from divergent ideals, now recognizes that it is better to help them learn the truth about other religions and to demonstrate the superiority of its own views in open comparison than to try to hide from their followers the facts about the existence and nature of other religions. Production of a volume satisfactory for this purpose must thus be regarded as a desirable achievement.

But when the unexcelled value of one's own sect has been proposed, such a book on comparative religions must express and demonstrate the sect's superior excellence. Here, "the truth" about other religions must respect the perspective from which it is made. Facts about other religions, such as dates, names, books, practices, quoted doctrines, can be objectively presented. Yet, when the question of the relative merits of these other religions is considered, a sectarian cannot admit either equality with or the superiority of other religions without thereby surrendering something essential to his own sectarianism. How can he face frankly and expose fully the virtues and successes of other religions without jeopardizing the hold upon the loyalty of his fellow believers?

Despite the predicaments tormenting authors of such books, the writing of works on comparative religion, in which one studies and judges other religions with his own taken as standard, appears to be a very healthy trend in religious literature in Western civilization and, indeed, in the whole world. This trend occurs not merely as a current fad ("Everybody's doing it") but marks a step in the development of religious ideals in Western thought, both within each sect, which thereby recognizes that it must now come to terms in an open fashion with other religions, and in the general religious milieu within which the well-read citizen finds himself. This trend will naturally beget another which, indeed, has already begun.

As more readers pick up books expressing the attempts of different sects to state not merely their own doctrines but to claim that their own perspective of other religions is the correct one, such readers will take upon themselves the task of assessing such books on comparative religion. The appearance of these books in increasing quantities naturally magnifies the problem of how to evaluate their relative merits. The point being made here is that, whereas earlier generations of readers confronted conflicting claims of exclusivistic proponents, current generations of readers now confront uneven quality in the fairness with which religious proponents deal with this problem of comparing religions.

Hence we now enjoy a new level of exposition and propagation of faiths and, in effect, dwell in a new dimension for judging different faiths. The sectarian must now take into consideration the effect that his success or failure in being objective and fair in dealing with other religions will have upon a better-informed and more highly sensitive generation of readers. The relative degree of objectivity that he can muster in presenting his comparative work becomes an item about which he must expect to be judged. Both his own colleagues and others increasingly realize that the more distortion that an author feels required to make in defending his own sect, the more it will seem to his readers that his sectarian doctrine cannot stand up in face of the full truth about other religions. Thus the presentation of a relatively fair volume on comparative religion has now become a serious responsibility to which each sect must attend. If it does not, its own devotees will wonder why it fails to meet in open competition on this score.

But what can *I* do for you? Although the work of preparing comparative religious texts expressing the perspectives of each sect will remain unfinished until volumes representing all sects and religions have been prepared, the production of another such volume is not my aim. As treatments of comparative religions from sectarian viewpoints multiply, there naturally arises the question of whether it is possible to compare religions on some basis that transcends sectarian perspectives. Is it possible to study religions in such a way that the claims of each can be stated in its own terms and that all can be compared on bases that they have in common? Or, if any one of them has some relatively unique virtues held up as standards, judgment of other religions by these standards will be balanced by an endeavor to judge such a religion by the unique virtues of other religions also upheld as standards.

A real issue appeared in concrete form at a recent meeting of the Southwestern Union for the Study of the Great Religions. Among the guests at this meeting were Christian professors from nearby seminaries. Their interest in comparative religion is genuine and their views are liberal, especially when contrasted with those of many staunch supporters of their particular denominations. Yet, the predominating view expressed by them was that "comparative religion" of necessity meant comparison of other religions with their own taken as standard. My own view is that "comparative religions" does not exist in its fullest and fairest sense until judgments are based upon standards common to all of them and until each religion that proposes a standard of its own by which to measure other religions is also measured by standards proposed by other religions. "Comparative religions" as a study cannot approach being an "objective science" until those who study it become willing to commit themselves to comparisons based upon "objective standards."

My own experience, after abandoning as inadequate the sectarian outlook in which I was trained, has consisted in teaching courses in comparative religions for a quarter of a century in state universities. In such an environment, not only relatively free from pressures of sectarian biases but suffused with an atmosphere requiring one to be fair to all of them, my own desire to be fair received both sanction and support. Although doubtless I cannot wholly escape the influences of my Christian training and of the Western civilization in which my mind has been nurtured and shaped, genuineness of commitment to democratic ideals has demanded of me that fairness and objectivity of treatment be extended from Western sects to world religions. Sympathetic study of them has revealed both virtues unsuspected by outsiders and broader bases for comparison. Prolonged accommodation to the task of trying to represent each religion in terms of its own perspective, and a personal philosophy that holds that there is some truth to all positive views, have made me no longer capable of supporting a sectarian bias, unless bias against bias is itself somehow sectarian.

I shall try to provide some aid in introducing you to that additional dimension in which comparisons of religions are based upon virtues common to all of them. Mine is not the first such attempt nor will it be the last. But positive support of thinking in this dimension is not yet general. The merits of this additional dimension need to be upheld, and I consider it my task and duty to do so. Doubtless several generations of thinkers committed to exploring and expanding upon the virtues of this dimension will be needed before mankind will be genuinely ready to tackle a further problem: that of religious amalgamation.

The Importance of Religion

To some, the importance of religion is so obvious that any remarks about it seem superfluous. To others, religion consists in superstition, which man gradually outgrows and which becomes increasingly unnecessary as science progresses to provide us with better ways of living than religion ever did or can. Neither of these views is correct, from the perspective in which this book is written. Religion is important, even though its significance is perpetually challenged and constantly in doubt. Religious values, like other values, must prove themselves again and again to each generation and to every individual.

Religion is important. It will never be outgrown. But its nature and significance do not remain perennially obvious and need to be rediscovered again and again. The particular forms, doctrines, and institutions through which the religious needs and experiences of some people have been expressed may become obsolete, and their continuance often becomes detrimental to healthy religion. Identification of religion merely with any of its specific forms is a mistake, because then, when these forms outlive their usefulness, people mistakenly infer that religion has outlived its usefulness. "Man is incurably religious." The needs in man that gave rise to his religious experiences and expressions in the first place remain inherent in his nature. But just as automobile and jet plane have replaced ox and horse, skyscrapers have supplanted caves, and wash-and-wear fabrics have superseded animal skins, so we should expect the modes of expression serving our religious needs in cosmopolitan society to be different from those which inspired the fearful shepherd, Moses, on a fiery mountainside or the wondering camel driver, Mohammed, in a Meccan cave.

Cultural lag, which naturally afflicts all social institutions somewhat, often characterizes religious beliefs and practices. The deeper, more profound, and more important our needs, the more we hesitate to disturb and revise institutions that have been long established for serving them, especially when we remain unclear about what alternatives will serve them better. Yet, the more obsolete and ineffective such institutions become, the more important does revitalization, *i.e.*, revision or replacement, become. We remain unprepared to do so as long as we identify religion with its obsolete establishments rather than with the need that gave rise to them in the first place. A study of the nature of religion in general, which can be derived better from examining and comparing many religions than from confining our insight to any one of them, may help to remedy our unpreparedness.

One unfortunate association, which has become fixed in the minds of many, both appreciators and depreciators of religion alike, is that of religion and magic. But "magic" belongs to "technology," not to "religion." Its association with religion derives from its being the kind of technology available to people at the time when early religious doctrines were formulated. Religion has no need for magic. The results obtainable from religious insight and practice will continue to seem "miraculous," *i.e.*, marvelous, to those who first do not and then do obtain them, but no violation of any natural principle is required to serve a very natural need.

Religion is important. But such an assertion continues to be unsatisfactory so long as we have not yet said what religion is. Thus far, we have considered only what religion is not.

Before we say what religion is, as conceived in the present volume, let us take a quick look at some of the difficulties in defining any comprehensive field. Following a procedure used in describing "philosophy" (See my *Philosophy, An Introduction,* Ch. I.), we distinguish six "components" of religion. These are: "problems," "attitude," "method," "conclusions," "activity," and "effects." Each will be explored in turn.

1. Problems: The problems of religion are value problems. Religion, which as an area of belief and practice is distinguishable from ethics, aesthetics, economics, and politics, shares with them concerns for values. All pertain to man's desire to increase good and reduce evil. All value-interests may overlap and interdepend, but the terms "religion," "ethics," "aesthetics," "economics," and "politics" designate different emphases in men's ways of creating, conserving, and consuming values. For example, when concerned with the nature of "oughtness" as an ethician, a person can and should then see how business ethics, political ethics, and religious ethics all constitute parts or branches of ethics as a general science having its own problems, standards of evaluation, and ways for reaching its own conclusions. So likewise, religion is something that comprehends ethical, economic, political, and aesthetic values within its purview. But we must guard against the tendency, more obvious in the behavior of others than in ourselves, to give any one of these fields, including religion, the right to dominate over other fields. The political scientist tends to see the course of history determined by political rather than economic factors, whereas the economist naturally views the evidence with which he is acquainted as favoring the economic determination of history. Ethicians, aestheticians, and theologians (not to mention astronomers, geologists, biologists, and dieticians) all tend to emphasize the primacy of their own field, and some even assert its exclusive predominance.

This note of warning is included not merely as a platitudinous generalization for every specialist, and for each of us as we too become more specialized, but as a bit of stage-setting before I plunge into my task of stressing the superior importance of religion in human affairs. This task is one I undertake willingly, just as in another volume I willingly attempt to state the claims of the superior importance of ethics when viewed in terms of its own problems and methods and its service in interpreting the good of mankind.

To say that religion is an area of life that has problems of its own is not, in itself, to say what those problems are. I should like, if possible, to avoid settling any dispute about what must be included among the problems of religion, at least until after the disputes have been examined. Here we merely mention one of the answers that have been given as to what constitutes religious problems.

Religion consists in man's concern for his ultimate value and how to attain it, preserve it, and enjoy it. The particular doctrines, institutions, techniques, and practices that we call "religious" have their origin, nature, and end determined by this basic concern. People, cultures, and philosophies may differ regarding what is man's ultimate value as well as how it may be attained. Some foolishly deny that man has any value at all, simply because they have concocted a scheme of the universe, based upon genuine but partial evidence, in which they find no place for value. Some posit a single ultimate value before which all other values must fade into insignificance by comparison. Some insist that ultimate values cannot be compared. And some design elaborate schemes for distinguishing higher and lower values, even higher and lower religious values. Since most of us have difficulty in appreciating abstract schemes, we prefer graphic, dramatic accounts of the nature and attainability of our ultimate values. Those cultural traditions which early adopted an appealing story have the additional virtue of seeing their account stand the test of time in its service to this basic human need. Yet cultural erosion plays havoc with pictures too primitive to be adaptable for integrating explanatory concepts and new varieties of personally experienced values into traditional schema. Each culture, and each person, must decide for itself how long it is best to pour new wine into old bottles and when it is best to adopt new bottles. But the problem of what to do about man's ultimate concern and how to attain it, preserve it, and enjoy it always remains. And this problem, at least, is fundamental to religion.

Another general characteristic of the problems constituting religion is that they are essentially practical problems, in contrast with the problems of philosophy and science, which are primarily theoretical. The philosopher and the general scientist seek understanding. What is done with his attainment is not, merely as philosopher and scientist, his concern. But since each philosopher and scientist is also a man, having practical concerns, he is interested in what use may be made of such understanding. If one cannot begin to approach practical solutions of religious problems without first understanding the nature of man and the universe, he is dependent upon philosophy and science for such understanding. Some of us today prefer to accept the science and philosophy of man's early yesterdays. Others demand up-to-date versions. But that religious practice depends upon some conception of the nature of man and the universe surely must be conceded. In this sense, religion as a practical endeavor depends upon philosophy for its theoretical presuppositions. Any weakness in philosophical foundations tends to make itself felt in the success, or lack of it, with which one pursues his religion.

Our philosophical task is to understand our ultimate nature and value; and our religious task is to attempt to attain that value. To the extent that we cannot successfully pursue our efforts without an adequate philosophy, our religion depends upon our philosophy. But to the extent that philosophy, having as its problem the understanding of such ultimate nature and value, derives its problem from man's practical, *i.e.*, religious, need for such understanding—and its usefulness as an actual guide to such attainment—it is dependent, even completely dependent, upon the conception of man as religious. There is only one thing a man can do with his religion, and that is to live it, practice it, and embody it in his life. If he does not, it is not religion. For religion is essentially practical.

Because religion is practical, its problems are practical problems. When a man becomes puzzled about an explanation to which he has given some assent, his disturbance is a practical disturbance. The need he has for settling his theoretical doubts is a practical need. Hence, the quest for certainty, which is the source of man's search for understanding, is a part of his quest for security. "Religion" is the name we give to those practical attempts to secure our ultimate values. We cannot be deeply religious without also being philosophical. But our philosophy is a means to our ultimate ends, not an end in itself.

We must leave our survey of problems as one component of religion without exploring the many particular problems resulting from various ways of conceiving the nature of man's ultimate value. These ways constitute the subject matter of the following chapters dealing with each of the world's living religions. But these problems, multifarious and seemingly incompatible as they are, are still all religious.

2. *Attitude:* Whereas essential ingredients in philosophical and scientific attitudes are "open-mindedness" and "ob-

jectivity," these are not essential to our religious nature, except as necessary means to the end of attaining a true understanding. Our feeling of security remains incomplete so long as we remain in doubt. Hence, a proper goal of religion is to eliminate doubt. But one cannot feel secure so long as he is aware that his system for eliminating doubt is itself dubious. Hence, for many, the shortest distance from doubt to certainty is through more and more doubting. Needless disturbance of those enjoying freedom from doubt is a mistake, unless their freedom somehow seriously endangers the welfare of others. But the crushing doubts which demand their due merely multiplies them and stokes the fires of desperation that may overwhelm one with fears of permanent insecurity. Nothing less than honest efforts to deal objectively with doubts can serve to settle them sufficiently in the long run.

But the attitude required before one can reach his religious goal is one of assent, not of doubt, one of affirmation, not of denial, one of assurance, not of uncertainty. One does not need to be open-minded in order to be religious. In fact, open-mindedness, so long as that signifies a feeling of failure to settle important questions about ultimate reality and value, prevents one from being completely religious. Yet to those so inclined, open-mindedness is felt to be necessary for attaining and maintaining a true view of life, and must be regarded as essential to the religious security of such persons. When one has committed himself to open-mindedness, he cannot feel honest when he knows that he has closed his mind to genuine evidence.

These two attitudes—that one need not be, even cannot be, open-minded in order to be religious and that one may be, even must be, open-minded in order to be religious—may appear contradictory to some. Yet in fact they are not. Both are intended to promote an affirmation of faith. Those who cannot feel secure in their faith until they obliterate all desire to question must seek to close their minds once for all as soon as possible. Those who cannot feel fully affirmative unless they first willingly face up to every doubt that presents itself as a challenge to their convictions and then settle it to their satisfaction, must demand of themselves that they remain open-minded forever. Other possibilities, such as remaining open regarding some questions and fully settled regarding others, may also better serve the needs of some. Or one may take the attitude that human ignorance and incapacity make it impossible for him to make up his mind as to whether it is best to retain an open or a closed mind and that "being religious" consists in resigning oneself to a state of perpetual uncertainty; but about this attitude too he may have closed his mind to alternatives other than so "resigning himself."

The foregoing apparent contradiction, revealing two or more different ways of being religious, constitutes additional evidence of difficulties in trying to reduce religion to some neat and simple definition that will serve for all purposes.

3. Method: Methods should be suited to problems. Just as philosophy and the sciences as fields of inquiry call for critical and exploratory methods, suspended judgment, rigorous restraint of wishful thinking, so the methods of religion, whose purpose is to attain assurance of achieving one's ultimate values, should be devised in a way to bring about such assurance. Since this assurance is greater when one feels that he already enjoys his ultimate value than when he merely believes he has attained the method that guarantees its future enjoyment, the more fully a person is convinced that he has already arrived at the goal of religion, the more fully religious he is.*

*If this latter statement be true, it may be possible to judge different religions as "more religious" or "less religious" in proportion to the ease and fullness with which they induct their members into feelings of having already attained life's goal. The Calvinistic doctrine of "election," for example, which has been gradually discarded as a too severe and unreasonable set of conditions for an all-powerful, all-loving God to have imposed, retains an element of psychological truth in it. One who feels he is already "elect" experiences much greater assurance than one who believes he must await some future "Judgment Day." Hindu culture is generally regarded as "more religious" than European culture. If this view is correct, it may be due to the fact that Hindus more commonly consider themselves as already divine and as lacking in final and full divinity only in ways that are within the power of each individual to eliminate. Western re-

Persons, and cultures, differ as to what seem to be the best ways of acquiring assurance. Some may wish to approach the matter empirically and learn for themselves. However, most individuals not only discover themselves inducted by birthright into a living community providing them with ready-made kinds of assurance, but also discover, when they venture out for themselves, that independent discovery is impossible. Whether highly integrated socially or temperamentally rebellious, persons soon learn to take advantage of short-cuts whenever they become available. The inquirer naturally appeals to those who know or claim to know. Thus, as we say, he appeals to authority. The greater or more reliable the authority, the greater his confidence in it tends to be. When an explanation and method are more ancient, primitive, original, and thus longer-enduring, they may seem more worthy. When a doctrine and technique are used approvingly by more people, they appear more workable and reliable. When a view of, and a way to, life's ultimate value have the approval of, and in turn sustain, more powerful social organizations, politically, economically, artistically, and intellectually, they gain a psychical force that promotes our confidence. Integration of "Church" and "State," *when* that means integration of religion and government, promotes the ends both of religion and of government.

Unfortunately, so often religious institutions become more institutional than religious, and their suffering either from cultural lag or from internal incompetence and politics makes them detrimental to the very cause they are designed to promote. Furthermore, antagonism between diverse religious institutions often makes necessary a separation of Church and State as a matter of wise political policy. Unfortunately, or perhaps fortunately,

---

ligions, or any religions, which picture man either as inherently incompetent to attain his own ultimate value or as forever dependent upon some external power whose dispensation regarding his ultimate fate remains uncertain, must be judged as "less religious" by this standard. Although, obviously, the standard itself is open to debate, if it obtains and especially if it is implied by presuppositions inherent in such religions, Western religions may now, as they compete increasingly with Hindu religions for men's allegiance, be encountering a challenge in which they will fall shorter than most of them yet realize.

"religion" need not be identified with "Church," for there may be more religion outside than inside churches, and long-established ecclesiastical hierarchies notoriously develop political interests and intrigues both inside and outside their churches. Even if separation diminishes an individual's feeling of assurance, it may be the best solution possible when the alternatives, *e.g.*, perpetual civil war or tyranny of one religious hierarchy over all others, are worse.

The authority appealed to is judged to be better if it knows more. Who is a better authority than the author of the universe? Somehow voiceless existence must be given a voice if man is to hear what his ultimate value is. Where God can be personified and persuaded to reveal his knowledge to man, assurance may be strengthened. However, the more ingenious and fantastic the stories of creation and revelation, the more a learned listener wonders and, reflecting, is given to doubt. It may be better to say we do not know what we do not know when religious children query us, for if we try to satisfy their childish questions with childish answers, then when they grow to intellectual manhood and "put away childish things," they may feel forced to abandon a religious tradition that deceived them by telling them too much. In a day when past revelations have proved themselves increasingly inadequate, and new revelations are prohibited by established hierarchies, appeals to such revelations have decreasing effectiveness in promoting the kind of assurance that religion needs to provide. No "science of religion" has yet "become of age." Ours is a time of transition, in which the marks of disintegration of our traditional religious institutions are clearly visible but in which the new forms of appeal have not yet come into sight. Those who identify religion with decaying institutions can see only despair, for they think that, as the church declines, religion will disappear. However, those who see the basis of religion in man's seeking his ultimate value, and not in particular institutions designed to serve that need, naturally have faith that this need will be met by newer, more vital forms in due time. A study of how these transitions have occurred in other cultures provides its own measure of insight into what to expect in the way of institutional resurgence to meet man's religious needs in our own culture.

What about wishful thinking as a method in religion? Presumably wishful thinking (misnamed "value-judgment") is an evil according to scientific method. However, plenty of evidence exists that scientists habitually wish the world were, or believe it is, more intelligible and amenable to their methods than it is. But is wishful thinking permissible in religion? Critics commonly complain that religious preachers claim more assurance of truth for their doctrines than is warranted. The fault, some of them say, lies in assenting too uncritically to "reasons of the heart." We more easily and more fully affirm a belief when and because it fulfills our desire than when it dooms us to disappointment or leaves us in a tortured state of uncertainty. Man is a credulous being. What is wrong with wishful thinking if, by wishing, we can bring ourselves closer to our goals? Of course, if wishful thinking sets up false hopes and false beliefs that must be painfully reconstructed, its evil is obvious. But it is evil not because it is wishful, but because we discover it to be false.

When we conceive the goal of religion to be beyond life, then the truth of our views about its nature and location and realizability become all-important. Faith in the reliability of our views is necessary to our feelings of security. But when the goal of life can be experienced here and now, intuitively grasped without the intervention of dubious doctrines, one's feelings of assurance can attain certainty. To the extent wishful thinking provides this intuitive grasp, it may be justified. A man is much more likely to be happy when happiness is self-induced than if he depends for it upon someone's arguing him into such a belief on "intellectual grounds." One cannot reach his goal, in either religion or science, without some degree of what William James has called "the will to believe" or without some measure of "faith in things not seen."

4. Conclusions: Philosophy and religion differ in emphasis regarding the role of conclusions or beliefs held. For philosophy, conclusions are its end product, and a philosopher may spend a lifetime in reaching them. But for religion, beliefs are presuppositions of practice and, except for the rebel, one finds beliefs already inherently present in any system of practices provided him by his cultural heritage. Whether one does or does not become critical of these beliefs, he needs them as bases for and guides to satisfactory practice. Generally speaking, the beliefs needed must give some explanation of the universe as a whole, of mankind generally and of the self in particular, and of good and evil. Regarding each of these, some account of its origin, nature, and end is included. Especially important is some view of the nature and attainability of ultimate value, since this is the goal of religion. Descriptions of the goal must not fail to provide some ideal of the best possible condition that man can achieve. It must be dubbed "the supreme value" or "the highest good" in some language or other. When the goal is depicted as not already present, some belief about its attainability and how to attain it, and what, morally, one ought to do to attain it, must be indicated.

These beliefs need not be either clear or detailed, but they should be convincing; they must be apprehensible and satisfying, and must clearly promise to serve man's need for some ultimate goal.

The term "religion" is comprehensive enough to include those beliefs serving both as ideals guiding the practices of an individual and as those which have functioned historically. When we investigate the varieties of established beliefs and practices that prevailed and evolved during the history of mankind, whether in our own or other traditions, we are "studying religion." But also, when a person seeks to learn the doctrines propounded by his own sect, he is "studying religion." And when a person critically reexamines, and perhaps reconstructs, the philosophical conclusions inherent in his religious outlook, he is "studying religion."

Conclusions or beliefs, then, constitute one of the necessary components of religion.

5. *Activity:* Religion consists in what people do when they are religious. When a person says that he belongs to such

and such a religion but does nothing about it, we incline
to judge him hypocritical. Joining a group is an activity, but
it is so minimal as to be insignificant if nothing else happens. If the goal of religion is the attainment of ultimate
value, then when a person makes neither effort nor progress toward that goal, he can hardly be considered religious
—no matter how much social and official responsibility to
ecclesiastical organizations he may take upon himself. The
monk, the yogin, the hermit may be much more religious
than the minister or priest if he devotes himself more fully
to *religious* activity.

There are three or four different kinds of activity, which
to some appear incompatible. Distinction needs to be made
between four stages that a person naturally goes through
on his way to the goal. In Western traditions, at least, he
often first discovers what religion is by being told that he
is "not religious" or that he falls short of some goal that
he ought to attain. The doctrine of "original sin" is an
effective tool for this purpose. Some teach that one cannot begin to be religious until he is first "convicted of
sin." Only then can he realize both the extent of his imperfection and that he must exert moral effort to destroy
it. Negative approaches of religion must instill fear and
consequently uphold various tabus. Although it is true in
a sense that religion began (and begins) in fear, this is a
shallow summary if it fails to depict clearly a prior recognition of some great value that one is then in fear of losing
or of not attaining.

Ignoring antecedent experiences, we will designate as
our "first stage" of activity a dawning awareness that one
does not now enjoy the goal of life. The more he believes
he remains distant from such a goal, the more fearfully he
may behave. He may cringe, weep, become distraught or
panic-stricken, depressed, discouraged. Especially if his
prior experiences were joyful, he may reject the view that
condemns him as evil. He may, indeed, rebel against his
teachers who tell him that he must learn to despise himself. If he accepts their dicta, he will then inherit a set of
directions as to what to do and what not to do. He becomes
aware of specific tabus as onerous and distasteful. This
stage consists in the discovery that the self is somehow
lacking in goodness—if not being actually evil—and the

discovery of negative and positive modes requiring unwilling assent, and the activities demanded as a consequence.

Our "second stage" of activity is guided by a desire to attain the goal and consists in efforts in that direction. Now one becomes interested, hopeful, zealous. He wants to know more about the goal and how to get to it. He becomes a seeker, a quester, a striver after a good that he does not yet know much about. He acts willfully. He becomes anxious and behaves conscientiously. He tends toward thoroughness in doctrinal understanding and in details of practice. His activity becomes lively, concerned, meticulous, if he accepts an established pattern, or he becomes moody, critical, reflective, and penetrating, if he feels he must find his way alone. But, in any case, our second stage is marked by zealous search and anxious effort. At later stages, zeal will be regarded as detrimental to religious attainment. But at this stage, zeal is necessary.

In our "third stage," willfulness gives way to willingness. Willfulness is needed for arousing sufficient effort to change things, if not the world, then at least oneself. Religious zeal is needed for improving one's knowledge, attitude, habits, and surroundings. But sooner or later one must discover that some things cannot be changed, no matter how intensely he wills to change them. What cannot be changed ought not be changed. One must learn to accept some things as they are, or are going to be, as the best that is possible. To these things one must become willing to say "Yes." Religion is essentially a matter of "yea-saying." With the Stoics, one must say, "I accept the universe." Christian tradition phrases this as "becoming completely willing to accept the will of God." Each of the world's religions has its own way of picturing for man his need for assenting to the truth that "what is is right"—a truth so easily misunderstood in languages where "is" contains ambiguity, denoting both "is present" as against past and future, and "is" in all tenses of all verbs. This latter meaning, not the former, requires assent. For if things can be changed for the better, such changeableness and future change are essential parts of "what is."

Acceptance of the universe for what it is involves a faith that man's ultimate value is to be found within it, that he will get as much as he deserves (especially since he may question whether he deserves anything), and that as much justice as possible will prevail. Must one not recognize, in one way or another, some ultimate justice involved in "God causes it to rain upon both the just and the unjust" and in the Shin doctrine that the thief has a better chance of being saved than the good man? Acceptance of the universe involves a willingness to accept paradox as somehow ultimate, and a confidence that ours is the best actual universe, and failure to enjoy its goodness is to miss life's ultimate value. At this stage, morality becomes subordinated to amorality, and the willingness to accept the ultimacy of an actual world that is amoral (whether both moral and immoral or neither moral nor immoral) is better than one of perfect morality without any taint of immorality. Hindu and Chinese religious teachers have succeeded better, on the whole, in enunciating ideals of amorality for common acceptance. Such ideals are fully present in Western religions, but Western teachers seem to emphasize morality. Idealization of amorality in daily practices reaches something of a pinnacle in the teachings of Lao Tzu, Confucius (mistaken so often as a mere moralist), and Zen.

Religious activity in our third stage consists in behaving in such a way that one obviously "accepts the universe" in his daily actions. He is no longer tormented with anxieties accompanying zeal and morality. He lives and acts with confidence that, even in the presence of such evil as exists, life is as good as it can be, especially after he has put forth his best efforts to improve it. To those whose religious insight and activity remain confined to our zealous second stage, the behavior of those in our third stage will appear as inactivity, as complacency, even as indifference. To the highly moral man, amorality seems a kind of immorality. But to the amoral man, any morality that implies intense antipathy to immorality is immature, for one who sets out to eliminate more immorality than can be eliminated thereby becomes immoral: he wants better than the best possible. He fails to realize that killing a killer does not diminish but only increases evil. The narrow moralist seeks to balance one evil against another—"an eye for an eye." The amoralist ignores unrealistic criteria of justice and not only forgives "seventy times seven" but prepares himself for the attitude that "even though he slay me yet will I love him." Our universe, which brings us all to death eventually, is yet a good, indeed the best actual, universe. The activity of our third stage consists in behaving in such a way as to appreciate this fact.

Our fourth stage consists in enjoying ultimate value. Here there exists no looking forward, no desire for more, no moral concern, no anxiety, no zeal, no conscientiousness. One does not look forward to reaching a goal that he has already attained. One desires no more when his desires are fully satisfied. Morality, anxiety, zeal, and conscientiousness become irrelevant when the ultimate value is fully realized. The "activity" constituting our fourth stage consists in intuitively apprehending and in enjoying ultimate value. Each philosophy, religion, and cultural tradition may have its own way of depicting such "activity." "Basking in bliss," "practicing presence," "beatific vision," for example, serve as phrases attempting to describe an ultimate condition that has been named, variously, "Heaven," "Nirvana," "Kaivalya," "Jivanmukti," "Pure Land," and "Zen." A duty of each religion is to make clear how the goal of religion is experienced after arrival, and one task of a study of comparative religions is to show how well each succeeds in this, as well as in how efficiently each brings its adherents to the goal.

If the end (enjoyment of ultimate value) justifies the means, each religion may be judged both by its goal and by its theory and methods for bringing men to that end. Individuals, sects, and whole cultures may be judged as "religious" according to their progress and attainment. Fear, zeal, yea-saying, and basking in bliss are all religious. But they constitute stages farther from or nearer to the goal. Full-grown religions exhibit all of the stages. Some revered authorities in the various religions speak more forcefully in support of one rather than another of these stages. Jesus, for example, gave emphasis to "this day" in which we should "care not for the morrow" because "the kingdom of heaven is within you," whereas Paul stressed fear, "lest ye be not ready," zeal in preparing for the future, morality and justice, as well as love.

These four stages are not mutually exclusive, nor need a person fully complete one before he begins to participate in the next. But one who cannot distinguish between them and their progressive sequence tends to feel confused when seemingly incompatible admonitions, such as "fear" and "fear not," are presented as equally authoritative demands upon him. And one who cannot comprehend the goal and its intrinsic value will have difficulty in seeing any good reason for "being religious" in the sense of fearing, being zealous, or of yea-saying.

6. *Effects:* Religion is what religion does. Since the time of John Dewey and other broad-gauged behaviorists, we have come to realize that a description of any phenomenon remains inadequate until we have viewed its nature in terms of its practical consequences. Thus, in addition to the activity of religious individuals, we must notice the effects of religious traditions, both as philosophical and practical systems, upon civilizations. Although one may repeat the common opinion that Hindu civilization has been more religious than Western civilization, he will be safer, perhaps, if he recognized that all of the four stages just outlined tend to be exhibited in each civilization. Older civilizations might be expected to place more stress upon the later stages. But here we enter a field of study that lies beyond the scope of our present purposes. However, we need to recognize that effects, the influences that a religion has upon other aspects of life, constitute one of the components of religion.

Religion as Yea-Saying

No attempt will be made here to present a complete or even adequate definition of religion. The nature of religion is much too complex, intricate, rich, to be capsuled fairly in a single book. Yet we need to select some basis for comparing religions in order to present a significant example of how religions may be compared to each other without taking as a standard some feature peculiarly outstanding in one of them. Religions are alike in some respects and different in others. Neither their likenesses nor differences should be overstressed. Ours is an age in which differences tend to be noted more than similarities and a counterstress upon similarities is needed to redress the imbalance. Which similarity shall we choose for exploration?

I have selected the third stage, that of "yea-saying," because all of the major religious traditions exhibit examples of this element.

What is "Yea-saying"? It is an attitude of appreciation that things are as good as they are. It may be contrasted with "Nay-saying"—the view that things should be better than they are. Nay-saying manifests dissatisfaction, discontent, dissent. It is natural to say: "But you can't say 'Yes' to everything. Evil exists, and evil is not something you can approve. Furthermore, things should be better than they are so long as we have the power to make them better." This view is true, but it is not the whole truth required by religion. Yea-saying, in its fullest sense, consists in saying "Yes" to things as they are where "things as they are" means things in all senses and verbs in all tenses, not just the present as distinct from future or past. If the future can be made better, then this "can be made better" is a part of "things as they are," to which we, being religious, may give assent. But if the future cannot be made better, then that "cannot be made better" is part of "things as they are," to which we need to give consent.

One may ask: "But how do you know whether or not the future can be made better?" Two kinds of replies are in order. First, if one cannot know whether or not the future can be made better, then this "cannot know" is part of "the way things are." Secondly, if by trying we may make the future better, then this "may" is part of "things as they are." Religion consists in genuine goodwill. Our will to goodness is not wholly genuine unless we put forth our maximum effort to bring it about. But when we do so exert ourselves, we find that some evil still exists. No matter how hard we try, we cannot eradicate all of it. Then, the existence of some evil that cannot be eradicated is part of "things as they are." For after the best has been done, to say that it should be better than it can be is, in effect, to deny that it is as good as it is. Such denial is a form of Nay-saying and is "irreligious."

Low Religion and High Religion

Religions have been rated as "low" and "high" on various scales or by numerous standards. We choose to employ the terms "low" and "high" here in a very specific sense and for a particular purpose.

By "low" religion we here mean living with an attitude that one can get, should expect to get, and should try to get more than he deserves. By "high" religion we mean enjoying life with an attitude that one should neither expect to get more than he deserves nor feel sorry for himself when he seems to get very little since, ultimately, he really deserves nothing anyway. It is a function of religion to help man to want only what he deserves and to enjoy what he gets as being his ultimate value.

When one wants only what he deserves he is already saying "Yes" to the universe. Although there may be other forms of Yea-saying, this one is basic. Both individuals and cultural traditions may be judged as supporting "low" or "high" religion according to their views about getting only what they deserve. "High" religion frees a man from all self-pity. Conversely, anyone who feels shortchanged, persecuted, fearful, or depreciated in his life, or who pities himself in any way, can be assured that he is indulging in "low" religion.

The particular way in which each religion handles this problem of helping men to enjoy their life as one in which they are already getting more than they deserve provides an important ingredient in its moral and religious atmosphere. The cogency with which a religion induces men to say "Yes" to the life they live determines whether such a religion is relatively "high" or "low." The peon and porter who says "Yes" to his load, not just as his day's work but as his life's work, may be enjoying "higher" religion than the high priest who wearies of hearing confessions.

Classifying Religions

The myriad varieties of religious beliefs and practices confront the student of world religions with the tremendous problem of selecting representative perspectives that will do justice to the numerous complexities and at the same time provide insights into the authentic vision of each major religious movement. The three greatest civilizations of mankind are the Hindu, the Chinese, and the European or "Western." Each has its own indigenous traditions, distinguishing characteristics, and long history of development. Each is complex in origin (and has borrowed from time to time from the others), yet each embodies some predominant traits that color its outlook on all things, including religion.

Hindu civilization is one of the most ancient, though its recorded history began primarily with the invasion of India by Aryans from the northwest. Orthodox Hindus today, despite wide differences in specific philosophies and practices, accept the huge and variegated bodies of traditional literature as inspirational. Jainism and Buddhism, originating in the sixth century B.C., objected to some ineffective local practices and have been declared heresies. Yet they express the dominating mood and logic of the Hindu mind in essentially the same way as other movements, and their achievements and teachings have been absorbed into the general Hindu cultural tradition. We have arbitrarily distinguished between "Hinduism," which refers generally to the whole span of thought and practice, and "Vedantism," which denotes its later, and possibly culminating, philosophies. "Veda" means "truth." Truth is one. So all who express the truth are "Vedantic." Its expression in those works now called "The Vedas" has been commented upon, explained, and elaborated into various schools of thought. "Vedanta" means "end of the Veda" or final formulation of the truth. Each of many different schools of thought calls itself "Vedanta," so this term also has a wide connotation.

Chinese culture, too, has most ancient origins. Again, the sixth century B.C. saw the famous and influential formulations by Lao Tzu and Confucius. Taoism and Confucianism, though names for somewhat differing emphases, constitute a single strain of thought that also has proliferated itself in amazingly intricate and voluminous ways. Importation from India of a foreign religion, Buddhism, stimulated centuries of struggle, compromise, and integration, so that Taoism, Confucianism, and Buddhism came to constitute "The Three Truths" of China. Their joint contribution to Zen and their intermingling with Shintoism, the indigenous religion of Japan, produced another luxuriant flower garden of religions in Japan.

Western civilization, which dominated Europe and the Americas for so long, had its roots in Egypt and Mesopotamia, and two different streams of cultural development contributed to its mainstream. These two were the Greek, which endowed it with rational, philosophical, and scientific tendencies, and the Hebraic, which provided a voluntaristic, aggressive, and theistic tone and literature. Judaism, Christianity, and Islam, all integral to Western culture, have been commonly misunderstood as "Oriental," because they originated at the eastern end of the Mediterranean Sea, the commercial and cultural spawning place of Western civilization. Islam, especially, has been misjudged as Oriental, because it spread into and dominated large portions of India. But ideologically Islam is a late (sixth century A.D.) product of the Hebrew and Christian traditions and shares with them monotheistic preconceptions typifying Western civilization. Humanism, although appearing elsewhere in the world, has received special emphasis in Greek, Renaissance, and Modern times as a nonecclesiastical religion whose pervasive success perpetually threatens the dominance of the three "God-centered" traditions. Some adherents call it "The Fourth Faith"; critics try to identify it with "secularism." Dualism, exclusivism, conflict, conquest, and missionary zeal have characterized the spirit of Western civilization and its religions somewhat more than those of India and China. But its dominant flavor has been theistic, and it continues to be disturbed by the relative indifference with which Hindu and Chinese peoples receive its appeals to the superiority of its theisms. Only gradually is the West coming to realize that it, too, has something to receive from the religions of China and India.

We are not yet ready to develop a "world religion" incorporating the virtues of all of man's religions. But surely it is time for us to become more fully aware of the problem as a problem. The last chapter of this book will consider the consequences of the increasingly intimate encounters of the world's living religions and whether man should seek to take hold of his religious needs and resources with a scientific and managerial spirit and deliberately modify the direction of his ideals and practices in a way that integrates the merits of each into a pattern conveniently available for all.

Chapter 2 **Primitive Religion**

Almost every day some Navajo or Pueblo Indian passes by my home on the University of New Mexico campus, to remind me of the omnipresent intermingling of primitive and Western cultures and religions in my city, state, nation, and world. Every year in Gallup, New Mexico, the Inter-Tribal Ceremonial Association sponsors an exhibition of sacred dances as well as personal and social achievements of native Americans representing such groups as the Zuni, Zia, Hopi, and Apache. Some of us wear jewelry and decorate our homes with pottery bearing designs symbolizing ancient wisdom. These examples of how primitive cultures affect us today may serve as a reminder that some one hundred and fifty million people, among the followers of the world's living religions, still adhere to ideals and practices classified as "primitive."

The terms "primitive" and "primary," referring to that which is first, mean both first in time (early) and first in development (foundational). "Primitive religion" is primary in both of these senses. Not only did "primitive religion" emerge first in time, thus being most ancient and yet most enduring since it persists in primitive cultures today, but also it provided the basis upon which other religious ideals and practices developed. Primitive religion contains all of the necessary and sufficient conditions for the existence of religion. Examination of the nature of primitive religion, then, provides a basis with which to compare "advanced" or "secondary" religions, such as Christianity, Buddhism, or Confucianism, so we may more easily discover what is essential and what is accidental to them as religions. Furthermore, since the more complex religions evolved out of their earlier antecedents, including their earliest and most primitive, by a relatively continuous process, we may gain much insight into the nature and purpose of our own contemporary religious beliefs and practices by discovering how our present needs were met by primitive religious concepts and acts.

Animism

Before citing particular details, I will summarize the philosophical and religious outlook inherent in primitive mentality generally. This view has now been named "animism," and misleadingly defined as "belief in spirits." *"Anima"* (Latin) means "breath of life," and "animism" captures the idea that the world is pervaded by living force or forces. Belief in such forces or powers is needed to account for the appearance and disappearance of certain experienced effects. These forces remain invisible for, like electric power, they are inferred to exist in order to explain how startling results occur. Each culture generates its own favored name or names to designate such power or powers. Anthropologists have catalogued these for us in amazing quantities. The reader may be familiar with many of them.

Algonquin, Iroquois, and Sioux Indians speak, respectively, of "manitou," "orenda," and "wakan." Arabic tales tell of "ginns" or "ginni." Japanese talk about "kami." Hindus enjoy a plethora of terms, such as "hari," "shakti," "nath," "at" or "atma," "brahm," "daeva" (etymologically related to our English "divine" and "devil"), "shiva" and "jiva" (related to our English "live"). Indo-European languages have the interrelated "th" and "de," observable as stems in "theos" and "deus," as pervasive power terms. "Th" not only developed into the general definite article, "the," to denote any entitive or active force, but became declined as "this," "that," "these," "those," "thee," "thou," "them," "then," "there," "thus," "thing," etc. The semitic "el," and its variants, "al," "il," "ol," not only continue as parts of personal names, such as "Daniel" or "Elizabeth," as parts of place names, such as "Beth-el" or "El Alamein," as parts of names for things, such as "oil" or "ol" (meaning "oil") as in "oleomargarine," as names for God, such as Abraham's "El Shaddai" and Mohammed's "Allah," but also as the general definite article in Romance languages.

Anthropologists, searching for some single term to stand for what all of these various names denote in common, adopted, perhaps arbitrarily, the Melanesian and Polynesian term "mana." The practical convenience of having a single term to signify some general meaning common to such a variety of terms should be obvious. Consequently, our literature now defines "animism" as "belief in mana." Readers unfamiliar with Polynesian details can entertain the term "mana" without reading into it preconceptions built into their minds as a result of late developments in their own culture and language. The Latin term *"spiritus,"* meaning "breath" (still evident in the English words "inspiration" and "expiration") and also connoting "life" as something identical with breathing, was adopted by early Christian anthropologists to designate *"anima"* or "life force." The translation was a good one, or would have been, if the term "spirit" had not absorbed additional connotations, which transformed its meaning—and consequently the meaning of "animism" defined as "belief in spirits"—into something not present as part of primitive mentality. This additional connotation grew out of our Greek-Christian heritage, which developed a sharp distinction between "spirit" and "matter," so sharp, indeed, that Descartes once claimed that spirit is everything that matter is not and matter is everything that spirit is not. This ideological division of the world into two exclusively different kinds of being is an advanced product of Western civilization that yields serious misunderstanding when read back into primitive mentality. Also, identification of the distinction between "matter" and "spirit" with another distinction between "natural" and "supernatural" introduces an additional mistaken preconception when applied to primitive religion. The world of primitive men is populated by natural powers, some more amazing than others. But slicing the universe in two by means of a "law of excluded middle" is not typical of the primitive mind. One who defines "animism" as "belief in the supernatural" obviously does not know much about his subject.

What Is Mana?

If the key concept in primitive religion is "mana," then what is it? Five characteristics may be described. First, mana is *invisible*. You cannot see it. That is, you cannot detect it directly through any of your senses. (This characteristic is a basis for attributing to it a "mysterious" quality.) Secondly, mana is *powerful*—more or less. It has the ability to make a difference or to cause effects. In brief, then, mana is simply invisible power.

If you should happen to wonder why anyone would believe in invisible powers ("If you can't see them, why believe in them?"), stop to consider why you believe in electrons or other atomic particles and in electricity. Today our whole scientific, technological, industrial, and commercial way of life depends upon our belief in electrons, *i.e.*, in invisible powers. In our generalized animistic language, these electrons are, or have, mana. What reasons do we today, as did early primitive man, have for believing in mana?

The reasons are simple and obvious, once we stop to think about them. Human minds, both ours and primitive minds, naturally employ cause-effect reasoning: "Nothing happens without a cause." Now whenever we see something happen and see something else that pushed it, stabbed it, clubbed it, or frightened it, we can see a cause for the effect. But when we see an event happen without observing any cause of its happening, we naturally wonder, "What caused it to happen?" If we look around and search in vain for visible causes, then we normally conclude that the causes remain invisible. Developing ideas about and names for such invisible causes follows inevitably.

How detect the presence of mana? By its effects. If mana is the power to produce effects, then you can tell whether a particular kind of mana is present by whether or not a particular kind of effect is produced. Primitive man was, to use a contemporary term, very pragmatic. According to pragmatic behaviorists, a thing is what a thing does. If you want to know what a thing is, observe the way it behaves. If it functions in a certain way, then you conclude that it is a kind of being with that kind of behavior. Primitive man, like modern man, found the presence of mana by observing each situation to see whether or not a thing supposed to have mana could produce the effects that such mana was believed to produce.

Perhaps the nature of mana can be clarified further by employing a simple analogy. When I was several years younger, the lingo of the times was pervaded with certain usages of the word "it." Anything that "had what it took to get the job done" had "it." A horse that won all its races and a car that went faster or farther on a gallon of gasoline had "it." Those were the days when Clara Bow was "The It Girl." Now what is "it," and how can you know whether anything has "it"? If a girl is attractive, how can you discover whether or not she is attractive? Very simply. Look at her. If she attracts you, then she is attractive. If you have any doubts about your own judgment, then observe how many others are attracted by her. If she attracts more men than other girls do, then she has attractiveness. She has "it." She has mana. Primitive people, then, had no great difficulty in detecting the presence of mana— at least some kinds of mana. Other kinds of mana, however, were more elusive. Then more complicated and elaborate methods of detection were needed, and the first of these may be regarded as man's earliest attempts at science.

Kinds of Mana

How many kinds of mana are there? As many as there are kinds of visible effects that need to be accounted for by invisible causes. Ask yourself the question, How many kinds of effects have I experienced for which I have not observed visible causes? Then do you not need just that many kinds of mana?

Yet, some think that there is only one Mana, one totality of universal Energy, or one God. Is mana one or many? To this question— "Is there just one great invisible power or are there many individual invisible powers?"—the primitive mind gave no consistent answer. But why should it? Even today we still do not know whether existing power is all one or whether it is distributed among dispersed parts. How can you determine whether mana is one or many? By the same empirical methods used to detect it in the first place. If two different effects can be produced by the same cause, then you need only one kind of mana for both. Primitive minds tended to require many causes, though the sharp distinctions we make today were not always present. For some purposes, simple polyspiritism is sufficient. But from it developed polytheisms, pantheons interrelating the gods, multiple-armed (indicating ability to produce many kinds of effects) gods, many-headed gods, trinities, duotheisms, hierarchical systems of gods or their incarnations, as well as varieties of monotheisms, pantheisms, and panentheisms. Desire for some simple solution to man's interpretive problems has favored idealizing a single ultimate power. Yet multiplicity also has to be accounted for, and the view that mana is both one and many, rather than merely one or many, recurs again and again even in the minds of those who prefer extreme monism or extreme pluralism. It may be that the problem, "Is mana one or many?" must find its solution as the problem of "the one *and* the many," which then presents itself as how the two function interrelatedly rather than as which of two unrelated ways of being we must accept.

If we review the history of physical speculations, we find a similar process. Today our chemists distinguish about one hundred and six different kinds of atoms and twenty-odd kinds of subatomic particles. Yet, at the same time, all seem to be only particular modes of behavior in a vast sea of energy. Are these atomic "particles" really particles, *i.e.*, little independent substantial indivisible parts (as ancient, and even modern, materialists believed), or do they consist rather in relatively persistent waves in a cosmic sea with varying fields of density or complexity of activity? Scientists continue to search for an explanatory principle that will unify all other general principles within a single formula. If they succeed, then the unitary nature of the universe of energy and its laws of behavior will presumably be demonstrated. Yet different kinds of forces exist: subatomic, atomic, molecular, electrical, physiological, psychological, social, geological, and astronomical. Discovery of some unity or uniformity will in no way diminish the actual plurality and variety; and thus evidence for mana, invisible power, being both one and many will remain.

Neither the primitive mind nor the contemporary mind is prepared to settle the issue, "Is mana one or many?" by choosing either exclusively.

Yet, our grasp of primitive mentality may be aided by sampling some of the varieties of ways in which mana manifests itself. Five types, here called "inanimate," "animate," "personal," "social," and "symbolic," will be illustrated.

Any inanimate thing that has power to produce results that other similar things do not have obviously possesses greater mana. The more sparkling stone, more enduring rock, more slippery mud, stronger wind, swifter current, louder thunder, or safer place has more of something invisible than other such things do. A liquid that burns or a piece of wood that refuses to burn has unusual qualities. A more successful club or bow, a more fearful or uglier face, the luckier phases of the moon—all may be observed as results caused by invisible power.

By "animate" we here mean both plants and animals. Some trees grow faster or taller or sturdier. Some plants produce edible leaves and fruits and berries and roots that have power to sustain life; others produce poisons that kill. The powers causing these different effects remain invisible, for one cannot know, merely by seeing, smelling, or tasting, whether or not a plant is nourishing or poisonous. Some animals seem more vicious, swifter, or higher flyers than others. Also, as one gains strength by eating plants, animals, or other men, so one needing to increase his own mana will seek to eat the most nourishing foods. Not only do we today calculate our calories and vitamins in accordance with our chemical schemes, but primitive man sought to replenish his strength by eating those parts of plants, animals, or other men in accordance with his own ideological scheme. The throbbing heart that sustained a strong animal or man often was considered a prime source of strength. Guided by such a conception, a victorious warrior ate his strongest enemy's heart as soon as he was able.

Some persons have more mana than others. The warrior who wins all his battles, the combatant who is more courageous, the elder who lives longer than others, the father of more children, the ascetic who fasts longer or lives without eating longer than others, the artist who paints more beautiful pictures, the thinker who knows more facts or foretells more events, the leader of his people—all have mana of some unusual sort. Citing examples of unusual powers should not be taken to imply that other persons do not have mana. Mana is everywhere, and a person must have mana in order to live. When his breath stops, when his power to move is gone, he dies. But exceptional powers signify exceptional mana, and by observing these more striking examples we may be able to draw conclusions about mana generally, just as some people require miracles in order to believe in a God whose greatest miracle, creation of the world and life itself, does not impress them, and just as scientists found clues to electronics in the dramatic effects of lightning and static electricity, when in fact energy is omnipresent.

Some social groups have more mana because they exhibit more power than their neighbors, whether tribes or clans or nations. The military posturings, space-rocket and hydrogen-bomb technology advances, and propaganda victories of contemporary nations illustrate faith in their mana, each visible demonstration being evidence of greater invisible power. Also, social groups have power to compel conformity on the part of their group members. Such moral compulsion seems at times to be very effective through invisible means. A person who feels compelled to conform, even when no one is present to tell him what to do, feels the invisible power of group mana over him.

Symbols, whether spoken, written, or gestured, have mana. That some sounds or words have more power than others may be observed if we but listen to people speaking in a foreign language; we notice that some words get startling results when others do not. The sounds and visual symbols are apparent, but their power, especially their difference in power to cause responses, remains invisible. The primitive mind, noting this, became greatly impressed by the invisible, and even inaudible, power of words, singly and in groups. The use of chants, and charms was a natural consequence. Patterns, forms, formulae may have more or less mana, as do ideas and ideals, which, though invisible, have power to cause us to act in one way rather than another. Mana is everywhere and in everything, but, as it prompts one kind of response here and another there, it appears as mana of different kinds.

Additional Characteristics

To the first two characteristics of mana, *invisible power*, we must add, thirdly, that its *location is not necessarily fixed.* It is dynamic and may come and go. A thing, place, person, or group may gain or lose mana. You yourself can testify to the common experience of sometimes having ability to accomplish certain results and at others not having such ability, even when you do not know why. Persons, animals, machines, or societies sometimes can and sometimes cannot perform expected functions. The obvious explanation is that mana comes and goes. It may remain in one place for a long time and then leave suddenly. How can you know? By the empirical test. Observe and see whether the conspicuous results are still produced. How can you tell whether the girl is still attractive? Look at her again, and if you are attracted, she still has power to attract. If you are not attracted, her mana is gone.

Another example is the mana of life—the power to keep alive. As long as a man lives, he breathes. When he stops breathing, his life mana is gone. Some who seem to stop breathing, start breathing again. Those who appear to be dead may thus come alive. This simple idea is, I suspect, partly responsible for the belief that soul and body are different and separable. Without necessarily believing that mana is imperishable, primitives did, and we today do, tend to believe that power persists in spite of its disappearance from some places.

Fourthly, mana is *not necessarily conscious, intentional, personal, or moral.* Mana is not, in itself, moral. Mana, as mana, intends neither good nor bad. Mana, as such, is conceived as neither conscious nor unconscious. Like liquor or electricity, however, it may have a role to play in good, moral, and conscious behavior. Whenever mana becomes embodied in a person, or whenever a person has mana, then such mana may be used for personal, including moral or immoral, purposes. Whenever a person obtains extra mana, or when mana manifests itself more in some persons than in others, we call these persons "gods."

How can you tell whether or not a person is a god? By the same empirical test. Does he have power to produce marvelous results? Those whose influence over the lives of others continues through many generations have more power, or are more godly, than those who have no such influences. Some of our ancestors seem to grow in power after their death as more and more people become influenced by them, their ideas, or their progeny. Their influence over us may seem intended.

Fifthly, is mana *controllable? Sometimes, sometimes not.* It is difficult to deal with because it is invisible. You cannot handle it, smell it, taste it, or hear it. You must infer its existence through its effects upon things you can sense in any way. Since the effects of mana upon us may be good or evil, may sustain life or cause death, we cannot help experimenting to find ways of controlling it. Some kinds of mana, such as that manifest in the wind, sun, stars, thunder, and time, seem beyond our power to influence. Other kinds, such as those manifest in rocks (jewels), plants (vitamins), animals (food) or persons (servants), we may direct to our benefit. "Engineering," "agriculture," "psychology," and "politics" are areas in which men try to influence the mana evidenced in things. Each primitive culture has its own name for persons especially adept at knowing how to gather, use, and predict mana. Today we lump these various primitive manipulators under the name "medicine men," and reserve the names "scientist," "pharmacist," and "physician" for specialists who perform these functions in our own time.

Ways of Controlling Mana

If several different kinds of manageable mana exist, each may require its own method of control. In describing our own culture, we refer to "technicians." In reporting methods observed in primitive cultures, we speak of "magic" (from the Persian "magi") and "magicians." Custom now distinguishes between two kinds of magic, sometimes called "contiguous" and "imitative."

"Contiguous magic" requires contact with some part of the thing being influenced. Striking to us is the example of believing that if you can obtain a portion of another person's body, such as a hair, nail paring, or, better, a finger, and destroy or harm it, you can thereby destroy or harm the person himself. Today we touch a button to switch on a distant light or twist a knob to tune in an invisible broadcasting station. Involved here is a principle that some things, such as hair or knobs, are parts of wholes, such as human bodies or electromagnetic wave systems, which may be manipulated in ways that influence those wholes. Physical contact with and mastery of some integral portion of a whole may enable us to modify the course of that whole.

"Imitative magic" presupposes the principle that "like produces like" or, as we call it today, the "principle of the uniformity of nature." Whenever you have a given set of causes that produces a given set of effects, we say then that if you have exactly the same set of causes again, you will get exactly the same set of effects again. Such a principle illustrates an inherent trait and tendency of the human mind, namely, to reason by analogy. In fact, all reasoning is reasoning by analogy. For logic and mathematics presuppose that if, for example, "(p implies q and q implies r) implies (p implies r)" and "Two plus three equal five" once, then the same relation will hold again and again because the conditions remain the same or analogous. Some analogies are "strong," others "weak." Primitive men, and you and I in areas of little experience, must get along with weak analogies until stronger ones come to be known. Rain dances in which one fills his mouth with water and squirts it out to imitate falling rain drops employ analogies that seem unreasonably weak to us today, though our more intricate climatological analyses and analogies and cloud-seeding efforts have not yet proved generally successful.

Goal of Religion

The nature of life, as conceived by primitive mentality, consists in having or being mana. In the obvious and continuous struggle for existence, an increase in mana seems advantageous. The greater the power that one being has over another, the greater his chances for survival in competition. Decrease in mana places one in danger, and complete loss of mana means death. One may have mana as inner strength (virtue), as power over things (wealth) or persons (political dominance), as shared power through family, clan, or tribe (kinship), or as miraculous power over unseen forces (divinity). Recognition of personal or tribal kinship with an animal tribe has come to be called "totemism," and consequently analogical reasoning yields contact and imitative behavior with animals of this kind similar to that with persons of the same kind or kin.

We have come to distinguish between a "priest," who has special abilities to influence mana external to self, and a "shaman," who possesses much mana within himself. Every man is both shaman and priest, though a particular person may become noted as being either a great shaman or a great priest or, sometimes, both. These two abilities do not necessarily develop equally. A person embodying greater mana is the holier of the two. One more skilled in manipulating mana is the craftier or more practical of the two. The more fearful and needy a person feels, the more he will seek the aid of a priest. The more confident and self-sufficient he feels, the more he experiences himself as a shaman; and the more unperturbed he remains under insult or attack, the more others recognize him as a shaman.

The goal of life is to enjoy continuing strength, and thus to possess internally and to control externally as much mana as possible or as much as nature or fortune brings one's way. Man, primitive and contemporary, "seeks the divine," but culture modifies conceptions of divinity by inventing different ways of explaining its nature. When primitive man eats, he eats mana, knowing that life is precarious and that danger is ever present. Modern man may be more confident about his control over some things, *e.g.*, grain and cattle, yet if he conceives some overarching Providence as a power determining his long-range destiny, he may still "say grace" at meals or "give thanks" at harvest festivals.

Christian "holy communion" services involving "eating the body and drinking the blood of Christ" signify man's need for becoming a shaman, for partaking of the substance of divinity, for attaining more mana. Recognition of its possession yields a feeling of confidence, of attainment of being, of ultimacy.

Comprehension of the psychology of primitive mentality

may yield a clearer vision of man's religious nature, motive, and goal than the study of intricate intellectual and ecclesiastical systems, provided we do not lose sight of the general nature of mana in examining the seemingly endless varieties of particular ritualistic practices. A surface study of primitive societies convinces us that they are "superstitious." But profound insight reveals similarities, as well as differences, between primitive and modern conceptions of mana. Some who, rejecting as inadequate modern ecclesiastical explanations and practices, believe they thereby reject "religion" may discover that their motive for rejection was itself religious. Man is naturally, "incurably" religious; but religion as a general trait and need of man may be hidden from view by the theoretical schemes elaborated by philosophers and theologians and by the peculiar language, literature, and traditions of particular religions. Knowledge of primitive mentality can provide a basis for grasping the nature of religion in general.

If one essential of religion is the attitude of yea-saying, how does such an attitude evince itself in primitive religion? When a man arises in the morning and finds himself able to stand, he recognizes the mana within him as power to stand. His very act of standing thereby constitutes an act of yea-saying to his ability to stand, as does his slumping into sleep at night exemplify a yea-saying to the diminution of his mana. If he must eat to live, he must say "Yes" to the need for eating, even when he remains sympathetic to the desires of his victim not to be eaten. His shaking with fear in face of crises exhibits a yea-saying to the presence and power of mana believed greater than his own. His walking and fighting with confidence shows his faith in his own mana and a yea-saying to power felt within. The coming and going of seasons, of birth and death, of day and night, of shifting patterns of wind, rain, thunder, and food, all must be assented to with considerable stoicism, though particular experiences result in specialized techniques of control formulated into rituals, tabus, sacrifices. Whenever his wishes or fears create anxieties to which he cannot say "Yes," he will then say "Yes" to seeking a priest or magician to foretell or influence events. When he bribes a priest to bring him more than he deserves, his religion is "low." When he accepts his lot for what it is, whether deserved or not, his religion is "high."

part i

Religions of India

Chapter 3 Hinduism

Hinduism is of outstanding significance to the student of religion because it combines so many durable characteristics in superlative ways. Several claims made for it command our notice. It is said to be the oldest, the most spiritualistic, the most influential, the richest and most complex, and the most informative example of evolution of all the world's great religions.

Is it the oldest? Although Hinduism has primitive antecedents and sources, and shares some common linguistic and ideological ancestry with European and perhaps even Chinese religions, it appears to be the oldest religion possessing the other characteristics mentioned. The Zoroastrian *Gathas* may be older, but the relatively dwindled numbers of Gabars and Parsees stand as evidence that the *Gathas* lack prevalence. The *Vedas* appear to be the earliest body of literature of any quantity that has had continuing influence upon the religious thought and practices of large numbers of people throughout the ages, including the present.

Is it the most spiritualistic? It has emphasized the ultimacy of spirit longer, more extensively, more persistently, and more intensively than either Chinese or European cultures. The Chinese have been predominantly naturalistic, and European civilization has tended to be dualistic, hierarchical, and realistic in its prevailing emphases. In Hinduism, ultimate reality and the goal of religion are to be sought inwardly, not outwardly.

Is it the most influential? Here the claim must be considered beside those for Chinese religion in light of the population masses of China, and for Christianity, which spread to the Americas and, through colonial and missionary efforts, throughout the world. Yet the facts that

India's own population is huge, that its culture pervaded Southeast Asia, and that it exported Buddhism throughout China, Korea, Japan, Tibet, and Mongolia, must be reckoned with. Influence of early Hindu ideas upon the mystery religions of the Near East and upon the Neo-Platonic backgrounds of Christian doctrines should be considered in the total picture.

Is it the richest and most complex? The origin of Hindu religion has been attributed to an intermingling of Aryan and Dravidian animisms. But richness derives not only from embodying in scriptures these early ideas that have survived to the present, but also from retaining them through myriads of commentaries, and commentaries upon commentaries, rather than discarding what fails to fit each new ideological scheme. Most later Hindu thinkers have designed systems that were modifications of their tradition rather than revolts from it and have incorporated rather than repudiated the various evolutionary stages that preceded them. Hindu philosophies have been appreciative, not merely critical; synthetic, not merely analytic; and perpetually felt as serving life rather than as irresponsible "ivory tower" abstractions. All known ways—works, faith, science, and trances—have been woven and interwoven into an amazing tapestry of ideologies and practices.

Is it the most informative example of evolution of religious ideas? Each investigator may have his own favorite examples. Yet the history of growth from animism and polyspiritism, through polytheisms, through various gropings for organized associations of gods, through a pantheon of thirty-three gods, through a trinity of gods that merged into a *trimurti* encompassing incarnations of all of the gods, to a monism so monistic that even distinction between the one and the many disappears, is one of the most elaborately documented of all histories of theological evolution. Despite the clear and constant tendency from multiplicity to unity and from objective plurality to inner oneness, counter tendencies also occur, and the extreme monism, or nondualism, which constitutes an epitome of mankind's attempts to think monistically, has met effective resistance and reversal in the direction of more humane and commonsense theisms. I propose, in the following, to sketch some of the outlines of this long, rich, complex, spiritualistic evolution of Hindu religious ideas.

The Vedas

"Veda" means "word." "In the beginning was the word." "Word" refers not merely to sounds (or, later, written letters) but to meanings contained in and conveyed by such sounds. Primitive minds tended to believe that words embody meanings rather than merely represent them. When one spoke he embodied things or powers in his speech by speaking. Once speech gets under way, our view of things becomes embodied in our words. So verbal expression of our vision is also "veda." "Veda" thus also means "view" or "vision" of what is. Vision of what exists is "knowledge," so "veda" means "knowledge" and also "truth." Thus "veda" refers both to words, writings, scriptures, and to knowledge of the true view conveyed therein.

Tradition has arranged the earliest writings into four groups, called *Veda* in Sanskrit and *The Vedas* in English. These groups were composed by many different people over long periods of time. When they began, we do not know. Some estimates extend their origins to 3000 or 4000 B.C., but most of the composing was done during the century and a half between 2000 and 500 B.C., after the Aryan invaders from the northwest, cultural relatives of the ancient Persians and thus also distant cousins of the early Greeks, conquered and settled among the Dravidian natives of northern India in the Punjab area.

The earliest, called the *Rig* or *Rig-Veda,* consists of a collection of poems in ten books comprising over a thousand pieces in all. Most of them are hymns of praise and petition addressed to particular gods or groups of gods. In each book, the hymns are addressed primarily to one god, though recognition may be paid also to some others and then to all the gods. The second, called *Sama-Veda,* consists largely of chants sung by assistants at sacrificial ceremonies. The third, *Yajur-Veda,* is devoted largely to prose formulas used by another group of assisting priests. A fourth, the *Atharva-Veda,* appears to be a somewhat later collection of primitive charms and magical formulas.

Two noteworthy characteristics of the earliest Vedas are the absence of local deities, indicating that their authors were migrants who had to leave local deities behind when they moved, and the fairly advanced linguistic development with which they addressed their deities. Along with animistic ideas, a fairly high development of polytheistic notions and a complex, even hierarchical, priesthood had evolved.

Being migrants, they had no temples, but needed to locate a suitable place, prepare and sanctify the ground, build an altar, gather and prepare proper foods or animals and other materials all in appropriate ways, before conducting a sacrificial ceremony. Since each phase of the complex rituals required specialists, many varieties of priests developed, each doubtless passing his skills on to his children in an hereditary fashion. Need developed for a head priest or master of ceremonies to coordinate all of the others. These priests, called "Brahmins," knowing the proper ways of doing things, became the hereditary scholars as well as priests and served not only as conveyers of some of man's earliest ideas but also as originators of some of its profoundest philosophy when they began to meditate upon and study critically the meaning of these hereditary rituals.

The main gods of the *Rig-Veda* were the great powers of nature that affect human welfare. The bright sky, the enlivening sun, the rosy dawn, the rain storm that dispels drouth, powers that influence people everywhere and thus have a universal character, all receive worshipful attention. Acquaintance with a few of these many gods may be worthwhile, for we shall meet them again and again, even if in modified dress, throughout later literary and theological developments.

"Agni," the name for fire in all its forms in heaven and earth, is one of the greatest. More than two hundred hymns were dedicated to him. He is the fire that lights the sky (sun), that streaks across the sky in storms (lightning), that burns forests. But his primary importance to Vedic ritualists appears in his occurrence as the hearth fire in household rituals and in the fires of the three great sacrificial ceremonies. Offerings of butter *(ghee)* are made to him, and sacrifices to other gods are given to his care so that he may convey them in his rising flames and smoke to their places in the heavens. Since sacrifice propitiates gods and removes guilt, and since fire purifies and expels evil influences, Agni came to be regarded as one who takes away sin and restores the sinner to favor. Thus Agni comes to have a moral character. He is a friend of men, a guest in every house with a hearth fire, a protector whose light and flames drive away demons. The births of Agni became favorite themes of poets. Agni is begotten on earth daily when fire is kindled by rubbing together two fire sticks; therefore he must be hidden in the wood. ("Agni" has an etymological cousin in our English word "ignite.") He is born of lightning shooting from clouds; therefore he must be hidden in the clouds. He is born each morning as the sun, flaming a straight path across the sky from horizon to horizon each day; therefore he hides in cosmic distance. He lights our way, warms our bodies and our hearts, cooks our foods, protects us from enemies, gives us vision and insight. Is he not the greatest of the gods?

Indra, to whom about one fourth of the hymns of the *Rig-Veda* are addressed, appears primarily as the rain-bringing and drouth-dispelling power behind and in storms. Indra must be distinguished from Rudra, the violent, destructive power that also manifests itself through storms. As a protector of people, Indra became a god who helped ward off and defeat both human and spiritual enemies. He is personified as a gigantic bearded figure who rides to battle on a chariot, wielding his thunderbolts. He is famous for slaying a dragon, Vritra, who had shut up the waters so none could have any. Accompanied by his friends, the Maruts (winds), he engaged in fierce combat, slaying the monster with his thunderbolt and letting out imprisoned waters. His heroic capacity for food and drink, gulping flesh of cattle by the hundreds and swallowing whole tubs of soma, provides him with energy for fighting and for holding up the sky and earth. His flirtations arouse jealousy in his wife, Indrani. Like other gods, he is addressed as the greatest.

Soma, an intoxicating beverage from the soma plant, not only is poured as an offering to the gods, but functions also as a god. A whole book of one hundred and fourteen hymns is dedicated entirely to him. As a drink of the gods, who can be influenced to grant favors to worshippers providing such drink, Soma was personified as a deity having power over other gods. He not only inspires others to valor but is himself a great warrior whose conquests bring many good things to those who worship him. He causes the sun to shine, generates heaven and earth, and displays unlimited power. Soma is powerful medicine that heals the sick, cures falsifiers, provides courage and strength, destroys enmity, and brings immortality.

Among the many other gods are Ushas, the rosy dawn; Surya, the sun; Vayu, the wind; and Varuna, cosmic law and order. Dyaus, the bright sky, sometimes called "Pitar" (father) and paired with Prithivi (earth) as mother, is related to the Greek Zeus-Pater and the Latin Jupiter. Vac, goddess of speech; Naga, the snake; Yama and Yami, the god and goddess of death; Hanuman, the monkey; Ganesha, the elephant; Rita, moral and social order; Mitra, related to the Iranian Mithra; and Vishnu, a minor deity destined to dominate the other gods later—all play their roles with amazing valor.

Persons having particular needs should be happy to have such a rich multiplicity of specialized gods to call upon for help. But priests and scholars, whose function it is to keep them all in mind and to give them proper attention, gradually find their tasks becoming onerous. As they taught their duties to apprentices, they were called upon for explanations of relations between the gods. Sometimes the gods appear together, as companions or as enemies; but their associates may change in different hymns. Do fixed relationships exist among the gods? Indra and Indrani and other husband-wife pairs remain together, yet not always. Ganesha, the elephant, usually accompanies Kubera, riches. But why? Various pantheons developed, but one that eventually gained favor and remained as a permanent feature of Hindu theological lore was that of "the thirty-three gods." Unlike the Greek pantheon, with Zeus as father, Hera as mother, Poseidon as brother, and Apollo and Athene as children, which was a family arrangement, the Hindu pantheon divided the gods into three atmospheric levels, those of the "upper air" (sky), "middle air" (atmosphere), and "lower air" (close to the earth). Eleven gods were assigned to each layer. Although I have never seen a complete list of such gods, the locus of some should be obvious to anyone who knows their functions. Surya (sun), chief god of the upper air, is accompanied by Dyaus (sky), Ushas (dawn), Mitra (light), and Varuna, Rita, and Vishnu, apparently ex-solar deities. Indra (thunder-rain god), chief of the middle air, has Rudra (destructive storm), Vayu (wind), the Maruts (breezes), and Parjanya (clouds), among his companions. Agni (fire), leader of deities in the lower air, shares this level with Soma (intoxicating beverage), and Prithivi (mother earth).

However, another kind of development was destined to become more typical, influential, and far-reaching. Once the Vedic hymns were stabilized in forms that the priest-scholars could study, some obvious characteristics became increasingly bothersome. For example, each of the many gods received praise as "the greatest." Now good reason existed for such appraisal. When faced with death from drouth, persons whose very life appeared to depend upon the god who brings rain addressed him as the greatest because, indeed, he was the greatest. When faced with conquest by enemies, persons in need of victory in war praised their war god as the greatest for, indeed, he was. In each kind of crisis, the gods whose specialty was demanded unquestionably became all-important and, for present purposes, all-powerful. For people with variable critical needs, submission to all-out honor of the god whose help is being sought involves no more inconsistency than putting forth a maximum of energy on each occasion of danger from animals or personal enemies. But when scholars noted that two or more gods were regarded as supreme, they first wondered whether they were, and then sometimes concluded that they were, really, the same.

This problem, and tendency, developed from the fact that several of the gods possessed overlapping or duplicating functions. As worshippers magnified their praises of each god, they added to his powers and thus to his functions. The more each god was aggrandized, the more each began to resemble the others in capacity and function. Thus, the kind of reasoning mentioned previously when discussing primitive culture—namely, that one can decide by empirical methods whether one or more gods is needed to perform a particular function—was natural also for Vedic scholar-priests. Thus Indra and Agni became Indragni; Mitra and Varuna became Mitravaruna; Indra and Vishnu became Indravishnu. Then, faced with Indragni and Indravishnu, scholars were moved to see Indra, Agni, and Vishnu as one god, though from such combinations, "Vishnu" emerged as the name that survived to designate the single deity who incorporated so many functions and thus manifested or embodied himself in so many different ways. As time went on, Vishnu became recognized as a pervasive deity incarnating many different gods, engulfing all of them into his own being. Vaishnavism, the sect regarding Vishnu as the supreme deity, became and remains today one of the most numerous and influential. We will hear more about Vishnu later, but now we must introduce the concept of "avatar."

Although the idea of the transmigration of souls and their reincarnation in other bodies apparently did not occur during the early Vedic period, when it did emerge it naturally applied to gods as well as men. The rebirths of Agni, god of fire, have already been mentioned. Embodiments of Vishnu in the sky, in the rain, and in fire again and again obviously appear as rebirths. So the idea of Vishnu's reincarnations came to have a special name, "avatar." As the literature of Vishnu's incarnations accumulated, the problem of relating and systematizing these arose, and, for whatever reasons, ten avatars attained special recognition and came to be called "the ten Avatars of Vishnu," even though Vishnu is said to have hundreds, thousands, even an infinite number, of incarnations. Each of these ten has an interesting story or series of stories associated with it, including the Fish, Tortoise, Boar, Lion, Dwarf, and first Rama Avatars. The seventh and eighth, or Rama and Krishna Avatars, which will occupy our attention when we discuss the Epics, stand out as most important, at least for later Hindu religion.

The tendency of Hindu thinkers to unify all things also manifested itself through the avatars of Vishnu in a very striking and significant way. If Vishnu is indeed the universal power, the supreme god, then whenever any heroic, wise, and influential figure arose in history, the followers of Vishnu naturally interpreted it as another expression of

Vishnu. So, when the fame and influence of Gotama, the Buddha, spread far and wide, Vishnuites easily accepted the Buddha as another Avatar of Vishnu, the ninth. The tenth, the "White Horse Avatar" of the future, was depicted as an incarnation in which Vishnu should appear at the end of a cosmic epoch riding a white horse, wielding a sword blazing like a comet, to create, renew, and reestablish purity on earth. When the power and influence of Jesus, the Christ, became known to the Vishnuites, especially after Christian British conquests of India, some of them were willing to accept Christ as the tenth Avatar of Vishnu. Thus the omnivorous Vishnu devours all the various gods within his being, or rather shines multifariously through his incarnations as all of the gods, including Buddha and Christ. Thus Hindus have no quarrel with Christians because Hindus conceive divinity as all-inclusive and unlimited in its manifestations. But Christians quarrel with Hindus when they insist that Christ is the *only* Son of God and that all other devas are really devils to be avoided and condemned. Having extended a hand of religious fellowship to Christians, Hindus have difficulty comprehending why Christians seem so ungracious in rejecting it.

Before leaving our story about the main line of Hindu theological development, we must mention Shiva and some additional kinds of syntheses that occurred. For whatever reason, Shiva also became the Supreme Deity for other Hindus, with his own history and numerous incarnations or "descents." (The term "avatar" usually has been reserved for incarnations of Vishnu, but once in common usage, this term was appropriated also as a general term for any incarnation of a deity.) Shiva, like Rudra, functions as the destructive storm god, sometimes depicted as a grotesquely horrible monster. However, when he developed into the supreme god of a major sect, his better side became magnified and his malevolent traits tended to pass over to his female and worse half. Shiva, like Vishnu, had consorts, a different one in each incarnation. Just as Shiva exists as one god with many incarnations, so his consort (or female half, for the two came to be regarded as inseparable in accordance with the unifying tendency in Hindu thinking) also manifested herself under different names, including

Devi, the goddess; Gauri, the bright one; Durga, the un-approachable; Bhairavi, the terrible; Barala, the horrible; Kali, the black one; Uma, Parvati, etc. Many of these goddesses were worshipped in their own right. Kali temples may be more popular than those of Shiva himself, though of course, being inseparable from Kali, he automatically becomes involved in Kali worship.

Shiva is usually depicted as having six arms, each one holding a different object and raised in its own posture, for each has a different function to perform. Shiva is not alone in being multiarmed, for the Hindu mind, which naturally thinks in terms of multifunctioning gods, pictures them as possessing many arms and hands for carrying out such functions. Four has become a usual number, but ideally the number of arms would be infinite if each of an infinite number of different kinds of activity could be represented by its own arm. (Some Mahayana Buddhist artists later succeeded in representing such enormous multiplicity in sculpture.) Shiva's outstanding characteristics, in addition to being author and destroyer of life and personification of the reproductive forces of nature, include being Lord of Dance. He is fond of hunting and drinking and orgiastic practices. Yet he is also regarded as the great Yogin who sits with matted hair and naked body besmeared with ashes in age-long self-mortification and meditation. He is regarded as a divine philosopher and sage, and skilled in grammar and in the literature of the Vedas. To Saivites, as the followers of Shiva may be called, he is the Supreme Deity and as such possesses all of the superior qualities and powers, and ministers to all human and cosmic needs.

How Shiva has come to be idealized by contemporary followers may be illustrated with quotations from an article by A. K. Banerjea, Principal of the Maharana Prata College at Gorakhpur, "The Contribution of Saivism to the Spiritual Culture of India," appearing in the October, 1954, *Bulletin of the Ramakrishna Mission Institute of Culture,* Calcutta: "Saivism is, perhaps, the oldest religious cult in India, based on the ideals of renunciation, asceticism, self-mastery, and self-realization." The idea of "compassion for all creatures has always been associated with the conception of Shiva. . . . He is not the God of the noble

men of society; He is the God of the masses. . . . He is the
God of the fallen and the depressed. He is the God of the
beasts and the birds, the God of the serpents and the tigers,
the God of the loathsome and the terrible. Among the gods,
Shiva is unique in his all-embracing love. Thus, Shiva has
all along been conceived, on the one hand, as the loftiest
and most transcendent of all the gods, dwelling in the in-
accessible height of spiritual perfection, and, on the other
hand, as the most liberal, cosmopolitan, and popular of all
the gods, most easily approachable by men, women, and
children of all classes, castes, and races. . . . He is the most
loving and lovable God to men and women of the lowest
strata of human society. . . . He does not make any demand upon His worshippers that they may find difficult.
He is the god of love and mercy. . . . The Worship of Shiva
does not require any elaborate ritual, or any correctly pro-
nounced Sanskrit *mantra,* or any valuable article for offering. . . . He seems to proclaim to all men as well as to all
the gods of the world, 'Give all the poison which you produce as the result of your bad actions to me, so that you
may enjoy the nectar which may be produced from your
good action.' "

With two major sects, each having one supreme deity
whose incarnations fill all the world and whose manifestations include all of the multitudes of gods that have appeared in history, how does the Hindu mind function? If
both are supreme and both pervade everything, may they
not be the same? Are not Vishnu and Shiva two names for
the same Supreme Deity? The complexity and richness of
the two traditions, and the distinguishable patterns of
practice and ways of depicting the gods developed by the
two sects, prevented so simple a solution. Rather, at one
time, the two were represented as one god having two
heads in a statue called "Harihara" ("Hari" is a common
name for gods), and many temples were dedicated to this
god. But another development took place that overshad-
owed this tendency, due to the presence of a third all-father,
namely, "Brahma." Brahma had only a few temples erected
to him and relatively few exclusive worshippers. No vast
literature of "juicy stories" of his exploits with susceptible
maidens in various incarnations grew up. Nevertheless,
somehow he came to rate along with Vishnu and Shiva as

one of three great all-pervading deities. Together these three reigned in the minds of some as a trinity of distinct gods, but soon they merged into a trimurti, the three forms or functions or faces or appearances of the Supreme Deity. Forever after, the Trimurti came to stand as the supreme synthesis of personified deities. Followers of Shiva can accept this synthesis and the name "Trimurti," but the three-in-one may still appropriately be called "Shiva." The followers of Vishnu likewise assent to the synthesis, but continue to call it "Vishnu."

The Trimurti, carved as a single body having three heads or three faces extending halfway out of a single head, is thought of as a single being with three general types of functions, namely, those of creating, preserving, and destroying. To Brahma was assigned the role of creator, to Vishnu the role of preserver, and to Shiva the role of destroying or consummating particular existences. The single being manifesting itself through these three functions remains a timeless, functionless, impersonal, pure unity whose perfect stillness baffles any intellect trying to grasp it. It may be called "Brahman" (to distinguish it from "Brahma," one of the three gods of the Trimurti, though unfortunately the existence of other ways of making this distinction in English may cause confusion). Brahman, as conceived by Advaita Vedanta, brought the Hindu tendency toward monism to its pinnacle of perfection. But we must reserve exploration of this subtle and abstruse philosophy until Chapter VI. Our summary of how Hindu theological ideals evolved has brought us far beyond its Vedic beginnings. Yet, as later monists fondly point out, expression of the idea of an ultimately complete unity was found already in Book X, 129, of the *Rig,* the earliest of the *Vedas.* Here the "Hymn to Creation" expresses perhaps mankind's first recorded appreciation of "That One," so unitary that no distinction, not even the distinction between nonexistence and existence, existed within it.

Although our sketch has been designed to portray the spirit of Hindu thinking as spiritualistic, where "spiritualistic" involves a preference for and belief in the greater ultimacy of unity as against plurality, we must remember also that Hindus appreciated a jungle-like proliferation and profusion of life forms, images, and desires. The hu-

man mind has difficulty in reconciling itself to the ultimacy
of a being stripped of all detail. Yet that very ideal provides a basis for unlimited varieties of things that would
appear as chaos were it not for the presence and power
of some such ideal. The prevalence of such an ideal provides an intellectual basis for a tolerance of the broadest
kind, a kind needed where varieties flourish in profusion.
Yet its presence as a principle of explanation compels
thought in a more spiritualistic direction. Hindu thought is
spiritualistic not so much because it maintains its Vedic
belief in numerous animistic and polytheistic powers as
because it retains an abiding faith that all are somehow
reconciled and joined within an ultimate unity.

A famous story in the *Upanishads,* condensed here, sums
up this spirit. When a teacher was asked, "How many gods
are there?" he replied, "As many as were mentioned in
the formula of the hymn of praise to the Vis-va-devas:
three and three hundred, three and three thousand." "Yes,
but how many gods are there really?" he was asked again.
"Thirty-three," he said. "Yes, but how many really?" "Six."
"But how many really?" "Three." "How many really?"
"Two." "How many really?" "One and a half." "How many
really?" "One." "But, then, what are these three and three
hundred, three and three thousand?" "Oh, they are only
the various powers."

The Upanishads

Hindu religious philosophy and practice underwent a gradual transformation from public ritualistic acts, properly
performed by priests propitiating animistic nature powers,
to private, silent, meditative self-intuition of ultimate reality and bliss. This transition, slow, subtle, and doubtless
unintended at first, eventually became so marked that the
names *"Karma-kanda"* and *"Jnana-kanda"* were used to
designate the vast difference that evolved. *"Karma"* pertains to deeds, acts, intentional efforts aimed at producing
results. The early Vedic sacrificial ceremonies consisted of
deeds or acts intended to avoid evils and to bring about
good results through the agency of the deity addressed.
These included physical health, freedom from physical
danger, prosperity, longevity here on earth, and perhaps

some future heavenly boons. *"Jnana"* is knowledge of ultimate reality itself, not so much knowledge *about* as knowledge *of* ultimate reality intuitively apprehended as embodied in one's own true self. The attention was transferred from looking outward toward external gods and prescribed, overt behavior where one's action can be publicly observed, to looking inward toward a pure, silent, peaceful unity felt as underlying all transitory appearances including desires.

This transition occurred so slowly and through such a complex maze of literature piled layer upon layer—with later strata consisting of comments upon the earlier— that the resulting views were believed to rest upon a solid foundation. Hence Hindu orthodoxy retains Vedic accounts of animistic slaughter ceremonies to the specific god Agni, for example, as basic to the literature and philosophy of its most advanced, contemporary sects and saints. Thus one needs to realize how the *Vedas,* the *Brahmanas,* the *Aranyakas,* and the *Upanishads* constitute not so much four distinct sets of writings as successive layers of commentary by scattered priests and seers whose inspirational bursts represent varying stages of development. The four *Vedas* themselves consist mainly of hymns *(mantra)* composed independently and only later gathered together *(Samhita)* in a collection. The *Brahmanas,* too, as first layers of commentary, also emerged sporadically, though they gained some semblance of system by the fact that they were comments upon specific *Vedas* or portions thereof. Each of the four *Vedas* consists mainly of prayers and hymns, while each attached *Brahmana* deals mostly with rules and regulations for the sacrifices and interprets the meanings of the prayers, which otherwise might be lost to later performers. These interpretations of meaning contain insights initiating further reflection.

The *Aranyakas,* a third level of comment, represent a somewhat sharper break in the development of thought due to the fact that these were derived from and designed for, dwellers in forests who were away from family, hearth fires, and priestly utensils and services. Thus far we have neglected to mention the "four stages of life" normal for each orthodox individual: First, that of childhood, when one learns to live, study, earn, and serve; second, that of adulthood, during which one marries, has children, earns his livelihood for himself and family, performs his duties to society and to the gods, and rears and trains his children for adulthood; third is a period of retirement from family duties, enabling one to study and meditate, a period often spent away from home in quiet forest settings; the fourth consists of a final period of meditation, trance, and attainment of the highest goal of life together with approaching death. Although one might study in a forest any time he was able, the third stage of life more naturally lent itself for this purpose. The *Aranyakas* contain allegorical interpretations of the Vedic sacrifices and functions of the gods. For example, Rudra, the destructive storm god, appears as a bringer of storms within man's soul. Agni, the god of fire, appealed to in the *Vedas* as the purifier of things from evil spirits, is felt as the purifier of one's own soul from evil thoughts. Varuna, Vedic keeper of cosmic order, may be seen as a power within the self to prevent the spiritual disorder inherent in excessive desire or overanxiety. Although such allegorical insights were impulsive and sporadic, their establishment in literature provided further authoritative bases for the speculations bursting into full bloom in the *Upanishads*.

The *Upanishads* themselves seem partly extensions of, comments upon, and later chapters in, a *Veda-Brahmana-Aranyaka-Upanishad* series. For example, the *Taittiriya Samhita* portion of the *Rig Veda* is followed by the *Taittiriya Brahmana*, at the end of which comes the *Taittiriya Aranyaka*, which is concluded by the *Taittiriya Upanishad*. But sometimes a *Upanishad* comments directly upon a *Veda (e.g., Isha Upanishad)*. The situation is complicated by the fact that there exist differing versions of the same *Veda* with different commentaries. Furthermore, portions of some of the *Vedas* seem to have been composed later than some of the earlier *Upanishads*. Attempts to organize the *Upanishads* have resulted in a tradition that claims authority for one hundred and eight *Upanishads,* ten or twelve of which seem most important, though many more writings called *"Upanishads"* exist. Regardless of seeming confusion and diversity of inspiration and speculation, Hindus regard them all as having both a divine or authoritative origin and as expressing a common fund of truth. When compared with Chinese and European scriptures, they do seem to have a common flavor peculiar to them. Acceptance of all as orthodox makes it incumbent upon later schools of thought to incorporate all of their basic insights or to explain them away. Since all four sets or layers of thought purportedly deal with the original Veda, Word, or Truth, all of them together are called "The Veda" or "The Truth." The philosophy of the *Upanishads* and of the later orthodox schools that claim to systematize and explain its philosophy is called "Vedanta" ("Veda-anta" or end of the Veda), indicating that it is the culminating expression of "The Truth." (See Swami Nikhilananda, *The Upanishads,* four volumes, for an excellent rendering and interpretation.)

Before taking leave of the *Upanishads,* we should mention that they too remain unsystematic. Collectively, they appear as a veritable sea of literature with waves of inspiration and speculation topped by occasional whitecaps of rich insight that call for quotation again and again. Yet "the Upanishads do not contain any ready-made consistent system of thought. At first sight they seem to be full of contradictions." (Swami Vireswarananda, *Brahma Sutras,* p. vi. Advaita Adhrama, Himalayas, 1948.) Hence there arose a need for systematizing such thought, and many attempts were made. The work of Badarayana, however, variously called the *Brahma Sutras* or *Vedanta Sutras,* became accepted as a standard authority to which all later commentators referred. We will not review its involved arguments. Nor will we here anticipate the final forms that Vedanta takes. These will be found summarized in the chapter, "Vedantism and Yoga," especially in the section on "Advaita." All agree that Brahman is the ultimate reality and that all other forms of deity, spirit, soul, self, and even body, are related to it, either as identical with it, or as only a little different from it, or as somewhat different but as continuingly dependent upon it. Hence the dominant philosophy of the Hindus is sometimes called "Brahmanism."

The Epics

A third major trend in Hindu philosophy and religion comes to prominence in "The Epics." Although historical

periods can be marked out in Hindu history only with
great difficulty and much guessing, because the Hindu
temperament has been much more preoccupied with appreciation of timeless being than with temporal processes,
gradual shifts in prevailing ideas and practices recorded
in literature do make possible some workable guesses about
major periods. If we "guesstimate" "the Vedic period"
(marked by the appearance of the *Vedas, Brahmanas, Aranyakas,* and *Upanishads*) as from about 2000 to 500 B.C.,
and "the Sutra period" (giving us the *Brahma Sutras* and
the *Dharma Sutras* containing the Laws of Manu) as from
about 500 to 200 B.C., we may speak of "the Epic period"
as extending from about 200 B.C. to 300 A.D., even though
the events in the stories may have occurred earlier. Some
distinguish further a "Puranic period" (the *Puranas* being collections of diverse materials, such as creation stories,
theories of the "ages" of the world, legends of the gods,
dogmas, grammar, medicine, and arts) from 300 to 750
A.D., a "Darshana period" (the *Darshanas* being teachings
of the six orthodox schools of philosophy from 750 to
1000 A.D., a "mediaeval period" from 1000 to 1800 A.D.,
and a "modern period" after 1800.

Although many epic stories occur in Hindu literature,
two stand out with major prominence not only as perhaps
the greatest in Hindu history but as among the greatest
epics of all mankind. They are called the *"Mahabharata"*
and the *"Ramayana."* The term *"Mahabharata"* remains
hard to translate into English but is a word as rich in
connotation for Hindus as the word "American," which
has vague and variable geographical, cultural, political,
literary, and spiritual meanings intuitively appreciated
by those at home in them. *"Maha"* means "Great" and
"Bharata" has a meaning variously signifying "Being" (such
as the cosmic being of mankind), "Bearing" (such as the
providential giving birth, nourishing, maintaining, protecting and bringing to worthy culmination of mankind), and
"Brotherhood" (not a collection of associated men but
variegated, emergent, sentient and desiring beings existing
as manifestations of a common reality in which they live
and move and have their being). *"Bharata"* may be translated as "India," not so much the geographical territory as
the spiritual Mother of people; not so much as something

opposed to other nations, cultures, or territories as an up-welling of spiritual consciousness in a persisting and providential spiritual cosmos. Those who prefer a more mundane translation may be satisfied to point out that the *Mahabharata* consists of the story of the descendants of King Bharata and that the title has no other significance. Yet, whatever the origin of its name, in the Hindu mind it is felt to have a very profound and sacred meaning. The term *"Ramayana"* refers to the god, Rama, and to enduring moral and spiritual values illustrated in Rama's character, which are preserved for our benefit as part of our cultural heritage.

Both epics differ from the *Vedas* and their commentaries, which the epics presuppose, by deifying personalities rather than by personifying nature powers. The main characters, now idealized and perhaps somewhat fictionized, doubtless were once real persons faced with human problems, temptations, vices, and virtues. The accounts of their lives, exploits, and attainments, especially moral victories, have been magnified as divine and their natures have become deified and often identified with cosmic deities. Krishna, for example, is regarded as an Avatar of Vishnu, and so the legends and philosophy of Krishna became amalgamated into the huge mass of spiritual literature in such a way that it is regarded as an inspiring expression of the same ultimate reality, Brahman, that manifested itself as the Vedic gods and as the *Atman* or *Purusha* (cosmic soul) intuited in yogic meditation.

Both epics differ from the *Brahma Sutras* in that they consist of stories about the lives of peoples faced with moral predicaments rather than arguments about textual meanings of early scriptures and about structural relations between Brahman and levels of deity and about the nature and fate of individual souls. Although the views discussed in the *Brahma Sutras* also were presupposed and generally accepted, the epics emphasize both principles of morality and devotion to persons. These two emphases, on devotion and morality, merge with, or rather remain unseparated from, each other and feelings of identity with Brahman, yogic methods of intuiting ultimate being, and participation in the sacred history depicted in and flowing from the *Vedas*. These epics dramatize interminglings of many different phases of Hindu philosophy and religion while adding poignant examples of moral virtues dressed in lovable personalities whose deeds and attitudes serve as ideals to be emulated in ordinary life. Thus these two epics join the great stream of Vedic and Sutra literature as part of the vast Hindu Bible.

The Ramayana

The story of the *Ramayana* is known to every Indian just as the life of Moses and the parables of Jesus are known to every European. King Dasaratha of Ayodhya had three wives and four sons, Rama, Lakshmana, Bharata, and Satrughna. When the sage Visumitra called for help from the King to stop demons from throwing dirt upon his ceremonially-clean austerity practices, the King, who could not come himself, sent Rama, who destroyed the demons. Rama thereby exemplified both unselfish service, defense of traditional holy values, and personal prowess. Rama then went on to pay a friendly visit to a neighboring king, Janaka, who happened to be offering his lovely daughter in marriage as a prize to the first contender who could lift a huge bow. Rama courteously deferred to all contestants until, after all others had failed, he stepped up, not only to lift the bow but to shoot it with unerring marksmanship, thereby illustrating the superior virtue of combining strength with modesty. He not only won the beautiful daughter, Sita, but provided the occasion for himself and his three brothers to marry four sisters in a glorious celebration.

The King wanted Rama for his successor, but the King's favorite wife, mother of Bharata, wanted her son to rule. She had previously obtained two boons or promises from the King; she now asked for the crowning of Bharata and the exile of Rama for fourteen years. Rama, despite his own, his father's, and the people's disappointment, voluntarily undertook to keep his father's word as a dutiful son should do, thereby upholding both the sacredness of honor and the ideal of filial service to parents. Although Rama desired to go into exile alone, to spare his wife Sita the dangers and discomforts of rude adversities and foreign afflictions, both she and his brother Lakshmana chose to

accompany him, thus portraying the virtues of loyal wife-
liness and loyal brotherliness. After the King died, Bharata,
who was duly called to the throne, believed Rama the right-
ful ruler and went to Rama in exile to beg him to return.
But Rama, still imbued with a sense of duty to his father's
solemn promises, refused. Bharata, also adamant, exemplifying courage to stand for fitness and justice against
conniving and favoritism, compromised by taking Rama's
sandals back and placing them on the throne while he
ruled as vice-regent until the end of Rama's fourteen-year
exile.

While wandering in exile, Rama was attacked by demons.
Repulsing them, he miraculously killed fourteen thousand
of them in forty-eight minutes, so powerful was he. This
deed enraged Ravana, chief of the demons, who contrived
to carry off Sita, Rama's wife, in revenge. As she was
being carried away, Sita tossed her ornaments to monkeys,
hoping they might serve as clues to aid Rama in tracing
her. But he searched in vain, giving vent to his grief and
pledging undying love in eloquent language oft-quoted by
Hindus, much as Europeans express their sentiments in
Shakespearean moods. Finally, having won through kindness the friendship of a monkey, Rama was inducted to
the inner circles of the monkey kingdom to seek help from
Sugriva, the monkey chief, who unfortunately was occupied in a battle to regain his kingdom from an evil brother.
Rama helped Sugriva, symbolizing further service on the
side of justice, more personal courage and strength, as well
as persistence and patience in his pursuit of Sita. Although
slow to do so, the monkey chief sent his monkeys out in
all directions to search for clues, to no avail, until Hanuman, the wisest among them and the friendliest to Rama,
discovered her safe but imprisoned on Ceylon. Hanuman
returned with the news to Rama, but not until he had
first warned Ravana, "You had better release Sita or you
will be punished." Aided by monkey bands and prodigious
leaps, Rama and his loyal brother Lakshmana built a bridge
of islands across two hundred and fifty miles of sea to
Ceylon. A ferocious battle between the armies of Rama
and Ravana narrowed to a violent hand-to-hand contest
between Rama and Ravana, in which the former was vic-

torious, demonstrating ultimate victory for those who persist in righteousness.

Although Sita was rescued amid rejoicing, Rama suddenly developed doubts about her loyalty and purity, and a concern for his royal reputation. Sita willingly submitted to a trial by fire, which burned her not, proving her innocence and exemplifying the virtue of wifely fidelity for all Hindu women to emulate. A triumphant return to Ayodhya, where his vice-regent brother, Bharata, was now able and glad to turn over the governing of a restless people to King Rama, brought the adventures of the heroic Rama to a lived-happily-ever-after conclusion. Later events also illustrate how misfortune falls upon the most deserving and how we may behave admirably even in the face of injustice.

Part of the significance of the story is the role played by Hanuman, the wise and friendly monkey, who also became deified as "man's best friend," giving scriptural justification for the customary treatment of monkeys as divine beings. Although in the story itself, the heroic Rama is not regarded as a cosmic deity, tradition has identified him as one of the ten Avatars (the eighth) of Vishnu, thereby enabling teachers to claim Rama's moral virtues as manifestations of the supreme deity itself. Thus in popular religion, the thrilling account of the life of Rama continues to be a source of interest and moral instruction in present-day India.

An example of how the message of the ancient *Ramayana,* authorship of which is attributed to Valmiki, has been adapted to support India's contemporary political and social system can be observed in an article by D. B. K. S. Ramaswami in *The Aryan Path,* October, 1949. The key to government guided by the ideals of the *Ramayana* is "a change of heart in human beings." "Valmiki's concept of the State was secular yet spiritual. He stood for a Dharmic State, a State wherein Dharma (moral principle) rules as King of Kings." "Valmiki's India was not a country of the modern capitalistic type or of that other modern type of regimented collectivism. It approximated more to the modern type of Welfare State of a democratic and constructive type of Socialism which chooses the middle way...." "I claim that the *Ramayana* society and State were of an evolutionary democratic Socialist type, based on reverence for personality and group interdependence and motivated by love and *ahimsa* (nonviolence)." It involves "extension of the family spirit to society as a whole."

The Mahabharata

The *Mahabharata,* composed of one hundred thousand verses, remains mankind's longest epic. It is a veritable library of dramatic episodes in a complicated historical struggle of a people typifying all mankind, failing to live at peace with themselves due to the greed and pride of a few otherwise decent noblemen. The whole gamut of human problems, and of joys and woes, afflicting good people caught up in the intrigues of a highly-placed schemer have been excitingly portrayed by the literary genius of Vyasa, who selected them out of the real lives of his own relatives. The *Mahabharata* is at once an historical account of the moral turmoils of the descendants of King Bharata, an allegorical drama of the battle within man's soul between his higher and his lower natures in which justice and virtue eventually win out, a summary of the major types of Hindu philosophy, and a religious documentation of how divinity both intervenes in and remains aloof from the affairs of men. The struggles depicted are human, all too human; yet the constant presence of Krishna, Avatar of Vishnu, who announces his divinity and dispenses divine wisdom, sustains the Hindu ideal that all men are more or less divine and that moral virtue and vice are themselves of greater or lesser divinity. As an epic, the *Mahabharata* combines great religion, great philosophy, great literature, and great drama.

The plot begins when Dhritarashtra, blind eldest son of King Bharata, was debarred from ruling by Aryan law, and Pandu, next in line, was enthroned. Pandu died prematurely, and his own five children, the eldest and heir being Yudhishthira, were cared for by their blind uncle, the debarred heir, and trained by Bhishma, a wise and unselfish granduncle. Duryhodhana, eldest and favorite son of the blind Dhritarashtra, jealous of the five Pandu brothers, contrived to have them entrapped in a flaming building. They escaped, disguised themselves as Brahmin beggars, and won a princess of a neighboring kingdom in competition with Duryhodhana while still in disguise. After the wedding they reappeared in their own kingdom before the blind vice-regent Dhritarashtra, who was persuaded by Bhishma to split the kingdom in half between his own sons, with Duryhodhana at the head, and the five sons of his brother Pandu, with Yudhishthira as their head. This was done, but the jealous Duryhodhana schemed to have Yudhishthira risk his kingdom in games of dice. Yudhishthira lost, which meant thirteen years exile for the five brothers, after which Duryhodhana refused to restore their rights or even to give them five little villages despite the pleadings of friends and relatives, including the wise and divine Krishna.

The grounds were thus laid for a "righteous war" wherein the virtuous but wronged sons of Pandu were forced to battle the vicious sons of Dhritarashtra in an all-consuming conflict that nobody wanted. The eighteen-day slaughter ended in victory for the sons of Pandu, vindicating righteousness and establishing a happy, justly governed kingdom. Although the *Mahabharata* remains a vast treasury of source materials for many purposes, including varieties of examples of courage, honesty, justice, charity, patience, perseverance, and other moral virtues for popular emulation, two characters stand out as examples for religious and philosophical instruction: Krishna and Arjuna. Both will receive further mention in our following section on *The Gita*. But stories about the life of the god Krishna embedded in the *Mahabharata* deserve some attention.

Krishna, a brother-in-law of Yudhishthira and Arjuna from a neighboring kingdom and possibly himself chief author of the *Mahabharata*, *i.e.* Krishna Vyasa, contributes a story of his own development through a series of dramatic episodes. Eighth child of a royal couple, whose birth, an omen had predicted, would kill a forewarned and watchful tyrant, Krishna at birth was transported miraculously from prison to a nearby herdsman's home and substituted for a girl born simultaneously. He grew up among the goats and gopis (daughters of goatherds), mischievously delighting all with his audacious pranks. During his early youth, from seven to twelve, Krishna spent happy years gamboling with gopis among the forests and pastures along the Jamuna river. "Their love-episodes in the woods and dales and meadows of Vrindavan [Brindaban] are still cherished by millions of Hindus and form an important part of India's mystical literature." (Swami Nikhilananda, *The Bhagavad Gita*, N. Y.: The Ramakrishna-Vivekananda Center, 1952, p. 30. This volume contains an excellent twenty-eight page summary of the story of the *Mahabharata*.) The tyrant, King Kamsa, having learned about Krishna's survival, inveigled him to a festival and involved him in a faked wrestling tournament before the assembled multitude. Krishna's superhuman prowess enabled him to dispose quickly of both his would-be murderer and King Kamsa. He then revealed his true self to his parents and the public, restored the kingdom to Kamsa's father, established a city and kingdom for his kinsmen, and became an adviser to kings in matters of government and war. He himself never ruled but developed a reputation as an impartial and wise counsellor.

It is significant to note how a person endowed with heroic qualities, unimpeachable moral insight and courage, and devoted to the service of all his people, became deified through the literary expression of ideals appealing to people. In contrast with the Vedic accounts of gods, in which natural phenomena such as the wind and sun and rain were deified and personified, through the story of Krishna we see how a person was deified and then identified with the great impersonal deity or superdeity, Brahman. We need be no more startled by Vyasa's depicting himself as god and Brahman than by Jesus's saying "I and my Father are one." Any seer who recognizes himself as an embodiment of cosmic wisdom is dishonest when he fails to express the truth about his embodiment, unless, of course, the place where he lives consists entirely of "stony ground" and among those who have ears that "cannot hear." Vyasa's self-deification was no act of arrogance but simply the expression of great virtues in ways that have inspired Hindus to nobler living throughout the centuries. He merely spoke in the already-established spirit of Hindu philosophy and religion, which regards all life as divine and its various turmoils as manifestations of cosmic degeneration or sport.

We turn next to the *Gita,* that small portion of the *Mahabharata* providing a literary summary of all major types of Hindu religious philosophy which serves as the "gospel" or "new testament" of Hindu religion.

The Gita

Strange and ironical will appear the selection of a battle-field as the setting for the expounding of a philosophy of peace. Stranger still will seem the divine advice of the god of peace that his moral hero should fight and kill un-flinchingly and without remorse. Here exists a god-is-on-our-side scriptural source that Hindu militarists have not yet finished using. But deeper penetration into the author's motive reveals the intention is not to justify war but rather to demonstrate a philosophy so all-sufficient that it can set at peace even the doubts of a warrior who must fight. It would be unrealistic of either an author or a di-vinity to ignore the prospects and practical necessities of war. The real-life plot of the whole *Mahabharata* weaves itself into a predicament making war inevitable; what bet-ter time than at the critical moment before plunging into a life-or-death struggle to take stock of the meaning and nature of life and the universe, and how its ultimate goal may be achieved? Also, allegorically, the significance of conflicting forces within man's soul may most readily be grasped when its crisis has reached a peak. With inge-niously masterful strategy, dramatist Vyasa chose the most exciting moment, the opening of his climax, to hold his audience while he surveyed all of the great ways to life's goal, ways that might escape attention if other modes of instruction were used.

Arjuna, chosen leader of the sons of Pandu forced to fight against the sons of Dhritarashtra, as already men-tioned, had the deity Krishna as his adviser and charioteer. While reviewing his forces just prior to the signal for both hordes to attack, Arjuna suddenly "got cold feet." He not only was risking the lives of his brothers, children, friends, and followers, but also was bound to destroy some of his beloved cousins, uncles, grandnephews—for the bitter battle was a family affair (even as all wars occur among members of the human family). A moral hero, he wanted not to slay anyone; he preferred to be killed rather than kill any of his relatives. Krishna restored his fighting morale by arguments giving the ultimate reasons for all living, acting, and desiring, and reasons that he should want to fulfill his own particular duties in the present situation. In doing so, Krishna surveyed all of the principal ways of living or paths to life's goal, thereby giving divine expression to the different varieties of philosophy prevalent in Hindu thought and providing another lasting example of how the Hindu mind incorporates, without being disturbingly inconsistent, the Many in the One. Let us summarize these chief ways of yea-saying by reducing each to its essential ideas. Each may be called a "Yoga" and each Yoga is a way of saying "Yea." We will call them "the Way of Knowledge," "the Way of Action," "the Way of Meditation," and "the Way of Devotion."

The Way of Knowledge

Krishna argues that Arjuna's faltering must be due to ignorance of the true nature of things. If you know the truth, the truth will make you free from all doubt and lack of confidence. If you know the truth, you will naturally act in accordance with it. The truth is that ultimate reality is permanent, unchanging, eternal, and similarly that what is ultimate about one's own self or soul, and about one's kinsmen, whether friends or enemies, is eternal and imperishable. Therefore, whatever happens to bodies in battle is merely a temporal event that has no real effect upon their ultimate nature. It is a mistake to take these perishable bodies as real when the ultimate good cannot be harmed by change of form. You cannot destroy souls by killing bodies.

But why, then, do delusions arise? Why do bodies seem real and the persons possessing them seem lovable in their unique shapes, particular location, and peculiar temperaments and traits? Illusion is caused by the three *gunas*. Ultimate reality, whether as pure Brahman or pure souls, remains perfectly still, undisturbed, changeless, without motion. But nature continues to be permeated by three tendencies (*gunas*), which cannot be eradicated. The first is the tendency to act, to initiate action, to stimulate interest, to arouse desire, to stir ambition, to excite passion, and to establish an insisting, demanding, willful, anxious character; it is called *"rajas guna."* The second is the tendency to remain steady, stable, calm, and unperturbed amid conflicting tendencies; this is called *"sattwa guna."* The third is the tendency to degenerate, decline, tire, give in, and give up; it is named *"tamas guna."* These three *gunas* not only permeate the whole of active existence but remain latent in ultimate reality in its pure and passive state.

When latent, the forces of these three tendencies remain in equilibrium so that no one dominates the other. But whenever *rajas,* the rousing *guna,* overcomes quiescence, it initiates disturbances that set in motion evolutionary processes that then produce the whole complex, dynamic, changing world of men, animals, and things. The very life force manifesting itself within us as a will to live, a desire to eat, and a wish to love, is an expression of the dominance of *rajas guna.* When *tamas,* the depraving *guna,* attains predominant control, stupefying degeneracy saps vitality. Sluggish intellect and deluded vision, which mistake the trivial, titillating, twinkling tinsel of life as its ultimate reality, result from the power of *tamas guna.* When *sattwa,* the stabilizing *guna,* assumes control, the excesses of *rajas* and *tamas* are held in check, the mind sees things in a clear light, a mood of confidence and trust reappears, and the self enjoys a feeling of comfort that tends to prepare it for full realization of its ultimate perfection. These three *gunas,* impersonal forces fatefully controlling our individual destinies, cause and control our insight and will, and thus determine our lot. Although personal wills are free in the sense that they are our own, the particular form and intensity they take are products of impersonal tendencies for which we are not responsible and the results of which we should not grieve about.

Since the concept of the three *gunas* may be unfamiliar to readers, some further acquaintance should prove worthwhile, especially since the *Gita* itself elaborates upon their pervasive presence. Three kinds of men, three tastes for food, three ways of giving, and three tendencies in knowing, for example, proceed from the ascendency of each of the three *gunas*. *Rajas guna* causes men to lust for power and wealth, *tamas guna* steeps men in superstitious fears of ghosts, while *sattwa guna* strengthens men to trust the sustaining powers of the universe. *Rajas guna* stimulates craving for spicy, piquant, tangy foods; *tamas guna* goads men to gluttony; *sattwa guna* predisposes men to prefer wholesome, healthy, and strength-sustaining foods. *Rajas* prompts giving for the sake of getting back more; *tamas* provokes a pretentious toss of the wrong thing to the wrong person at the wrong time; *sattwa* motivates benefiting of the needy who cannot give anything in return. The *rajas*-dominated knower sees things as different; the *tamas*-deluded knower mistakes a trivial part for the whole of truth; the *sattwa*-enlightened knower sees an ultimate indivisibility uniting all things that appear divided. Thus, one who diligently pursues the Way of Knowledge gains and retains deep-seated serenity about the course of temporal processes because he knows that good is good, evil is evil, *rajas* is *rajas*, *tamas* is *tamas*, *sattwa* is *sattwa*, and *Brahman* is *Brahman*. Instead of being anxious and ambitious (*rajas*-motivated) or fearful and despairing (*tamas*-overwhelmed), he remains confident (*sattwa*-sustained) that divine providence prevails in the end despite appearances to the contrary.

The ultimate reality of the whole Universe *(Brahman)* exists eternally without change or modification. The ultimate reality of the individual soul *(Atman)*, being identical with that of the Universe (*"Atman* is *Brahman"*), also exists eternally without change or modification. Appearance of change in body or mind flows from *Maya*, the deluding veil beclouding vision as one drifts away from perfection under the influence of the *gunas*. The Way of Knowledge *(jnana-yoga)* leads to freedom from delusion and thus to intuitive acceptance (yea-saying) of one's own ultimate reality as eternal and of man's helpless and yet self-helpful journey through the vicissitudes of time, to be observed and surveyed with deep-seated unconcern. As we shall see, action undertaken undisturbedly may itself exemplify attainment on the Way of Knowledge.

The Way of Action

Karma-yoga, progress toward the goal of life by way of good deeds, is the easiest Way to apprehend and undertake. But it involves a long path threading mazelike through countless lives, through tantalizing distractions by myriads of delightful objects, through several subtle layers of ignorance as to how, when, where, and why to act, and requiring constant alertness to appropriate nuances regarding every intention and·effort. *Karma-yoga,* the Way of Action, presupposes the "Law of Karma," known to every Hindu as part of common sense. It is the principle of reciprocity, *i.e.,* that for every action there exists an equal and opposite reaction, which permeates all activity. Consequently every good deed or intention begets its reward, sooner or later, and each evil deed or intention stores your future with a stock of "bad karmas" that ripen in due course as fruits deserved. One's station in life, *e.g.,* enjoying high or low economic and social status, one's condition in life, *e.g.,* having a beautiful or ugly, healthy or diseased body, and one's experience of life, *e.g.,* as joyful or miserable—all result from deeds in previous lives. Thus one's present experiences and the prospects of a future escape from the miseries of *Maya* all depend upon freely willed intentions and actions (as well as the *gunas*). Every act of good will assures improvement and progress on the Way of Action. Ill will or neglect, even in slight degrees, snags and subtlety snares an impassioned soul into backsliding unawares.

Paradoxically, an action done for the good of others without concern about reward for oneself brings greater good to oneself than an action selfishly intended. By a trick of fate, those who do good for the sake of reward come to concentrate more upon the reward than upon the doing of good. What does one actually receive when his action has been motivated by the wish for a reward? Calculations about amounts of rewards tend to degenerate into bargaining, distrust, cheating, quarreling, and, eventually, noncooperation. What do you wish for those who make a gift to you without wanting or expecting anything in return? Are you not embarrassed to find another who is more generous than yourself? Do you not automatically love him for his gift and want to express your love by giving in return? Empirical observation of how these psychological principles work is available for those to whom they are not intuitively, even instinctively, clear. Hence, when the divine Krishna speaks the truth about *karma-yoga*, he admonishes Arjuna to desire to do his duty without desiring rewards. "Renounce attachment to the fruits." "Do your duty for duty's sake, not for sake of rewards." Then a reward greater than all rewards will become yours without your asking.

Another profound paradox involved in *karma-yoga* appears when we realize that "action" includes not only acting overtly but acting covertly (truly intending: "As a man thinketh in his heart, so is he"), not only initiating action but intending to refrain from action, and permitting these actions and intentions in others. One who intends to resist temptation thereby acts; and such intentional resistance to action builds up one's store of good karmas as truly as intention that ends in overt behavior. Furthermore, there exists still another level of profundity involved in this paradox. For higher than intending to act and intending not to act is intending not to intend. That is, allow the *gunas* to run their course, or intend that processes, whether natural or divine, fulfill themselves any way they must, in and through you as well as in and by means of others. Unselfishly renounce your self as actor, thereby also renouncing any right of your self to rewards as actor. Will inactivity of will while observing the activity of life evolving under the direction of the *gunas*. Such inactivity is not cessation of activity and is not inertia or laziness; it is active intending to "let nature take its course" in temporal action, knowing that willingness not to disturb the course of action is more akin to the quiescence of ultimate reality than is willingness to steer the course of events in a direction conducive to greater rewards for self. Hence, Krishna speaks: "He who sees inaction in action, and action in inaction, he is wise among men, he is a yogin, and he has performed all action." (Nikhilananda, *The Bhagavad Gita, op. cit.,* p. 132.)

The Way of Meditation

Of the four ways, *raja-yoga* is both the most uniquely Hindu and the least developed in the *Gita*. It is the way of ascetics, of the aged during the last of the four stages of life, and of full-time yogins who concentrate upon attaining Nirvana in their present life rather than through countless future lives. It is well-known to Hindus as the way of its holiest of holy men. Thus Krishna, speaking to Arjuna about the ways to the goal of life, could not fail to include it and summarize its nature. Yet, it remains the least dramatic, least popular, and least conducive to spurring a warrior to engage in a crucial battle. But a presentation of *raja-yoga* not only is needed to complete the summary of ways but to show Arjuna that the goal of temporal action is to be found in eternal being bereft of all temporal considerations. *Raja-yoga* is the way through which intuition of ultimate peace can be approached most directly.

No satisfactory translations of *"raja-yoga"* into English exist. Commonly called the "Way of Meditation" or "Way of Concentration," it seeks to still all bodily and mental activities by acts of concentrating attention upon an immovable object, by eliminating all sense experience through becoming unresponsive to sensory stimuli, by restraining memory, imagination, reflection, and desire, after attaining bodily self-control through posture and breathing exercises. We shall explain *raja-yoga* later, but we should mention here that Chapter VI of the *Gita* summarizes as well as any popular work the kinds of conditions and efforts needed for "practicing yoga." (See, for example, P. C. Roy, *The Mahabharata*, Vol. V, pp. 72–75.) Yet, for the author of the *Gita*, details about a secluded place, stable seat, reduced eating, restraining senses, indifference to objects, etc., all remain subordinate to the spirit of equanimity, indifference to temporal events, and steadfast faith in the attainability of ultimate quiescence, which is the same spirit required for attaining perfection by the Ways of Action, Knowledge, and Devotion. The same goal and means to be found in all of the Ways are appealed to as evidence in convincing Arjuna to fight "for duty's sake," indifferent to personal temporal rewards.

The Way of Devotion

Bhakti yoga is a way common to all theisms and, next to *karma-yoga,* the easiest to practice. *Bhakti* (devotion) consists in worship involving a willing surrender of self and its interests to the interests of something, often a god, whose intrinsic value is regarded as greater or even greatest. Man's perpetual problem, of preventing his seeking what is best for himself from turning into a selfishness that becomes self-destructive (each man is his own worst enemy), here receives solution not by self-destruction but by self-abandonment. One does not eliminate his will but surrenders it to willing good for god; one does not diminish desire but magnifies it through wanting what is best for that being which is most good. Emotion becomes full-bodied rather than suppressed. Yet, here too, as in duty for duty's sake and in putting forth effort to attain effortless meditation, one desires to become desireless—not in the sense of having no desires but in having the good desired entirely for the better being to which one is devoted.

To what should one be devoted? The particular manner in which the object of devotion is conceived does not matter. The important consideration is attainment of selflessness through such devotion. As if in answer to countless questions raised by those hearing claims that one should be devoted to this rather than to that god, Krishna details a long list of identities so there will be no mistaking that all are manifestations of ultimate reality. He says, "I am Vishnu, I am Indra, I am Shiva, I am Rama, I am Varuna," etc., reviewing all of the well-known names of god and mentioning that to all the lesser names for deity there is no end. "I am the beginning, the middle, and the end of all creation." "I am the killed, the killer, and the instrument which kills." "I am the cunning of thieves and the purity of the good, the misery of suffering and the joy of happiness, the silence of deepest secrecy and the noise of trivial jabbering. I am the desirer, the desire, and the desired, the frustrater, the frustration, and the frustrated. I am everything and everywhere." "One cannot worship without worshipping me." Hence, to mistake universal deity as if existing wholly in some particular and partial deity is to be blind. But deity must also say, "I am the blinded, and blindness, as well as the being which the blind cannot see." So "even those who cast slurs upon me worship me in the best light they have and thereby devote themselves as best they can, and I accept their ignorant worship for what [good] it is." "One may worship me by worshipping and serving humanity, as mother, sweeper, scholar, or soldier." Thus devotion to duty as a military leader is devotion as much as any other kind, provided, like other kinds, it is selfless and without mental reservation.

What are the proper ways of worshipping? It should be clear already that the particular method or form is not of primary importance. Some worship many particular gods and spirits, through the ritualistic practices outlined in the *Vedas*. Some worship through knowing the identity of Atman and Brahman. Some worship through withdrawing the senses and mind. Some worship through austerities, fasting, and bodily torture. Some worship through sexual ecstasy. Some worship through reading scriptures, chanting verses, singing hymns, enacting plays, pilgrimages to shrines, composing poems, and wondering about the stars. All are ways, even if somewhat indirect, for attaining selfless devotion to that ultimate eternal value which transcends and endures beyond, as well as in, mortal beings. Yet, each particular person must worship in his own way and in light of his own insight and capacity. "Even a wise man acts according to his own nature." (Roy, *op. cit.*, p. 66.) But, obviously, some ways are better than others. Those which reduce hatred, bias, preference, and passion, and those which conduce to profound rather than surface indifference, are superior. One who slays a sacrificial animal or a martial enemy with great disinterest may embody a profounder and more ultimate peace than a secluded ascetic embroiled in inner wrestling with uncertainty and doubt. "Therefore, Arjuna, dedicate yourself entirely and unquestioningly to me, and fight."

The four Ways, of Knowledge, Action, Meditation, and Devotion, may appear to be different ways, even though all lead ultimately to the same goal. Yet, a deeper insight into them reveals that they not only support each other but that each entails the other in very intimate ways. (1) Selfless devotion—to deity, or to duty, or to study, or to meditation—yields knowledge that what is is, and that selfish desire to distort what is into what is not continues to be self-defeating. And one cannot progress far on the Way of Knowledge before discovering that what he seeks is a knowledge that is not knowledge but rather an intuitive awareness of having fully realized his being. (2) Acting or intending to attain knowledge, acting or intending to diminish mental activity through meditation, acting or intending to diminish selfishness through devotion, all are ways of acting and automatically yield karmas. And one cannot progress far on the Way of Action without discovering that the reward he seeks is enjoyment of a condition transcending all concern for rewards. In doing duty for duty's sake he seeks a reward that is not a reward. (3) Success in meditating not only presupposes having finished one's other duties, devotions, and quests for knowledge, but one who studies, acts, or worships with sufficiently profound selflessness and disinterestedness is already "meditating" to the extent that self and self-interest are forgotten. And one cannot advance far on the Way of Meditation unless he discovers that "meditation" is not so much a "way" as already "the end itself"; hence he seeks "a meditation which is not a meditation" by "questing for questlessness." (4) The devotee may devote himself with as complete abandonment to his study, to his duty, or to his meditation in worshiping or serving any god or cause or man, for total surrender to the good may be made on one path as upon another. And one cannot proceed far on the Way of Devotion without realizing that, to be effective, one must devote himself to some ultimate devotionlessness, to an ultimate reality that is what it is, existing as an intrinsic value, without devotion to anything else.

Knowledge that is not knowledge, action that is inaction, meditation upon meditationlessness, and devotion to devotionlessness—these profound paradoxes remain beyond common comprehension. Yet they underlie and permeate the predicaments of man who remains confused, perplexed, and uncomprehending until he becomes enabled, by whatever means, to perform (with faith, without doubt, unhesitatingly) whatever action is presented to him now as his to enact. Arjuna ought to lead his people into battle courageously now. Each man should say "Yes" to the actualities confronting him, just as the universe as a whole exists as a being that must say "Yes" to itself because it has no other real option. Even one who says "No" must say "Yes" to his saying "No." Thereby he is forced to say "Yes" even while saying "No." The four Ways, or *Yogas,* appear as merely different ways of saying "Yes." One must say "Yes"; and the more fully, the more automatically and the more profoundly he says "Yes," the less he suffers and the happier he becomes.

Chapter 4 **Jainism**

Jainism has survived for at least 2500 years and has grown both in numbers of adherents, to about a million and a half, and in complexity of philosophical erudition, to rate as one of the world's major philosophical and religious systems. Like Buddhism, which it preceded by from thirty to three hundred years, it has been regarded as heretical because it rejected as authoritative the teachings of the *Vedas* (which include animal sacrifices). But unlike Buddhism, it retained a vigorous following that distinguished itself from other movements within India. Buddhism, as an organized movement, died out in India and prospered elsewhere as a result of missionary activity. But now, while Buddhism is struggling to reestablish itself in India, Jainism, especially through the efforts of the Jain Mission Society, is extending itself to other parts of the world.

How did Jainism get started? Although we cannot be absolutely certain, we now consider Vardhamana, who after attaining stature as a religious man and teacher came to be called "Mahavira," the "Great Man" or "Hero," to be its chief founder. Mahavira lived from 599 to 527 B.C., according to our best guessing, and was probably a contemporary of Gotama, The Buddha, but somewhat older, perhaps as much as thirty years. Because he conquered the delusions and inclinations infecting degenerate human nature, he, and other Jains before and after him, came to be called "Jina" meaning "The Conqueror." He did not conquer and enslave others. Each man is his own worst enemy and conquest of self is a man's greatest victory. Now, every man who attains self-mastery is a conqueror, a Jina, or, more commonly, a Jain.

Jain tradition holds that Mahavira was preceded by twenty-three other holy teachers or *Tirthankaras* (Saints).

His immediate predecessor was *Parsva* (or *Parshva*) who lived about two hundred and fifty years earlier, presumably during the hundred years 877 to 777 B.C., which would put the origin of Jainism in about the ninth century B.C. and make it one of the world's oldest religions. The fantastic periods of time that Jain tradition claims elapsed between the appearances of the twenty-two earlier *Tirthankaras* forces the careful scholar to leave that matter unsettled for all but the Jain faithful.

Two sects developed from an issue that, to outsiders, seems trivial, perhaps. One sect, the *Digambaras,* believe in humility and practicing austerities to the extent of wearing no clothing and giving up all possessions. Their name means "sky clad," and they regard nudity a natural requirement of their religious beliefs. The other sect, the *Svetambaras,* or "white clad," do wear white robes and behave somewhat more accommodatingly to many of the human frailties. But on major doctrinal issues the two sects remain in substantial agreement. What are these?

Jain tradition conveniently summarizes its views under nine headings, principles, or categories. Single words serve as mental handles for them: "soul," "non-soul," "virtue," "vice," "inflow," "bondage," "checking," "shedding," and "freedom."

I. SOUL (*Jiva,* a Sanskrit term etymologically related to the English "live," the French "vivre," the Spanish "viva," and the Russian "zhiv") is the life principle. A soul is an inherently conscious, independent agent. An infinite number of souls exist. Each is eternal (hence imperishable), formless, and spatial. When a soul obtains a body it pervades the whole body and thus assumes the size and shape of that body. When released from all bodily connections, a soul ceases to have any appreciable size of its own but nevertheless continues to exist in a celestial space.

Souls may exist in two kinds of conditions: freed (*mukta*) or bound (*bandha*). The freed state is the ideal goal to be obtained, if not at the end of one's present life, then at the end of a series, or several series, of lives, if one eventually succeeds in becoming a "conqueror." It is a condition of perfect bliss, life's ultimate objective.

The bound condition consists really in a whole range of degrees or levels of bondage that may be thought of as levels or degrees of imperfection. A soul does not become imperfect, but it loses intuitive insight into its own perfection by becoming entangled in material entities that obscure the clarity of its vision of itself and the universe. These levels of obscurity may be correlated with the capacities for knowing exhibited in different kinds of animals, for example. Whereas in a freed state the soul is omniscient, since nothing obscures its vision, in a bodily state it submits to apprehending itself and other things with the aid of the various senses. Men normally perceive through five senses, commonly called touch, taste, smell, hearing, and seeing, as do cows, elephants, monkeys, birds, frogs, etc. But some animals have only four senses, since sight is presumed to be missing in mosquitoes, for example. Some have only three senses, for hearing seems absent from ants, lice, and certain insects. Some have only two, for worms and snails supposedly cannot smell. Finally, we come to beings with only one sense—touch. Vegetables belong to this class, though since souls pervade everything—earth, air, water, and fire—these seethe with souls whose capacity to know has been reduced to that of contact.

Bound souls mistakenly cling to obscuring conditions as if they were good. Not only continuation in the same body (which may change and develop from birth to death) but in many different successive bodies is a natural consequence. Desires that merit evil consequences intensify a soul's debasement; desires that merit rewards enable a soul to attain clearer insight and rise to higher levels. In order to account for this view a theory of the universe has been developed. We turn, next, to the second heading under which five additional kinds of substance are presented.

II. NON-SOUL (*"Ajiva,"* a Sanskrit term joining the "a" meaning "not" with *"jiva"* meaning soul or life) is of five kinds. These again may be designated by single names: "Matter," "Motion," "Rest," "Space" and "Time."

A. **Matter** *(pudgala)* exists in two forms: atomic *(anu)* and aggregate *(skanda)*. Each atom is indivisible, indestructible, and hence eternal. It occupies one point in space, but does not extend over two points. It is formless, yet serves as the source of all form. All atoms are alike or homogeneous, having no qualitative differences.

Each possesses certain qualities that function as the ultimate source of our sensory experiences of them. Each has "one taste" (there are five kinds: bitter, pungent, sour, sweet, astringent), "one color" (five kinds: blue, yellow, white, black, red), and "two tactile qualities" (eight kinds: softness, hardness, heaviness, lightness, cold, heat, smoothness, roughness). Atoms remain imperceptible but have qualities that produce perceptions when they are gathered together in aggregates that are big enough (but not too big, for we cannot perceive the whole earth, for example).

Aggregates of atoms may be large or small, can grow or decrease, and constitute the bodies of all perceivable material beings. Matter functions as the basis for a soul's body, for speech, for respiration, and for mind. It makes possible sensuous pleasure and pain, and life and death. Matter is knowable and enjoyable. Karmic particles are also classed as material. This feature of Jain metaphysics seems especially important since it provides a reason for the emphasis upon austerities in Jain ethics. Although karmic atoms embody both "good karmas" and "bad karmas," one cannot attain the final goal of liberation until his soul is freed from all matter, including all karmas or karmic particles.

B. **Motion** *(dharma)* is really a principle of motion, a principle that makes motion possible, without itself moving or causing anything to move. A soul cannot move up and down in the levels of imperfection of vision without some principle that makes such motion possible. The soul, although an agent in the sense that it can will, does not embody any principle of motion in itself. Hence some non-soul principle of motion seems needed to account for the upward and downward movements of souls as well as all other kinds of movement.

C. **Rest** *(adharma)*, the opposite of motion, is also a principle that makes rest possible. Not only do physical things remain at rest for long periods, but a soul itself may eventually come to rest in its ultimate free state. Thus a non-soul principle of rest seems needed.

D. **Space** *(akasa)* is of two kinds. One is the space of the world, including all of "the three worlds": the upper or celestial world with sixteen heavens; the middle world, with its innumerable rings of continents and oceans; and the lower world, seven "earths." These three worlds serve as a ladder of degrees of imperfection that a soul may climb or descend through hundreds of thousands of lives. Freed souls rise to the top where they remain eternally. The number of bound souls is infinite and the number of freed souls is infinite. But all souls exist in space, even though freed souls no longer have size since they no longer have bodies. The second kind of space is that outside of "the three worlds" and contains nothing. It is pure space and performs no significant function in the structure of the universe.

E. **Time** is of two kinds: "Absolute" or "real" time (*kala*) and "relative" or "empirical" time (*samaya*). Absolute time is that principle which makes endurance or continuance of things possible. It is eternal, formless, and without beginning or end. Relative time is that principle which makes change, novelty, growth, and aging possible. It has beginnings and endings. It consists of many varieties, such as moments, days, and months, which have different durations.

All five kinds of non-soul are substantial and eternal. They, like souls, were neither created nor can they be destroyed. They exist together and mutually penetrate or pervade each other. Together they provide conditions within which souls become bound and may again become free.

III and IV. VIRTUE (*punya*) and VICE (*papa*) are good and evil karmas that lead to right and wrong conduct. Good karmas produce pleasant experiences and bad karmas unpleasant experiences. Although we desire good karmas and desire to avoid bad ones, paradoxically both good and bad karmas must be eliminated before we can attain liberation since, in a liberated state, we become freed from all desiring, including good karmas. The ultimate goal consists not in a life of virtue but in a condition freed from both virtue and vice.

V and VI. INFLOW of karmic particles into a soul, and the BONDAGE of a soul and these particles to each other, occur when a soul becomes emotional. A soul may cease to be emotional and attract no more new karmic particles without releasing itself from bondage to those already

present in it. Causes of inflow and bondage may be arranged into four groups, pertaining to "wrong belief,"
"vowlessness," "passions," and "activity."

A. **Wrong belief** is of five kinds: One-sided conviction; perverse belief; doubtful belief; ignorant belief;
blind devotional belief.

Our will to believe that we know truly when we do
not leads to hasty generalization and to "one-sided conviction." Each thing has many sides or aspects. To accept some and reject others as revelatory of its nature
constitutes a one-sided view. Jain logic emphasizes a
nonabsolutistic knowledge of things and lists seven
kinds of statements that can be predicated of each
thing: (a) In a sense, X (any substance, such as "a
table") is A (*i.e.*, has some aspect or quality, such as
"is brown"). (b) In a sense, X is NON-A (where
"NON-A" means some qualities or aspects other than
A; *i.e.*, no one quality or set of qualities can exhaust all
of the qualities of X). (c) In a sense, X is both A and
NON-A. (d) In a sense, X is indescribable. (That is,
no matter how many qualities have been included in
A and NON-A, there is more to X, including more
qualities of X, than can ever be described. Hence, in
addition to all the ways in which a thing can be described, there is also something about it that cannot be
described.) (e) In a sense, X is A and is indescribable.
(f) In a sense, X is NON-A and indescribable. (g) In
a sense, X is both A and NON-A and indescribable.
Jain logic has been designed to help prevent one-sided
belief, which mistakes partial apprehension for total
or absolute apprehension.

"Perverse belief" may be illustrated by the conviction
that killing animals is good (whether for food or as sacrifices to the gods, as the *Vedas* teach) or that a soul·is
material and destructible. "Doubtful belief" may be exemplified by doubts about the existence of soul, non-
soul, etc., or about the nine principles of Jainism here
being discussed. "Ignorant belief" is belief without the
effort to understand what it believes in. "Blind devotional
belief" is clinging to convictions even in the face of evidence of falsity.

B. **Vowlessness** refers not to the failure to swear an

oath but to the failure to develop character tendencies that carry out the five virtues of non-injury *(ahimsa)*, truthfulness, non-stealing, chastity, and renunciation of possessions. *Ahimsa* (or *ahinsa*), that typical Hindu ideal of nonviolence, is emphasized by Jains as much or more than by any other group of Hindus. *Ahimsa* includes not merely killing of all kinds (from which vegetarianism follows logically), and physical injury of any kind, but also intention to disturb another's mind with unpleasant thoughts or to harm his reputation or spiritual condition in any way. A committed Jain carries a brush for gently removing ants or crawling insects from his path whenever he goes out walking. Some even wear masks to protect flying insects from the danger of being inhaled.

C. **Passions,** mainly of four kinds—anger, pride, deceit, and greed—may again be subdivided into twenty-five kinds, depending upon their intensity and duration, but including also fear, hate, sorrow, and sexual passions. Submitting to emotional disturbances naturally leads to turbulent thought and conduct.

D. **Activity,** whether of mind or body, that disturbs the soul with desires, whether good or bad, binds additional karmas to it. Passionless thought, and consequently passionless speech and conduct, will stop further inflow and bondage. Hence one should seek to embody in himself humility, forgiveness, honesty, truthfulness, purity of heart, self-control, penance, charity, and nonattachment. He will, further, seek to live calmly and peacefully, suffering the unavoidable troubles of hunger, thirst, cold, heat, abuses, dishonor, and the like. Finally, he will meditate upon the transitoriness of worldly phenomena, the painful nature of wandering in the world, and the way to liberation.

VII and VIII. CHECKING and SHEDDING of karmic particles require efforts that not merely oppose but also reverse the processes of inflow and bondage. In order to check inflow and bondage, one must seek to attain right belief, commitment, passionlessness, and calm behavior. In order to shed already bound karmas, one must seek nonattached thought-activity by concentrating upon the purity of his soul. Such concentration may be aided by practicing certain austerities *(tapas):* fasting, eating less than is required, giving up rich and tasty foods, sitting and sleeping in solitary places, accepting penalties for violating rules or vows, devotion to the true path, service to those on the right path, reading scriptures, disregard of body and its surroundings, persistent meditation, etc. The clinging power of karmas can be loosened through practicing such asceticism; and when they drop away finally, the soul is freed from their knowledge-obscuring powers. After a soul has shed all such infecting karmas, it automatically rises above them and enjoys its own pure, blissful, omniscient state.

IX. LIBERATION *(mukti)* is a condition attained after all foreign karmic particles have been removed. In its freed state, the soul is pure. It also enjoys omniscience, perfect faith, omnipotence, and utter bliss. It does so eternally, for once a soul becomes released from the rounds of rebirth, it does not return into them. "Omniscience" consists in knowing all things precisely as they are. Such knowledge is clear and complete. "Perfect faith" enjoys absence of all doubt. Omniscient knowledge apprehends all things intuitively so all doubt must disappear. When one has arrived at and intuitively enjoys the ultimate goal of life, doubts about his arriving there have been eliminated automatically. "Omnipotence" means power to remain perfect. Nothing can force or tempt a freed soul out of its pure or perfect condition. Omnipotence is not power to control other things, for the moment one developed an interest in meddling with or influencing other things, his own disinterested condition would disappear. Thus, perfect omnipotence is not power to control things but power to remain uninfluenced by any foreign element. The "utter bliss" that a freed soul enjoys remains, of course, beyond description. No terms, such as pleasure, joy, or ecstasy, that describe our experiences in a bound or bodily state, can capture the all-pervasive, overwhelming, eternal bliss constituting the soul in its freed state.

Jainism is atheistic. At least it believes that all of the nine principles or categories just reviewed remain eternal and uncreated. No God is needed to create an eternally existing world. Each soul must work out its own salvation, so no God is needed to help. Each soul in its liberated state itself becomes omniscient, omnipotent, and the highest possible value, so no greater knowledge or power or value is possible. However, if this condition is characteristic of God-hood, then every liberated soul is a God and every bound soul, whether existing as a man, as a mosquito, or even as a rock, is potentially just such a God whose realization of its Godhood is prevented by karmic particles, which ob-scure knowledge.

If Jainism is atheistic, how can it be a religion? many will ask. Religion is man's quest for his ultimate value. Jainism acclaims the ultimate value of man, describes a way to attain it, and explains why so many souls have not yet arrived at their goal. Comparing Jainism with other reli-gions, we may observe that it conceives each man as having potentially greater ultimate value than do those religions that depict him as forever inferior to the value of a Su-preme Being Whose goodness he may enjoy by coming "face to face" with it. If "man's last end" exists outside him, even partly, then he has less to hope for than if he can realize ultimate perfection entirely within himself.

If religion involves yea-saying, how do Jains conceive man's way of saying "Yes"? A review of the doctrines already mentioned reveals them as designed to promote yea-saying. First, the doctrine of self as a living principle *(jiva)*, translated into English as "soul," is something that a man cannot help but say "Yes" to. Unless given to despising himself, a person naturally accepts himself as enduring and worthwhile. Secondly, being afforded the means of hope for the soul's liberation from its entangle-ment in a round of rebirths in a world of delusion, is an essentially optimistic view to which a person can say "Yes." Thirdly, the view that each soul can attain perfection, a perfection attributable only to God in many other religions, is an ideal to which a devotee will naturally say "Yes." Fourthly, by locating the source of obligation within each self and having no external force to antagonize men, this system eliminates man's natural resistance to externally imposed "don'ts" or tabus to which he instinctively says "No." Fifthly, the specific means for pursuing the religious goal include particular suggestions for yea-saying. For example, it commends one to "right belief," and everyone wants right belief. It advises an attitude of "calmly and peacefully suffering unavoidable troubles." Finally, in addition to the varieties of yea-saying available to a person bound in his present body, Jainism idealizes the condition of a soul in its liberated state as having "perfect faith" or an attitude in which yea-saying is complete. If a soul attains unending omniscience, omnipotence, and bliss, which are directly intuited, it can have no doubts, no "Nays," no lack of complete, perfect, and perpetual affirmation.

Does Jainism exhibit both "low" and "high" religion? It has no doctrine of grace whereby one may hope for better than he deserves. Its law of karma operates relentlessly and one can expect no rewards unless he works for them and unless he deserves them. A man's present condition as well as his future prospects are conceived as determined by his own actions; hence he alone is responsible and he receives and will receive precisely what he deserves. Jain ideals clearly exhibit "high" religion. "Low" religion doubtless occurs in the dissatisfied attitude of those who, inheriting a low and frustrating station in their present life, attribute their unhappy condition to the misdeeds of a soul in antecedent lives. Or, if one pursues his desires today, disregarding their consequences for himself either in this life or in later lives, he acts as if he believes he can later escape the evil he deserves. It exists, also, whenever one fails to realize that he does not deserve to attain his ultimate goal until he not only habitually prefers to act so as to produce good karmas but also becomes habitually willing to surrender his attachment to all karmas. That is, one must not only affirm that he deserves justice, if the results are painful, but also that he has no right and should have no desire to demand justice, in terms of reward, if he is to rise from "low" to "high" religion.

Perhaps I should not confess that my investigation of Jainism has produced some doubt as to the universality of my thesis that all mature religions exhibit four stages, characterized primarily by fear, hope, assent, and joy. I have difficulty finding examples where Jain teachers make any overt appeal to fear. It is true that a traditionally accepted Jain picture of the cosmos has "seven earths," each with its own "hell." But these appear more as graphic representations of kinds of suffering due to increasing stupor resulting from knowledge-obscuring conditions as a soul becomes embodied in lower forms, than as progressively painful torture chambers designed to frighten the indifferent man. Fear of failure to attain one's ultimate goal is, of course, implicit in the system. But my thesis is safe only if Jain parents and teachers in fact appeal to fear in order to arouse in their children and wards a concern for their religious welfare.

In closing the present chapter, I cannot refrain from mentioning that my summary sketch fails to convey the intricate ways in which Jain practice has become involved in the industrial and metropolitan complexities of contemporary life. If we can trust a news report, we urbanites may sympathize with a current Jain predicament. After eight months of collective bargaining, more than one hundred Jain priests from twenty-one temples in Ahmedabad won most of their demands. Their agreement provides them with forty days of leave annually, with substitutes employed for their days off. Such annual leave may be accumulated up to three years. Retirement pay will be provided for priests with more than ten years of service.

Chapter 5 Buddhism

Estimates of five hundred million Buddhists in the world, including about one hundred and sixty-five thousand on the North American continent, do not begin to tell the story of the importance of Buddhism today. Although Buddhism died out in India as an organized movement, most Indians still regard Buddha as India's greatest figure. Buddhism spread not only throughout Southeast Asia, where it continues to be the dominant, even official, religion of many countries, but into Tibet, China, Korea, and Japan where it remains a stalwart force resisting Western, including Communist, penetration. Having lived a half-millennium earlier than Jesus and having influenced two of the world's three great civilizations, Buddha has been more widely known and has reached more people than Christ. In the West, Buddha has become the best-known Oriental, and, even though his teachings remain unclear, acquaintance with statues of Buddha has become almost universal.

Certain puzzles confront Westerners trying to learn about the teachings of Buddha. In addition to difficulties in comprehending Oriental outlooks generally, which tend to be antilegalistic and antivoluntaristic, and to the fact that paradoxes, inherent in all philosophies, seem to stand out more bafflingly in those of foreigners than in our own, and to poor idiom-to-idiom translations between languages constructed on different conceptual schemes, we find many versions of his teachings. Keeping in mind two things may alleviate our predicament. The first is that Buddhism has had a long history, half a millennium longer than Christianity, and has suffered modifications through two different civilizations, Hindu and Chinese. The second is that Oriental sectarianism remains unobtrusive because of an inherently pacific nature. A live-and-let-live attitude prevents sects from fighting and seeking to suppress or annihilate each other. Thus antagonism of one sect toward another does not become a part of the doctrine of each sect, as seems so often the case with Western religions. Usually they simply ignore each other. In the process, many Buddhists belonging to one sect remain ignorant of the existence of other Buddhist sects and may be as puzzled as Westerners about such differences.

The point being made here is that one cannot begin to understand Buddhism until he learns that major as well as minor sects exist, with varying emphases among the main branches, so that he will be able to assign different views to specific movements rather than remain bewildered by an amazing diversity, or accuse Buddhism of a contradictoriness that disappears as its more distant branches become clearly differentiated from its stem and roots. In what follows, we shall distinguish between Theravada (the main philosophy of Hinayana Buddhism), Sunyavada (an outstandingly subtle philosophy of Mahayana Buddhism), Shin (a somewhat theistic type of Buddhism), and Zen (an antiphilosophical practice of immediate attainment). This sample omits even some of the main types, such as Tibetan Lamaism and Tantric Buddhism. But before we glance at the central doctrines of these four movements (for each has its own history and varieties), we will try to grasp something of the philosophy of Gotama, the Buddha—the man himself.

The Philosophy of Gotama

In June, 1955, I arrived at the University of Rangoon, Burma, as Fulbright Research Scholar in Buddhist Philosophy, to study firsthand the teaching and practices of people in a Buddhist country. Buddhism has now become the officially recognized religion of Burma. My interest in studying Buddhism grew out of two decades of teaching comparative religions during which I became gradually convinced that apparent discrepancies between formalized doctrines, which had an opaque and wooden quality about them, and stories revealing deep insight into human nature, which had a lively and self-evident quality about them, were clues to a puzzle that challenged solution. My presence in the University of Rangoon, with its library and teaching resources and opportunity for devoting full time to studying Buddhist literature, enabled me to discover, to my own satisfaction at least, a living philosophy of one of the world's wisest men, which cannot be refuted and which has universal appeal, once the crusts of tradition have been removed.

The sources of my information consist primarily of the Pali *Pitakas*, which now appear in English translations in the *Sacred Books of the Buddhists* series and of the Pali Text Society publications. The *Pitakas* are collections of sayings, dialogues, discourses, and studies handed down by monks for centuries until recorded on palm-leaf manuscripts in Ceylon and carved in rock tablets later in Mandalay and Rangoon. Pali is a language closely allied to Sanskrit. Sometimes it resembles Sanskrit so closely that one may regard it as Sanskrit spoken and written "with a Harvard accent," *i.e.*, with the "r" dropped, so that *"karma"* becomes *"kamma," "dharma"* becomes *"dhamma," "sutra"* becomes *"sutta"* and *"nirvana"* becomes *"nibbana."* The *Pitakas* are really three collections (or "baskets"): the *Vinaya Pitaka*, emphasizing rules for monks; the *Sutta Pitaka*, a repetitious compendium of dialogues, discourses, and remembrances; and the *Abhidhamma Pitaka*, a later systematization of Theravada doctrines presumably summarizing the essence of previous teachings.

The predominating doctrine expounded in the *Pitakas*, especially the *Abhidhamma Pitaka*, will occupy our attention later when we explore Theravada, the main philosophy of Hinayana Buddhism. But my discovery and confirmation of another philosophy embedded in the first two *Pitakas*, pieced together bit by bit from scattered references, resulted in its statement and demonstration in my *Philosophy of the Buddha* (N.Y.; Harper and Brothers, and London; Rider and Co., 1958. Reprinted as a paperback by Collier Books, N.Y., 1962.). A life-affirming, sensitive, startling, profound philosophy lies all but hidden in the repetitive layers of remembered and embellished discourses expressing a philosophy that, by comparison, seems relatively life-denying, unrealistic, and bafflingly inadequate. But first we should glimpse the life of Gotama.

Siddartha Gotama, c. 567-487 B.C., prince of the Sakya

clan and kingdom, was reared in luxury and pleasure by his kingly father, who feared his only son might be tempted into monkhood and leave him without an heir. But despite a surfeit of delicious foods, dancing girls, lovely music, games of war, and isolation from the misery and suffering of others, Gotama (or Gautama) wearied of such pampering. Faithful to his filial duty, he married and provided his father with a grandson and heir, before departing, at the age of twenty-nine, in quest of the true way of life. One night, after a fond look at his sleeping wife and child, he rode with his servant to the borders of his kingdom, took off his royal robes and ornaments, and sent them back to the palace with his servant. Then he went on alone, with begging bowl and loincloth, in search of wisdom. For seven years, either by himself or in company with five advanced ascetics, he practiced meditation, trances, mortification, and fasting, but all without success. One day, while recuperating from a particularly debilitating fast, he attained an insight that revealed to him the reasons for his failures and the way required to attain happiness. From this insight, called his "Enlightenment" (Sanskrit: *Buddha;* Pali: *Bodhi*), comes his honored name and "Buddhism," a collective name claimed by various movements that attribute their doctrines directly or indirectly to him.

His insight may be epitomized in a single psychological principle: "Desire for what will not be attained ends in frustration; therefore, to avoid frustration, avoid desiring what will not be attained." (*Ibid.*, p. 15.) An observation so simple and obvious compels acceptance by all who hear it. Unhappiness consists in not getting what you want. If you get what you want, you will be happy. Of course, if you want what you get, you thereby get what you want. And when you do not want what you get, you thereby do not get what you want. In sum, the reason for human unhappiness lies in failure to want what one receives and the way to human happiness is to be found in wanting what you receive.

When, as a young prince, he dined on delicacies and danced with damsels, he was unhappy, because he still desired something more. When, as a vigorous ascetic, he forced himself to suffer until he was fatigued, and fasted until he fainted, he experienced unhappiness because the goal he sought evaded him and he still desired something more. The goal can be found, he concluded, neither through self-indulgence nor through mortification but in some middle way. What is this middle way?

After a person discovers and assents to Gotama's principle, he naturally tries, at least as an experiment, to avoid wanting what he will not get. In doing so, he desires to avoid such desiring, and thereby involves himself in another kind of desire, namely, this desire to avoid such desiring. For example, one who wants more money than he will obtain becomes frustrated when he does not obtain it. If he then desires to stop desiring more money, he tends to be frustrated here also (because he desires a cessation of his desire for more money than he will acquire). Furthermore, if he then desires to stop desiring to stop desiring money, etc., he succumbs to an infinite regress. Thus in order to escape frustration completely, one must not only accept what he gets as what he wants but also accept the desiring that he has as the desiring that he wants. In effect, he must say "Yes" to his desires that will be frustrated as well as to his desires that will be satisfied. Only when one gives up caring whether his desires are satisfied or frustrated can he become completely happy. Few people can do this. Such a view does not aim to eliminate desire, but only the additional desire to have one's desires satisfied and not frustrated. It is this additional desire, which we may call "desirousness," "avidity," or "anxiety" *(tanha)*, that brings us misery.

The "middle way" turns out to be "the way things are." "The way things are" here means "are in the universe, past, present, and future," not just "are in the present as against past and future." It means "are in the present, including present opportunities for changing things in the future" as well as "are unchangeable in present or future." "The way things are" thus includes "are" in all tenses of the verb "to be" and, indeed, of all verbs. One who wants the past to be different from what it was is frustrated. One who wants the future to be different from what it is going to be will be frustrated. One who wants the present to be different is frustrated. Unhappiness results from wanting to change that which cannot be changed, or from wanting to keep the same that which cannot be kept the same.

But what if, by desiring and acting on our desires, we can make the future better than it would be without such desiring and acting? critics will ask. Go ahead. Gotama sees no objection to desires that will be satisfied, including desires to make the future better. In fact, whenever an opportunity arises for improving things and a desire to use such an opportunity arises, then such an opportunity and such desire are themselves parts of "the way things are." Superficial critics feel that Gotama discourages ambition. Not so. If the ambition to gain does result in gain, no problem of unhappiness arises. Not ambition but over-ambition is the cause of suffering; it is wanting to gain more than one will gain that causes frustration. Where one is due to lose, acceptance of the fact causes no frustration. But wanting to lose less than one will lose begets frustration. Hence, the "middle way" is also a way between wanting things to be more than they are or less than they are. It involves desiring to have one's desires satisfied or frustrated to the extent that they are. The "middle way" consists in saying "Yes" to life as it is, was, and will be, to its opportunities for attainment as well as to its limitations.

"But," the critic will persist, "how can we know whether or not our desires can be satisfied and how can we tell when we are overambitious?" When you do know, from past experience perhaps, no problem arises. When you do not know, then the problem of unhappiness occurs all over again, this time in the form of desiring to know more than you can know; and such unhappiness can be removed only by becoming willing to replace this desire by an attitude that accepts your ignorance for what it is. When, in the face of uncertainty, you must gamble, then if you are willing to accept the outcome, whatever it may be, no frustration occurs; but if, when you gamble, you insist that it come out the way you favor, you will suffer disappointment when it does not.

Gotama has a reply for all who want to know more than they can know. Such people suffer from "greed for views." His fellow monks quizzed him again and again about questions for which they wanted answers but about which no sure answers can be given. Tradition records "the ten questions" then much debated: Is the world eternal? Is the world not eternal? Is the world finite? Is the world infinite? Is the soul the same as the body? Is the soul one thing and the body another? Does one who has gained his goal live on again after death? Does he not live again after death? Does he both live again and not live again? Does he neither live again nor not live again? To each of these questions, Gotama gave the same reply: "That is a matter on which I have expressed no opinion." Why? Because taking sides on issues regarding which I do not know the answer merely commits me to unhappiness.

When his fellow monks persisted, he patiently reiterated his general psychological principle, his *dhamma,* in a more specific form suited to the person asking the question. One day an impatient young monk demanded that Gotama answer the question: "Is there a soul or is there not a soul?" threatening to abandon further association with Gotama if he failed to answer. Gotama not only refused to answer but pointed out to the young monk that he was desiring and expecting more in the way of answers than he had any right to desire and expect and that he was, therefore, merely making himself unhappy. Gotama's principle in effect promised a way to eliminate all unhappiness; but it did not promise to answer unanswerable questions. He refused to affirm not only the existence or nonexistence of a soul, the existence or nonexistence of God, the existence or nonexistence of a next life, but even whether the Law of Karma holds or does not hold. He neither affirmed nor denied the truth of the *Vedas,* though his refusal to affirm was widely misinterpreted as a denial, and he was branded as a heretic, just as his refusal to affirm the existence of a soul was mistaken as implying that he denied its existence.

Consider, for example, the issue of whether or not there will be a next life. If you desire a next life and there is a next life, you have no problem. If you desire a next life and there is no next life, you will be frustrated. If you desire no next life and there is no next life, you have no problem. If you desire no next life and there is a next life, you will be frustrated. For those who seek happiness, the important issue is not whether there is or is not a next life, but whether they are willing to accept it whichever way it comes. Regardless of whether there is or is not a next life, whoever now attains a willingness to take what comes,

however it comes, has already reached the goal of life
(Nibbana) "in this very life." When you acquire such willingness, such yea-saying, then, as English translators report the record, "to whatever place you go, you shall go in
comfort; wherever you stand, you shall stand in comfort;
wherever you sit, you shall sit in comfort; and wherever
you make your bed, you shall lie down in comfort." (*The
Book of the Gradual Sayings,* Translated by E. M. Hare.
London: Luzac and Co., Ltd., 1955, Vol. IV, p. 200.)

If Buddhism consisted simply in assenting to Gotama's
principle, surely you and I would all be Buddhists. However, the insights of Gotama have been conveyed to us
through the minds and writings of persons who interpreted
them as they understood or misunderstood them and applied them and explained them in ways of which Gotama
could not entirely approve. Each person who heard Gotama
had to respond to what he heard in terms of the perspective
and preconception and power to grasp that he brought with
him. Belief in karma and reincarnation were part of the
common sense of his time and persisted in the views of
his interpreters and their successors. The natural tendency
to generalize hastily and carelessly and to infer that between two opposites there exists no middle ground (*e.g.,*
either you are a theist or an atheist), even though more
careful thought reveals a middle ground (*i.e.,* those who
remain undecided, ignorant of the issue, or unwilling to
commit themselves), caused some to insist that Gotama
did take sides on issues that he persistently held in abey-
ance. Since Buddhism includes *all* of those doctrines and
practices which multitudes of sects attribute to him, no one
of us, nor even any devoted Buddhist, can accept them in
their entirety. Whatever additional merit or demerit these
additional doctrines may have must be judged in terms of
their own insights and successes in helping men to attain
their ultimate goal.

Theravada

Before summarizing the most orthodox doctrines of
Hinayana Buddhism, a movement prevailing in Ceylon,
Burma, Thailand, and Cambodia, we must take a further
glance at the life of Gotama, the Buddha. While medita-

ting upon his insight or "Enlightenment," Gotama wondered whether he ought to tell others about it. It was obviously contrary to prevailing views as to how to go about attaining life's goal. Although simple, Gotama's principle was
also subtle and hard to grasp, as the reader himself may testify by the critical questions it raised in his own mind. Furthermore, according to Gotama's principle, one should accept the world as he finds it and thus accept other people as
they are in their ignorance of the true way. Yet he recalled the struggles that he and his five ascetic companions
had together and their mutual promise that, if one of them
found a way, he would share his findings with the others.
He went to them and, despite their resolve to snub him for
deserting them, they were converted upon hearing him.

Although he still refused to regard himself as an evangelist for a new way, he did respond to questions that people
addressed to him. The astounding obviousness and irrefutability of his principle led his hearers to tell others; and
so he became sought after both by earnest seekers and
by the curious. His hearers marveled. His fame spread.
When monks devoted to full-time questing heard about
him, their interest was naturally aroused. When teachers
of monks heard about a competing doctrine, they were
moved to inquire and to challenge. Thus he became involved in repeated occasions for expounding his doctrine,
although actually disinclined to do so.

One of the most significant events in his life, so far as
perpetuation of his teachings is concerned, was his meeting the three Kassapa (Kashyapa) brothers, each the head
of an established order of monks. These three brothers
had five hundred, three hundred, and two hundred "matted
hair ascetics" as followers, according to the record. (*Book
of the Discipline,* Translated by I. B. London: Horner,
Luzac and Company, Ltd., 1951. Part IV, pp. 32–33.)
Gotama met Kassapa of Uruvela, leader of the three, on
a walk and stayed overnight and then settled in a nearby
grove for awhile. Marvelous occurrences led the three
brothers and all of their thousand monks to recognize
the superiority of Gotama. Although he made no effort to
lead these monks, neither did he resist their wish to consult
him on any occasion. Many of them regarded him as the
actual leader of their order, but he repeatedly referred them

back to the Kassapa brothers for directions concerning their order. He did, however, offer advice when asked, and such advice as he gave was remembered by monks and incorporated into their collection of rules.

After he had stayed at Uruvela as long as he wished, he set out for another place and found himself followed by "all those same thousand monks who had formerly been matted hair ascetics." *(Book of the Discipline, op. cit.,* p. 45.) Although others, singly and in groups, chose to accompany him also, he remained associated with the Kassapa brothers and their orders as long as he lived. At his death, when disputes arose as to his teaching that could no longer be settled by asking him directly, it was Kassapa of Uruvela who gathered the monks together to try to remember what he had said and to agree upon some common interpretation of his teachings that they would then try to preserve. This gathering is regarded as "The First Council" in Buddhist history. The accounts presented did not all agree in detail. Many somewhat different versions persist to this day in the Pali *Pitakas,* to say nothing of versions added later. Those who violently disagreed with the prevailing consensus left in a huff. How many of these were responsible for sectarian differences we do not know. But at least twenty distinguishable sects developed by the third and fourth centuries after Gotama's death. (See Y. Sogen, *Systems of Buddhist Thought,* pp. 100ff.) We cannot explore all of these. Many of them eventually died out. We must content ourselves with a summary of the doctrines of the predominant group, who call themselves the "Theravadins."

Who were, and who are, the Theravadins? *"Vada,"* like *"Veda"* and *"Vidya,"* means truth, vision, view, word, or theory. Today we prefer to speak of theories or views or doctrines or philosophies, since we normally distinguish between a theory and that which it is about. In earlier times when vision of truth was believed to be direct, the distinction that we demand was either not recognized or not considered significant. *"Theravada"* is the truth as viewed by the Theras. I prefer to speak of it as "the philosophy of the Theras," but "Theravada" has become a recognized English name so we will use it. Who, then, were the *Theras?* They were the elders in the teaching order of monks. Kassapa of Uruvela was a *Thera*. In fact, as reverence for him grew, he came to be called *"Mahathera,"* "the Great Elder." Although, so far as I know, scholarship has not yet demonstrated the following, I cannot refrain from expressing my suspicion that Mahathera Kassapa, leader of an order of five hundred to a thousand monks already established before Gotama came along, manager of the first council that presumably collected and preserved Buddha's teachings after his death, and chief elder and teacher of the order for some time after, was primarily responsible for the modified form in which Gotama's teachings appear in the bulk of the *Pitakas*. Other monks who accompanied Gotama and whose discourses also have been preserved doubtless contributed some share. They too are regarded as *Theras*. Furthermore, all who became learned and elder teachers down through history and all of the most learned monks today are called *Theras*. They and all laymen today who subscribe to the doctrines attributed to these *Theras* are properly regarded as Theravadins.

Without reviewing the many factors affecting the course of transmission, study, and systematization of the teachings of Gotama (for which see Chapter II of my *Philosophy of the Buddha, op. cit.*) we will proceed directly to Theravada as it is taught in the University of Rangoon and other Theravada centers of learning. His teaching is first summed up under "The Four Noble Truths" and "The Eightfold Path" and then explained in terms of both the traditional doctrines of karma and reincarnation and of two new doctrines of impermanence and no-soul. A seemingly endless elaboration of varieties of distinctions have been evolved in explaining how these doctrines account for our ordinary everyday experience.

Gotama's principle—"Desire for what will not be attained ends in frustration; therefore to avoid frustration, avoid desiring what will not be attained"—needed to be spelled out in more simple steps so that humbler minds could grasp and retain it more easily. Four such steps have become traditional. My summary of them is: (1) Everyone is unhappy. (2) Unhappiness consists in wanting what you do not have. (3) Unhappiness ceases when you want what you have. (4) "Wanting what you have" includes wanting to have the desires you have, with their frustrations as well as satisfactions, and some middle way between wanting and wanting to stop wanting what you do not have. These principles apply in all areas of life.

Let me comment upon each before turning to Theravada interpretations of them. (1) Everyone naturally wants more than he has. Man is by nature a desiring being, and to desire is to desire something that one does not have. "Our reach exceeds our grasp, or what's a heaven for?" To have ideals is to have ideas of goods yet unrealized that ought to be realized or that we ought to want to have. Everyone, at all or most times, has desires, overt or latent, that remain unsatisfied. Except for rare moments when we feel fully satisfied, we find ourselves looking forward to the future and motivated by desires to attain goodness in it. Hence, generally speaking, everyone is at all times unhappy, at least a little bit. Unhappiness prevails everywhere.

The Pali word *"dukkha,"* meaning "bad to bear" or en dure or experience, which is opposed to *"sukkha,"* meaning "good to bear" or enjoy or experience, has been rendered into English in many ways, none of them quite satisfactory. Such words as "pain," "unpleasantness," "illness," "dissatisfaction," "frustration," "anxiety," "anguish," "unhappiness," and "suffering" have all been used. Some translators select a single term and stick to it repetitiously. Others, to avoid monotony and to capture probable delicate nuances, adopt different English terms in different contexts. As new terms appear in English, such as "negative feeling tone," new translations will be required. Some term general enough to signify the whole gamut of meanings from petty annoyances to mournful misery and intolerable torture is needed. In the meantime, we should recognize something of the general and variable significance of the term "suffering," used in a standardized rendering of the first step as "All is suffering."

(2) The second step diagnoses the cause of unhappiness: Unhappiness consists in wanting what we do not have. This wanting what we do not have comes in varying degrees and extends to all kinds of wants. It exists as an enduring tendency as well as a momentary impulse. Some careless translators say simply that "the cause of suffering is desire." But not all desires cause suffering, *e.g.,* those

which become satisfied easily and those which stir us so feebly as to arouse no disturbed feelings when they disappear unsatisfied. Theravadins rightly distinguish between *"chanda,"* calmly experienced motivation (such as that which causes us to put one foot in front of another when we go for a meditative stroll), and *"tanha," "thirst,"* impatient anxiety pervaded by an overwhelming fear that we will not get there quickly enough no matter how fast we rush. *Chanda* (quiescent pursuit of our natural needs) causes no suffering until we become anxious, desirous, intense, and possessive. *Tanha* (the feeling of urgency, insistence, or passion) may take any form, such as *lobha* (greed, lust, avidity) or *dosa* (hate, revulsion, anger). Perhaps our English words "willingness" and "willfulness" differentiate as well as any the general distinction between *chanda* as quiescent desire, which causes no unhappiness, and *tanha* as overzealousness, which automatically leads to frustration. The second step, even when stated as "the cause of suffering is desire," refers to the latter.

(3) The third step states how to eliminate unhappiness. Unhappiness ceases when you want what you have. So, "to remove suffering, get rid of the cause of suffering, namely, desire" or desirousness. More briefly: "To remove suffering, remove desire."

(4) The fourth step purports to tell how to "remove desire." This is the most subtle and difficult of the four steps and has received the greatest elaboration. Gotama described it as "the middle way." Both of two universal features cause considerable confusion in the minds of listeners. First, Gotama's principle applies to all things, including all desires. In order to avoid unhappiness, one must be willing to accept the inner desires that he has as well as the external conditions that he confronts. Where desires conflict, as in both desiring more than you have and desiring to stop desiring more than you have, you must seek a middle way in which you may gradually and progressively and calmly reduce your avidity. One can become completely willing to accept things as they are only by becoming willing to accept "becoming completely willing to accept things as they are." (For further exposition of dialectical subtleties involved, see Chapter 8, "Dhyana," of my *Philosophy of the Buddha, op. cit.* Grasping these

subtleties seems to me to be necessary for a full under-standing of Zen.)

Secondly, Gotama's principle of the middle way applies in all areas of life. Memorizers and teachers adopted a convenient series of eight areas that were sufficiently com-prehensive for the needs of beginners. These areas, which came to be interpreted as constituting a progressive series, have been traditionally designated and translated as "The Eightfold Path":

(1) Believing should be characterized by neither cre-dulity nor scepticism, neither hasty generalization nor agnosticism. Such middle-of-the-way belief *(sammaditthi)* has received a standard translation as "right belief." (2) Aspiring, resolving, intending should be characterized by neither insistence nor half-heartedness, neither avidity nor hopelessness, neither inflexibility nor indecision. Such will-ing *(sammasankappa)* has been translated "right resolve." (3) Expression of thought in speech should be neither verbose nor reticent, neither too vague nor too meticulously detailed, neither meaningless nor intended to say more than can be said. This speech *(sammavaca)* is now called "right speech." (4) Action should be neither too energetic nor too lethargic, neither too quick nor too slow, neither in-adequate nor prolonged. Such action *(sammakammanta)* now reads "right conduct." (5) One's way of living and attitude toward life and its continuance should be neither too reckless nor too cautious, neither too violent nor too apathetic, neither too scornful of danger nor too fearfully clinging. This kind of moderate living *(sammaajiva)* appears in translation as "right livelihood." (6) The effort with which one pursues his endeavors should be neither too strenuous nor too lazy, neither too vigorous nor too weak, neither too enthusiastic nor too apathetic. Such endeavor *(sammavayama)* is known as "right effort." (7) Remember-ing and keeping in mind what one has learned should be characterized by neither too much retentiveness (by memorizing everything in complete detail) nor too much inattention, disregard, or negligence. The middle way be-tween constant alertness and heedless stupor *(sammasati)* comes to us as "right mindfulness." (8) Even our most general and most important need, that of eliminating un-happiness itself, should be pursued moderately. Our quest

for happiness should be characterized neither by anxiety to remove unhappiness nor by hopeless indifference to unhappiness. Our final approach to the goal *(samma-samadhi)* is now referred to as "right concentration."

The Eightfold Path thus embodies eight generalizations illustrating Gotama's single general principle. Teachers, finding the level of generality still too difficult to comprehend, gave specific illustrations with which their pupils were already familiar. Many were able to remember the illustrations when they could not grasp the principle. As these illustrations multiplied, there came the opportunity for incorporating all of the standard mores into the eight collections. Once the authority of the great Buddha could be enlisted in support of customary moral sanctions, these sanctions and the memory of the Buddha tended to sustain each other. Gotama's great insight that happiness is to be found in the middle way, *i.e.,* being neither too much nor too little concerned about morality, was transformed into a catechism for teaching mores, a characteristic especially well conveyed by translating *"samma"* (middle-of-the-way) as "right."

Furthermore, the orthodox interpretation of the Eightfold Path involves another transformation. Although *samma* emphatically names each of the eight areas, thus denoting it as an area of calmness and rest rather than of anxiety and progress, interpreters found in the arrangement of the areas—"belief," "resolve," "speech," etc., ending in "mindfulness" and "concentration"—a suggested order, sequence, and direction capped by *samadhi,* the traditional goal of yogic endeavor. Those feeling pressed into conformity with their fellow monks welcomed an interpretation with which they already agreed. Some concluded that direction was intended and that, instead of middle-wayness itself being the way, the eight successive steps laid out a direction that constituted a path. References to the middle way became deemphasized and gradually disappeared from the center of attention. The eighth "step" becomes elaborated into a series of four steps, the fourth of which involves four more, so the character attributed to the "Eightfold Path" cannot be missed by the followers of *Theravada.*

Turning from how Gotama's principle was first expanded into "four truths" and "eight folds" and then transformed into an efficient tool for promoting morality, to current *Theravada,* let us now explore two new concepts and then present its version of the "four truths" and "eight folds." The two concepts are *anicca,* "impermanence," and *anatta,* "no soul."

The problem of understanding permanence and change has plagued mankind from its beginnings. Many have become familiar with the puzzles and predicaments baffling some of our earliest Western philosophers, Parmenides and Zeno, and the history of repeated attempts to solve these puzzles. Every philosopher, indeed every person, has to deal with them. We cannot here explore how other Hindu philosophies stand on the issue, but two main Buddhist movements, *Theravada* and *Sunyavada,* hold seemingly opposing views on the subject, though, as usual, subsurface similarities modify the sharpness of the opposition. Whereas Gotama refused to take sides on the issue of whether existence ultimately is permanent or changing, *Theravada* not only favors change as ultimate but explicitly and repeatedly asserts an extreme view: "All is changing." *Sunyavada,* as we shall see, regards ultimate reality as devoid of all change. Part of the significance of *Theravada* in world history is that it stands out as a relatively rare type of philosophy in holding such an extreme position on change. Others have held extreme positions, but the way in which its implications regarding "no soul" have been worked out in the context of Hindu subjectivism remains significant as a unique contribution.

The problem, "Is there a soul or is there not a soul?" also has plagued mankind ever since it could comprehend the problem. In Hindu tradition, where belief in the existence of the soul has remained so central, the Theravadins appear as extreme radicals. No soul exists, they say. Yet, since they accept traditional notions of karma and reincarnation, a plethora of paradoxes arises as to how there can be reincarnation of a self if no soul exists and how a self can suffer from accumulation of bad karmas or profit by gaining good karmas if no soul exists. Great ingenuity and many subtle distinctions developed through their answers. An intricate psychological analysis emerges to support their conclusions, and the result is amazing. How a no-soul doctrine can serve as the foundation for a religion will startle many. Theravadins are also atheists; existence requires no creator, and the doctrine of impermanence eliminates an enduring God as well as an enduring soul. Salvation is attained as *nibbana (nirvana)* when an illusory ego gives up its mistaken attachment both to a world mistaken as real and permanent and to a soul mistaken as real and permanent. The law of karma, or of causality (or "dependent origination"), explains how such illusions arise and why several rebirths of consciousness may be needed before it can be eliminated. A self must say "Yes" to its nonexistence before it can free itself from bondage to its illusory existence.

How does *Theravada* interpret "the Four Truths"?—

(1) "All is suffering, because all is change." A really nonexistent self, in mistaking itself as a soul or permanent existent, clings to its belief in and desire for its permanent existence, thereby wanting what it cannot have. Its attachment to itself leads to attachment to other things; it believes it has an enduring body, lives in an enduring world of other persons and things, and can acquire and own enduring possessions, of wealth, honor, and children. Belief in their attainability and greed for acquiring them grow out of this mistaken belief in their permanence. If, or since, all is changing and there is no permanence, recognition of the fact that neither things nor self are permanent will lead to no desire for them, and thus to an elimination of all frustration that comes from realizing that we cannot have them. The phrase, "All is suffering, because all is change," should be expanded to explain that all is suffering because what is really changing is mistaken as permanent, and desires to retain permanence are doomed to frustration.

The need for explaining the doctrine, "All is suffering, because all is change," occurs at two levels, one popular and one technical. Popular exposition appeals to items already obvious in common experience. The way in which universality of suffering was demonstrated may be summarized by a typical quotation: "Birth is suffering, decay is suffering, disease is suffering, death is suffering; grief, sorrow, lamentation, pain, and despair are suffering; to be connected with things we dislike is suffering; to be separated from things we like is suffering; not getting what we want is suffering; in short, all existence and attachment to existence is suffering."

Technical explanation is summed up in "the five aggregates," temporary, even if persisting, associations of phenomenal elements mistakenly accepted as substantial. The five are corporeality, feeling, perception, mental tendencies, and consciousness. The first makes up the world of material objects; the last four constitute mind. "Corporeality" is the visible form of four invisible, inseparable elements or forms: extension (earth), cohesion (water), energy (fire), and motion (air). A material thing is not a substance but a temporary aggregate of these elements. "Feeling" (pleasant, unpleasant, indifferent), "perception" (through the six senses, including recognizing things as belonging to kinds), "mental tendencies" (fifty types of mental formations, including aptitudes, prejudices, ideas, and volition generated by past experience), and "consciousness" (awareness of all the other factors together) comprise mind. Mind is no substance and involves no soul but survives as a temporary, constantly changing flux of these aggregates in shifting combinations. Further analysis must be omitted here.

(2) "The cause of suffering is desire." "Desire" here means desirousness *(tanha) of* all kinds (ambition, acquisitiveness, attachment, greed, insistence) and *for* all kinds (pleasure, the well-being of self and others, and survival). But how can desire arise in a nonexistent self or soul? Although the ultimate reason that things come into existence is as mysterious for Theravada as for any other philosophy, "twelve links" have been distinguished in analyzing stages in the emergence and development of desires: (1) ignorance of the truly impermanent nature of beings exists; (2) volition emerges from ignorance as a will to endure; (3) awareness emerges from volition; (4) consciousness of objects and ego emerge from awareness; (5) the five senses and mental processes emerge to provide qualities of objects and thoughts about objects; (6) the seeming reality of sense qualities and objects of thought emerges from sensing and thinking; (7) feeling about such qualities and objects as pleasant or unpleasant, good or bad, arises from their seeming reality; (8) desire (craving) for pleasure and for avoidance of pain emerges from such feelings about ob-

jects; (9) clinging results from craving; (10) endurance results from clinging; (11) rebirth results from endurance; (12) suffering (birth, aging, dying, with grief, lamentation, and despair) results from rebirth.

(3) "To remove suffering remove desire." At the popular level, this means to stop desiring, or at least to stop being greedy, lustful, avaricious, demanding, fearful, hateful, or ambitious. So avoid temptations, allurements, sweets, sexual stimulation, submission to passions. At the technical level, the "twelve links" must be reversed. One must first remove ignorance by realizing the truth of the doctrine of impermanence, including the doctrine of impermanence of self (*i.e.,* no soul). Removal of belief in permanence will remove willing the endurance of what does not endure. Removal of such willing will remove awareness. Removal of awareness will remove awareness of objects and ego. This will involve removal of senses and mental processes, which will remove sensations and thoughts about objects and self, which will remove the appearance of their reality, which will remove having feelings about them as good or bad, which will remove our craving for them as good, which will remove our clinging to them, and our desire for endurance, which will remove our rebirth and thus remove all the suffering involved in rebirth.

(4) "The way to remove desire is the Eightfold Path, consisting of right belief, right resolve, right speech, right conduct, right livelihood, right effort, right mindfulness, and right concentration." Although accounts may mention that this is called "the middle way," they assert that it consists in "the Eightfold Path" or in a path with eight steps. *(a)* "Right belief" (or "right views" or "right understanding") consists in understanding and believing the "Four Noble Truths." Such belief involves knowing that "all is suffering," that "all is impermanent," that suffering arises from mistaking the impermanent as permanent and thus the doctrine of "the five aggregates" and "the twelve links" of causation, which involves the doctrine of "dependent origination" or law of karma and reincarnation. *(b)* "Right resolve" (or aspiration or thought or "mindedness") consists in embodying in self a disposition to nonattachment and freedom from ill will and harmfulness toward any sentient being. *(c)* "Right speech" embodies right dispo-

sition through refraining from lying, gossip, slander and harsh and frivolous talk. *(d)* "Right conduct" refrains from killing, stealing, and sexual perversion. Opportunity exists here for extending the doctrine to include family and local mores and the use made of it varies with different teachers. *(e)* "Right livelihood" is interpreted as proper ways of earning a living. Since one should not kill or harm, he should avoid occupations such as hunting, fishing, butchering, selling intoxicants or guns, robbing, or misrepresenting goods. *(f)* "Right effort" involves a fourfold constant striving. Negatively, one should try to root out old evil dispositions and avoid yielding to new temptations. Positively, one should seek to acquire and develop new good thoughts and to retain them continuously. *(g)* "Right mindfulness" emphasizes the need for constant alertness and attentiveness to our ignorant condition, to the impermanence of self, body, values, and the world, and to missing no opportunity for resisting regress and making progress. Intellectual self-searching and contemplation of death, the transitoriness of life, the unreality of the soul, the mere aggregation of body particles, and the futility of desire all enter here.

(h) "Right concentration," regarded as the last step, is most difficult. It may receive two kinds of treatment, one for laymen and one for monks. For laymen, attainment of the goal, *nibbana,* is practically impossible, so they are urged to reemphasize the first seven steps and, when possible, to concentrate upon further details of the seventh step, "right mindfulness." For monks, a lifelong endeavor leading progressively to *arhat*ship is in store. This eighth step becomes transformed into a ladder of four more steps, each more subtle and difficult, the last of which may involve four still more subtle stages. These are called *"jhanas"* (Sanskrit, *dhyana).* The four: (1) A state freed from desire, in which reasoning and investigation continues. (2) A state freed from reasoning and investigation, in which a feeling of joy in tranquility prevails. (3) A state freed from joy, in which consciousness of existence at ease remains. (4) A state freed from consciousness of existing at ease, in which perfect insight, *nibbana,* is attained. From *nibbana* there is no returning into the mundane world of suffering. Life is at an end or, for rare *arhats (arahat,*

arahant), life may continue in such a way that all danger of returning to mundane suffering has been eliminated *(jivanmukti).* Though most accounts of *jhanas* stop with four, the fourth has been described as progressing through four stages of insight beyond the insights one has attained of the existence one is leaving. In these, awareness is characterized, progressively, by: (1) absence of distinction, (2) infinity of space, (3) infinity of consciousness, (4) awareness that nothing really is. Attribution of supernormal powers of vision and action at these stages appeals to the imaginations of some, but seems to be generally discouraged.

Hinayana Buddhist religion actually involves much more than Theravada philosophy. Except for knowledge of the Four Truths, the Eightfold Path, karma and reincarnation, and unclear notions of impermanence and no-soul, the vast majority of citizens in Hinayana Buddhist countries leave both the more abstruse philosophy and the more austere practices to the ordained monks while they busy themselves with ordinary affairs, keeping more or less in mind the need for doing good in order to improve their store of good karmas and chances for becoming ordained monks in a subsequent life. Since "doing good" is basically a mental attitude, one may do good by thinking good thoughts. Of course, genuinely good thoughts result in action when opportunity arises. But the action itself, when carried out, needs to be accompanied by good thought in order to have its maximum effect. One may wish to help others, including animals, but especially monks, who are entirely dependent upon free gifts of food and robes for their sustenance. One may also give money to build or maintain shrines, such as pagodas and Buddha statues, which commonly appear with goldleaf coverings. On holidays or at any time, one may come to a pagoda or statue to entertain good thoughts. Bringing flowers and sometimes food as an offering gives substance to one's thoughts. The example of the Buddha in attaining enlightenment and showing the way to men may be appreciated not only in the presence of statues but in the presence of monks who should be venerated for their devotion, especially those monks who have progressed far along the way.

Sometimes people pray. According to Theravada, Gotama

has reached Nirvana and cannot hear, so cannot answer prayer, and would not if he could, since, according to his teaching, each person must "be a lamp unto himself" earning his own way. Yet, in fact, many people, in great need, in deep distress, in desperate hope, do pray that one so marvelous in insight might somehow show them the way out of their personal predicament. "Lord Buddha" serves as a god to many who do not comprehend the more subtle doctrines. When people do pray, if they ask for more than they deserve, they practice "low religion," a practice condemned by those aware that the law of karma favors no one and that each person's suffering is due to his own greed. Therefore, to pray for what one does not deserve begets bad karmas. One who kills, knowing full well that he must suffer dire consequences and being willing to suffer them, may be practicing "higher" religion than one who prays for a minor boon he does not deserve. In practice, Buddhism intermingles with local beliefs, *naths* (spirits), and customs (holidays, festivals), in ways that baffle foreigners.

Although monks (about ninety thousand of them in Burma today) devote most of their time to self-improvement as outlined by Theravada, some of them teach or donate their presence when needed at ceremonies. Once monks were practically the only source of instruction in Burma, but since the introduction of public education facilities, their teaching is normally confined to Buddhist doctrine. Orthodox Buddhist families expect their boys to enter the *sangha* or society of monks for a trial period for educational purposes. The lenient Burmese require only a seven-day minimum, whereas Thai boys stay about fifteen days, and Cambodian boys about two months. Those who remain in the *sangha*, or those who enter it later in life, abandon a majority of their citizenship rights, such as right to own property, to work, to marry, to hold public office, to vote, or to be tried in court. Although these are national regulations that may vary from country to country, Buddhist countries tend to provide isolation for monks who maintain befitting behavior. They cannot be arrested or brought to court, except for a major offense, such as murder. They must beg for their food, not by asking but by approaching and standing mutely and unlongingly. If nothing is given, they must depart ungrudgingly. Gathering food and eating must be done between sunup and noon. Monks are expected to remain in their monasteries at night. Women may become nuns, but few do.

In taking our leave of Theravada, perhaps we should note that its particular reasons for atheism and its frank and explicit rejection of theism seem very striking to others. The Jains and Sankhya-Yoga schools accept a doctrine of eternal souls and reject the need for a god, because the universe is eternal and needs no creator or causal agent. Theravadins, however, reject all permanence and eternality, including both permanent souls and any permanent God. Their universe also has neither creator nor causal agent, for ignorance and volition are self-originating in each temporary, illusory individual. Although Theravadins do not go about preaching atheism or attacking other beliefs, for to do so would constitute having bad thoughts, there is a scriptural passage denouncing theism: "Owing to the creation of [the idea of] a Supreme Deity men will become murderers, thieves, unchaste, liars, slanderers, abusive, babblers, covetous, malicious, and perverse in views. Thus for those who fall back on the creation of a God as the essential reason, there is neither desire to do, nor the effort to do, nor the necessity to do this deed or abstain from the deed." (*The Book of the Gradual Sayings,* Translated by F. L. Woodward. London: Luzac and Co., Ltd., 1951, Vol. I, p. 158.) Few theists will recognize the charge as warranted, though why theism should be so regarded by a stable, orthodox, well-motivated, and "high" religion may give them pause for thought.

Sunyavada

Mahayana Buddhism evolved for more than twenty centuries into a massive jungle of theories and practices spread throughout the Far East. Like Hinayana, Mahayana originated and developed in India before expanding beyond its borders. Mahayana Buddhism proliferated in China, Tibet, Mongolia, Korea, and Japan. Despite their apparent intricacy and elusiveness to Western minds, Hinayana beliefs seem simple and clear when compared with that sprawling but intertwined maze of strands of thought comprising the vast literature known as "Mahayana." All we can do here is to paint a few strokes on a large canvas, indicating some general differences between Hinayana and Mahayana, and sampling three relatively cohesive religious philosophies: Sunyavada, in the present section, and Shin and Zen in a later chapter.

The best way to differentiate summarily between Hinayana and Mahayana is to compare the Hinayana idea of an *arhat* with the Mahayana ideal of a *bodhisattva*. The goal of life for a Burmese monk is to become an *arhat*, a condition in which his attainment of *nibbana* and cessation of the rounds of rebirth are assured. His achievement of such a goal remains his alone. Others who help him on the way do so as a means of acquiring good karmas so that they too may attain the goal, each for himself. Thus, achievement of the goal is essentially an individual affair. Although a monk may be aided by provisions of food and conditions of isolation, and may have had to express generosity and good thoughts for others as a prerequisite, the main struggle for the goal is entirely his own, as is its enjoyment after it is attained.

The ideal of a *bodhisattva*, on the other hand, entails both embodiment of compassion and sharing the goal. Mahayanists generally regard attainment of arhatship as a prerequisite for becoming a *bodhisattva*. That is, one must, through individual effort, achieve that condition of being in which his eventual attainment of *nibbana* is assured. But becoming a *bodhisattva* requires a vow that one will not actually enter such *nibbana* himself until he has, out of overwhelming compassion for the welfare of others, spent an indefinite period of time trying to help others achieve the goal. Thus, whereas Hinayana remains essentially a self-help religion, in the sense that there is no God nor other person who can help one in his personal struggle, Mahayana, in requiring extensive compassion by each person who becomes a *bodhisattva*, leads others who are far from the goal to expect benefits from such compassion. Furthermore, whereas the reverence of Hinayanists is directed primarily at Gotama, the Buddha, an historical person now dead, the reverential attention of Mahayanists may be devoted to any one or all of many *bodhisattvas*, any or all of whom may now be living.

Hinayana statues normally depict Gotama alone, though several statues may be needed to illustrate different phases of his life and teaching. When there appear statues of his colleagues, the *Theras,* such as Ananda, Sariputta, or Kassapa, are regarded as historical companions rather than as "living buddhas," even though they, too—to the extent that they understood and practiced Gotama's teachings—embodied his Enlightenment or *Bodhi* and thus were *bodhisattvas* in the sense that such *bodhi* was embodied in their being *(sat).* But when, in Mahayana, *buddha* or *bodhi* is conceived as an all-pervasive cosmic principle, it comes to be regarded as reembodied in all things and to become alive and effective again and again in the minds of *bodhisattvas.* Hence, a worshipper may seek his benefits from the apparently nearest or most conveniently available *bodhisattva.*

Although the benefits that a *bodhisattva* can bestow remain ultimately only those which will help a person to comprehend and attain *nibbana,* the mysterious power and compassionate attitude attributed to him becomes something to which ordinary people appeal whenever they find themselves in dire need. Mahayana philosophies continue to be too abstruse for most common people to comprehend, so they seek aid from the *bodhisattvas* in terms of their own needs as they conceive them. Thus, in popular practice, the various *bodhisattvas* function as so many gods of a veritable polytheism, with specialized types of compassion and blessings, such as mercy, wisdom, fortune, health. But one does not understand Mahayana philosophy until he realizes how the seemingly endless numbers of *bodhisattvas* (every person can and will become a *bodhisattva* eventually) represent merely ripples on a single boundless sea of *nibbana.* (Artistic representation of the multiplicity of *bodhisattvas* has been accomplished by packing statues of one thousand and one Kuan-yins in a single room.)

Before investigating *Sunyavada,* perhaps the epitome of abstruseness in Buddhist philosophy, we will glance at its close cousin, *Yogacara,* which may be easier to understand. The *Yogacara* school of thought, expressed in the writings of Asanga, Vasubandhu, and Dignaga, also calls itself *"Vijnanavada,"* the theory that ultimate reality is Consciousness. This Consciousness *(vijnana)* is universal *(alaya)*. It is an all-pervasive unchanging source of the constant flux of appearances that occupy our apparently individual minds. Like *Theravada, Vijnanavada* holds that both the things constituting the world of objects and the ideas clustering about our subjective egos are temporary illusions. Hence, whereas Theravadins refuse to comment upon the nature of *bhavanga* (a flux of being underlying conscious illusions), the Vijnanavadins assert that the ever-changing stream of cosmic consciousness is identical with an eternal, undifferentiated Consciousness. Your mind, which has ripples (objects, desires, attachments) of its own, is a ripple in the Cosmic Consciousness. Thus you and your objects remain not merely inseparable from, but never cease to be identical with, this Cosmic Consciousness.

Buddha or Bodhi—Enlightenment—consists ultimately in the intuitive apprehension whereby the Cosmic Consciousness realizes its undifferentiated eternality as both different from and at the same time identical with its waves —individual minds and their objects and desires. An individual mind becomes a *bodhisattva* or an embodiment of such intuitive apprehension, which retains compassion for other minds that do not yet embody it.

Turning to *Sunyavada*, the philosophy of Voidness, which also calls itself *"Madhyamika"* (The Middle Way), we find a still more subtle and baffling system formulated best in the writings of Nagarjuna. Here ultimate reality is called *"Sunya"* or "Void." But *Sunya* is emptiness, not nothingness. It is empty of all distinctions, as is *Alayavijnana* of the Vijnanavadins, and in addition, it is empty of anything so distinguishable as "Consciousness" or "Universal." *Sunya* is indescribable because description distinguishes, whereas *Sunya* remains without distinction. *Sunya* cannot be grasped by intellect, so any attempt to do so must end in failure.

The best way of meeting the insistent demand of those who persist in asking questions about it is to say of it that it neither is, nor is not, nor both is and is not, nor neither is nor is not. The Sunyavadins did not invent this "principle of four-cornered negation" which was repeated again and again in the Pali *Pitakas* and is employed at times by every important school of Hindu philosophy. This "principle of four-cornered negation" is as characteristic of what is ultimate in Indian philosophy as the "law of excluded middle" is a clue to something ultimate in the nature of Western mentality. This principle, a negation of all negation (and thus in a sense more negative than an excluded middle), at the same time asserts something more positive (in that all negation, or all exclusiveness, is excluded from it). This principle supplies the answer to any question that may be asked about *Sunya.*

Is *Sunya* existent or nonexistent? It neither is, nor is not, nor both is and is not, nor neither is nor is not, existent. Is it permanent (Jain Soul and Non-Soul are eternal) or impermanent (Theravadins say all is impermanent)? It is neither permanent nor impermanent nor both nor neither. Is it conscious? It is neither conscious nor unconscious nor both nor neither. Is it one or many? It is neither one nor many nor both one and many nor neither one nor many. Is it distinct from you and your desires and objects? It is neither distinct nor indistinct nor both nor neither. What is the "Middle Way" and why do the Sunyavadins call themselves "Madhyamikans"? *Sunya* is itself "the middle way," the way between being so or not so or both or neither with respect to any question about ultimate reality that may be asked. For Gotama and Theravadins, the middle way was a way between wanting too much and wanting too much to cease wanting too much. It was psychical and pertained to individual happiness only. For *Sunyavada,* "the middle way" is metaphysical; ultimate reality itself is a middle way wherever apparent distinctions arise. It is also a middle way between appearance and reality, a way that can be grasped adequately only through the doctrine of *Tathata,* "Thatness" or "Suchness."

"Suchness" seems a strange doctrine to those not familiar with it. Yet, once apprehended, an intuitive comfortable at-homeness in the universe is felt as flowing from it or rather present in it. Suchness consists in apprehending things as they are in themselves. Each thing is what it is, has its own nature, and, to be known truly, has to be known as it is in itself. You can see that this is true of "the universe as a whole." Nothing exists outside of the universe in terms of which it can be understood. To be understood, it must be grasped as it is in itself. So with all things. To say that a chair is not a table tells you nothing about what a chair is in itself. Since ultimate reality, *Sunya,* continues to be void of distinctness, the ultimate reality of a chair is void of distinctness as is the ultimate reality of a table. To apprehend as distinct two things—table and chair—that in ultimate reality are indistinct is to misapprehend them. However, let us not forget that the indistinctness ascribed to *Sunya* is not something that is distinct from distinctness. Of *Sunya* we can say that it is neither distinct, nor indistinct, nor both distinct and indistinct, nor neither distinct nor indistinct. Intellect must be willing to remain baffled in order to grasp that *Sunya* is present in both chair and table apprehended as Suchness; and that the indistinctness of *Sunya* from them is just as indistinct as their indistinctness is from it, so that *Sunya* is present in everything, no matter how distinct, but not present as distinctness.

Sunyavadins distinguish two kinds of knowledge, ordinary knowledge, which discriminates one thing from another and one kind from another, and absolute knowledge, which apprehends things as Suchness. The goal of life, and of religion, is attainment of such absolute knowledge, or *bodhi.* If one waits until he dies and is not reborn, he may then become indistinct and thus become *bodhi.* But one need not die. He need only apprehend things and himself as Suchness. But, so long as he is a slave to his ignorant intellect, he cannot wholly succeed. Although the Four Noble Truths are intended as aids to prepare one to succeed, one cannot fully succeed until he realizes that any distinctness between truth and reality, or between four truths and reality, or between one truth and another, is a product of intellect and therefore mistaken.

The intellect-baffling consequences of *Sunyavada* include the realization that "there is neither suffering nor its cause nor its cessation nor the way towards its cessation. . . . There is neither the Order [of monks], nor Religion, nor the Buddha. Nirvana itself is an illusion." (Chandradhar Sharma, *A Critical Survey of Indian Philosophy,* London: Rider and Co., 1960, pp. 92–93.) And all Buddhist doctrine, including *Sunyavada,* is illusory.

Is *Sunyavada* theistic? No, not unless God equals *Sunya,* the Void. Yet, it follows also that in whatever sense there is a God, *Sunya* is indistinct from it. Hence, one cannot say that *Sunyavada* is atheistic. For *Sunya* neither is, nor is not, nor both is and is not, nor neither is nor is not God. At the level of absolute knowledge, one cannot distinguish between *Sunya* and God. But at the level of ordinary knowledge, one can distinguish between *Sunya* and God. Insofar as any *bodhisattva* embodies in himself an apprehension of *Sunya* as indistinct from God, he too is indistinct from God and may be intuitively apprehended as such by those apprehending Suchness. But popular religion, guided by intellectually formed characteristics of the nature and power of *bodhisattvas,* fails to apprehend reality when it interprets a *bodhisattva* as God. Even so, since a *bodhisattva* is the most godlike being he can apprehend, man has little choice but to worship *bodhisattvas.*

How is yea-saying exemplified in *Sunyavada?* One must first say "Yes" to the Four Noble Truths and the Eightfold Path, the first step of which, "Right View," leads him ultimately to say "Yes" to the illusoriness of the Four Noble Truths and the Eightfold Path. He must say "Yes" to *Sunyavada,* which leads him to say of *Sunya* neither "Yes" nor "No" nor both "Yes" and "No" nor neither "Yes" nor "No." He must say "Yes" to the "principle of four-cornered negation" and to perpetual and utter bafflement of intellect. He must say "Yes" to Suchness, or to accepting things as they are in themselves. At the level of popular religion, a person must say "Yes" to the need for and goodness of becoming a *bodhisattva* and to the way to become such. A person may also say "Yes" to any grace that benevolent *bodhisattvas* can bestow.

Whoever realizes that he deserves nothing and that his duty is to attain *bodhi* entirely by his own efforts and then compassionately to help others as much as they need (even though they too must work their way entirely by their own efforts), thereby giving without deserving anything in return, and then becomes indistinct from or identical with the Void wherein no deserts can be distinguished, pursues "high" religion. But one who believes that he has some inalienable right to grace (which *bodhisattvas* perforce must bestow) is mistaken. In *Sunya* there exist neither rights, nor duties, nor obligations, nor grace. He who pursues his religion believing that becoming or attaining *nibbana* or identity with ultimate reality is a "reward," follows "low" religion. Only from the level of ordinary knowledge is *nibbana* seen as a goal to be reached and as a reward to be obtained. When one attains *nibbana* or *Sunya,* absolute knowledge or ultimate reality, distinctness of reward from its opposite disappears. One in *nibbana* will not know that he is being rewarded, for his condition will be apprehended as neither reward nor no reward, nor both, nor neither. On the other hand, one who apprehends any present thing or moment as Suchness is already enjoying *nibbana,* the goal that, when attained, neither is, nor is not, nor both is and is not, nor neither is nor is not a goal. Zen, as we shall see in Chapter IX, emphasizes enjoyment of present Suchness.

Chapter 6 Vedantism and Yoga

We now resume our quest for insight into orthodox Hinduism, after side trips surveying Jainism and Buddhism, commonly regarded as heretical movements. Orthodoxy, in Hinduism, consists in accepting the *Vedas* as authoritative, though the myriads of interpretations contain divergencies greater than those found in Jainism and Buddhism. Hinduism began with the Veda and ends, presumably, with Vedanta. "Veda" means "Truth" and "Vedanta" (Veda-end, or end of the Veda) means fulfillment or "Culmination of Truth." In the beginning was The Veda (The Word), and, according to the Mimamsa School of thought, The Veda was with God and The Veda was God, or was a self-expression of divine being. The books (now that they have been written down) containing the first accounts of the Veda are now called *"The Vedas,"* as we saw in Chapter III. The growth of insight into the truth expressed in them appears in the *Brahmanas, Aranyakas, Upanishads, Brahma Sutras,* Epics, etc.

After centuries of speculation, six orthodox schools of philosophical thought distinguished themselves, each with its own complex history. The advocates of each of these schools regard their own doctrines as yielding insights first adumbrated in the *Vedas*. Each school regards itself as a culmination of the Veda. Yet tradition attributes the name "Vedanta" to only one of these six schools. The others retain more descriptive names. Two of these schools, Nyaya (logical realism) and Vaisesika (metaphysical pluralism), constitute a closely allied pair, the former emphasizing ways of knowing and the latter stressing kinds of being. Sankhya (metaphysical dualism) and Yoga (psychical methodology) also constitute an integrated pair, the former depicting details of cosmic evolution and the latter elaborating ways and methods for attaining liberation. Mimamsa (literal fundamentalism) justifies Vedic ritualism, not by idealizing the printed word, but by intuitively experiencing divinity in the chanted, ritualistically enacted, lived "Word." Westerners will find curious its combining the polytheism described in the *Vedas* with a superior atheism in the sense that the words themselves are eternal, hence uncreated or planned or uttered by any God, while the gods spoken of attain their being and significance as words in rituals. Vedanta (which brings the monistic, spiritualistic, and pantheistic tendencies to a high pinnacle) exhibits some of the world's most amazing yet logically precise speculation together with several divergent (*e.g.*, both atheistic and theistic) explanations of man's nature and religious goal.

We must confine our exploration here to a limited number of schools. Somewhat arbitrarily, we choose to describe (1) Yoga, as a major avenue to life's goal, conceived in terms of the Sankhya-Yoga scheme, (2) Advaita Vedanta, the masterpiece of Hindu monistic philosophy, which also appropriates Yogic ideals and methods, and (3) Theistic Vedanta, which rivals, or surpasses, Advaita in practical profundity and serves as the theological explanation for the major popular sects such as Saivism and Vaishnavism.

Yoga

As we have already seen in Chapter III, four main kinds of Yoga receive emphasis in Hindu life: *karma-yoga,* the process of working your way to the goal by performing good deeds that build up a favorable balance of good karmas in accordance with the Law of Karma, is known and practiced more or less by everyone; *bhakti yoga,* the Way of Devotion—not merely devotion to parents, teacher, spouse and children, but to God—will be discussed later when we consider Theistic Vedantism; *jnana-yoga,* the Way of Knowledge—involving a study of scriptures, philosophical systems, rational argumentation, and gradual growth in the ability to intuit ultimate reality as conceived by Advaita Vedanta, especially—will be stressed when we examine Advaita; *raja-yoga,* the method of pursuing the goal as directly as possible, focuses all efforts upon attaining complete self-control through physical self-mastery (*hatha-yoga*) and psychical self-mastery by concentration. *Raja-yoga* is the supreme Way in that all, before attaining the goal, must experience concentration (*samadhi*) and in that those who devote themselves full-time to seeking the goal normally pursue this way. Although the methods of *raja-yoga* are not exclusively allied with any one type of philosophy (some Buddhists, Jains, and Advaitins use them also), the classical formulator of Yogic doctrine, Patanjali, did so with the Sankhya philosophy in mind. We shall, therefore, explain the Sankhya system, after summarizing the teachings of Patanjali.

When Patanjali lived and composed his *Yoga Sutras,* we do not know. Sankhya-yoga ideas already appeared in the *Upanishads* and *Gita.* But the first systematic commentary upon the *Yoga Sutras* that has come down to us, Vyasa's *Yoga Bhasya,* appeared during the fourth century A.D. We shall skim the view expressed in Patanjali's *sutras* (phrases summarizing thoughts) by explaining the "eight limbs" of Yoga. (For further details, see my edition of the *Yoga Sutras* entitled *Yoga: Union with the Ultimate.* N.Y.: Frederick Ungar Publishing Co., 1961.)

Typically, Hindu thinkers picture the goal of life as one of perfect quiescence, commonly called *"Nirvana."* The term *"Nirvana,"* meaning "no wind," suggests cessation of disturbance. Almost every Hindu philosophy, including Jainism and Buddhism, conceives the goal in terms of relief from disturbance. Patanjali depicts the individual soul (*purusha*), a pure eternal bit of awareness, as somehow having come in contact with the natural world (*prakriti*), whereupon two things happened. First, the natural world, also eternal and perfectly quiescent in its undisturbed condition, begins to evolve a capacity for consciousness (*chitta*), which in turn produces objects, ego, desires, organs of perception and action, and to assume mistakenly as its own an awareness shining forth from *purusha.* Secondly, the eternal soul, powerless to cause or be caused, finds itself reflecting the evolving activities of *prakriti* as in a mirror, and identifying itself with (or failing to distinguish itself from) such activities. All such activities constitute disturbances *(vritti)* that enslave the soul in rounds of rebirth from which it can escape to its ultimate freedom *(kaivalya)* only through the practices of *raja-yoga*.

The "first limb," ABSTINENCE *(yama)*, consists in establishing a disposition that naturally refrains from injuring, lying, stealing, sensuality, possessiveness, or whatever magnifies involvement in worldly troubles.

The second, DEVOTION *(niyama)*, reverses this direction and advocates positive effort. Desire for purity, serenity, self-discipline, self-study, and attainment of the ultimate goal should not only occupy one's mind but should become ingrained dispositions.

The third, POSTURE *(asana)*, pertains to ease and steadiness of body movements and resting positions. Since progress in eliminating more subtle psychical disturbances can hardly advance so long as bodily discomfort distracts attention, one must attain such complete mastery over his body that it will remain an undisturbing factor for long periods. Patanjali's work contains no instructions about postures except that they should be held easily and steadily without tensions. Followers have elaborated in such great detail upon kinds of posturing that *hatha-yoga*, concerned mainly with posture and breath control, has become a relatively distinct, even separate, branch of yoga with its own emphases. One may benefit from the mentally relaxing and physically healthful effects of *hatha-yoga* quite apart from any interest in other aspects of yoga. (See my *Yoga for Business Executives and Professional People.* N.Y.: Citadel Press, 1965.) The "Lotus Posture," in which one sits in a firm, cross-legged, feet-on-thighs position, is most famous and has become, in the popular mind, the trademark of Jain and Buddhist as well as Hindu yoga.

The fourth "limb" BREATH CONTROL *(pranayama)* aims both at removing irregularities in breathing that may function as distractions, and at attaining a disposition toward quietude through regularizing and slowing the breathing rhythms. Proper breathing not only relaxes the mind and produces an abundance of energy-giving oxygen in the blood and brain, but the slow-swinging rhythm of regularized breathing serves, like a long-beat musical drone, as a subconscious psychical pendulum that sustains stable attentive power.

The fifth "limb," RETRACTION OF THE SENSES (*pratya-hara*), functions as a means to self-control whereby one becomes unresponsive to stimuli and thereby undisturbed by things external to himself. This condition is necessary before one can make much progress in eliminating all, including inner, disturbances. To observers, the yogin appears to be in a trance, a condition retained throughout the remaining three "limbs." Display of power to lie without pain on a bed of spikes is disapproved by orthodox yogins as exhibitionism involving a degenerate interest in the external world and its approval, rather than a withdrawal from such a world into one of inner peace.

The sixth stage, FIXATION OF ATTENTION (*dharana*), aims at steadying the mind by focusing its attention upon some stable entity. One may, before retracting his senses, practice attending to a single inanimate object. After such retraction, some inner means of focusing may help. Rolling the eyes upward and holding them together, as if attending to a spot in the center of the forehead, or downward, as if attending to the navel, or forward, as if attending to the tip of the nose, have become well-known techniques. The particular object selected has nothing to do with the general purpose, which is to stop the mind from wandering —through memories, dreams, or reflective thought—by deliberately holding it single-mindedly upon some apparently static object.

The seventh phase, FUSIVE APPREHENSION (*dhyana*), further unifies consciousness by combining clear insights into distinctions between objects—and between the subtle layers of veils that becloud intuition—with an awareness of their more basic indistinctness and irrelevance to ultimate freedom. Discrimination includes differentiating among the mind of the perceiver, the means of perception, and the objects perceived (See *Yoga: Union with the Ultimate, op. cit.*, pp. 64–67), between words, their meanings, and ideas (*Ibid.*, pp. 67–69), and between all the levels of evolution of *prakriti* (*Ibid.*, pp. 69–72). Clear discrimination is a means to apprehending them as being really fused in an undifferentiated continuum. One must apprehend both subject and object clearly in order to intuit their indistinctness, for a clear grasp of real identity of two apparently different things presupposes a clear grasp of their seeming difference. Thus "fusive apprehension" is apprehension of real identity among ostensible differences.

The final stage, FULLY INTEGRATED CONSCIOUSNESS *(samadhi)*, realizes what it is to be an identity without differences, and how a liberated soul can enjoy pure awareness of this pure identity. The conscious mind drops back into that unconscious oblivion from which it first emerged. The final stage terminates at the instant the soul is freed. The absolute and eternal freedom of an isolated soul is beyond all stages and beyond all time and place. Once freed, it does not return to bondage.

Yoga is a religion aiming at the perfection of yea-saying. Each of the eight "limbs" is a different area in which to pursue and practice yea-saying. One must say "Yes" to the "Five Abstentions" and to the "Five Devotions," to the needs for physical self-mastery, for purifying self from sensuous distractions, for single-mindedness, clear apprehension of ultimate reality and final assent to freeing the soul. The soul itself in *kaivalya,* utter freedom, entertains neither desires nor doubts; it is beyond saying "Yea" or "Nay," for its awareness is without questions or answers. The mind, before freeing the soul, has to say "Yes" to the soul's isolation from all yeas and nays as a superior condition to that in which the soul is occupied wholly with the mind's total commitment to "yea." Thus, like Job (13:15), who said "though he slay me, yet will I trust in him," Patanjali pictures mind as trusting the need for cessation of its own consciousness so that the soul may regain completely undisturbed awareness.

Yogic practitioners must begin with yoga as "low religion," for one cannot free himself without desiring to do so. One must say "Yes" to his desire for freeing himself from desires. But, since complete freedom from disturbances can come only after attaining freedom from desire itself, indifference to deserved fruits must be attained before such fruit can be experienced. Yoga idealizes "high religion" in requiring final assent to the superiority of indifference to rewards. The perfected mind does not say that the soul deserves its perfected freedom but only that everything is actually better when the soul is free and the mind is unconscious of deserts.

The original Sankhya-yoga conception of the universe

was essentially atheistic. Some souls *(purusha)* never become entangled in the process of the comings and goings of
the world *(prakriti)*. Their permanent isolation serves as
an ideal for those seeking to restore isolation. Such a soul
is thus admired as a "Great Soul" *(Mahapurusha)*, and
if the word "God" *(Ishwara)* is to have any meaning at all
in this system, it may be attributed to such an unfettered
soul. But, there are many such *Mahapurushas*. And neither
any one of them nor all of them together have any contact
with or influence either over the evolution of the world or
over the entanglement or freeing of other souls. Both souls
and *prakriti* in all its nature are eternal and uncreated. So
no *Mahapurusha* can create. Each entangled soul must be
freed solely by its own mind. So no *Mahapurusha* can
function as savior. Each isolated soul is utterly free of all
awareness of the world and other souls. So no *Mahapurusha* can know anything about the world and its entanglements, let alone be omniscient regarding them. Only omniscience in the sense of intuitively enjoying perfect freedom (which is all a perfected being needs to know), and
omnipotence in the sense of having the power to prevent
its entanglement in the world, may be attributed to *Mahapurushas*.

But some theists attracted to Sankhya-yoga tried un-
successfully to graft on theological ideas. Granted that
Sankhya-yoga has no satisfactory explanation of why some
perfect souls do and some do not drift into contact with
a disturbing world and activate its evolutionary processes.
But postulating a *Mahapurusha* as a God meddling with
the automatic processes creates more paradoxes and predicaments than it solves. Besides, its assigned function of
upsetting the pristine equilibrium of *prakriti* is superfluous,
since each *purusha* already does this automatically by its
own presence. It has no will; otherwise it would be imperfect. It cannot know the world or care about afflictions
of other souls, otherwise it too would be reflecting the
world's misery and thus be imperfect. It cannot aid any
disturbed soul by an act of grace for it would thereby upset
karmic justice and destroy the self-help principles essential to Sankhya-yoga. Thus it is powerless to save and has
no useful religious function to perform.

Attempts to introduce theistic ideas into Sankhya-yoga

appear to stem from a fear that its "high" religious demand
that each person must work his way by his own efforts
throughout will appear too hard to beginners who must be
enticed by a "low" religious hope that an even external
and isolated "presence" of God will provide a way out of,
as well as into, the entanglements of the world. But to
attribute to a *Mahapurusha* faint powers to lure souls in
and out, making it both the author of evil and the savior
from evil, a Devil as well as a God, would hardly constitute a gain for religious purposes and, in addition, would
destroy something of its ideal nature as a being to be emulated.

Advaita Vedanta

Advaita Vedanta is claimed by its proponents to be the
greatest philosophical system produced in India and, indeed, in the whole world. There is some justification for
this claim. The tendency of the human mind, exploited
perhaps more fully by the Hindus, toward belief that ultimate reality is unitary has been carried further and
developed in greater detail here than in any other system.
Granted that it had long histories of developments to build
upon, including the Buddhist *Sunyavada,* and that it remains too abstruse for common comprehension, nevertheless it does pursue certain directions in man's thought
about himself and his universe beyond other systems. In
doing so, it may, of course, be regarded as extreme. It can
be accused of overemphasizing the intellectual approach
(*jnana-yoga*) to man's religious goal at the expense of
raja-yoga (which we have just reviewed) and of *bhakti
yoga* (which we mentioned when discussing the Epics in
Chapter III). It will deny these charges, since it incorporates these other ways within its scheme. But its critics
will contend that this incorporation functions more intellectually than spiritually and that it diminishes rather
than promotes hope for personal salvation. Let us see for
ourselves how Advaita elaborates an amazingly intricate
multitheology and then subordinates it so completely to a
nontheistic ultimate reality as to be classified as "atheistic."

The term *"advaita"* is a compound of *"a"* (meaning
"not"), *"dva"* (meaning "two"), and *"ita"* (translated as

"ism"). The Sanskrit *"dva"* is etymologically related to the Latin *"duo,"* the Spanish *"dos"* and French *"deux,"* and the English "two." The Sanskrit suffix, *"ita,"* etymologically related to the English "ity," is employed here to name a system of belief as well as a condition of existence, and may thus be equated to the English "ism." *"Advaita"* thus means "nondualism." Chief formulator of the view was Shankara (or Sankara) who lived from 788 to 820 A.D. Both he and his predecessor, Gaudapada (600 A.D.), regard their ideas as already present in the *Vedas, Upanishads,* and *Brahma Sutras.*

The central term in this philosophy is "Brahman." What, then, is Brahman? When an inquirer asks, "Is that tree Brahman?" "Is the sky Brahman?" "Is my soul Brahman?" "Is God Brahman?" his teacher will reply "No" to every question. Brahman as the ultimate reality underlying all particular things or appearances, is beyond specification. Brahman is no particular thing. Yet, on the other hand, when an inquirer asks, "Is that tree Brahman?" "Is the sky Brahman?" "Is my soul Brahman?" "Is God Brahman?" his teacher will reply "Yes" to every question. For the reality of everything is to be found in Brahman. Thus, Brahman has two aspects, even though Brahman is not two realities. Distinction is made between "Nirguna Brahman," or Brahman without *(nir)* qualities *(guna),* and "Saguna Brahman," or Brahman with *(sa)* qualities *(guna).* Nirguna Brahman is the ultimate reality of which nothing specific can be truly stated. Its nature is such that it exists as pure indistinctness. Yet, since it is the only true reality, whatever reality Saguna Brahman has is not different from it, because its reality is the reality existing in or as all other things.

Saguna Brahman includes everything in the universe from its most general and most enduring nature to the minutest detail and briefest instant of experience, and all levels of existence in between. Saguna Brahman might be regarded as a kind of pantheism except that divinity in general as well as the specific gods emerge within it rather than serve as sources of it. In its most unitary level of existence, it may be described as being *(sat),* awareness *(chit),* and bliss *(ananda)* in their purest states. In Saguna Brahman, these ultimate aspects of existence may be distinguished, whereas in Nirguna Brahman, being, awareness, and bliss remain completely identical rather than distinct in any sense. Inherent in the nature of Saguna Brahman, either latent or active from its highest to its lowest levels, are "the three *gunas*," previously discussed *(rajas, sattva,* and *tamas),* the tendencies to initiate activity, to maintain being, and to degenerate. However, at its highest level, Saguna Brahman is potential existence prior to actual existence. The nature of each particular thing exists implicitly in Saguna Brahman prior to its creation.

Actual existence emerges first as a kind of cosmic consciousness, a bare awareness of being without awareness of anything specific. Then, as such cosmic consciousness grows active due to its *rajas guna,* it becomes aware of itself as an agent of such awareness, and thus becomes conscious of itself as a conscious being. Since awareness is useless unless it functions as awareness of something, objectivity (awareness of objects) emerges naturally. In this way the universe of objects comes into being. However, such emergence occurs not merely once but many, even an infinite number of, times, and it does so through the coming into being of particular selves *(jiv)* each of which becomes self-conscious and conscious of its own range of particular objects, some of which may be shared by other selves. Self-consciousness generates ways of experiencing objects (called *"pramanas"*) including sensing (through the five senses) and thinking about them (through *manas,* mind), and desiring to preserve and possess them. The processes of creation have been elaborated by Advaitins in detail that cannot be repeated here. Analogies with the manifestations of *prakriti* as described in the Sankhya-yoga system seem obvious. Subtle and gross objects, rounds of rebirth for selves greedy for ownership and endurance, the caste system, and creation and destruction of the actual universe ("Days and Nights of Brahman") can all be accounted for as manifestations of Saguna Brahma.

But this whole process of cosmic, personal, and physical evolution must be regarded as illusory so far as any awareness judges it to be real. The existence, nature, and activity of Saguna Brahman, and of everything within it, are referred to in Advaita as *"Maya,"* illusion. The reason given for describing existence as illusory is that, ultimately, there are not two realities (Advaita is Nondualism). If Nirguna Brahman is reality, then when Saguna Brahman is distinguished from Nirguna Brahman, it seems to be distinct from reality. We cannot call it "unreality" because it exists. We cannot call it "another reality" because there are not two realities. Therefore, we must speak of it as an illusory manifestation of something that is real. We may speak of the created universe as a "real illusion," if we thereby mean that it is an illusory manifestation of a real being, Nirguna Brahman. Its only reality is Nirguna Brahman. It itself is merely an appearance. Thus, the created universe must be regarded as illusory or *Maya*. Advaita goes on to distinguish between cosmic illusion and the differences between our seeing mirages and "real lakes." But the differences between what common sense calls a "real lake" and a "mirage" and a "dream lake" are all genuine distinctions within *Maya*, but the reality underlying all of them remains pure indistinctness.

Now, although all processes of evolution and devolution take place naturalistically (*i.e.*, in accordance with the nature of Saguna Brahman), Advaita Vedanta is committed, as an orthodox school, to accepting the revelations of the Vedic scriptures. Since numerous gods and numerous names for gods and God appear in these scriptures, all of these gods and names must somehow be incorporated into the Advaita scheme. This is accomplished with great ingenuity. The enormous detail of the Advaita accounts may be summarized under three headings, each corresponding to the levels of Saguna Brahman already outlined. Let us glance at each of these briefly.

"*Ishwara*," the most general name for God in Hindu thought, is identified with the highest level of Saguna Brahman, *i.e.*, as all things are potentially prior to their actual creation. *Ishwara*, so conceived, is omnipotence in the sense that it is the power required to bring things into existence actually. It is omniscience in the sense that all possibilities of actual existence are latent in it as a cosmic awareness not yet aware of their not-yet-actual existence. Thus *Ishwara* is the omniscient, omnipotent ground from which the world is created. It is perfect being, perfect awareness, and perfect goodness. The three *gunas—rajas, sattva,* and *tamas*—remain in equilibrium within it.

"Hiranyagarbha," God as the totality of all "subtle objects," is identified with the second level of Saguna Brahman, or with the actuality of all things at its most general level. That is, the emergence of cosmic "consciousness" (awareness of all actual objects and subjects together, as distinguished from awareness of them prior to their actual existence, which is *Ishwara*) constitutes a second level of God. God at this level is identified with the Trimurti, the three forms of deity that function in the actual world. God at this level is the creator *(Brahma)*, the preserver *(Vishnu)*, and the consumer or destroyer *(Shiva)* of the actual world. Since Vishnu has many incarnations, such as Krishna (described in the *Gita*), Rama (described in the *Ramayana*), and perhaps as Buddha and Christ, all of them exist as manifestations of *Hiranyagarbha,* the most inclusive and ultimate form of deity in the actual world. Individual souls emerge within it and generate their own ways of experiencing self-consciousness and awareness and desires for objects. Each individual self must discover for itself the illusoriness of its evil predicament and work its way, by the various yogas, especially by *jnana-yoga,* to a realization of the true nature of ultimate reality, which it then automatically will seek to attain. Thus all of the historical deities—Surya, Soma, Agni, etc.—and all selves or sentient beings owe their existence to their being particular manifestations of *Hiranyagarbha,* which is pantheistic so far as the actual world is concerned.

A third level of deity, called *"Vaisvanara"* consists in Hiranyagarbha's functioning as the principle animating all beings, including plants, and fires, winds, and stars, as well as sentient beings, individual souls, and even physical things, such as mountains and rivers insofar as they are dynamic. *Vaisvanara* is the principle of vitality manifest in all activity. It is the Mana of primitive religion expressing itself variously here and there; it is cosmic energy.

However, although Advaita thus elaborates one of the most intricate and inclusive syntheses of varieties of theism ever devised, it regards all such varieties as levels of *Maya,* the cosmic illusion. Hence, it regards all of the gods and all of God as illusory. Only Nirguna Brahman is ultimately real. One may then, if he wishes, distinguish a fourth level of deity, called *"Parabrahman,"* which is simply another name for Nirguna Brahman viewed as that ultimate reality which is superior to all distinct being. But this level is regarded by Advaita as really superior to all deity. Hence, despite its elaborate theology, Advaita regards itself as essentially atheistic where ultimate reality is concerned. Advaita does not say there is no God, but only that God is *Maya*. Yet, since Advaita maintains nondualism of ultimate reality, the reality of God and the world are not different from the reality of Nirguna Brahman. Nirguna Brahman alone is ultimate reality. God and the world and souls, as parts of Saguna Brahman, have no reality as such.

Why Nirguna Brahman manifests itself in such an illusory fashion remains an ultimate mystery. Why a perfect being expresses itself in imperfect ways remains as much a mystery for Advaitins as for others. The emergence of levels of deity cannot be explained (except as a consequence of the operation of the inexplicable *gunas*); instead the concept of Brahman, Nirguna and Saguna, and the levels of *Maya* and deity are used to explain our predicament as unhappy living beings. One may wonder how the Advaita scheme can serve man's religious needs, for how can one become interested in arriving at an awareness of ultimate indistinctness? The Advaitin answers that its incorporation of all of the gods makes it as much available as all of the varieties of polyspiritism, polytheism, pantheonism, trinitarianism, and monotheism together, and at the same time appeals to man's demand for a perfect intellectual solution *(jnana-yoga)* to his predicament. It regards itself as both inclusive of and superior to all other ways. Nirguna Brahman, that ultimate identity of perfect being, perfect awareness, and perfect bliss, is something to which man must automatically assent with a complete intellectual yea-saying. One may not succeed immediately in bringing his practical will into complete agreement with his intellectual assent, but only because he recognizes that he does not yet entirely will what he knows is best for himself. Persistent attainment of the intellectual goal of both philosophy and religion, *Brahmavidya* (knowledge of Brahman), conditions one to assent more fully to willing and acting in whatever way is needed to reattain one's being as Nirguna Brahman—"the fearless goal of life."

Theistic Vedantism

The term "Theistic Vedantism" here serves as a collective name for several varieties of theism, all formulated after, and in opposition to, Shankara's Advaita. Each also claims to be Vedantistic, *i.e.*, to finish filling out doctrines begun in the *Vedas*. These theistic schools also trace other predecessors and serve as theological explanations for popular movements such as Vaishnavism, the followers of Vishnu, and Shaivism, the followers of Shiva and consorts. We must restrict our account of these varieties to three, namely, those formulated by Ramanuja, Madhva, and Nimbarka. The views of Vallabha, Chaitanya, and Aurobindo must await some other occasion.

(1) RAMANUJA (1017–1137 A.D.) accepted Shankara's Nondualism with important modifications. Hence it is called "Visist-a-dva-ita" or "Modified Nondualism." Brahman is indeed the ultimate reality and it is not two. But since the relation between Nirguna Brahman and Saguna Brahman is one of identity, then Saguna Brahman must itself be as real as Nirguna Brahman. Hence, Saguna Brahman is not illusory but real, and everything in it is also real. Saguna Brahman is *Ishwara,* as Shankara had claimed. But since Nirguna Brahman is not different from Saguna Brahman, the distinguishing terms, "Nirguna" and "Saguna," become irrelevant. Brahman is *Ishwara* and *Ishwara* is Brahman. *Ishwara* has two aspects or levels—the first consisting in the universe, or multiverse, unmanifest; and the second in the multiverse manifest—which are, in reality, indistinct. Ramanuja's system is a kind of pantheism in which *Ishwara* both transcendentally unites all plurality and is each detail of the plurality. Thus God is a one-in-many, a unity-in-diversity, a whole of many parts. (*See* Jadunath Sinha, *History of Indian Philosophy,* Vol II, pp. 658–663, for comprehensive description.)

Ishwara manifests itself in two kinds of parts that, though different from each other, are not different from *Ishwara,* just as two parts of a whole differ from each other without being different from their common whole. These two are spirit (*chit*) and matter (*achit*). *Achit* is akin to the *prakriti* of the Sankhya-yoga school in being an uncreated, eternal reality that contains *rajas, sattva,* and *tamas gunas* and that stirs into evolution consciousness, self-consciousness, mind, the senses, and their objects. But it differs in that it remains inseparable from God and functions as his body in response to his will. *Chit* is akin to the *purusha* of the Sankhya-yoga school in being awareness, atomic, eternal, and capable of reflecting suffering by connection with body. But it differs in that its existence remains inseparably dependent upon *Ishwara. Chit* manifests itself as many *jivas* or selves, whose births are due to *avidya* (ignorance) emerging from association and false identification with bodies, and also from false belief in its independence from God. Each *jiva* has free will but not will that is completely independent from God's will. *Jivas* collectively do not constitute the mind of God. They differ from *Ishwara* in being created, ignorant, and eternally saved by grace, whereas *Ishwara* is creator, omniscient, and savior. But they also remain the same as *Ishwara* in that they have no independent reality in this Modified Nondualistic system.

A soul may attain release from its bondage to ignorance by devotion *(bhakti yoga),* which, for Ramanuja, takes the form of a constant remembrance of God. Performance of duties, services, sacrifices, moral behavior, prayer, chanting, meditation, etc., all may aid. But only when devotion reaches a state of complete self-surrender can a soul be freed. After freedom, it does not lose its individuality in transcendental *Ishwara-Brahman* but persists as a knower, possessed of infinite knowledge and bliss, enjoying the "infinite sport of God."

(2) MADHVA (1199–1278) champions Dualism *(Dvaita),* thereby becoming the archenemy of Shankara's Nondualism *(Advaita).* Both God and the world are real, uncreated, and indestructible. God, Brahman, or *Ishwara* is identified with Vishnu, chief deity of the Vaishnava sect. The world consists of two kinds of beings: souls (of an infinite number) and matter *(prakriti),* depicted as the body of God, as the will of God, and as Lakshmi, the eternal consort of Vishnu. God remains perfect in all respects, infinite in power, creator, controller, destroyer, giver of grace and bliss, and omniscient. He is personal, but his personality is of an absolute kind. He has no purpose in creating

the world, but does so spontaneously and continuously, since creative activity is essential to his nature. He creates the world, not out of nothing, but out of *prakriti,* the eternal material cause, by molding it as he wills through first evolving the three *gunas* and then through the stages already outlined in discussing the Sankhya-yoga system. Souls were neither created by God nor do they form part of the body of God; but they depend upon him. Each soul is eternal and without parts. It dwells in the body and experiences happiness and misery. Merits and demerits determine rebirth; when they wear off, bodily existence ceases and the soul becomes liberated. However, three classes of souls may be distinguished: those which were always free, those which have become free, and those remaining in bondage. Of the last, some, pervaded by *sattva guna,* will be liberated; some, dominated by *rajas guna,* will wander continuously from life to life in the world; and some, saturated by *tamas guna,* are doomed to a miserable life in hell. Among the Hindu religions, the doctrine of eternal damnation is peculiar to Madhva and Jainism.

Madhva's Dualism is not completely dualistic since its two kinds of reality—God, on the one hand, and souls and *prakriti,* on the other—are unequal in many respects. God is independent; souls and matter depend upon God. God is perfect; souls and matter, although eternal, are imperfect in knowledge and self-movement, respectively. Five kinds of differences, each eternal in nature, are required to account for Madhva's Dualism, namely, differences between God and souls, between God and matter, between soul and matter, between one soul and another, and between one material thing and another. God, matter, and soul remain eternally irreducible to one another. Their differences really exist; yet souls and matter depend upon God. By maintaining a constant awareness of this dependence upon, and nonidentity with, God, a soul may liberate itself. Such awareness, manifest through worship of Vishnu, pleases God, who gives his grace to those who love him most dearly. Thus, by grace, as well as self-help, man is saved. Here again, by saying "Yes" to the truth, now conceived as assenting to one's lot (different from body and from God, dependent upon God, and redeemable through reverent awareness of God), one believes he can attain the goal of life.

(3) NIMBARKA (dates uncertain) criticizes the Nondualism of Ramanuja and Shankara as failing to recognize the reality of differences between Brahman and the world of souls and matter. He also objects to any Dualism that considers differences as absolute. He regards both difference and nondifference (identity) as real, and equally real, in constituting relations between God and the world. Hence, his view has been called "Dualistic Nondualism" *(Dvaitadvaita)* and the "Difference-Non-difference Theory" *(Bhedabhedavada)*, where *"bheda"* means "difference." We will not review the details of Nimbarka's theory that regards the transformation of Brahman into the world—which continues to depend upon him—as a real transformation. Brahman eternally transcends the world *and* creates a world really different from him in which he becomes immanent. The significance of Nimbarka's view for us consists in its illustrating another variety of Theistic Vedantism apparently indigenous to orthodox Hinduism. Religious yea-saying must now assent to an identity-and-difference philosophy, in contrast with the pure identity (nondistinct, or nondualistic) view of Shankara, with the modified identity (identity-in-difference) view of Ramanuja, and with the difference (or dualistic) view of Madhva.

Popular Religion

Technical differences between theologies seem to bother worshippers very little. The Supreme Deity may be worshipped in any form and in any temple as well as at home. Reverence for the Supreme Deity as the Divine Mother, a Tantric interpretation, has become common. The Divine Mother of her own free will divided herself, for purposes of creation, into the dual aspects of male and female. The male aspect, which is predominantly spiritual in nature *(purusha)*, appears as Shiva, for example; and *shakti,* the power of the female aspect, which functions as the primordial bodily energy *(prakriti)*, appears depicted in the forms of the consorts of Shiva, such as Kali. These two aspects of the Divine Mother remain inseparably related, so worship of Kali automatically involves worship of Shiva, and vice versa. To the devoted worshipper it matters little whether the Divine Mother be called Shiva or Vishnu or Brahman or Ishwara or Krishna or Durga, for all are various manifestations of the same ultimate reality.

Customary ways of expressing religious feelings include *japa,* the repeating of the names of deity or of sacred phrases *(mantras)* in a chant; *homa,* the placing of oblations into consecrated fire; and *tarpana,* the worship of deity with offerings, including food and flowers. These may be accompanied by suitable gestures and postures. Temple worship often requires the services of trained priests, who conduct services with precision.

Perhaps I may report my own experience in observing a portion of a ceremony in the Kali temple on Bogyoke Street in downtown Rangoon in 1955. Loud clanging of bells, part of an ongoing ceremony, aroused my curiosity and, removing my sandals, I went in and stood with six or eight others observing two priests moving gradually around several small candle-like fires on a raised platform. They appeared to be touching each of the flames in a purificatory process that ended with one of the priests carrying a platter of ashes sanctified by prayers and refined by flames. I was somewhat startled when the priest approached me with his platter. I happened to be standing first in the row of people, and I did not know what was expected of me so I merely stood watching. The priest, engrossed in his activities, had not seen me enter. Walking with his head down in a humble position and with his attention focused upon the holy ashes, he did not observe me until, when I did not partake of his offering to me, he looked up also somewhat surprised. When I still did not respond, he moved on to the next person, who placed his finger tips in the ashes and rubbed some on his forehead. Then I realized that this was a holy communion service where not bread and wine symbolizing the body and blood of Christ but ashes refined from several sacred flames symbolized the union of mortal man with the eternal Divine Mother, the ultimate cosmic reality. Here was one of mankind's most ancient rituals, permitting personal participation in the cosmic unity. The ceremonies occur only at regular times, when one may step in out of the busy marketplace, the city traffic, and the business of bartering, and pause to partake of a spirit of holiness. The worshipper leaves the temple with the ashes still on his forehead, signifying his sharing in a bit of permanent peace amid daily struggle, thus reminding others who see him of the omnipresence of the Divine Mother and enduring destiny.

Festivals and sacred days are numerous, and, although not everyone can celebrate all of them, the idea of having so many seems welcome all around. As everywhere, solar and seasonal changes require appropriate markings, and birthdays of great saints and gods receive recognition. There are great variations in the times and deities cele-brated in different localities in India. But each may stir the individual out of his personal troubles and arouse in him a feeling of community with others, with the gods, and with the universe. (My own personal experience at the University of Rangoon remains vivid. Apparently I have an unfailing tendency, both at home and abroad, to go to a library when it is closed. At any rate, I was at first perplexed about why there were so many holidays. Here, in a predominantly Buddhist university, it is customary to celebrate not only Buddhist holidays and national holi-days, but also Hindu, Christian, and perhaps even Mos-lem, holidays. And why not? Not only "the more the mer-rier" but also "the more the holier," for holiness is not the private preserve of any one religion. One who recog-nizes the interest that others take in holiness thereby be-comes reminded of his own interest in holiness, even when he does not participate formally in the ceremonies peculiar to each religion. But there are limits to the number of holidays that can be celebrated, even in Rangoon.)

Acquaintance with Indian religious practices leaves one impressed with the amazing range as well as complexity of appeals to man's religious needs, varying from the primi-tive magical pursuit of personal spite to the generous and sustained support of world peace through world culture. I recall, for example, another Hindu festival celebration centering around a fire-walking ceremony. Going for a stroll near the University of Rangoon, my daughter, Elaine, and I noticed a crowd of gaily dressed people in front of a Hindu temple, where a garlanded sacred cow was standing. As we walked back of the temple into a five-acre field, in the middle of which was a small (perhaps twenty-five by fifty feet) plot surrounded by a tall stiff wire fence, some Indians hailed us and waved us into the enclosure. By then we realized, from the approaching crowds and flaming fires in the center of this enclosure, that we not only had stumbled upon a significant occasion but that we were invited, with other non-Indians, to take a "ringside seat," *i.e.,* to stand or squat, doubtless because we had cameras. Once inside, we discovered the purpose of the wire fence. The moblike throng, now standing outside the fence, would have pressed forward and prevented us from seeing anything. Without the fence, we should have been pushed progressively toward the fire and the participants in the ceremony could not have carried on at all.

In the center of the enclosure was a trench, about twenty-five feet long, ten feet wide, and a foot and a half deep, with a shallow pool of water extending about four feet from one end. In the middle of the trench were three huge log fires flaming high. After some time, when the highest flames had exhausted themselves, straw was thrown on the fires to damp the burning for the logs to disintegrate entirely into live coals. Meanwhile, about fifteen specially dressed (mostly nude) persons filed into the arena and marched solemnly around the flaming trench a few times and then took their places at the far end of the enclosure, awaiting further directions from a master of ceremonies. When the fires were ready for the next step, the master directed his aids to spread the coals out evenly over the trench, excepting the pool of water. The coals were shifted by long-handled rakes, which, when they caught fire, had to be dipped into metal barrals of water brought to the arena for this purpose. After allowing this glowing pathway to sparkle for awhile, until remaining flames had subsided, the fire walker first in line was permitted to approach the trench. He, and each successive walker, was held by his arms by two supervisors, who gave him a "go" signal and released him when they thought he was ready. Apparently each had received some kind of narcotic that affected his balance, his resistance to pain, and possibly his judgment as to just when to do his deed. Whenever one appeared to be too unsteady, he was eliminated from the line.

The first anxious walker permitted to go needed only four or five long rapid strides to reach the watered pool and the arms of waiting attendants to catch him at the end of his brief run. I must confess that although prepared by stories about fire walkers, I could not keep from marveling at the actual event. Granted, these men always went barefoot, were accustomed to pulling heavy carts on scorching pavements, and were under narcotic influence; but those glowing coals were still so hot as to pain the faces of roasting spectators several feet away. The first walker (*i.e.*, runner) received loud cheers from the crowd as he ran. Steadied to his feet after a brief cooling in the pool and inspection of his soles, he marched, with the aid of attendants, back to the end of the line of waiting walkers, prepared to take his turn again. Some of the walkers went through the fire several times. The second also ran, and the third and fourth. Soon, after footprints of previous walkers had depressed the coals a bit in spots, and, I suspect, did something to reduce the extreme heat, one brave person really walked, a fast walk to be sure but a walk and not a run, through the coals. He received the loudest cheers. Thereafter almost everyone walked. Then someone carried a weight upon his head as he walked, pressing his feet upon the coals. Then a young boy was carried piggyback. Then a shoulder-high platform was carried, resting upon long wirelike needles sticking into carrier's flesh at various places down his front and back. And there were many who had one or more spikes stuck through their tongues or noses. Finally the image of some deity, decorated with flowers, was carried through the coals in this shoulder-high platform.

What, the reader may wonder, did all this seemingly gruesome torture have to do with religion? Neither my remembered account nor my interpretation may be completely accurate. But I gathered that such ceremonies, performed annually or oftener, have a complex significance, expressing penance for misdeeds, expiating evils due to karmic demerits, offering a kind of personal sacrifice to the gods, demonstrating courage and faith in god, as well as providing a kind of sustenance to the order of the universe. The custom, handed down by special training generation after generation through tribe and family from

time immemorial, is just a part of the way things are—
even as we today celebrate Halloween, Thanksgiving, and
Christmas without raising much question as to whether it
might be otherwise. The expiation of sins need not be
merely personal, but felt as both a duty to and a benefit
for the whole community and for all mankind. Only the
calloused onlooker, realizing that such an elaborate public
ceremony of self-torture is done intentionally partly for
his spiritual benefit, can fail to appreciate the goodwill
of the firewalkers.

My Hindu friends reminded me that fire walking is
something that appeals only to the lower, largely illiterate
classes. I witnessed also a different sort of ceremony when
invited to the home of Professor N. C. Das, Lecturer in
Philosophy at the University of Rangoon. The occasion
was a celebration honoring Sarasvati, the Goddess of Wisdom and Learning (naturally patronized by professors),
whose gleaming white marble statue had been imported
from Calcutta for the ceremony. The statue of the goddess was enthroned on a screened porch, banked with
flowers, surrounded by candles, and suitably situated amid
lights and shadows so as to produce a beautiful, hallowed
glow. After a banquet at rows of tables on the lawn, with
convivial fellowship and some goodwill speeches, sacred
dramas were enacted upon a stage erected at one end of
the yard, accompanied by appropriate music, dancing, and
songs.

part ii

Religions of China and Japan

Chapter 7 Taoism

Surely the reader already knows that Chinese civilization is one of the world's oldest continuous major cultures. Many indigenous and foreign springs have contributed to the mainstream of the great Far Eastern cultural river with its many estuaries making permanent donations to mankind's rich cultural ocean. Less familiar, perhaps, are the nature and significance of its donations. Many Westerners have become aware that Hindu culture is highly spiritualistic. They may regard as understandable the claim that Hindu civilization is "the most religious" of the three great civilizations, even when they do not accept it. Westerners who define religion as "belief in God" (a definition common to Judaism, Christianity, and Islam) usually regard themselves as "the most religious." They often consider Hindu and Chinese cultures as "superstitious" and interpret Confucianism as a primitive form of "ancestor worship" confusedly intermingled with "dragon worship." Hence any claim that Chinese culture is "the most religious" may well seem strange.

Whereas Hindus are spiritualistic, Europeans dualistic and "God-centered," the Chinese are naturalistic or Nature-centered in their religion. Religion has been naturalized, or rather never was denaturalized, in China. Westerners traditionally have idealized God as "supernatural," as above and beyond nature, implying that the source and goal of life has a kind of foreignness or "otherworldliness." Western religions typically require a man to "deny himself," to recognize his natural existence as "total depravity," to "repent," and to submit his will utterly to the Will of a Higher Power. These concepts are foreign to the spirit of Chinese religion. But then, these concepts tend to make religion foreign to man. When religion is natural to man,

man is naturally religious. He does not have to deny himself, change his nature, become a "new man," in order to be religious. He is religious already. Both Hindus and Chinese regard man as naturally religious, though the Hindu goal, *Nirvana,* can be realized by most only in some other life or beyond life.

Chinese culture regards man as good, *i.e.,* man as he is now is as good as he can be, and the goal of life is to live happily in the actual present. Religiously, each man has already arrived at the goal of life, if he can but recognize the fact and enjoy it. Persons coming from other cultures, expecting the Chinese to be religiously oriented toward a future and a beyond that will be better than the present, are pained to find "the heathen Chinee" not even looking for anything better. Hindus, believing that one should look within and beneath commonsense appearances to some underlying, indistinct unitary reality *(alayavijnana)* or void *(sunya),* exported Buddhism in order to "provide religion" for the Chinese. Westerners, especially Christians and Moslems, have sent missionaries to convert the Chinese "to religion." But, despite the spread of Buddhism throughout China and "rice Christians" whose children have become staunch believers, the general temper of Chinese culture remains naturalistic. There is nothing unnatural about life. The goal of life, and thus of religion, is to be realized by recognizing and assenting to "the importance of living."

The Three Truths

We of the West should know more about, even when we cannot accept, Chinese religions. Not only have these religions already played an enormous role in human history, indelibly shaping the ideals of huge masses of population, but they will continue to influence any world culture, world government, and world religion despite our tendency to ignore them and despite Marxist efforts to erase them by wholesale revisions of written history. Indigenous religious concepts structure the language with which Chinese minds think, and China cannot be wholly Westernized without acquiring Western linguistic structures. Chinese religious influence has not been confined to the mainland, but has shaped the ideals of Korea, Japan, and many island cultures in the Pacific. But also, these Chinese religions constitute some of mankind's most important religious experiments.

In addition to the numerous animistic ideas and practices which continue to persist tenaciously in every culture, the multifarious strands of religious developments in China may be grouped for convenience under three headings. These three, which have come to be called "the Three Truths of China," are Taoism, Confucianism, and Buddhism. Taoism and Confucianism, as we shall demonstrate, seem very much alike from foreign perspectives. Their minor, but genuine, differences have become magnified by serving as rallying philosophies for conflicting personal and social interests. Growth in misunderstandings, proliferation of branches and sects, and accumulation of libraries of only partly comprehensible literature, have led to divergencies more superficial than deep. The main rift in Chinese minds developed when they were inveigled into hoping for gifts from Buddhist *bodhisattvas* and for greater insight into ultimate reality by studying the subtle speculations of Buddhist writers. Despite centuries in which it has been one of "the Three Truths," Buddhism is still generally regarded as a foreign import that may be sloughed off without one's risking disrespect from culture-loyal Chinese compatriots. Buddhism itself became modified under the influences of Taoism and Confucianism, so much so that scholars must now distinguish between "Chinese Buddhism" and "Buddhism in China." Zen, as we shall see, owes as much to Taoism and Confucianism as it does to its nominal ancestor, Indian Buddhism.

Yang and Yin

Before examining the central ideas of Chinese thought, let us glance at some of the conditions in early Chinese history that produced them. Three must be noted: animism, agriculture, and family life, though treatment of the latter will be reserved for our chapter on Confucianism.

Like all early peoples, primitive Chinese were animistic, believing that observable occurrences without visible causes have invisible causes. The presence or absence of water, winds, rain, thunder, the changes of day and night and of the seasons—all natural phenomena, in fact, called for explanation. Since the dark was fearful and daylight brought visibility and dispelled fears, the sun was welcomed for its fear-relieving functions as well as for its heat and light. The cock, which crows in the morning to announce the coming sunrise, was thus regarded as a herald of good. Earthenware cocks came to stand as symbols of beneficent powers, as did the ugly dragons whose images, used to scare away evil spirits, came to be posted as guardians of entrances and rooftops. Bonfires and torches, and later lanterns and candles and noisy firecrackers, served a similar purpose. Chinese festivals even today properly require firecrackers, lanterns, and huge dragon floats to celebrate good fortune in surviving the evils that beset us in the course of our lives.

Observing also that one day and night is like others, and yet differs as more sunny or cloudy; that one year is like others in having four seasons, yet differs in floods and drouths and relative abundance or scarcity of food; and that one life is like others, yet differs in that some children die young while others live long, Chinese too noted analogies not only between cyclical phenomena of the same kind, such as days, but also between those of different kinds, such as days, years, lives, and even dynasties. Since life and death depend upon such analogies, the early Chinese sought ways of predicting, even if not of controlling, both regular and irregular behavior of nature and its powers. They noted, for example, that all cyclical changes have beginnings, periods of growth, periods of decline, and endings, and they soon discovered ways of generalizing about and symbolizing these stages.

Two of the broadest generalizations should be noted. The first consists in observing that phenomena appear in pairs of opposites. Not only do things and events have beginnings and endings, growth and decline, increase and decrease, expansion and contraction, but they participate in other oppositions. Parent-child, husband-wife, king-subjects, master-servant, and sky-earth appear as opposites. Up and down, hot and cold, north and south, light and dark, wet and dry, hard and soft, right and left, forward and backward all oppose each other. Opening and closing, advancing and retreating, creating and destroying, giving and receiving, desiring and becoming satisfied, arousing and subsiding, leading and following are other polarities. Odd and even, good and bad, love and hate, fear and confidence, stimulus and response, youth and age, affirmation and denial, all stand opposed to each other. Our first generalization, then, is that opposition exists everywhere.

The second, perhaps a bit less obvious than the first, consists in noting that for each pair of opposites one of the two has a kind of priority over the other. Just as a person with two hands, which oppose each other, also tends to be either right-handed or left-handed, so one of every pair of opposites appears to be somewhat dominant. Yet this dominance is temporary and what dominates comes to be dominated in the normal cyclical course of events. In generalizing about priority, the Chinese noted that in any process one phase comes first and another follows, or that one stage is initiative and another completive, or that one aspect is active and another passive. Today we would say that one is positive and the other negative. Two terms, "Yang" and "Yin," came to designate these positive and negative traits of opposites. Review each of the pairs mentioned in the previous paragraph and observe for yourself how natural it is to conclude that beginning must precede ending, parents must precede children, that advancing must precede retreating, that desire must precede satisfaction, and that a thing must be new before it can become old. Although no single interpretation of Yang and Yin can suffice to convey all of their general significance, I suggest that an adequate summary may be found in a concept combining initiation and completion, including activity and passivity. Once this is done, then one may notice some consequences flowing from its application.

When you interpret Yang, connoting initiation of action, and Yin, meaning completion and cessation, as male and female, how does the analogy fit? Does the observation of male-female polarities corroborate and support the Yang-Yin generalization? Physiologically men usually are stronger, larger, more active, more aggressive, and women usually seem smaller, weaker, more quiet and submissive. Men tend to initiate courtship and women to respond. He is the lover and she the beloved. He bestows and she receives. When he is aroused, she can quiet him. When you compare the Yang-Yin polarity with the Heaven-Earth polarity, again the morning sun arouses earth to activity, plants turn toward the sun as it journeys across the sky, rain comes from the sky to vitalize and fructify the earth, the stars retain an orderliness despite seeming chaos on earth. Heaven is Yang and Mother Earth is Yin. Hence, the terms "Yang" and "Yin" apply to many things, to all pairs of opposites, and Yang should not be interpreted as "Heaven" or "male" merely.

Still another generalization has to do with the mutual dependence and supplementary aspects of opposites. Beginning and ending involve each other, for a thing cannot end that does not first begin, and if a thing begins it cannot reach its perfection without coming to its end. Although beginning is prior to ending, ending eventually dominates over beginning—"the last of life for which the first was made." Desire has its end in satisfaction. He chases her until she catches him.

Not only are opposites complementary, but they succeed each other. Not only does ending come after beginning, but a new beginning follows each ending—otherwise existence would cease. Day is followed by night, then night by day. Spring is followed by fall and winter, but winter is followed by spring. Desire ends in satisfaction, only to eventuate in another desire. Thus Yang and Yin succeed each other cyclically, each taking its turn in the natural course of things. Such mutual dependence, mutual supplementation, and mutual succession of Yang and Yin have been symbolized by the *Bah-Kua:*

Not only does a day begin to end as soon as it begins, but there is something of it still ahead and yet to begin, until it has ended completely; and not only does one cycle terminate both day and night, but within each day some anticipations of the night occur, and during each night there is an accumulation of energy to be used during the day.

We should note in passing that the line between Yang and Yin in this symbol, although clear enough to differentiate between opposites, does not depict a straight line that cuts opposites into contradictories. The clue to Chinese logic, and to the Chinese mind, is to be found in "both, and" (Yang *and* Yin) rather than in the "either, or, but not both" (true *or* false) that characterizes Western exclusivism, or in the "neither is, nor is not, nor both is and is not, nor neither is nor is not" that shapes Hindu ideals. Thus the *Bah-Kua* is a logical symbol, connoting opposition without contradiction, difference without exclusion, and succession without cessation, as well as a metaphysical symbol, signifying the constitution of existence by supplementary opposites, and as a value symbol, indicating the equal goodness of good (Yang) and bad (Yin), each being good in its own way. Despite their differences, male and female, initiation and completion, desire and satisfaction, birth and death, are all good. Nature is good, man is good, opposites are good.

Differences in the ultimate logical ideals of Western, Hindu, and Chinese cultures provide clues to differences in ultimate metaphysical ideals to which religious persons in each culture must say "Yes." Western logic has traditionally idealized "three laws of thought," centering about "the law of excluded middle." The inevitable result is dualism, of good and bad, right and wrong, true and false, sin and salvation, God and man. That strict dualism cannot be maintained in practice does not prevent its continuing as an ideal. Man is compelled to say "Yes" to his difference (imperfection) from God (perfection) forever, and to glory therein. His dualism of Heaven and Earth requires him to give up all hope of reaching his goal in life on Earth, to wait in the hope of "drawing nigh unto God" in Heaven.

Hindu logic has opposed Western dualism by idealizing an indistinctness so extreme that all distinctions must be regarded as illusory. Man is compelled to say "Yes" to his indistinctness from ultimate reality.

Chinese logic retains a duality of opposites without ever adopting a dualism of exclusive contradictories. Opposites are to be found everywhere, but always supplementing rather than excluding each other. Chinese logic retains some indistinctness by rejecting complete exclusiveness between opposites. But it refuses to shut its eyes to the obvious differences between Yang and Yin. Chinese logic is thus middle-wayed regarding the existence and sharpness of distinctions. By comparison, the logic of the so-called Madhyamika (Middle-Way) School of Buddhism represents an utter extreme. Although the Chinese mind may be no more able than Hindu or Western minds to pursue its logical ideals to perfection, its ideal does commend it to say "Yes" to distinctions that are not too distinct and to indefiniteness that is not wholly indefinite. One who has grasped this general spirit of the Chinese mind will more easily accept its additional ways of symbolizing analogies by means of hexagrams.

Hexagrams

Symbols for Yang and Yin, doubtless among the oldest of mankind's most general symbols, are "—," an unbroken line, and "- -," a broken line, probably first represented by twigs or sticks. Thus "—" signifies initiation, activity, advancement, while "- -" signifies completion, passivity, subsidence. Although these Yang and Yin symbols can be used to signify whole or gross phenomena, such as male and female, day and night, spring and fall, the demands for a more subtle symbolization produce greater complexity. The Chinese way of doing this consisted in using these same symbols over again for additional subordinate oppositions. Hence, an aggressive male can be symbolized by ═ and a submissive female by ══, and a bashful male by ══ and an aggressive female by ══.

The symbol for the most basic or most general Yang or Yin trait takes the bottom position in the diagram, and the symbol for the additional Yang or Yin trait appears above it. When a third pair of opposing traits enters a picture, the two symbols are employed a third time. A male who is not only aggressive but also ambitious or insistent in his aggressiveness can be symbolized by ☰ , whereas a male who is less so may then be symbolized by ☱ . Our aggressive female may be symbolized by ☲ when she is unrelenting and by ☳ when she abandons her pursuit. The third symbol takes the top position of the three. When the symbol ☷ denotes a patient, submissive female, femaleness is represented by the bottom line, submissiveness by the second, and patience by the top. Three such lines constitute a standard unit of interpretation, and they have come to be called, in English, "trigrams."

The simplest bit of calculation will reveal that there can be only eight trigrams:

☰ ☱ ☲ ☳ ☴ ☵ ☶ ☷

Let us see what happens when the eight trigrams are used to symbolize the eight stages of a complete cycle of change such as a day and night, in a clockwise manner. First, day may be regarded as light and rousing and coming first, so day is naturally symbolized by an unbroken line. Then night, which is dark and quiet and the opposite of day, is naturally designated by a broken line. Now the day also can be divided between forenoon and afternoon, so the forenoon can be represented by two unbroken lines and the afternoon by a broken line on top of an unbroken line, thus signifying completion of the first half, or the beginning part, of the day. Then the first half of the forenoon is symbolized by three unbroken lines because it is the beginning (first half) of the beginning (forenoon) of the beginning (day) of the day-night cycle. The remainder of this process may be traced on the diagram on page 160. The stages of any cycle, such as the weeks of a month, the seasons of the year, the periods of life (childhood, youth, maturity, and old age), the reign of a ruler or the history of a dynasty, may be symbolized by these eight trigrams. They may also be used to designate the "four corners of the earth" or the directions of a compass. So there is apparently no limit to the practical applications of trigrams as interpretive symbols.

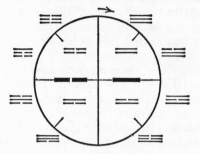

Although the number of general analogies found in the eight trigrams may seem sufficient for most purposes, human curiosity and need for greater detail press the system of trigrams further. Instead of using four lines, however, and then five-lined diagrams, Chinese tradition jumped from three to six lines or from trigrams to hexagrams. Yet even so, a hexagram consists not of six lines piled one on top of another but rather of two trigrams, one above the other. Hence, one must already be familiar with the general nature of each of the two component trigrams in order to grasp the added meaning indicated by their conjunction. There are exactly sixty-four hexagrams. All of them may be used to indicate units of a cycle having sixty-four degrees (whether a cycle of change or a static circle). Together they constitute a very rich set of general analogies that may be used for interpretive purposes.

The *I Ching (Yi King)* or *Book of Changes* consists of these sixty-four hexagrams together with interpretations, commentaries upon the interpretations, and additional commentaries upon the first commentaries. These layers of commentary are called "the ten wings." The hexagrams were first used for divination, including predictions made on the bases of cracks appearing in the stalks of milfoil plants, or lines on the back of tortoise shells, etc. But historical developments have produced many ways in which trigrams and hexagrams have functioned to shape the Chinese mind. They now permeate several phases of its culture. Musical notation, for example, is expressed in trigrams. The angles of triangles and the corners of cubes may be symbolized by trigrams. The figures and moods of the syllogism may be represented by trigrams. Those who are curious may find an analysis of the binomial cube and other mathematical analogies in Z. D. Sung's *The Symbols of the Yi King*. An appreciative evaluation of ways in which ancient methods of conceiving natural oppositions have been employed in contemporary America is found in the volume written by a Chinese scholar-scientist working in a United States research laboratory: *The Tao of Science:* An Essay on Western Science and Eastern Wisdom, by Ralph Gun Hoy Siu. (Boston: The Technology Press, Massachusetts Institute of Technology, 1957.)

The Five Elements

In every civilization, early attempts at generalized principles of explanation have resulted in singling out five elements that have fundamental significance. A comparison of how these five elements have been treated in different civilizations can be very instructive in providing clues to typical traits of those civilizations.

Western civilization remembers the picture that its Greek progenitors painted of earth, water, air, fire, and ether, ranged in an hierarchical order. The principle of the arrangement can be found by mixing any two of these together and letting them then seek their own level. When muddy water rests, earth settles to the bottom and clear water rises to the top. Mix water and air together; then notice that all the bubbles of air rise to the surface. Air and fire together result in mounting flames and heat with cool air descending. These may be pictured also as occupying concentric spheres, with ether occupying the rarest and outermost sphere. The hierarchical structure typical of Western theology, logic, and science can be found already embodied here.

Hindu civilization has tended to identify earth with odor, fire with visual form, water with flavor, air with touch, and ether with the medium for sound, thus giving a subjective sensuous source for the five elements. Its habit of interpreting all things in spiritual terms is typified by its non-hierarchical association of the five elements with the five senses. Neither Greek nor Chinese cultures accept such association as having any basic significance.

In Chinese civilization, "the five elements" are "water, fire, wood, metal, and soil." The function of water is to moisten and descend; that of fire, to flame and ascend; that of wood, to be crooked and straight; that of metal, to yield and be modified; that of soil (or earth), to provide for sowing and reaping. But these are conceived not only as general principles or powers or agencies, each with its own nature and mode of functioning, but also as related in a serial and cyclical order, such as that which we have just been discussing in connection with the hexagrams and *Book of Changes*. Analogies derivable from the natures of these elements may be noted in our own usages when we describe persons as wet or depressing, as fiery or exciting, as stiff and as bent, as malleable, and as reciprocative. By associating these characteristics with analogies suggested by trigrams, an ingenious mind can discover many sorts of interesting similes.

Serial and causal relationships between the five elements have become standardized as follows: wood, fire, soil, metal, and water. On the one hand, we can observe how wood, when burned, becomes fire; how fire, when it dies down, becomes ashes (soil); how soil becomes impacted and may be mined as metal; how metal, when melted, becomes water (liquid); and how water, when absorbed by trees, enables them to grow into wood. On the other hand, "wood overcomes soil" (uses it for growth); "fire overcomes metal" (melts it); "soil overcomes water" (absorbs it); "metal overcomes wood" (chops it); and "water overcomes fire" (extinguishes it). Impressed by the pervasiveness, profundity, and obviousness of this serial set of relationships between the elements, the Chinese mind has used it as a basic pattern from which to draw interpretive analogies. Once similarities between seasonal cycles, life cycles, and historical cycles and this basic set have been noted, one may then find other similarities also.

The typical functions of each element, previously mentioned, may be regarded as general tendencies that may be symbolized by arrows. Water descends ↓, fire rises ↑, wood (annual growth of tree rings) expands , metal (when dented or melted) contracts —>⟨— and soil

(through planting and reaping, receiving and giving) recip-

rocates ⇆ , or ↓↑ . Notice the pairs of opposites present
in these five functions, and how soil, or mother earth, embodies both of two opposing directions and thus is the
most self-contained and self-sufficient of the five. Note
how these arrows denote stages in a person's life cycle
when the wood-fire-soil-metal-water cycle of elements is accepted as typifying such stages: The first stage of life, from
conception through youth, is one of expanding (like wood)
by growing in size; the second, from youth through young
manhood, is one of rising (like fire) in the world of
affairs; the third, middle age or maturity, is one of recipro-
cating, of producing and consuming, of fructifying and
having children (like soil or earth); the fourth, old age,
is one of contraction (like dented metal) evidenced by
shriveling muscles and wrinkling skin; and the fifth, death,
is (like water) a descent into the earth. One must not
press analogies too far. But by employing them with restraint, *i.e.*, by accepting them as involving "distinctions
which are not too distinct and indefiniteness which is not
wholly indefinite," one may discover a measure of usefulness.

Perhaps the Chinese themselves have carried these analogies too far. But with simple ingenuity they noticed
that the seasons and the points of the compass both exhibit
associations with the five elements. Spring (like wood) is
a time for expansive growth of plants. Summer (like fire)
is hot. Autumn (like metal) is a time for contracting growing things back to their source. Winter (like water) is a
time when all life has descended toward or into the soil.
Earth, the all-inclusive reciprocator, is common to all
seasons, and the summer and winter (rising and descending) opposites and the spring and fall (expanding and contracting) opposites together function as earthly recipro-
cators. The four directions have functions that may be
related to the five elements. East, the direction of sunrise,
like spring and wood, is connected with growth and ex-

pansion, as those who have been asleep arise and extend themselves through activity. South, like summer and fire, is hot, when the sun reaches its zenith. West, like autumn and metal, is the direction of sunset, the dying day, which contracts activities back again into stillness. North, like winter and water, is cold and damp, dark and dead. Again, earth is the common denominator of them all, reciprocally containing them as dynamic polarities.

The beginnings of a theory of color relationships have been drawn from the foregoing analogies. East, spring, wood, childhood, and expansion suggest green. South, summer, fire, youth, and ascent seem arousing and red. West, autumn, metal, age, and contraction are white or gray. North, winter, water, death, and descent are black. Earth, the common source and goal of all else, is yellow in all its shades, which separate out into the other four colors.

It is important to realize that these analogies have formed the Chinese mind, its literature and philosophy, its temperament and its goals. We blind ourselves to the enduring strands in that grand tapestry constituting Chinese culture when we ignore the significance which it actually has. Too, we may attain valuable insights into our own cultures by comparing them with the key analogies in Chinese and Hindu cultures.

Religious ideals built on the basis of the foregoing analogies must be expected to be different from those presupposing dualism and hierarchy, and from those worshipping indistinctness and quiescence. Ultimate reality is not a God different from and superior to the natural world. Ultimate reality is not Nirguna Brahman, a common indistinctness in the center of the soul and of the universe. Ultimate reality is Tao, which, as we are about to see, is a natural, present, immediately observable, dynamic, cyclical process of giving and receiving, initiating and completing, in which we participate. Man must say "Yes" to himself as a process in a world of process, and take what comfort and joy he can from observing how the five elements embody themselves in the successive stages of his life, even as they do in the pageants of the seasons and the dramas of history.

Lao-tzu

The earliest and greatest classic of Taoistic philosophy, and one of the greatest classics of all mankind, is the *Tao Teh King (Tao Te Ching)*. The date of its composition and its author remain uncertain, but probably it was written during the sixth century B.C. by Lao-tzu, an elder contemporary of Confucius. Whoever was responsible for assembling the ideals therein must be regarded as one of the greatest religious thinkers of all time. The ideals themselves grow out of the agricultural experiences and rural wisdom of ancient China, wherein men had to recognize their dependence upon the ongoing processes of nature. Lao-tzu, reported as having been a court librarian, attributes his ideas to Huang-ti, a legendary civilizer of China who is supposed to have ruled about 2697 B.C. The ancient wisdom expressed is so simple that anyone, even the humblest mind, can understand it, yet sufficiently profound that the most sophisticated must pay their respects to its penetrating insights and the soundness of its principles.

The *Tao Teh King* is a book *(King)* about Nature *(Tao)* and its intelligence *(Teh)*. Tao, which remains incomplete without Teh and Yang and Yin, is the most fundamental concept in all Chinese philosophy. It has been rendered into English in many ways, *e.g.*, as God, Logos, Reason, Brahman, The Absolute, *Élan Vital*, Truth, Way, Path, Method, Mana, and Existence, none of them quite satisfactory. My personal acquaintance with various translations of this classic—some reading into it a Buddhist message, some interpreting it with a Western theistic slant, some explaining it as yogic in intent, all trying to transform indigenous Chinese ideas into those native to foreign cultures so as to make them "intelligible"—left me dissatisfied. Efforts of various authors to "explain" apparently simple and self-evident ideals in terms of Stoic, Spinozistic, Hegelian and Bergsonian analogies, and a further tendency of some to interpret the simple ideas of Lao-tzu as if they already contained the more sophisticated dialectic of Chuang-tze and metaphysical presuppositions of later

Neo-Confucianists, provoked me into preparing my own edition: *Tao Teh King, Interpreted as Nature and Intelligence*, N.Y.: Frederick Ungar Publishing Co., 1958. The following quotations will be from this edition.

Tao is Nature, with a capital "N," and consists of many taos or natures, such as yours and mine and that of horses, dogs, and plants, which come and go. "To look for an external source of Nature is foolish, for Nature is the source of all else." "Nature contains nothing but natures; and these natures are nothing over and above Nature." "Consider how Nature operates. Some things precede while others follow. Some things blow one way while some blow another. Some things are strong while others are weak. Some things are going up while others are going down." "Nature's way is a joint process of initiation (Yang) and completion (Yin), sowing and reaping, producing and consuming." "Nature alternates dynamically. When it completes what it is doing, then it starts all over again. All that is springs from such alternation." (Pp. 75–76.) Nature's action is self-action or spontaneous action, for nothing exists outside to cause it to act, and any inner motive is already its own. Nature acts naturally, or in accordance with its own nature. Whoever acts naturally is a part of Nature's self-action. Nothing within Nature can fail to emulate Nature since each thing is a manifestation of Nature.

Teh is the power of Nature, and of any part of nature, to act naturally. Now if Nature acts naturally, and if Teh is the power of Nature to act naturally, Teh is nothing different from Nature. True. Yet, some things in Nature, or some parts of Nature, seem at times to act artificially. By "artificial" here is meant that a thing acts in accordance with a nature not its own. Horses and men, for example, have different natures, even though they are both parts of Nature. When a man tries to act like a horse—run on all fours, eat hay, carry a heavy load—he is acting in accordance with a nature not his own. That horses should have hoofs is natural; but that horses should have harnesses is artificial, for then they are forced to act in accordance with men's natures rather than their own.

Lao-tzu idealizes each thing acting wholly in accordance with its own nature. Thus he advocates shunning all imposing upon and being imposed upon by others. He rec-

ommends that all activity be self-activity, meaning thereby
the activity inherent in one's own nature. Whatever has
the ability to so act has Teh. To the extent that anything
is imposed upon by other natures, it lacks Teh, and to
the extent that it imposes upon other natures, meddles in
the affairs of others, it lacks Teh. Also, one who tries to
change or modify his own nature, by lengthening or shortening his life, or by lengthening or shortening his stature,
lacks Teh. "Those too eager for activity soon become fatigued. When they exhaust their vigor, they age quickly.
Such impatience is against Nature. What is against Nature
dies young." (P. 87.)

Teh is not inactivity, but inner activity or self-activity.
It is the ability of things to keep within limits, to remain
self-sufficient as Nature is self-sufficient (*See* p. 90.), and
to achieve without effort. Teh is intelligence, for intelligence
consists in attaining one's genuine goal, which is to be himself, to live his own life, to fulfill his own nature, to live
as the self that he is. Trying to emulate other natures, to
live as if one were someone else, or to act as if he were
different from what he is, is unintelligent. Teh is the ability
to accept one's own nature as it is, and as good or as bad
as it is, without desiring to change it.

Thus Teh is the power of man to be religious, to say
"Yes" to things as they are or are going to be for him.
One who has Teh thereby says "Yes" to both his own
nature, to Nature of which he is a part, and to the natures
of all other things, which he, as religious, permits to go
their own several ways without his meddling. Teh is one
of mankind's greatest religious ideals, because whoever
has Teh succeeds religiously, for by saying "Yea" to the
actual he thereby automatically actually attains all he
wants. If "to idealize" means wanting things to be different from the way they actually are or are going to be, then
to idealize means saying "No" to the inevitable and to
make trouble for oneself. But if, on the other hand, when
one "idealizes the actual" (meaning wants things to be
the way they actually are), he says "Yea" to them.

Teh is the power to say "Yea." Hence, Lao-tzu's Teh
joins the Mosaic Yahweh's "I am that I am" (Exodus 3:
14), and the Hindu Buddhist *"Tat Tvam Asi"* (That Which
Is), and Jesus' "I am the way" as one of the great religious

ideas of mankind. Nature acts wholly naturally and intelligently; only man acts unintelligently part of the time. But man, when he discovers his own artificiality and unintelligence can, if he chooses, renounce these and "emulate Tao," *i.e.*, act naturally and intelligently all of the time. The Taoist does not "sin," where "sin" is willing to go against the "Will of God," for if God is a "thou" or something other than man, to act in accordance with such an other or external will would be "artificial." If, on the other hand, "God's will" is interpreted as wanting what is actually best for each individual, then that will and the individual's will are actually identical and God is not a "thou" but one's own self (as Hindus so persistently maintain) recognizing itself as part of its own larger whole. Jews, Christians, and Moslems "sin," whereas Taoists, like Greeks, "act unintelligently" or not in accordance with their own best nature. Both are ways of saying "Nay" to what is believed to be actually best for the individual.

Lao-tzu's analysis of man's predicament explains our distinction between "high" and "low" religion in terms of "having Teh" and "lacking Teh." Each nature is what it is. To raise the question of whether or not it "deserves" to be what it is involves initial doubt about whether one should say "Yes" to his being as he is. Such doubting involves "acting unintelligently" or "lacking Teh" to some degree and thereby constitutes the beginning of "low religion." Only after one realizes and acts upon his need for saying "Yes" to whatever he gets as being what he deserves, or as more than he deserves, can he attain "high religion." Religion is "highest" when one realizes that living is not at all a question of deserving but is a question of enjoying whatever nature and conditions obtain. How Lao-tzu might discuss questions about "deserving" may be inferred from his remarks about giving and receiving. "The generous giver gives because he wants to give. The dutiful giver gives because he wants to receive." "Nature's way is to take from those who have too much and to give to those who have too little. Man's way, on the contrary, is to take away from those who have too little in order to give to those who already have too much." The intelligent man "gives his gift without desiring a reward, achieves benefit for others without expecting approbation, and is generous without calling attention to his generosity." (*Ibid.*, p. 95.)

"Religion" is sometimes said to be concerned with "the mystical" and "the mysterious." This is true, but only because "the mystical" and "the mysterious" both exist as part of human experience. Unfortunately, "the mystical" and "the mysterious" have become confused in popular thought. A "mystery" involves ignorance whereas "mystical" means direct insight. Thus these terms have opposite meanings. The message of the *Tao Teh Khing* is not mysterious. Neither did Lao-tzu advocate that we regard the world in which we live and of which we are a part as mysterious. Granted that we cannot know all about it; but then, if we trust it, as we must anyway, we do not need to know all about it. Our natures, like the natures of plants and water buffalos, are self-active; they are born, grow, decline, and die, all without needing either external direction or explanation (description of their nature in terms of something that is external to or other than their nature). Explanation is artificial and like all artificiality should be shunned. When one accepts himself and his world as he intuits it, grasps it directly (*i.e.*, mystically), he will experience no mystery. If the goal of religion is to replace fear of the mysterious with confident acceptance of the obvious, then the way of life according to Lao-tzu is one of the simplest and most direct ways to attain that goal. When one occupies himself with the mystical (direct apprehension and appreciation of present experience), thereby losing all sense of and fear of mystery, the goal of religion has been reached. For Lao-tzu, the Naturalist, religion is natural, and only by becoming artificial (interested in the mysterious) do we lose that confidence which constitutes living religiously.

Chuang-tzu

Neither Taoism nor Taoist philosophy stopped with Lao-tzu. The philosophy of Lao-tzu, like that of Jesus, Gotama, and Confucius, was clear, compelling, and wise. One wishes that all of these philosophies could have come down to us uninterpreted and uncontaminated. But without lesser minds to appreciate, remember, and retell their sayings, we might never have benefited from their wisdom. Modifications naturally occur as other minds revise and expand earlier ideas to suit new situations, as worshippers appreciate and eulogize what they do not fully comprehend, as vested interests in institutionalized versions induce both formalization and political authoritarianism, as biased scholarship seeks to "prove" inherence of later conclusions in the texts of ancient authorities. Taoism is no exception to these general rules, and the beginnings of change can be found already in the writings of two other famous early (fourth century B.C.?) Taoistic philosophers: Yang-chu and Chuang-tzu.

Yang-chu and Chuang-tzu extend the ideas of Lao-tzu in opposing directions. Yang-chu, emphasizing the self-sufficiency, self-activity, and self-interest of each individual (tao), ignored both the naturalness of recognizing each individual as part of the larger universe (Tao) and the naturalness of having interest in the welfare of others. Lao-tzu opposed meddling, *i.e.*, imposing one's nature upon others, but accepted the naturalness of having good will toward others whenever such an occasion arises naturally. He did not object to giving. The intelligent (teh) giver "gives because he wants to give" and "gives his gift without desiring a reward." Yang-chu, on the other hand, seems to have maintained that "though he might have profited the whole world by plucking out a single hair, he would not have done it." (Fung Yu-lan, *A Short History of Chinese Philosophy*, p. 61. See also *Yang Chu's Garden of Pleasure*, tr. by Anton Forke, Ch. XII.)

Chuang-tzu seems to have paid more attention to Tao from which our taos come and back into which they return. The transcendental Tao, perpetual mother and permanent grave of all things, deserves our recognition, attention, and appreciation. Or, we ought to recognize, attend to, and appreciate our own source and end: "That which has taken care of my birth is that which will take care of my death also." Some translators interpret him as seeing man "embraced in an obliterating unity" (Herbert A. Giles, *Chuang Tzu*, London: George Allen and Unwin, Ltd., 1961, p. 46), but he seems to be more concerned about trustfully appreciating his dependence than about obliteration, and about his providential birth and death than about ultimate unity. Most will agree that he is more subtle and had greater dialectical skill than Lao-tzu, but then perhaps he needed to have such abilities in order to respond tellingly to the revered critics and sophists who had arisen to condemn Lao-tzu in the meantime. Lao-tzu merely needed to state his view in opposition to other views. Chuang-tzu had to argue for it against a battery of skilled debaters. His dialectical ability may be illustrated by his arguments against arguing: "Whom shall I employ as an arbiter between us? If I employ one who takes your view, he will side with you. How can such a one arbitrate between us? If I employ someone who takes my view, he will side with me. How can such a one arbitrate between us. And if I employ some one who either differs from, or agrees with, both of us, he will be equally unable to decide between us. Since then you, and I, and a man, cannot decide, must we not depend upon Another?" *(Ibid.)*

Futility of claims to certainty was demonstrated by Chuang-tzu in a way that will be a classic for all time: Once I dreamed I was a butterfly, fluttering about from blossom to blossom. Then I awoke. Now I do not know whether I am a man who once dreamed he was a butterfly or a butterfly now dreaming I am a man. Another unsurpassed classic is his burial philosophy. When he was about to die, some disciples began preparing for the customary ceremonies. But Chuang berated them. "With heaven and earth as my coffin and tomb, with the sun, moon, and stars as my burial regalia, and with all creation to escort me to the grave, are not my funeral paraphernalia already at hand?" When his disciples pleaded that, unburied, he would be eaten by vultures, he sardonically replied: "Above ground I shall be food for vultures. Below ground I shall be food for worms. Why rob one to feed the other?" Thus Lao-tzu's yea-saying to Tao was advanced further through the dialectical subtleties of Chuang-tzu.

Four Streams

Taoist philosophy persisted in various forms, partly absorbed by the thoughts of many thinkers, partly by being syncretized into other systems (later it was used to interpret and modify Buddhism), partly by being criticized by opposing schools, and partly by degenerating into a "school of pure conversation." Too, the name "Taoism" was adopted by a "hygiene school" that cultivated longevity through breathing exercises, gymnastics, collecting herbs for medicines; by a "magic school" that engaged in alchemy for a drug that prevented death and in expeditions to enchanted islands where ambrosial foods assured perpetual youth; and by a "Taoist church" whose popes presided over political destinies as well as religious ceremonies, with egregious results. Holmes Welch, a U. S. Government official stationed in Hong Kong, has produced an excellent summary of these "four streams" which "were separate when they flowed into history in the middle of the fourth century B.C." (*The Parting of the Way*, Boston: The Beacon Press, 1957, p. 83.) From 220 to 120 B.C. they "met to form a broad river." (*Ibid*., p. 97.) Pantheons of thousands of gods appeared in, or joined, this cultural river which gradually expanded, meandered, intermingled, and branched into estuaries flowing into the Chinese culture of today. Despite a "burning of books," the Taoist "Canon" or Bible has accumulated more than a thousand volumes, a veritable sea of literature in which we can fish for an amazing variety of curious ideas.

Taoism Today

Evaluation of the extent of Taoism in China today must be guesswork. Built into the Chinese language throughout the centuries, it is ineradicable so long as this language remains. Yet the influx of foreign ideas, from India and Europe, involved in commerce, science, technology, literature, and politics, added to the myriads of indigenous developments, have made Chinese metropolitan life so complex that the Taoist influence must be declining. It remains, or did until the advent of Marxist efforts to reorganize life, one of the "Three Truths" of China. Lin Yutang, in describing "the Chinese character" (*My Country and My People*, Ch. II), mentions "mellowness," "patience," "indifference," "old roguery," "pacifism," "contentment," "humor," and "conservatism,"—all traits reflecting the Taoist spirit. His delightful book, *The Importance of Living*, conveys something of the Taoist spirit in a way that we can all appreciate. He estimates that "among scholars who know the Orient, there are more devotees of Laotse than of Confucius." (*The Wisdom of Laotse,* N.Y.: Random House, 1948, p. 3.) "Every Chinese is a Confucianist when he is successful and a Taoist when he is a failure." (*My Country and My People, op. cit.,* p. 117.)

Chen Li-fu, former Minister of Education in Chiang Kai-shek's cabinet, illustrates, in his *The Philosophy of Life* (N.Y.: The Philosophical Library, 1948), how a contemporary leader combines many of the ideas we have outlined with those of Confucianism, which we have yet to treat, and adapts them to contemporary social problems. He states the ancient idea that individual taos emerge from and return to Ṭao in contemporary language: "Thus the universe is forever losing its order and equilibrium and forever recovering them, forever possessing differences and forever seeking to wipe them out, only to bring about the cycle of life." (P. 45.) He explains that "The Tao and the Teh are not an outer bondage but something from within which satisfies the deepest demand of man." (P. 66.)

Tomé H. Fang, Professor of Philosophy, National Taiwan University, in his recent *The Chinese View of Life,* (Hong Kong: Union Printing Co., Kowloon, 1957, pp. 22–23.), summarizes the Chinese temperament: "Man lives in Nature where the passage from the primordial to the consequent stage is an overflow of Life, getting and spending with its inexhaustible energy. Should anyone come in contact with this directional energy from without, he would feel that something has encompassed him with hardness. Like a raindrop falling into the river, it is being borne away and forever lost. Nature encountered by any one individual man in this way is felt to be an encumbrance and blind necessity. But when the drops of water have been deeply merged in the river, they become ingredients in its wave. Now they are one surf, rising and falling in the same rhythm as the lover and the beloved beat their hearts together in the same measure of music. The force of propulsion in the ongoing process of Nature passes into an ideal excess, swinging in concurrent motion, as it is displayed in an elegant dance, full of the sense of joy. The feeling of restraint and compulsion entirely expires in a new ecstasy of freedom. Therefore, Nature, confronting Man as necessity, is finally transformed into communal fellowship fostered through the magic of felicitous sympathy. Nature is a continuous process of creation and Men are concreators within the realm of Nature. Nature and human nature are two in one, giving form to what I have called the comprehensive harmony, a harmony between ingrowing parts as well as a harmony with surroundings. In this form of primordial unity, all that seems various and antipathetical is so intrinsically related that it strikes together sympathetic chords to the accompaniment of a song of love, which is an encomium of life."

Chapter 8 **Confucianism**

Confucianism is a religion. In fact, Confucianism, considered as all of those beliefs and practices attributed to Confucius and Confucians which have accumulated during the two and a half millennia of its history, may be regarded as several religions. Gradual development of ideas about the nature of man and the universe yielded varieties that may be regarded as distinct, and the name "Neo-Confucianism," for example, denotes some major shifts in doctrinal viewpoint.

The task of putting Confucianism into proper perspective for Western readers, becomes further complicated due to the fact that several misconceptions about Confucianism as a religion have grown out of attempts by theists to evaluate Confucianism in terms of their conception of "religion as belief in God or gods." These attempts have begotten several interpretations of Confucianism: as not a religion, as agnostic about religion, as an insincere animistic religion, as ancestor worship, as deification of Confucius, and as deliberate use of Confucian doctrines by ruling classes to maintain the status quo. Although some basis exists for each of these interpretations, all of them miss being accurate evaluations of Confucianism as a religion. The thesis presented here asserts that the philosophy of Confucius—even if not that of all his followers who called themselves "Confucians"—is a great religion, perhaps the world's greatest religion, and that what makes it so is a fundamental trait almost entirely overlooked by Western interpreters.

Confucius

Discussion of Confucianism must begin with Confucius, his life, his background, and his philosophy. Confucius lived between 551 and 478 B.C. He flourished during the sixth century B.C., which was also the century of Lao-tzu the Taoist, Gotama the Buddha, and Mahavira the Jain, before the time of the great Greeks, Socrates, Plato, and Aristotle, before the assemblage of the Hebrew Pentateuch, and half a millennium before the appearance of Jesus Christ. His own scholarly interests centered in the history and traditions of his and neighboring kingdoms, and the ideals he expressed were attributed by him to men of earlier times. He regarded himself as a transmitter of ancient wisdom rather than as an innovator. Such reforms as he proposed were pictured as a return to the more virtuous ways of old. We cannot be sure just when or how the ideas he propounded began. Furthermore, his own teachings were recorded mainly from memory by followers after his death, sketchily and with some modifications. However, a philosophy did emerge that is clear in its general outlines. Whether it is precisely what Confucius thought, we may never know. But that it flowered early as one of the great philosophical insights attained by man appears beyond doubt, and its attribution to Confucius is a practice convenient to follow.

Sketching the little we know about his life, we may infer that he had a good education for at the age of twenty-one he began to teach, by the time he was thirty he had reached settled opinions, at thirty-four he visited the capital of the empire and saw the places where the great sacrifices to Heaven and Earth were offered and the ancestral temples of the rulers. He spent much time collecting and editing available literature about ancient customs and beliefs. At fifty he became the chief magistrate of a city where he put his theory of government into practice with such telling effect that it became a model town within a year. The duke was so pleased by the transformation that he made him minister of justice. Laws fell into disuse because there were no criminals. People came from elsewhere to study his methods. Thus he became famous. But other advisers to the duke became jealous of his success and diverted the duke's attention so that he no longer paid heed to Confucius. Finally, Confucius gave up and quit in disgust. Then he traveled from court to court, offering his services, with little success. He spent the later years of his life studying and finishing his collections. He died at the age of seventy-three.

As background essential to understanding his views, the facts of rural life, family life, court life, animistic beliefs, pictographic writing, the development of hexagrams and their symbolic interpretation, and the Taoistic philosophy of Lao-tzu need to be mentioned. The role of nature and of men's arising and declining as parts of the ongoing processes of nature, described by Lao-tzu, were incorporated into the philosophy of Confucius. However, the nature of family life, which also forms a backbone of Chinese culture throughout its history and which was largely ignored by Lao-tzu, and the nature of courtly life and government, which was shunned by Lao-tzu, became central problems for study by Confucius. Animistic practices, calligraphy, scientific prognostication by means of hexagrammatic analogies, concern for music and poetry, and burial and memorial traditions that were carried on in courtly society constitute important parts of the cultural milieu within which Confucius found his task of understanding the nature and goal of life.

Since both popular and scholarly evaluations of Taoism and Confucianism typically represent them as extremely antagonistic, our first duty in summarizing the philosophy of Confucius is to demonstrate how much it is like that of Lao-tzu. Basically their philosophies remain essentially the same. Both accept the ideas of Tao or Nature, Yang and Yin as principles of initiation and completion, the cyclical character of Nature's processes, the naturalness of man and the goodness of each man's living out his own life in accordance with his own tao. Religiously, they are also similar, since both idealize spontaneity, self-activity, and an unquestioning affirmation of life. Their differences appear in ethical, social, and political philosophy, as we shall point out later. But these differences will be more accurately understood if the Taoism of Lao-tzu is pictured as roots and trunk of a tree out of which the philosophy of Confucius grows as a major branch than if they appear as separate, unrelated plants. The philosophy of Confucius was a necessary supplement to that of Lao-tzu; for as Chinese culture emerged farther from its agricultural bases, through its family and courtly systems of association and control, with their social and political principles of operation, the naturalistic Taoism had to be adapted to account for the "tao of society," that is, the nature of man in his social relationships. Faced with inescapable facts of family and courtly life, one cannot, as Lao-tzu recommended, run away and hide. If Lao-tzu's function was mainly that of describing Tao, then the function of Confucius was chiefly that of describing the "tao of society." Lao-tzu was primarily a metaphysician, Confucius primarily a social scientist. But both were in agreement about saying "Yes" to nature's way, whether as the universal Tao or as each person's own tao. Lao-tzu simply lacked comprehension of that tao which man has as a social being. Confucius, in filling this lack, was a more complete philosopher.

In describing Tao and tao, Nature and human nature, Confucius expresses ideas similar to those of Lao-tzu but in somewhat different language. The opening passages of the *Chung Yung*, one of "The Four Books" presenting Confucian ideas, summarize Taoistic ideals upon which Confucius takes his stand. "What Nature [*T'ien,* or that nature which transcends man] provides is called 'his own nature.' Living in accord with one's own nature is called 'self-realization.' Proper pursuit of self-realization is called 'maturation.' One's own nature cannot be disowned. If it could be disowned, it would not be one's own nature. Hence, a virtuous man attends to it and is concerned about it, even though it is invisible and inaudible. One's visible exterior is nothing more than an expression of his invisible interior, and his outer expression reveals only what is inside. Therefore, the virtuous man is concerned about his own self." (Section I.)

"The wise man retains his true nature. The foolish man does the opposite. A wise man retains his true nature because he is wise; and he is wise because he retains his true nature. A foolish man does the opposite because he is foolish, and he is foolish because he fails to appreciate what is good." (Section II.) "One's true nature is self-sufficient, but few people can maintain it for a long time." (Section III.) "I know why the course of one's true nature is not pursued. Men of accomplishment try to rise above it. The inept fail to come up to it. I know why the course of one's true nature is not understood. The ambitious overestimate it. The lazy fail to appreciate it." (Section IV.) "Nature's way is to be genuine. Man's way is to become genuine. To be genuine is to act truly without effort, to attain without thinking about it, and automatically and spontaneously to realize one's true nature. Such a man is wise." (Section XX.)

However, Confucius goes on to assert that mere self-concern is not sufficient for realizing the fullness of life. Man is also a social being who finds his fullest expression only through his associations with others. Section I, quoted above, concludes: "Being undisturbed by [attitudes toward others involving] pleasure, anger, grief, or joy is called 'one's true nature.' Being stimulated by [such attitudes] each in its appropriate way is called 'one's true social nature.' This 'true nature' is the primal source [great root] from which all social affairs develop. This 'true social nature' is the means for attaining happiness by all humanity. When our 'true nature' and 'true social nature' prevail uninterrupted, conditions both above man and below man remain wholesome, and everything thrives and prospers."

Section XXV reiterates: "Genuineness is self-sufficient. And its nature is self-directing. Genuineness pervades being from beginning to end. Without genuineness nothing could be. This is why the wise man values becoming genuine above everything else. Genuineness not only promotes self-realization; it is the means through which one develops his relations with others also. Self-realization involves associating with others [*jen*]. Developing one's relations with others involves sympathetic insight. Both associating with others and having sympathetic insight are abilities which anyone has for realizing his own nature [*teh*]. One's whole nature [*tao*] integrates both external (social) relations and internal (individual) processes. Hence, genuineness is fully genuine when both of these abilities are appropriately integrated." (Author's versions.)

Confucius was a Taoist who believed the tao of man involved him in human association and that he was not wholly human until his social nature was fully developed also. Although he would not have spoken of a "tao of society," thereby giving society a substantial status and nature of its own, he did discriminate between a man's social tao and his individual tao as integral and continuous portions of his whole tao. Confucius devoted his life to being a social psychologist, by observing the practices of various courtly societies and studying the records of previous societies, to discover the most successful ways of organizing human relationships and the kinds of attitudes needed for conducting them. These ways were then held up as ideals for others to emulate. Thus Confucius became a teacher of customary morality as it had prevailed in the happiest kingdoms. We will not here review details of those customs which have now become obsolete. But we should investigate the ethical philosophy that he developed by generalizing upon his observations, and the general theory of human nature, which, supplementing that of Lao-tzu, remains one of the grandest and most penetrating philosophies of all time. In developing it, Confucius expounded one of the profoundest, possibly the most perfect, philosophy of religion that has ever emerged. Let us see how he did it.

We can summarize the philosophy of Confucius by developing his four characteristics of the ideal man, sometimes called the "Sage," whom we shall speak of as the "wise man." The "wise man" as here described remains an ideal that few ever attain to perfection. But it is an ideal that all may use in improving themselves. These four characteristics are referred to as *yi, jen, li,* and *chih.*

(1) YI is the best way of doing things. We must keep in mind the basic tenet of Lao-tzu and Confucius that nature and human nature are good. Whenever anything is allowed to live in accordance with its own inner nature, all will go well, provided, of course, that it does not try to overdo, underdo, or modify it artifically. *Yi* is the way things behave when they act in accordance with their own natures; and this is the best way for all things to act. No man is wise until he understands *yi.* He may not completely understand the nature of all things, but he should grasp the fundamental truth that Nature provides each being with a nature that is self-sufficient and self-fulfilling and thus as good as it can be. To try to make it better than it is involves trying to change it; trying to change it is artificial; making it artificial will bring it to an unnatural end. Reading Lao-tzu's eulogies of behaving naturally serves as an

excellent background for comprehending the presuppositions underlying Confucius' conception of *yi*.

But, since human nature is also essentially social, the
best way for human beings to behave is as social beings.
What, then, are these best ways? What are the principles
of social behavior that each person can discover operating
in his own way of doing things? We summarize these under
two headings, "the principle of reciprocity" and "the principle of sincerity."

(a) *The principle of reciprocity* is a basic principle
of the universe in which all activity involves both initiation (yang) and completion *(yin)*. Today we formulate it
as a physical principle: for every action there is an equal
and opposite reaction. But early Chinese thinkers, like
early Hindu ("law of karma") and European ("retribu-
tive justice") thinkers, did not separate the physical
out of the natural world and castrate it of values, as
European materialists have done. Whatever is natural is
good. Since it is natural to come into being, so it is good
to come into being. Since it is natural for what comes
in to go out, so it is natural, and good, to go out of
being, in due time and in proper course. To resist this
reciprocal behavior of Tao, which is both the source
and the culmination of the goodness of each thing, is
bad because it is against one's own nature.

The principle of reciprocity not only operates throughout Nature and each individual nature but also in and
through man's nature socially. One person gives and
another receives. One who receives responds by giving
in return. In this way, social interaction occurs. Recall
how, when someone snubs you, you automatically want
to snub back. If civilization has already built restraints
into you, try to remember how you once responded by
observing the normal behavior of little children. When
someone does you an unexpected favor or pays you an
undeserved compliment, do you not feel a desire not to
be outdone in doing for others what they do for you?
The simple psychological principle involved is obvious to
anyone who takes time to observe its operation, and
peoples of all cultures have formulated it in one way or
another in their lore. Christians speak of it as "the Golden
Rule," "Do unto others as you would have them do unto

you," thereby formulating it as a "commandment" or "rule" rather than as a "principle." The Confucian way of stating the rule, unfortunately regarded as "negative" and therefore inferior by proud Westerners, is more subtle and is based in the Taoistic philosophy out of which it grows.

In addition to stating the principle as a rule—"Do not require of another what you would not have another require of you"—Confucius added a phrase that reveals his insight to be more penetrating. As we shall see, Mo Ti, a critic of Confucius, rejected this additional phrase; and it is generally neglected in other cultures. The phrase is: "if you were that person." That is, "treat another as you would be treated if you were that person." People are unequal. A child and his parent differ. A wife and her husband differ. A sick person and a healthy person are different. A mother should treat her child as a child, not as if her child were another mother. And she should treat her child as she would like to be treated if she were her child. A man is not a woman and does not wish to be treated as if he were a woman, and a woman is not a man and does not wish to be treated as if she were a man. A man should treat a woman as a woman, and treat her as he would like to be treated if he were a woman. More particularly, he should treat each person as if he were that person. This kind of treatment considers actual differences between persons and takes them into account in deciding how to act according to the principle of reciprocity. It is important to notice that greater insight, *i.e.*, sympathetic insight, is needed in order to act on this principle. For one needs to make the effort to think about the nature and feelings of the other person in order to know how he would like to be treated if he were that other person.

The Taoistic spirit upon which the philosophy of Confucius is founded presupposes that if each thing lives in accordance with his own inner nature, all will go well. Whenever one is imposed upon by others, his inner or natural course may suffer. Hence, the most "positive" way of formulating the principle of reciprocity is to say "Do not interfere with the good natures of others in ways that you do not want to have your own good nature interfered with." Each person has his own vital flow, his own tao, with his own desires, wishes, or will. Therefore, as a minimum, "do not" will to interfere with his will.

By his observing that the principle of reciprocity is an essential trait of men as social beings, Confucius was able to advance beyond the "shun all association as artificial" doctrine of Lao-tzu. For Lao-tzu, the ideal life was one in which each person would stay as far away from all others as possible, since contact with them involved impositions of each upon the other. But Confucius, steeped in the facts of living in large families, clans, tribes, and nations, recognized both the necessity and naturalness of people living together and thus "imposing upon" each other. He looked for, and found in the principle of reciprocity as he formulated it, a principle of human nature that is just as natural and necessary as any other natural principle.

A child cannot be born without depending for his conception and gestation upon his mother. A child cannot survive without milk, which must come from his mother, who, by then, is "another." A child cannot survive without protection and care, which, in practice, require many varieties of dependence upon others. Each such act of dependence upon others would be a kind of imposition if such dependence were not also natural to the inner (social) interests of the person depended upon. Thus the inner interests of a mother in her child make her already, automatically, and naturally, a social being. Her inner and outer interests are continuous with one another rather than being contradictory in nature. Hence, the principle of reciprocity grows out of a mother's own inner nature. It is not something forced upon her from the outside as "artificial." So with the child. His coming into being, his own nature, his own survival, the molding of his own interests and character, all grow naturally out of his associations with his mother. Her interests are his interests, for if she dies he dies, unless he can find someone else to take an interest in him.

The principle of reciprocity, which is so obvious in intimate family relations, continues to work as one's horizons widen, and include persons in a larger family. Discriminating observation reveals that one's relations with others vary. Consequently, one may question whether the principle is the same in relations with different people. Here again, one should observe with care. Brothers quarrel and become jealous of each other and of parental favoritism. Different families compete for the food available from a particular plot of land. Exchange of goods between families or between strangers does not always come out equally. Kings attack other kings, even when they are not attacked. Yet, what alternative is there to the principle of reciprocity? Perhaps in response to questions by his pupils, Confucius elaborated details about applying the principle to all kinds of social relationships. He was especially concerned about those between rulers and subjects. But his advice about rulers grew naturally out of the general principle, which he found working at all levels of interaction. For purposes of instruction, all such relationships were conveniently summarized into five kinds, namely, those between parent and child, between husband and wife, between an older brother and a younger brother, between a ruler and his subject, and between friend and friend. Recognition of differences among these five kinds of relations provides a foundation for extending such discrimination to grandparents and grandchildren, to a husband's brothers and to a wife's sisters, to older sisters and younger sisters, to rulers and subjects, to less intimate friends, casual acquaintances, strangers, and even to enemies. Mastery of the principle of reciprocity in these five prepares one for discriminating use of it in all social relationships.

However, since one may not be able to trust it as a general principle until he first becomes aware of its operation in his most intimate relationships, the relation between parent and child receives special emphasis. Not only may one grasp it intuitively and surely in such a relationship but if either a child or a parent fails to accept the principle here, family life will come to disaster. Hence "filial piety," as English translations customarily name the need of a child to treat his father as he would be treated if he were his father, has a basic significance. Since failure here will lead to failures elsewhere, its recognition is essential.

(b) *The principle of sincerity (hsin)* is a second principle of the tao of association. Some rate it as a fifth characteristic of the wise man. It follows naturally from the first for, according to the principle of reciprocity, if you are insincere in your dealings with others, the most you can expect is insincerity from them. Since you do not wish to be dealt with insincerely, you must treat others sincerely. If you merely pretend to respect others, the most you can expect in return is pretended respect. But deceit begets deceit, distrust distrust, fear fear, and you soon find yourself in a situation that is not best for yourself. Hence, being sincere is a part of *yi*, the best way of doing things for yourself in your association with others.

(2) JEN is goodwill; it is willingness to do what is best socially. Since acting in accordance with one's own nature is what is best for each person, goodwill consists basically in allowing each person to act in accordance with his own nature. This means not interfering with him or wanting him to be different from what he is. A man of goodwill accepts each person for what he is. *Jen* is simply willingness to act according to *yi*. *Yi* is the best way of doing things, and *jen*, goodwill, is willingness to do, or to have things done, the best way, individually and socially.

Two requirements of goodwill may be easily overlooked. The first is insight. Where persons in intimate relationships act interdependently, each can know how to treat others only if he has some insight into their natures. If, for example, a parent wants what is best for his child and wishes him to develop naturally, must he not try to put himself in the child's situation so he can realize how much or how little to require of him in the way of social behavior? If a parent works hard all day gathering ten bushels of rice, should he treat his eight-year-old son as an equal and expect the same hard work and the same ten bushels from him? Or should he develop sufficient insight into the nature and capacity of his child to recognize the child's limitations? Does not genuine goodwill require action toward another in terms of that other's own nature and ability?

The second requirement is sympathy. Insight is necessary,

but it is not enough. Not only must one recognize how others feel when treated in certain ways, but one needs to try to promote good feelings if he has goodwill. One who desires to torture another may be more successful if he has insight into how another responds to such torture than if he does not have such insight, but sympathy means actually sharing the feelings of another, so far as possible. Insight *and* sympathy assure *jen* or genuine goodwill. The principle of sincerity together with the principle of reciprocity require genuine goodwill.

(3) LI is propriety, or the appropriate way of giving overt expression to inner attitudes. Involved here is a basic principle, namely, that one's inner nature and one's external behavior are correlative, or should be correlative when one's intentions are sincere. Only a deceiver or an ignoramus will behave toward others in such a way that they misunderstand his intentions. To act with good intentions in a way that others will take to be bad is a wrong way of behaving. In order to be sure that one is conveying his good intentions to others, he should, in addition, behave in such a way that the other cannot mistake his intentions. Now, do some ways convey intentions more clearly and precisely than others? Yes. At least so Confucius concluded from studying the behavior in different families and courts, both in his own time and as recorded in history. If customs have developed with regard to specific ways of expressing respect, such as bowing, saluting, or handshaking, one who wishes to be understood will automatically employ these ways. They are the best ways of behaving because they actually convey one's true intentions. Hence, understanding *yi,* the best way of doing things, involves not only having *jen,* but also *li,* or knowing and practicing the best ways of behaving so as to accomplish the intended result.

Now unfortunately, once appropriate etiquette has been formalized, deceivers may also use these forms. Consequently, one who has been deceived by use of them may come to distrust them. Also, when parents try to teach their children appropriate manners before they recognize the need for such manners, the children may feel externally forced to conform to a convention that has for them no inner meaning. To learn forms of behavior without learning their inner meanings is artificial, not natural, and so is not a part of the best way of doing things. Not only Lao-tzu but Confucius, too, advised us to shun the artificial. But Confucius conceived the artificial as behaving in any manner that fails to express inner intentions. Hence, one should avoid formalism. For each *yi*, the best inner way of behaving, there exists a *li*, the most effective external manner of behaving. *Li* and *yi* should be correlated if one seeks his fullest self-realization through his tao of association. External expression is false unless one both knows *yi* and has *jen*. *Hsin*, genuineness, requires the desire to be free from all such falsity.

Now *li* may also be called "propriety" or the proper way of behaving. We also speak of this as the "right way" or as "right conduct." Many of us have forgotten that "rite" and "right" have similar meanings and that rituals were originally intended to be the right, *i.e.*, best, ways of doing things. When social intercourse becomes too complicated for us to keep in mind the value of all social rituals, the latter tend to become ritualistic, *i.e.*, forms without meaning. Confucius not only warned against artificiality, formalism, or ritualism, but he also sought to discover more details about right behavior as social relations become more complicated, as they do in larger families and more intricate systems of government.

Recognizing that persons holding different political offices also require different external forms of behavior to express the different responsibilities inherent in each office, he sought to discover the forms that custom had already developed for these purposes. Then he systematized them and taught them for the purpose of expediting efficiency. Just as in science today we idealize precision in performing our experiments, so Confucius sought precision in modes of behavior, which we call "punctiliousness." "Punctiliousness" is conscientious behavior, not formalism. Unfortunately stupid formalists mistook means for ends and demanded performance of rituals even after their meaning had been lost. Consequently, Confucius, who preached *against* formalism, has come to be considered its proponent.

Another important phrase in the language of Confucius is "rectification of names." If we regard "rectitude" and "rectification" as merely stiff-necked or artificial, we will misunderstand Confucius again. His interest here is also in "the best way of doing things." Names and natures should be correlated. If two things are the same, *e.g.*, two children, they should have the same name, *i.e.*, "child." But when two things are different, *e.g.*, a child and a man, they should have two different names, *i.e.*, "child" and "man." Each different kind of thing (chair, table, house), each different kind of person (father, wife, eldest daughter, baby), and each kind of office (ruler, minister, scholar, guard) should have its own name. Use of names can be relied upon only if two principles are followed.

First, each thing, person, and office should be called by its right name. For to call a guard a "ruler" or to call a child a "man" is to use words falsely. Secondly, each person who has a name should live in accordance with it; otherwise either his life or his name is false. To call a person a "ruler" when he has ceased to look after the best interests of his subjects is wrong. Such a person should no longer be called a "ruler" but should be deposed. To call a woman a "wife" when she runs about after other men and no longer behaves like a wife is to misname her. According to the principle of the "rectification of names," fathers who neglect their fatherly duties and scholars who do not study should be treated no longer as fathers and scholars. These two principles—that persons should be called by their right names and that persons should live up to their names—together constitute the principle that names and natures should be correlated and further illustrate "knowing and practicing *li*," the principle that external expression (*e.g.* "names") should appropriately represent inner nature and intent.

Whereas Lao-tzu advised the shunning of naming, Confucius recommended shunning the misuse of names. According to Lao-tzu, "No name can fully express what it represents." "In seeking to grasp what is, the intelligent man does not devote himself to the making of distinctions which are then mistaken to be separate existences." (*Tao Teh King, op. cit.,* pp. 11, 12.) He appears to regard all naming as artificial. Confucius, on the other hand, recognizes the social necessities of noting differences between persons and of distinctive names for those differences. But he warns that "Not acting according to one's nature and name, is to act artificially. Hence, the best way for a person to act is in accordance with his actual nature and right name." (*Ibid.*, p. 111.) Right names are thus an essential part of *li, jen,* and *yi* and of the tao of human relationships.

(4) CHIH is wisdom. No man is wise until he is happy. Wisdom consists in confident living. Living confidently involves consenting to things as they are, *i.e.,* to *yi, jen,* and *li,* three characteristics of the wise man. Wisdom does not require encyclopaedic knowledge. It does require knowing that allowing each one to act in accordance with his own nature is best for each, and that differences among the natures of the persons upon whom he depends and who depend upon him, must be respected if he is to live in harmony with them. Achieving *chih* requires knowing *yi.* If one cannot live confidently until he has, and knows he has, genuine goodwill toward others, then he cannot achieve *chih* until he fully embodies *jen.* If one cannot live confidently until he knows all of the appropriate external manners needed to express his true intentions toward others, then he cannot achieve *chih* until he knows and practices *li.* Yet merely knowing *yi,* having *jen* and knowing and practicing *li* is not enough.

Chih is an ideal to be approached by degrees. One's assurance grows as he learns more. One's confidence increases as he frees himself from fears of inadequacy. One's trust in nature's ways—Nature at large, one's own inner nature, and one's social nature—develops as he desires less and less to deviate from their inherent norms. One will achieve *chih* fully only when *yi, jen* and *li* have become embodied within him so completely that he responds in each occasion, social and private, with perfect spontaneity. In *chih,* one lives according to habit, without question or reservation. *Chih* involves *hsin,* complete unwillingness to deceive oneself or others. *Chih* epitomizes yea-saying, thereby making the ideals of Confucius among the greatest religious ideals of all mankind. It is Confucius' ideal of *chih* that makes Confucianism a great religion, not the deification of Confucius by later admirers nor his teachings about "ancestor worship." *Chih* is wisdom because a person having achieved it responds to his opportunities and responsibilities so unreservedly, so automatically and spontaneously, that he never for a moment abandons the habit of living confidently. *Chih* is such a high religious ideal that Confucius himself complained that he was never able to reach it even though he tried the best he could throughout his life.

What is "ancestor worship"—as followers and critics of Confucius call it? Did he recommend specific ways for revering ancestors? Yes. Did he believe in the continued existence of departed ancestors in some incorporeal form? To this question, as to questions about the existence of spirits of any kind, he gave no positive answer. His reply, which has become familiar to us in a stilted form of pidgin English, was "Not know life; how know death?" Why, then, should he have bothered so much about specific ways of revering ancestors? You already know the answer if you can apply *yi, jen* and *li* to your relations with your own ancestors.

Consider, for example, how the principle of reciprocity applies here. Do you expect to die and become a departed ancestor? Yes. Do you desire to be forgotten as soon as you die? No. How long do you desire to be remembered after you are dead? Should you not then, according to the principle of reciprocity, desire to remember your ancestors in the same way as you desire to be remembered when you become one? How should you express your remembrance of the goodness and greatness of your ancestors? In the same manner and for as long a time as you desire to be so remembered? Since you doubtless do not wish to be forgotten too soon, especially by those dearest to you, nor remembered too long, especially by those who were never acquainted with you, you may find some socially accepted and culturally established manner of enacting such a remembrance.

Thus what appears to others as superstitious ancestor worship was for Confucius a natural expression of self-respect by socialized individuals. When we recognize additionally that one's social tao involves *hsin* or sincerity, we will then want to remember our ancestors as sincerely as we desire to be remembered. Do our ancestors still really exist? The principles of reciprocity and sincerity require that we regard our ancestors as existing in the same way in which we now desire others to regard us as existing after we have become departed ancestors. The naturalness of this desire makes it appropriate to set up tombstones, memorial days, tablets, halls, gardens, ceremonies, etc., which flow from our nature as social beings.

Confucius did not regard men as victims of determinate processes of Nature. Men become agencies that help to determine the course of Nature. But "it is only he who is completely genuine in the affairs of this world who can develop his nature to its fullest. If he can develop his own nature to its fullest, then he can help in the full development of the natures of other men. If he can help in the full development of other men's natures, then he can help in the full development of the natures of all animate and inanimate beings. If he can help in the full development of the natures of all animate and inanimate beings, then he can help in the production and maturation activities of Nature above and Nature below. When he helps in the production and maturation activities of Nature above and Nature below, he becomes a third kind of agency in the universe." (*Chung Yung,* Section XIII, author's interpretation.)

Critics of Confucius

The most famous and perhaps most influential rival of Confucius was Mo Ti. Mo Ti was a soldier in charge of instructing and commanding those who guarded the land. A good soldier must protect all equally and so must be willing to serve all equally and to die, if necessary, for all equally. Mo Ti claimed that *jen,* or genuine goodwill, must regard all persons without discrimination. He accused Confucius of teaching, if not an immoral, then at least a low moral, doctrine, namely, "discriminating love." A discriminator refuses to treat people alike because he claims that different people should be treated differently. He will not care for his friends as much as he does for his family. Consequently, he will not do very much for his friends. But a nondiscriminator will regard all people as alike and will do everything he can to help his friends, just as in the case of his family. He will have that "all-embracing love" which alone can assure peace and tranquility.

But Mo Ti did not end his criticisms by disagreeing about the nature of *jen.* He went on to say that there are four ways in which Confucian principles will ruin the whole world. (1) Confucianists do not believe in the existence of God or of spirits. Consequently God and the spirits are displeased. Mo Ti was himself a theist who believed that both an omnipotent but loving God and lesser spirits punish men who discriminate. As a soldier, he advocated absolute rule by a chief ruler who had power to reward and punish people; and he recognized the need for a supreme deity who would reward and punish any ruler who failed to love impartially. (2) Confucianists place so much emphasis on ritual that even those living a long life cannot encompass the learning needed to become acquainted with all of the formalities, and even those with the vitality of youth cannot perform all of the ceremonial duties. For example, the elaborate preparations for funerals and the persistence of acts of mourning for three years after death of a parent require so much wealth and energy that people do not have enough left over for ordinary living. (3) Confucianists advocate learning to play and listening to music. But the time and energy devoted to music is so wasteful that not even those who have amassed great wealth can afford to do so in the way Confucius recommended. (4) Confucianists seem resigned to a predetermined fate, which makes them lazy rather than productive. This latter criticism, at least, is hardly justified, since Confucius held that only after a person has done all that he can for himself should he resign himself calmly to the inevitable.

Commentators upon the controversy between Confucianists and Mohists delight in pointing out apparent inconsistencies on both sides. Mohists believed in the existence of spirits yet failed to perform ceremonies designed to please them. Confucianists punctiliously conducted ritualistic ceremonies for spirits even though they refused to believe in the existence of spirits. Yet such apparent inconsistencies disappear when we remember certain facts. The Confucian reason for conducting these ceremonies is not based on the assurance of the existence of spirits but upon the assurance of the principle of reciprocity inherent in the tao of association; that is, one should treat the spirits of his ancestors just as he would like to be treated if he were such a spirit. Consequently ceremonial expression of respect for spirits grows naturally from an extension of self-respect. The Mohist reason for belief in spirits is not based so much on evidence for their existence or for concern about their welfare as upon need for assurance that those who fail to love everybody indiscriminatingly will be punished by superhuman powers whenever human powers fail to guarantee such love.

Another critic of Confucius, Hsun tzu, was really a follower of Confucius in most respects. But he objected to the Taoist and Confucian doctrine that nature, including human nature, is essentially good. A child is born selfish and needs to be socialized. He does not at ·birth have an interest in the welfare of others. This he has to acquire and he can acquire it only by being taught. Human nature is not originally good, but it has to be made good by effort. Therefore the teaching of morality must be imposed upon new individuals by an external agency. Hsun tzu argued that rules of morality originated not so much as an extension of man's internal nature as from the fact that men cannot live together without some kind of social organization that requires social rules, and that men cannot defend themselves against enemies unless they have such an organization and rules. The rules of morality are designed to set limits upon the desires of those whose natural selfishness and aggressiveness would disrupt social harmony; in order to insure order such rules must be imposed upon everyone. It is the function of *li,* appropriate conduct, to establish these rules.

Han Fei-tzu, culminator of another classical school of Chinese philosophy, studied under Hsun tzu and agreed with him that human beings are born selfish and need to be controlled if welfare and stability are to be maintained. Han Fei-tzu was an administrator or minister of internal affairs. Thus he represented the viewpoint of a civil servant. Like his predecessor, Shen Tao, he argued that without authority an administrator cannot govern no matter how good he is, whereas with authority he can govern no matter how bad he is. Therefore a ruler's power must be absolute. Like another predecessor, Shen Pu-hai, he argued that a ruler should delegate his responsibilities to ministers, who will be rewarded if they succeed and punished if they fail. Therefore a ruler need not be either a wise or a highly moral man. Like a third predecessor, Shang Yang, he argued that uncertainty concerning laws leaves people unclear about their duties and that leniency and favoritism weaken a ruler's power. Therefore laws must be enacted on all subjects, made clear, and enforced with impartiality upon those high as well as low in social rank. Thus Han Fei-tzu and his school disagreed with the Confucian doctrine that knowledge of *li,* the best way of externally expressing one's inner nature, is sufficient for good government. They insisted that rulers should have absolute authority to impose conditions upon people so that they would be forced to be good.

Another attack on Confucianism, which occurred centuries later, was that by Buddhists. Confucian naturalism offered no hope of individual survival after death, no metaphysical explanations about the nature of the universe, no doctrine of grace whereby one might obtain special favors from powerful deities, and no escape from the rigorous moral duties detailed for each position in the family hierarchy. Buddhism, as it came from India, brought ideals of reincarnation and thus hope for rebirth, survival and eventual attainment of beatific Nirvana whereas Confucius and Lao-tzu believed death to be final. Buddhism brought speculations about the ultimate nature of cosmic reality and value, including ages of the world, levels of being, psychological processes, subtle dialectic, and even hells, which stimulated imagination and expanded intellectual horizons. Confucius, on the other hand, had maintained a simple, naive picture of experienceable nature and an agnostic attitude about invisible powers. Buddhism brought doctrines of Karma, with its accumulation of merits, and of *bodhisattvas,* who graciously sought to aid all who came to them in need; Confucianism did not include special favors from invisible divinities or rewards to be collected only in a future life. Buddhism brought ideals of monkhood, celibacy, and monastic isolation from worldly, including family, affairs, which permitted those suppressed in a family hierarchy to escape to a morally freer way of life; Confucianism allowed no opportunity for relief from domination of inferiors by their elders. Buddhist metaphysical, psychological, and logical ideas about the ultimacy of indistinctness ran directly counter to Confucian ideas about the genuineness of regularity and the orderliness of natural processes, about the need for appreciating the ultimacy of one's present duties whatever they may happen to be, and about discriminating among different persons, offices, and things. Buddhism regarded interest in external affairs, including government and ritual, as illusory, and thus attacked Confucianism at almost every level. The conversion of rulers to Buddhism, and its spread and partial domination of China for almost a thousand years, was perhaps the greatest threat to the survival of Confucianism that occurred until recent times.

Defenders of Confucius

Chief defender of Confucianism in early times was Mencius (372?–?289 B.C.). Critics of Confucius, both before and after Mencius, emphasized problems connected with spirits, ancestor worship, agnosticism, ritualism, and discrimination to such an extent that the positive contributions of Confucius, which were too subtle for many of them, tended to be ignored. The teachings of Confucius constitute some of mankind's greatest religious ideals, but these are not to be found in the interpretations given by his critics. His great religious ideal was *chih* or wisdom. This ideal received such scant attention among his critics that many accounts omit it entirely. It was the chief task and achievement of Mencius to defend and expand this great ideal.

Before we show how Mencius did this, let us show how he defended the position of Lao-tzu and Confucius that human nature is basically good. Such a view seemed so obvious to Confucius that he never felt called upon to discuss it. The Taoistic view that whatever is natural is good was so much a matter of common sense that it did not need questioning. Evil consists in deviation from one's own nature. Save a man from deviation and good automatically ensues. But after the bitter criticisms of Mo Ti, who believed that men naturally remain selfish rather than social, Mencius was called upon to defend the goodness of man in a way Confucius had never done. Mencius argued his case by citing evidence available to everyone. We find, for example, an unwillingness in men to see other men suffer. To illustrate this, Mencius recalled how, when you happen to see a child about to fall in a well, you suddenly feel alarmed and distressed. The universality of such feelings of alarm stands witness that men are instinctively concerned with the welfare of others. That is, men are by nature social and not, as Mo Ti, Hsun tzu, and Han Fei-tzu claimed, merely selfish beings.

Further details of his argument include pointing out that we feel such distress regardless of whether the child is our own or that of a stranger. One tries, if he can, to rescue the child, not because he desires praise or reward, and not because he fears being blamed and shamed if he refuses. His response and efforts occur so spontaneously that he has no time to think of these possibilities. The sense of shame itself, also something universal in men, implies concern for one's reputation in the eyes of others and presupposes some inherently social nature. A person lacking in instinctive compassion and shame is not really human.

Our instinctive feelings of compassion are the source of our adult good will *(jen)*. Our instinctive feelings of shame are the source of our interest in the best way of doing things, *i.e.*, the principles of morality such as reciprocity and sincerity *(yi)*. Our instinctive feelings of modesty are the source of our desire for appropriate modes of social interaction *(li)*. Our intuitive sense of what is so and what is not so, or of genuineness and artificiality, is the source of our religious ideal of yea-saying or wisdom *(chih)*. (See *Mencius*, II, A. 6.)

Mencius elaborated upon Confucius' ideal of *chih*, not for the purpose of modifying it but to explain it. The simple *chih* of Confucius becomes the complex *hao jan chih ch'i*, sometimes rendered into English as "The Great Morale." (*See* Fung Yu-lan, *The Spirit of Chinese Philosophy*, pp. 24–28.) Confucius' *chih* is that ideal condition of life in which we have perfected our knowledge of *yi*, fully achieved *jen*, intuitively know and habitually practice *li*, and no longer act with any doubt, mistrust, or hesitation inhibiting the perfection of our yea-saying to whatever life offers.

To explain Confucius' *chih*, Mencius seems to have added first the concept of *ch'i*, morale. Now one might have morale in isolation from others in the sense that when alone on a journey he maintains his hope that he will complete the journey successfully. But what Mencius means is that kind of morale which people have together when their joint confidence serves as a mutually sustaining force. His description calls to mind Jesus' ideal of that "Kingdom of Heaven," which is at once within you and among you and is pervaded by that love "which casteth out fear." *Chih ch'i* is no momentary festival of convivial togetherness in which usual animosities have been temporarily forgotten. It can be attained only by the gradual growth of profound respect for the common interests of people who have lived together for long periods of time. It manifests itself as an habitual response to both the present and continuing needs of others as if fulfillment of them were as much to be expected as of one's own needs. That Confucius' *chih* was essentially a social morale is something that Mencius explicitly reemphasized.

But a second, possibly more significant, addition for those seeing religion as cosmic at-homeness appears in the terms *"hao jan,"* meaning "great to a supreme degree." *Chih* is the affirmation not merely of self and of society but of the cosmic universe, of Tao, of *yang* and *yin,* of *T'ien* (that Nature which is above man), of the Five Elements, and of the cyclical processes that brought mankind into being and that conduct each man into and out of existence in due course. Hence *hao jan chih ch'i* consists in the perfect embodiment in men of an unquestioning confidence in the natural course of cosmic as well as human events. After Mencius, no doubt should have remained that *chih* as an ideal epitomizes, perhaps, mankind's greatest religious idealism. Yet, to people troubled with animosities, hunger, or doubts, and especially to those who hope for more than they deserve, this supreme ideal is, as Mencius admits, "difficult to explain."

Later defenders of Confucius, throughout more than two millennia of Chinese history, were numerous. "The Four Books," expressing ideas attributed primarily to him, and "The Five Classics," commonly associated with him, became required subjects for official examinations for civil service positions in 125 B.C. His supporters prompted various special Imperial honors from time to time. In 1 A.D., he was given the title "Duke." In 59 A.D., sacrifice in his honor in all schools in larger cities was decreed. In

422, a temple honoring him was erected at his place of birth. Successively, he was entitled "Foremost Teacher" (609), "Foremost Sage" (628), "Prince" (739), and "Grand Perfection and Ultimate Sage" (1308). Thus a gradually growing tendency to deify Confucius gained momentum until he was finally accorded the same ceremonious sacrifice by the Emperor as was made to *T'ien* or Heaven. Confucianism became a kind of state cult. Yet reverence for his greatness never went so far as to interpret him as a god, a creator, a savior, or a transcendental power. Not only did acceptance of Confucian doctrines by ruling dynasties help to spread his fame and influence, but too close identification of his teachings with the status quo led many to reject his tenets as not only conservative but as reactionary when times were ripe for revolutions inspired in part by Western scientific, political, and economic ideals.

"Confucianism" has come to mean a whole long complex history of cultural developments. Confucian philosophy was modified again and again by later interpreters, both under the increasingly intricate criticisms of Buddhist and Taoist thinkers, who themselves held modified views, and under the attempts of supporters—such as the famous Neo-Confucianist, Chu Hsi (1130–1200 A.D.)—to transform the Confucian *li* (meaning "form" as well as "propriety") into a Platonic "Idea" or essence. Speculations about cosmic "Reason" and about transcendental realities added new dimensions of thought to the broadening stream of Confucianism. The practices of political etiquette growing from modifications dictated by changing times continue to be called "Confucian." The misunderstandings of critics, which find their place in literature and history, also bear the name "Confucian." Present perspective suggests a double fate now in store for Confucius: a deliberate annihilation of such evidences of his influence in China as seem "imperialistic" and "reactionary" to Communist rulers and a growing absorption of his ideals as part of the wisdom of mankind. Will the teachings of Confucius, like those of Gotama, the Buddha, in India, and those of Jesus Christ, in Judea, suffer a declining in interest in his homeland while it grows in magnitude throughout the world?

Chapter 9 **Buddhism**

Buddhism entered China from India probably during the first century A.D. Its growth was minuscule at first but its gradual expansion with the help of converted emperors, brought it to a dominating role for six or seven centuries. Some refer to its "conquest of China." It finally became widely recognized, along with Taoism and Confucianism, as one of "the Three Truths" of China. As Lin Yutang has emphasized, "every Chinese is a Confucianist when he is successful and a Taoist when he is a failure." (*My Country and My People, op. cit.,* p. 117.) Buddhism, however, provided a supplementary "emotional outlet for the Chinese people." (*Ibid.,* p. 131.) It also offered hope for another life, a monastic escape from political turmoil into a realm of metaphysical speculations that had been largely neglected.

But it met opposition, early and late, that countered its advances with tragic defeats. As early as 200 A.D. objections against it were formulated and proclaimed. First of all, it was a foreign doctrine, and people then as now often reject the strange and the new. Its ideal of monkish life, including celibacy, leaving home, begging for food, and nonemployment, clashed head on with the strongly established ideals of family life where everyone works according to his ability. It created scepticism by promising reincarnation in another life, in the absence of any evidence for the return of the dead. It argued that the Buddha was the greatest teacher, thereby lessening the glory attributed to Confucius and Lao-tzu. It required monks to shave their heads, whereas Confucian practice called for leaving one's body intact. Celibacy of monks left women without husbands and led to unfilial conduct in sons who had no desire for progeny. Later, when Buddhism became so favored by an emperor that more than two hundred thousand men became monks, decline in production and in tax collections led to a terrible persecution in 845 A.D. that closed more than four thousand cloisters, forcing monks back into ordinary life.

The volume of literature accumulating around Chinese Buddhism is tremendous. The early trickle grew until, in 518 A.D., 2,213 works were listed in a catalogue, most of which (all but 276) have been lost. By 972, all three of the *Pitakas* had been translated into Chinese, though versions often differed widely from those appearing in the Pali editions. In addition to scriptures translated from Sanskrit, those attributed to Chinese authors are said to total more than seven hundred times the size of the Christian Bible. Since Buddhism in China is chiefly Mahayana, the more important works represent different aspects of this complex movement.

For example, *The Awakening of Faith* is perhaps the earliest influential work. Although authorship remains uncertain, it is associated with Ashvagosha and was translated into Chinese about 170 A.D. Books emphasizing *Sunyavada* include the *Prajnaparamitra Sutra* (translated into Chinese by Kumarajiva), *Madhyamika Sastra* and *Mulamadhyamika Karika* by Nagarjuna, and the *Lankavatara Sutra* (used by Zen). Books expressing Yogacara ideals include the *Mahayana-sutra-lankara* and *Bodhisattvabhumi* by Asanga, the *Abhidharma-kosa* (used by Kusha and Jodo sects in Japan) and *Sukavati-vyuha* (used by Shin), both by Vasubandu, the *Avatamsaka Sutra* (used by Kegon), the *Diamond Sutra* by Kumarajiva, the *Saddharma-pundarika (Lotus of the True Law)*, sometimes called simply *"The Lotus Sutra"* (a chief sutra of Tendai and Nicherin schools but used by practically all schools), and the *Sutra of Hui-Neng*, "the Sixth Patriarch."

We will select two outstanding contemporary schools for illustration. The Yogacara and Sunyavada philosophies, already sketched in Chapter V, pervaded China and provide necessary background for the two selected schools, Shin and Zen, that emerged and continued in China, flourished and proliferated in Japan, and have been most influential in the United States.

Shin

Shin (*Shin-shu,* meaning "Shin Sect") should not be confused with Shinto (*Shen-tao,* the "Way of the Gods," *Kami-no-michi*), the indigenous religion of Japan. Shin is a variety of Buddhism that traces its intellectual ancestry through many Mahayana teachers and scriptures back to Gotama and his Hindu antecedents. But since it advocates a doctrine of grace, and of faith as against works, in which one is completely dependent upon an "Other Power," in contrast with other forms of Buddhism and with more typically Oriental "self-help" religions, it stands out as a unique kind of Buddhism. Shin is a product of Mahayana *bodhisattva* ideals whereby a person already meriting, through its own works, attainment of Nirvana, must then vow compassionately to help others to the goal. Amida-Buddha (*Amitabha, Omito Fo*), the Buddha of Boundless Mercy, stands above all other *bodhisattvas* not only in vowing to persist until all sentient beings, animals as well as men, reach the goal but also because, through countless eons of time, he had himself earned sufficient merit to share it with all who need it. Now that the necessary work has already been done by Amida, all that men need to do is accept the gracious granting of salvation that Amida, in order to fulfil his "Original Vow," wants us to accept.

Not only is faith in the saving power of Amida sufficient, but arguments against works are presented to support the view that faith alone is enough. The ordinary person lacks ability to accumulate enough merit (good karmas) by himself to work his way to perfection. Hindu ("all is suffering"), Chinese (men meddlesomely deviate from their nature), and Christian ("original sin") doctrines all testify to man's inherent incapacity to do what is best for himself. Hence, if ordinary men are to be saved, they cannot attain salvation merely by their own efforts but must rely upon some superior "Other Power," namely, Amida. Evidence of faith in the gift of grace naturally expresses itself as affirmation by repeating the "name of Buddha," *"Namu Amida Butsu"* (*Namu Omito Fo*), customarily shortened to *"Nembutsu."* Repetition without faith remains ineffective;

if faith continues despite the absence of repetition, the goal will still be attained.

Shin ministers and laymen use long and short strings of beads to aid them in reciting their prayers. Religious services, including sermons, are held regularly (on Sundays in the United States), with three holidays celebrating the life of Gotama and three for remembering the life of Shinran-Shonin, chief founder of the Shin sect. Ministers marry (unlike Hinayana and early Mahayana monks). Children attend Sunday School, and a Young Men's Buddhist Association has functioned for some time. Striking similarities between Shin Buddhism and Christianity (especially Lutheranism) raise questions, not only in the minds of Christian scholars but of Shin Buddhists themselves. Disregarding late developments, perhaps adaptations resulting from influx into the United States, some evidence seems to exist of influence by Nestorian Christianity, apparently the only Christian movement penetrating the Orient early enough to make belief in such influence (fourth century A.D.) reasonable. But roots traceable to Hindu sources and the ideal of compassionate vows inherent in the Indian conception of *bodhisattva* would seem to indicate an independent origin. Similar ideals, like that of the rosary, could have arisen out of similar practical needs. Rosaries have appeared elsewhere in the world. One undaunted Buddhist remarked, in reply to questions about adopting the rosary from Catholics: "We think they got it from us."

The idea of seeking salvation through worship of Amida can be found in Hindu scriptures. *Karma-yoga,* the Way of Works, whereby one accumulates good karmas by doing good deeds, was contrasted with *bhakti yoga,* the Way of Devotion, whereby one may dissipate all self-interest by surrendering himself to wholehearted devotion to a god. Hindu ideas of re-incarnation, *karma, bhakti,* and *nirvana* are all retained in Shin Buddhism, as is Mahayana pantheism. Influences from Chinese Taoism and Confucianism are evident also. A selection from *The Tannisho* (See *From the Shin Sect,* Kyoto: The Eastern Buddhist Society, 1937, p. 38.) reads: "The Nembutsu is 'no-deed' and 'no-good' when viewed from the point of its followers. It is 'no-deed,' because when they practice the Nembutsu, they do not practice it of their own accord. It is 'no-good,' because it is not an act of goodness performed of their own accord. Since it is solely due to the Other Power, and beyond their self-power, it is 'no-deed' and 'no-good' when viewed from the point of its followers. . . ."

Is Amida a god, not a god, or *the* God? Amida is not the creator of the world, but he is the savior of man. Although historically belief in Amida developed relatively late, Shin doctrine, inheriting the Mahayana idea of *bodhisattvas* destined to return to identity with Ultimate Reality *(Sunya, Bohdi,* or *Nirvana),* and of some Buddhas as never losing such identity, interprets Amida as more completely identified. Although other Buddhas and *bodhisattvas* exist, they all are regarded as manifestations of Amida. Gotama, the historical Buddha born prince of the Sakya Clan, was only one such Buddha sent by Amida to reveal his nature and vow to the Hindu people. Consequently, Shin Buddhists regard Gotama as an advocate of compassion and interpret his forty-five years among monks and laymen as an expression of such compassion. (For a dissenting view on this subject, see my *Philosophy of the Buddha, op. cit.,* pp. 147–148.) Theravada interpretations of Gotama's Enlightenment, when he rejected the opportunity to enter Nirvana in order to instruct his friends, tend to support the Shin view.

Once Amida becomes recognized as the ultimate source of all power for salvation, all other historical, contemporary, and future advocates of compassion, including Jesus, may be regarded as particular manifestations (or *avatars,* to use the traditional Hindu term) of Amida. With Amida as the infinite, everlasting, and omnipresent power for salvation, Shin need not be jealous of other religions that advocate salvation by grace and faith in an "Other Power" because all such "other powers" may be viewed as incarnations of Amida. When Amida is identified with *Sunya* he is impersonal, but when pictured as the compassionate savior of mankind, he appears as the ideal person.

What is the goal of life? Nirvana. But what is Nirvana? Whereas Theravadins and Sunyavadins agree that individual selves are temporary, illusory disturbances in an ultimate calm, these disturbances having to disappear before the ultimate goal can be reached, Shin Buddhists believe that each individual self, although a seemingly continuous entity but actually a flux of flickering experiences during its temporal existence, becomes immortal upon reaching "The Pure Land." The goal, Nirvana, is pictured as a place, a "Western Paradise," to which all saved souls go. They continue as conscious beings, aware of each other's enjoyment of the benefits of Amida's compassion. Details of such existence are missing, though persons do enjoy "an enlightened body" and have no desires except through sharing wholeheartedly in Amida's compassionate desire that all sentient beings, without exception, be saved.

The name "Jodo," meaning "Pure Land" (or "Pure Realm," since it has no specific geographical or cosmic location), applies not only to Jodo Shin-shu, the Pure Land Sect, founded by Shinran-Shonin (1173–1262), which we have been calling simply "Shin," but also to the Jodo Sect founded by his teacher, Genku, also known as Honen-Shonin (1133–1212), and others. Japanese followers trace their origin to the Chinese writer T'an-luan (476–542), though Chinese followers ascribe the founding to the earlier Hui-Yuan. "In Japan today, more than half of the Buddhists belong to the Pure Realm sects, some 18,500,000 people. Of these seventy percent are Shin Buddhists, sixteen percent are Jodo Buddhists, the rest belong to the sects known as Seizan, Ji, Yuzu Nembutsu, and Shensei." (*See* Kenneth Morgan, *The Path of the Buddha*, N.Y.: The Ronald Press, 1956, pp. 332–33.) Shin itself has subdivisions and one of these, the Hongwangi, has two branches. Of the 165,000 Buddhists on the North American continent, about 60,000 belong to the Hongwangi sect in the United States, which calls itself "The Buddhist Churches of America."

The form of yea-saying that Shin Buddhism takes is that of an act of faith in the "Original Vow of Amida." This involves the intellectual acceptance of Hindu and Chinese Buddhist history as interpreted by Shin, the emotional acceptance of an attitude of compassion toward all other persons as well as an appreciation of Amida's gift, and the participation in the customs and ceremonies (including Nembutsu and rosary) expressing these assents. To a completely free gift of undeserved eternal life of bliss, one can hardly say "No." Shin is described as the "easy" way, wherein all one has to do is to say "Yes" to a free gift, in contrast with the "hard" way of Zen and other self-help religions wherein one must work for and earn by himself every step of the way. What can be easier than to say "Yes" to the "easy" way?

But if our distinction between "high" and "low" religion is warranted, and if religion is "low" when it leads one to expect more than he deserves, than either Shin exemplifies "low" religion, in this sense, or it must somehow show that man deserves to be saved by grace. Yet the very concept of grace implies receipt of something undeserved, and Shin makes explicitly clear its view that men lack worthiness when left to their own insights and efforts. One Shin document (*From the Shin Sect*, pp. 35–36) seems to argue that the more undeserving a person is the better his chances of getting into the Pure Land: "People generally think that even a wicked man is reborn in the Pure Land, and how much more so with a good man! Though this latter way of thinking appears at first sight reasonable, yet it is not in accord with the purport of the Original Vow, the faith in the Other Power. The reason is as follows: He who undertakes to perform good deeds by relying on his own power has no wish to invoke the Other Power, he is not the object of the Original Vow of Amida. If, however, by discarding his reliance on self-power, he invokes the Other Power, he can be reborn in the True Land of Recompense. We who are fully burdened with passions have no means to escape the bondage of birth and death, no matter what kind of austerities we performed, and this formed the original motive of Amida for making his Vow. For this reason, Shonin said that if even a good man is reborn in the Pure Land, how much more so with a wicked one!"

When confronted with the seeming paradox involved in this quotation, an able Buddhist remarked that the source was recorded some time after Shonin's death, and its exposition should be reserved for advanced students. The point of the quotation was not to provide an excuse for wickedness, which dull minds might unwittingly infer, but to exemplify the utter completeness of Amida's compassion. He might have pointed to Jesus' parable of the Prodigal Son as an analogy. Yet how can one escape feeling that

Shin not only promises but encourages belief that one should expect to get more, even infinitely much more, than he deserves? Despite the promised ease—as Shin is doubtless the "easiest" of all major religions—some, who have been convinced that justice is more ultimate than grace, will have to say "No" to it.

Zen

Recent association of Zen with American "Beatniks"— a name that has captured contemporary fancy—has aroused curiosity without yielding much comprehension. Search for an understanding of Zen yields a bewilderingly complex history of foreign and mysterious men, books, and doctrines, *koan* nonsense, tasteless tidbits of *haiku* poetry, unexplained and seemingly boring tea ceremonies, and a paradoxical "philosophy of no philosophy." The fact that Zen itself aims to baffle the intellect exasperates beginners The apparently irresistible temptation of writers to tease their readers with absurdities, claimed to be historically famous and profound, balks prospective insight into what many judge to be the world's greatest religion.

We may evade these mistakes by appealing to certain aspects of our own personal everyday experience, which reveals clues to understanding Zen. Zen itself is mysterious ultimately not because it originates in a foreign culture but because it emphasizes attention to omnipresent values so simple and obvious as to be transparent. They remain hidden from us because, like our eyes, we see *through* them rather then see *them*. Just as our ever-present breathing and pulse disappear from attention when we focus on objects and problems, so the omnipresent goal of life is lost from view as we look for values elsewhere, in the future, or even in the past. Let me suggest some clues to that "kingdom of heaven which is within you" and "at hand" by citing some familiar experiences. My suggestions fall conveniently under two headings: "Zen is easy." "Zen is hard."

ZEN IS EASY. It is as easy as falling off a log. It is easier, in fact, since, when falling, you try to resist the result whereas in Zen all resistance is missing. Recall how, when you tripped and fell, it all happened before you fully realized what was happening. If your automatic reflexes responded instantaneously to ease your landing, you may well wonder with amazement at the speed and efficiency of your response mechanisms. If you have not fallen lately, at least you can recall having dropped something and catching it before actually realizing what was falling, how far it had fallen, and whether or not it could be caught. You intuited the falling and your reacting: your responses were not preplanned. You had no time to think about the matter. You became aware, upon reflection, that, in the flick of a second, your whole complex intricate body adapted itself automatically with sureness and precision. The result was better than it would have been if you could have taken time to think through the whole procedure before and planned the movement of each limb in a specific way.

This spontaneous way of behaving, exhibiting unquestioning confidence in the wisdom of nature, serves as an important clue to the spirit of Zen. Living in Zen is indeed like falling off a log, except that you willingly assent to, rather than resist, your falling, your experience is more akin to joy then fear, and you continue on and on in the same alert appreciative spirit at all times and places and with respect to everything you do. In this sense, Zen is both universal and practical.

Bicycle riding also provides a glimpse into the nature of Zen. After you have acquired sufficient skill to ride unconcernedly and attend to sights and sounds along the way, chat with other cyclists, or daydream, you find your bicycle almost operating itself, without your constant attention to it. Your arms and legs move and your weight shifts quite automatically as you adjust your balance to meet changing circumstances, such as pebbles, holes, slippery mounds, or converging vehicles. You do not have to attend to each stone or rut with nervous anticipation, as when learning to ride. Adjustment occurs so automatically that, except for rare occasions, steering ceases to be a problem. You intuitively grasp the whole visual scene without careful attention to each detail. Such riding is relaxing, restful, comforting.

But note what is happening. The bicycle seems to steer you instead of you steering the bicycle. You continue without anxiety and yet the steering is done. Your muscles respond strenuously and yet effortlessly in the sense that all the straining is done before you become aware of it. This is the way one experiences living in Zen. Life lives itself and presents itself for enjoyment. When you intentionally interfere by trying to control the course of events and change it to suit plans of your own devising, you will have to worry about every intruding item that may spoil your plans. You must then attend to each new detail and consciously choose whether you will accept it or reject it.

The more you desire to manage your life according to some preconceived pattern, the more you find you cannot do it. The more you insist on meddling with things, bending them to your will, the more irritated, frustrated, and fearful you become. Like a novice bicycle rider who wants to force the obstacles out of his way by an act of will, you unrealistically create difficulties for yourself. If, on the other hand, you accept life as it is, as enjoyable and interesting and comfortable, willing to be steered through life's course, your troubles, at least your self-made troubles, will disappear. The same obstacles occur, but they no longer appear as worrisome. The same rocks and ruts confront the expert cyclist and the learner, but appreciative confidence replaces constant anxiety. In Zen, life steers the self rather than the reverse.

Yawning may provide another clue to Zen. Try planning a yawn. You can't do it. The harder you try the more improbable success becomes. But when a time comes for yawning, you yawn. *You* yawn. Yawning takes control of you. You accept it as your own, or as yourself in action. You can hardly resist a yawn, once it starts. If you try to resist, you feel frustrated, experience discomfort, and become apprehensive. When an urge to yawn arises spontaneously, what is the best thing to do? Try to stop it? No. Try to hasten it? No, this merely retards it. Accept it, submit to it, allow it to take its course. Let yourself be carried along by it, or with it, or through it. The more whole-heartedly you accept it, the more smoothly and comfortably will it occur. Zen is as easy as yawning for one who is willing to say "Yes" to his yawn, and so neither resists nor hastens it when it comes. Sokei-an, an American Zen Master, is author of a book, *Cat's Yawn* (N.Y.: First Zen Institute of

America, Inc., 1947). Few will be willing to see in a yawn, much less a cat's yawn, a symbol of high religion. But there is nothing occult, complex, or unobtainable about Zen experiences. However, it does require the same spontaneous willingness to say "Yes" to details of each present moment as is needed to enjoy a yawn when it comes.

ZEN IS HARD. Did you ever try falling off a log? That is, did you ever deliberately plan an unplanned fall? You can't do it. Not only is it hard; it is practically impossible. When you begin to think about falling, you become conscious of various inhibitions, uncertainties, fears. The more fears you develop, the more you believe you must carefully think through ahead of time just what should be done. How should you place your hands to prevent undue jarring? How will you feel as you fall? So long as these premeditated factors becloud your consciousness, you are not in Zen and not on your way to Zen.

Try harder. Scheme as cleverly as you like. Still you cannot bring yourself to trip and fall spontaneously. The harder you try the worse your failure—the greater your fear, worry, concern, anticipation, tension, effort. Zen is effortless living. So the more effort you put forth to attain it, the less can you achieve it. Zen is spontaneous living. But spontaneity cannot be planned. It can arrive only with a cessation of planning. The complete spontaneity enjoyed in Zen presupposes utter surrender of all desire to plan.

Zen consists in being fully and alertly occupied with living in the present, not in looking toward the future. Zen is like falling off a log only because this happens so suddenly that you do not have time to plan for the future. When your experience of falling lasts long enough for you to become afraid, it no longer resembles Zen. If you are seized and crippled by fear, you crash like a lifeless lump instead of snapping into your adjustment like a nimble cat.

The goal of life is to be found in living, not beyond life. So quit searching for the goal of life. It can be found only in living life without searching for a goal. This truth finds expression in a Zen remark about "Riding an ass in search for an ass." Such a search is said to involve two mistakes. The first consists in seeking that which one already has. Present life may be enjoyed as fulfillment of purpose rather than suffered as a slavish struggle toward an unattainable goal. The second is "being unwilling to dismount." That is, many who realize the Zen truth that the present may be enjoyed for its own sake still persist in looking for ultimate values in the future. Western culture urges man to put off enjoyment of living until some tomorrow. "Our reach exceeds our grasp, or what's a heaven for?" Says Robert Louis Stevenson, "It is better to travel hopefully than to arrive." Thus Zen interprets Western mentality as committed to "riding an ass in search of an ass."

Zen is hard in at least three ways. It is hard to get into, hard to stay in and hard to know when one is in.

(1) ZEN IS HARD TO GET INTO because one cannot attain it by any standard ways. Neither will, nor intellect, nor works, nor faith can get you there, and no one else can help you.

(a) *You cannot will your way into Zen,* because Zen consists in surrender of individual will. One cannot arrive in Zen until he has ceased wanting to get in. The seemingly suicidal will to stop willing repels everyone with a strong will. The harder he wills the farther away he becomes from entering Zen. The ardent novice must lose his ardor before he stands a chance of success.

(b) *One cannot reason his way into Zen,* because Zen is entirely, or basically, intuitive. Intellect abstracts parts, separating them from each other and from the whole, and reconstructs by relating such parts into an artifice of its own making. But Zen is antirational in the sense that it grasps the concrete presentation intuitively and without abstraction. Intuition is prior to reason, for reason must begin with something given, some immediately apprehended data. To believe that reason is prior to intuition is a mistake, and to believe that one can reason his way back into intuition is a greater mistake. Intuition is self-sufficient; to try to attain intuition in a way that makes intuition depend upon reason is to be misled. After one intuitively grasps Zen, then he can realize that reason can be of no help. But the seeker who asks "Why?" wants a reasonable answer. When he asks "How can I attain Zen?" he expects a rational reply. But Zen masters, knowing the unattainability of Zen by rational means, have been forced to devise ways of making the asker realize that he cannot be answered through reason. Any problem given to a seeker, the solution to which cannot be reached intellectually, is called a *"koan."* A *koan* is a technique for driving an aspirant into an intellectual impasse, thereby forcing him to abandon efforts to reason his way into Zen. Needless to say, they do not all succeed. Intellect finds it hard to surrender itself.

(c) One cannot work his way into Zen. Neither accumulated merit nor exertion of effort can bring him there. *Karma-yoga* does not suffice, for no amount of merit from past efforts can help. Being in Zen is unmerited. In Zen, one is essentially beyond morality, beyond duty and obligation, beyond reward and punishment. Murderer and healer may have equal opportunity and success in getting into Zen. So one cannot expect to enter Zen until he realizes that, no matter how much good he does, he will not receive Zen as a deserved reward. No matter how unfair it may seem that a wicked man may enter immediately and enjoy immensely while a virtuous man may remain shut out, one cannot enter Zen until he loses interest in such an injustice. Also, no amount of present effort can help one to attain Zen. Zen is effortless living, and the harder you work to get in, the farther you drift from its entrance. No amount of merit given in grace by some Other Power can be of any assistance either.

(d) Faith that one can and will attain Zen is useless. Faith, either in one's own power or in any other power, helps not a whit. It is true that one cannot be in Zen without having complete faith in Zen. After one is in Zen, such faith is automatic, inherent, all-pervasive. But before being in Zen, faith that one will get in provides no assurance. It is true also that attainment of faith in living, in living confidently in the sense that one intuitively grasps and accepts life without resisting it, may bring one, unwittingly, into Zen. But faith that one has the power to attain Zen is self-defeating. For when in Zen, life steers the self and provides potentialties for enjoyment that egoism immediately destroys.

Thus Zen is hard to get into because its attainment involves at least four simultaneous types of suicide.

These are: a will to surrender will; an intellectual assent to surrendering intellect as a means; a moral acquiescence to the superiority and self-sufficiency of bliss that is unmerited; and faith that a self can and will attain Zen must be replaced by awareness that such assurance of attainment can occur only after one has attained it. This fourfold suicide consists in the abandonment of all anxiety; all concern for future attainment must be dismissed before one can devote attention wholly to present enjoyment.

(2) ZEN IS HARD TO STAY IN, because life automatically presents us with desires, interests, wants; and the moment we allow these desires to occupy our attention and take over the direction of our life, we become future-oriented. Desires turn into dreams and dreams involve schemes, and self emerges as a wanter and master of its wants. Since to live is to desire, being in Zen continues only precariously. "While there's life, there's hope." "Hope springs eternal in the human breast." Zen is momentary unless one can pacify his desires, humble his ego, and care not for the future.

So far, we have been describing Zen as something absolute and without degrees. Yet, as we shall indicate in detail below, Zen may overlie and supervene upon practical interests. While in Zen, one may entertain interests, examine ideas, consider hopes, experience desires, work for tomorrow, and cling to his faith, all without losing his Zen experience completely. Even though maintaining the Zen experience becomes more precarious as more interests present themselves for consideration, a Zen expert can retain a Zen attitude toward them. But one will have to develop skill in retaining Zen, in reassenting to quadruple suicide, and in resisting total revitalization of intellect, will, morality, and ego. Zen is hard to stay in, but the skill to do so can be acquired.

(3) ZEN IS HARD ALSO BECAUSE ONE MAY, WITHOUT REALIZING, ALREADY BE IN ZEN, just as one in Zen may slip out without noticing it. This points up a difficulty in understanding Zen. When "understanding" and "knowing" mean having something as an object distinct from a knower, "understanding Zen" involves experiencing Zen as an object of knowledge. Since in Zen there is no or little distinction

between subject and object, making Zen an object of knowledge eliminates the knower from being in Zen. Hence, one who *knows* he is in Zen is not in Zen, and one who is in Zen *knows not* he is in Zen. One intuits being in Zen; intellectualizing the condition destroys it. Hence, Zen can never be "understood," that is, conceptually apprehended. Not only the novice who seeks to understand but also one who has been, or is, in Zen cannot understand it. He can only understand that it cannot be understood, but while he so understands he is not in Zen. Zen is hard.

Paradoxically, despite the fact that Zen cannot be "understood," the whole purpose of writing about Zen is to help you understand it. Thus far we have tried to convey ideas about Zen itself, or Zen in some absolute sense. For some Zennists, Zen *is* absolute, there being no degrees of Zen. Were this so, Zen could have no practical applicability. But since Zen may also be employed in daily experience and utilized to increase efficiency, not only in war and business but universally, some discussion of how this can be is required. For most of us most of the time, Zen, if experienced, must be experienced in some degree rather than as something absolute. Zen may be an aspect of experience, rather than the whole of experience. Zen pertains to the appreciation of what is present as present. But Zen does not prevent the content of what is present from having a future orientation. One whose whole attention is toward the future is not in Zen. But one who enjoys as a present value the prospect of future values can remain in Zen to the extent that the present enjoyment prevails. Being in Zen may be a matter of degree, or being in Zen may be an aspect of experience even when it is not the whole of experience. If this interpretation of Zen is not orthodox, then I shall be happy to claim it as my own.

Zen is universal. This does not mean that Zen is omnipresent, but only that there is no kind of experience that cannot be approached with a Zen attitude. It is true that experience occupied with emotional crises, egotistical pride, excruciating pain, overwhelming fear, intricate analyses, and consuming curiosity tend to exclude Zen. But the Zen expert can resist these impingements. I propose to indicate Zen's universal and practical aspects by surveying a few areas of experience, such as war, industry, art, and love.

War involves combat situations that may be illustrated by fencing, archery, *jujitsu,* and *kamikaze* piloting. Samurai warriors adopted Zen as a means to efficiency and survival. Trying to outguess an opponent's sword-stroke, by anticipating where he will thrust and placing a defensive guard there before he strikes, ends in fatality with a single false guess. One cannot afford to risk his life by anticipating plans of attack and defense. Rather he must alertly await attack and respond intuitively by automatic withdrawal or defensive movements so quickly that the intellect has no time to function. Staccato-like thrusts must be parried instantaneously in a present so fully occupied with action that it has no room for desire to win. One's spontaneous evasion and counterthrust are guided by his opponent's sword, not by his own intellect. Nimble efficiency, with lightning-flash responses—like those of a cat dropped upside down close to the floor that still manages a four-footed landing—is needed. When fighting in Zen, a warrior is neither brave nor timid, has neither fear of death nor thought of survival, can pause neither to size up his enemy nor evaluate his own strength. His responding must all be done before he has time to reflect.

D. T. Suzuki devotes almost a third of his excellent *Zen and Japanese Culture* to Samurai and swordsmanship. He points out how, in intuiting glittering gestalts of flickering swordplay, a swordsman identifies himself with his sword. "It acquires a soul," becoming indistinguishable from the spirit of the combatant. His sword comes to stand in everyday life as a symbol of his religion: the unquestioning loyalty, self-discipline, self-sacrifice, and devotion to duty required in combat permeate his ordinary activities. The unreserved yea-saying attitude demanded in combat extends into daily living, or rather one can hardly succeed in training for swordsmanship without first embodying within himself a similar attitude toward noncombat duties.

Eugen Herrigel, a Westerner, describes in *Zen and the Art of Archery* his own exasperating induction into Zen and how acceptance of an intuitive Zen attitude during archery practice perfected his target skill beyond that attainable by steady, muscle-straining, eye-focusing, perfectly controlled methods. *Jujitsu,* wrestling techniques exploiting possibilities for turning an opponent's aggressive movements into self-defeating falls and one's own weakness into unsuspected strength, also proceeds more smoothly when performed in Zen. *Kamikaze* pilots during World War II developed a remarkable reputation for succeeding where they should have failed; Zen training, added to their Shinto loyalties, has been given credit. Boxing and competitive games, such as basketball and football, can profit from the same principles.

Industrial uses of Zen are endless. Machine operation may be eased and speeded through Zen techniques. Money spent on efficiency experts and on time and motion studies remain inadequate until the financial possibilities of Zen attitudes have been exploited. The reader probably has some personal skill so fully perfected that he can recognize himself slipping into a Zen attitude during moments of peak performance. A glowing awareness of efficient mastery yields an enjoyment of automatic self-and-machine manipulation quite apart from interest in production goals. The semi-euphoria that a speedy typist can experience while maintaining sustained performance may be attained in other fields.

Those who have forgotten how they enjoyed their acquired automatic reflexes as cyclists may be aware of self-satisfaction while driving an automobile: the brakes go on and off, the throttle is moved with sensitivity to motor capacity and acceleration needs, the car is swerved and steadied, and the comfort of occupants intuitively cared for by acquired instincts. One driving a car with a Zen attitude maintains wide-eyed alertness undistracted by irrelevancies. Those unfamiliar with Zen mistakenly believe it to be a trance leading to drowsiness and sleep. One may go to sleep with a Zen attitude; when he does, he will go to sleep quickly and without hesitation. But a driver maintaining a Zen attitude toward his driving is less likely to go to sleep than one whose intense efforts at jerking his attention toward every distracting movement fatigue his muscles and drain his energy. Where complex, sensitive, and rapid responses are needed in machine operation, attainment of a Zen attitude reduces strain and fatigue, and increases enjoyment.

Art—meaning all of the fine arts, including painting and

calligraphy, flower arrangement and gardening, *haiku* poetry and other literature, music and drama—is an area of life reaping enormous riches through Zen attitudes. If aesthetic experience means something enjoyed as an end in itself, then Zen experience is always aesthetic. The Zen spirit, which looks not beyond the present, interprets every experience as intrinsically aesthetic. Zen is a religion that automatically transforms life's anxieties about the uncertain future into confident appreciation of the present. Zen is a religion that transmutes the dread of duties yet undone into persistent awareness that "the Kingdom of Heaven" is already at hand. This religious appreciation of present intrinsic value disposes the mind to see beauty everywhere. The "art of living" becomes self-evident in Zen.

Although some designing may intrude itself into art, just as calculating confronts us in business, art is at its best when artistic inspiration burgeons spontaneously and executes its result before the intuition springing out of the genius of nature becomes straitjacketed by a tyrannical intellect. Since intellect works rapidly, artistic execution must occur quickly. A slow artist, beginning with one insight and experiencing surgings of many additional insights, encounters problems of "harmonizing" discordant elements. His end product often represents a hodgepodge of inspirations; he must struggle to make them live together in one piece. Western aestheticians idealize harmony so much because disharmony is such a constant problem with Western artists. A simple work of art, executed to completion in a flash, during a Zen trance pervaded by a single intuition, involves no problems of harmony. Its insight is self-contained and self-organized; it embodies no internal inconsistencies and regards all comparisons with external standards as irrelevancies.

A Zen painter may be urged to paint by some vague impulse to which he responds unquestioningly. He reacts to his first brushstroke not with a critical eye (Did it flow along precisely as I intended it?), but with an alert, sensitive imagination that snatches each suggestion, apparent in the line as drawn, as a spontaneous contribution to the whole, which emerges, as it were, out of the canvas rather than out of the mind of the artist. The developing work

of art steers the artist more than the artist guides the development—at least in the most original works. Just as the
Zen swordsman acts to evade a sword thrust that is coming toward him, so the Zen artist instantaneously incorporates seemingly accidental suggestions into his creation. He
works so fast that he has no time to compare his present
inspiration or execution with any previous scheme. He
must complete his work before his unitary insight becomes
infected with additional insights that may destroy its in-
nate wholeness.

The foregoing sketch of a Zen ideal should not mislead
the reader into believing that Zen artists are incapable of
more extensive works or that execution of Zen inspirations
may not be prolonged. The Zen ideal may function as an
aspect of artistic endeavor even when it cannot dominate
completely. Common themes of birds and trees and mountains and lakes recur. Old familiar themes emerge in a new
dress that unites in a single intuition both the familiar and
the new. But complex subjects must subsume themselves
under some dominating insight that incorporates all that
is visible into a pleasing whole; if any item appears as if
in an unintended war with its neighbor, or if the vision as
a whole expresses a struggle with its external environment,
the work is a failure. Western critics may insist that harmony is present; but such harmony is not something meas-
urable by any objective standard, for it is a harmony of
mutually self-sustaining insights. Each artistic insight,
whether fully expressed in a few seconds or manufactured
laboriously over a period of years, manifests a self-contained gestalt that serves as its own internal standard of
construction.

Flower arrangement, itself a fine art (*See* G. L. Herrigel's *Zen in the Art of Flower Arrangement*) performed
with intuitive simplicity, may also incorporate symbolism
regarding man's significance in the universe. Typical Japanese flower designs contain three stalks—an upper, a
lower, and a middle—signifying sky, earth, and man respectively. (*See* Rachel Carr, *Japanese Floral Arrangement*,
for numerous examples.) Great sophistication, acquaintance with the varieties of traditions in standard types of
composition, and a knowledge of ingeniously specialized
tools are needed to appreciate and create prize-winning

displays. Many of these go far beyond Zen in nature and significance. Yet Zen, as universal, lends itself to the intuitive appreciation of complex creative insights, symbolic as well as nonsymbolic, in all of the arts.

Poetry readily gives itself to enlightenment by the Zen spirit. *Haiku,* a three-line seventeen-syllable form, is, despite its limiting formalism, especially adaptable to Zen intuition. It is short enough to express a single pulse of inspiration, yet long enough to include as much complexity of content as may be needed to give body to such a simple pulse. But the Zen spirit may remain a persisting aspect of more intricate poetic endeavors. And one may even wonder whether it is possible to enjoy poetic experience at all without the presence of Zen as an aspect. (*See* R. H. Blyth, *Zen in English Literature,* and D. T. Suzuki, *Zen in Japanese Culture,* Ch. VII.)

Love requires both an object of love and, in so many cases, concern for the future. How can it be embraced by Zen which tends to erase the distinction between subject and object and the limiting of appreciation to what is present? First of all, Zen exists as love of life, of life in its present, concrete condition without any trace of anxiety, fear, or lack of trust. Some will regard Zen as the perfect love of life and of all that appears in it.

If we turn from love in general to lovemaking in particular, we may recall how the scheming courtier creates distrust, which balks his advances, whereas an innocent smile of appreciation may stir a deep and genuine demand for irrevocable commitment. When a shy love-sick youth dreams how he will court his beloved with phrases of undying love, he finds his efforts to carry out his plans blocked by nervous, awkward, stumbling, fearful failures. Overwhelming embarrassment may make expression impossible. But the indifferent extrovert who "plays by ear" may, in being ever ready to recognize each smile or rebuff for its present value, conveys an air of confidence in which those in need can place their trust. Patient, instantaneous, automatic appreciation of accidentally presented little things reveals an enduring tendency to love. In Zen, the lover is led by emerging circumstances. Nature invented love and presents it to man at particular times. Man

who impatiently modifies and hastens nature's gift destroys
its delicate values and thrusts himself into a madness firing
his passion for a more intense and violent love. The anxious courtier is his own worst enemy. In Zen, the lover
remains alert, appreciative, considerate, patient. He enjoys
the confidence that what is in store for him he will receive,
or is receiving, and what is not in prospect is not his to
have anyway. He is so preoccupied with savoring present
feelings that he loses all anxiety about future ecstasies
or frustrations. With anxiety gone, satisfaction is complete,
continuingly complete.

No account of Zen as religion is adequate without mention of "The Tea Ceremony." And no self-respecting tea
drinker should claim he knows what he is doing when
drinking tea until he has read Okakura Kakuzo's *The Book
of Tea.* "Tea began as a medicine," "grew into a beverage,"
"entered the realm of poetry," and finally became ennobled
"into a religion." The Tea Ceremony may be enjoyed alike
by Shin, Zen, Confucian, and Shinto devotees and refuses
to be sectarianized, unless devotion to Tea Ceremonialism
may itself be regarded as an independent sect. A Shin
spirit of gratitude for Amida's grace, a Confucian spirit
appreciating cosmic and social orderliness symbolized in
ceremonial perfection, and a Shinto recognition of ancestral divinity manifesting itself in a constantly reliable
morale, join with Zen in sustaining the Tea Ceremony as
a supra-sectarian communion service.

In Zen, the Tea Ceremony is at once a direct, immediate,
nonsymbolic experience *and* symbolic both of the ultimacy
of Zen enjoyment and, by implication, the failure of so
much of life to be lived in Zen. For Zen, this ceremony is
not a formality representing an extrinsic value, but itself
constitutes a concrete embodiment of ultimate value. The
spirit of peace, of *nirvana,* is not so much symbolized as attained, not so much implied as enacted, not so much hoped
for as actualized. Its readiness to intuit present intrinsic
value constitutes Zen as a great religion. The ingenious
simplicity and naturalness characterizing tearoom, tea-
house, and tea garden design, and the silent, courteous, de-
corous cooperation and mutual sharing of worshipful ecstasy in which social, physical, and psychical factors blend,

not just harmoniously but also intuitively, defy description. Like all great religious experiences, Zen must be lived in order to be comprehended.

Zen is high religion. It brings yea-saying to a pinnacle. It needs no God, no church, no future heaven, because it finds its goal immediately at hand. Zen is not atheistic, because Zen is not against anything. Whether thoughts of God or thoughts of no God present themselves, its yea-saying response is the same. Zen, as universal, can adapt itself to the forms, ceremonies, beliefs, and circumstances of any other religion, to any form of government, as well as to any occupation. Zen has no need of creed, but in Zen one can assent to a creed more efficiently. Zen is not forward-looking, but one may say "Yes" more quickly and fully to his prospective fate when in Zen.

We have neglected thus far to mention the history of Zen. When one is in Zen, concern for the past and hope for the future are absent. Zen is a branch of Buddhism that professes disregard for Buddha and the *bodhisattvas*, for scriptures and teachers and monasteries, for history and doctrine. One may, of course, find Zen historians, Zen teachers, Zen temples, and Zen books. But these occur as social phenomena—just as do banking, manufacturing, governing, and homemaking—rather than as essentials of Zen. One may attain full enjoyment of Zen without any awareness of history or doctrine. Yet those interested in comparing religions may see Zen as a culmination of one of the most intricate religious histories, involving not merely the myriads of Buddhist sects, doctrines, and scriptures but also both Taoistic and Confucian conflicts and compromises and Shinto practices merging into an amorphous whole. The influence of Zen upon other cultures, including American, continues and provides materials for yet-to-be-written chapters of an unfinished story. But one cannot be sure he understands Zen apart from its historical sources in Hindu thought (*karma, samsara, yoga, dhyana, nirvana*), in Buddhist history (Gotamavada, Theravada, Sunyavada, Yogacara, and Shin), in Chinese philosophy (Taoism, Confucianism), to say nothing of Hindu, Chinese, and Japanese linguistic and social structures, and the peculiar line of teachers and monastic institutions that contributed to its survival and development. Yet it is true that Zen refers to something essential in human nature that exists quite apart from any particular historical development.

Zen has taken root in American culture and, excepting perhaps the following of Shin by citizens of Japanese stock, is the most popular of all Oriental religions in the United States. American interest in Zen is due to many factors, not the least of which has been the presence and persistent lecturing by D. T. Suzuki, whose many books have been widely read. The baffling character of *koans* irresistibly teases curiosity. Interests in Japanese art, architecture, poetry, flower arrangement, *jujitsu,* and fighting methods have all found some explanation through literature involving Zen. By penetrating American minds in many different ways, Zen is stimulating new varieties of thinking that partly merge with and partly contest the growth of Existentialism.

With regret, exploration of the numerous other Buddhist sects in China, Korea, and Japan, to say nothing of Tibet and Mongolia, and their many effects upon Confucian, Taoist, and Shinto developments, must be neglected here. Ryubo Shinto, whereby all of the many Shinto deities came to be regarded as *bodhisattvas* or incarnations of the Buddha, has its own interesting and instructive lessons. The intermingling of Christian, Moslem, and Jewish peoples in China and Japan and the mutual influence of commerce, science, industry, travel, and Buddhist religions provide other facets of our vast and intricate subject. Although lack of translation leaves many corridors still closed, great halls of learning about Buddhism have been opened up for Western investigation, and many tantalizing insights into human nature and man's religions await whoever has the curiosity and courage to enter them.

Japanese religion, with which Americans have become more familiar than other Oriental religions as a result of contacts resulting from World War II, has indigenous roots in a typical animism. Japanese cultural history provides us with another clear example of how religious ideas evolve. One virtue of Shintoism for purposes of studying the evolution of religion may be found in that it still retains animistic and polytheistic elements as prominent features. In some respects, it has remained a more conservative religion, until recently; and thus in it we may observe how a relatively primitive polytheism may survive and adapt itself to contemporary society on a large scale.

Kami-No-Michi

The Japanese name for mana, invisible powers, spirits, or gods, is *"kami."* With great simplicity, early Japanese thought personified each observable cosmic function. The original significance of names that have come down to us through the sacred records, the *Kojiki* and *Nihongi*, may be lost or modified, especially in English translation. But the functional nature of deified powers should be clear from these names: Prince-Rock-Earth, Foam-Calm, Sky-Mirror, Bubble-Wave, Sky-Mist, Princess-Clay-Easy, River-Weed, Rock-Splitter, Dark-Water, Great-Thunder, Ugly-Females-of-the-Land-of-Night, Princess-Listen, Trouble-Master, Open-Mouth, Ocean-Bottom-Possessor, Great-Sky-Shiner, Brave-Swift-Impetuous-Male, Long-White-Leaf, Prince-Measure-Knowing, Great-Palace-Female, Wondrous-Shining-Jewel, Grand-Ears, Water-Sprinkler, Princess-Calm, Great-Stone, Sky-Deer, Princess-Fragrant. (*See* Post Wheeler, *The Sacred Scriptures of the Japanese*, N.Y.:

Henry Schuman, Inc., 1952, for details.) The profusion of nature powers has been woven into an episodic narrative of creation, both of the world in general and of particular things: "From the crown of her [Jewel-of-Storehouse–Rice] head, the ox and horse and the mulberry tree; from the top of her forehead, millet; from her eyebrows, silkworms; from her eyes, panic; from her nose, small beans; from her belly, rice; from her vagina, barley, wheat; from her buttocks, large beans." (*Ibid.*, p. 21.)

The story of the creation of man, taught with all seriousness to children during periods when national solidarity seemed to need officially inspired loyalty, is one of the most delightful myths that the mind of man has produced. Originally, sky and earth and male and female principles remained undifferentiated in the universe. Later, distinctions occurred: lighter, purer nature easily formed the sky, then the heavier, earthy natures merged with greater difficulty, and then from an extensive white cloud appearing between them, the *kami* emerged. First to appear was Mid-Sky-Master, which begat High-Producer and Divine-Producer, who together were called the Three-Creator-*Kami*. In the following imaginative stages of divine lineage, two deities stand out as having special importance. They are Izanagi (He-Who-Invites) and Izanami (She-Who-Invites), male and female principles. They descended from the white cloud, "the floating bridge of heaven," to an island that came into existence as they descended. Here they presented the islands of Japan with a complete pantheon of deities, including the gods of earth, water, plains, mountains, trees, food, fire, etc. When the fire god was born, his mother, Izanami, lost her life and went down into the underworld, the land of Yomi. Izanagi followed her but, against her warning, he lighted a torch to see. She became angry that he should behold her in such loathsome corruption, so she and other hideous females chased him. By hard running he escaped and barred the exit. The things that he threw away in flight turned into gods, including the water in which he washed off the dirt of the underworld. He retired to an island to play no further part in creation.

Skipping details of the births of the various *kami*, we come to a story of the birth of the sun and moon. When Izanagi returned from the underworld and washed himself, from the water of his left eye sprang Amaterasu, the Sun Goddess; from the water of his right eye sprang Tsuki-Yomi, the Moon God; and from the washing of his nose sprang Susanowo, intended as god of the sea and storms, who asked for and obtained rulership over the empire of the dead. Susanowo, before descending to his underworld, paid a visit to his sister in the heavens. By crunching jewels, swords, etc., and blowing out fragments, he produced a number of children to whom various noble families trace their lineage. He then went on a rampage, ripping up his sister's rice fields, tossing manure on her banquet table, and throwing a rotting carcass on clothes she was weaving for deities. Outraged by her brother's conduct, Amaterasu shut herself in a cave, leaving the world in utter darkness. The gods, needing her light, resorted to various devices to entice her from the cave, without avail, until someone did an obscene dance that caused inextinguishable laughter. When, out of curiosity, Amaterasu opened the door halfway, the god Stronghand seized her and pulled her out. An erected barrier, preventing her from going more than halfway back in, seems to have provided a mythical explanation for day and night.

Susanowo was punished by a council of the gods and banished to his underworld. On his way, he visited Korea and Idzumo, slaying a dragon and rescuing a distressed maiden. Susanowo's son, Ohonamochi, became ruler of Idzumo; but because he followed his fathers advice to destroy his eighty bad brothers, he was dethroned. Then Ninigi, grandson of Amaterasu, received from her a commission to rule the world, with a promise of eternal duration for his dynasty. Japan has, in fact, been ruled by a single dynasty from the beginning of its recorded history until the present. Ninigi descended not on Idzumo but on Kyushu, from whence Jimmu Tenno, his son, the first human emperor, set forth to conquer central Japan. He established his capital in Yamato in 660 B.C., according to the records, though recent scholars have become inclined to place the date at a later time. The first of several generations of gods receive no overt homage in developed religious practices but serve primarily to provide a respectable pedigree for the Sun Goddess, the unbroken line of emperors and the royal or divine natures of not only the leading families but of all the Japanese people, as well as the land, majestic mountains, vast oceans, beautiful landscapes, and fertile fields.

State Shinto

The amazing complexities of Shinto deities become manageable only if we follow a now customary practice of distinguishing between State Shinto, Domestic Shinto, and Sect Shinto. Although the myth of creation is needed by all who wonder about the origins of life and the universe, it serves especially to provide support for the ruling dynasty that has governed Japan since early times. In some respects, the Japanese regard themselves as a huge national family all of whom can appreciate their divine ancestry as descendants from Amaterasu and Susanowo or other procreating deities. Recognition and celebration of such divine origins continues in one hundred thousand nationalized shrines, with ceremonies conducted by about ten thousand government-appointed priests. Japan's first major military defeat in World War II shocked the prevailing belief in divine invincibility of the Japanese people and their hitherto unconquered emperors. But restricted political power, rather than humiliating deposition, of the emperor has served to maintain Japanese morale and to continue, even if in modified form, a grand cultural tradition. Facile judgments about destroying Shintoism as a religion must be countered by an awareness of the facts of the intricate and specialized divisions of various religious functions. State Shinto priests do not, for example, perform marriage ceremonies. Their functions remain more like those of persons who officiate at American celebrations of George Washington's birthday, together with flag-saluting and allegiance-pledging ceremonies. Because American political origins are so recent, they lack long traditions of entrenched beliefs in the semidivine nature of political leaders, though national celebrations do not lack "in God we trust" features. Other aspects of men's religious needs are cared for through different religious customs and institutions. But before we look into these, let us glance at some outstanding features of State Shinto.

Most honored of all the Shinto shrines is that at Ise. It

enshrines the Grand Goddess Amaterasu, regarded not only as the greatest ancestress but also as the Almighty of Japan. She is described as that divine virtue which consists of peace, love, purity, righteousness, and generosity. Although once housed in the emperor's palace and worshipped by the emperor himself, she was moved to her own shrine at Ise. A special princess, assisted by seventy-three priests, is appointed to preside over daily services, though on the occasions of the great festivals in February, June, October, and December, the emperor sends a special messenger to Ise to offer prayers and invocations for national peace and popular welfare. The Harvest-Praying Services, the Rice-Plants-Transplanting Ceremonies, and the Divine-Tasting-of-New-Rice Services included in the great festivals are reminders of how dependent man is upon nature. The inner shrine is itself a simple building, a testimony to its antiquity, which has been ceremonially rebuilt with great precision every twenty years. It houses a mirror, a sword, and some jewels—sacred symbols of the Sun-Goddess. Entrance to this, as to all shrines, is through a *torii*, a sacred gateway supposed to represent a gate upon which a cock crew on the occasion when the Sun Goddess emerged from the rock cave and relighted the world.

Buddhism, which came to Japan in 552 A.D., influenced Shinto in many ways. First, the awareness of differences between Shinto and Buddhism aroused concern for studying the nature and history of Shinto and was probably partly responsible for the work leading to the writing of the *Kojiki* and *Nihongi*. The very name, "Shinto" (or *"Shen-tao"*), came into being in order to help distinguish *Kami-no-michi*, the Japanese Way of the Gods, from "Butsudo" (*"Buddha-tao"*), the Way of the Buddha. The coexistence of a growing interest in foreign *bodhisattvas* with the indigenous national family *kami* was an uneasy one. The new ideas, psychological insights, ancient literature, belief in afterlife, law of *karma*, and modes of worship stimulated interest partly because they had a broadening and enriching character. Yet, as devotion to *bodhisattvas* competed with reverence for Shinto deities, concern about conflicting tendencies was natural. Singular events foreshadowing amalgamation occurred in 715, when a Buddhist temple was annexed to a Shinto shrine, and in 750, when the

Shinto god of war was brought to pay his respects at a Buddhist temple where he then remained as a guardian in a specially constructed shrine. In 735, a desperate emperor, seeking to forestall further ravages of a smallpox epidemic, erected a colossal statue of the Buddha at Nara; the Buddhist patriarch, Gyogi, sent to Ise to request blessing for the project, received a favorable oracle, and the emperor himself dreamed that the Sun Goddess declared herself identical with Vairochana, the Great Mahayana Buddha. In 806, Kobo Daishi, a famous Buddhist priest, declared that all of the various aboriginal *kami* of Japan were really *bodhisattvas*. Henceforth, the common man was enabled to consider himself a Buddhist and a Shintoist at the same time. Although not all chose to do so, allegiance to Ryobu Shinto, the Twofold Way of the Gods, became common. In this way, Buddhism came to supplement, rather than merely compete with, State Shinto. And some Shinto shrines acquired statues of Buddha and *bodhisattvas*.

Still another striking development has taken place. Confronted not merely with political, commercial, and military challenges to traditional belief in invincibility but also with foreign (European, Hindu, and Chinese) metaphysical systems having superior profundity, complexity, and apparent adequacy in satisfying man's intellectual curiosity about the ultimate nature of things, Shinto thinkers have developed ideas that some call "Neo-Shintoism." Disturbed by an apparent lack of any unitary cosmic principle encompassing and explaining the profusion of deities, these thinkers recalled that the myth of creation began with the appearance of the Mid-Sky-Master, which was the source from which all the other deities sprang. The Neo-Shintoists then proceeded to declare that this deity was really the same as the god recognized as supreme by the other great religions, *i.e.*, as Jehovah (Yahweh), God, Brahman, Buddha, and Tao. So Japanese religion was in line with, or rather ahead of, other religions right from its beginning. The original Shinto deity was asserted to be not only the animating principle in all life but also the power that motivated Buddha, Lao-tzu, Confucius, and Jesus to become missionaries, even though they may not have been clearly aware of the Shinto origins of their missions. Thus Neo-Shintoists opened the way for Shinto to become a world religion, one to which anyone might adhere because it open-mindedly incorporated all good and powerful persons and movements as manifestations of the ultimate cosmic unity.

However, nationalistic fervor induced some of them to go on to proclaim Shintoism the most superior form of world religion, since its ruling dynasty had remained both unbroken from the beginning and undefeated militarily, and to declare the Japanese emperor the living will of the Spirit-Behind-the-Universe. The World War II military defeat blunted this movement, but postwar apologists have revived and extended it. Chikao Fujisawa, in his *Japanese Global Philosophy: Kotonarism,* (Tokyo: 1954, p. 2), says: "We Japanese feel called upon to reintegrate all sectarian religions into one global philosophical faith which ought to be embraced by all mankind." The cosmic basis, "the everlasting center of the Cosmos, which exhales differentiatingly and inhales unifyingly," continues to be represented through personification in the emperor. (*Ibid.,* p. iv.) Shinto is "the Way of the one and the many Gods, instead of 'the Way of the Gods'. . . . Its monotheistic phase is revealed unmistakably in the contractively all-unifying function displayed by the Heaven-Middle-Lord-Deity (Mid-Sky-Master), invisible and intangible, while its pantheistic phase is revealed in the expansively differentiating functions of a galaxy of eight million gods visibly peopling nature." (Fujisawa, *Concrete Universality of the Japanese Way of Thinking,* Tokyo: The Hokuseido Press, 1958, p. 50.) He goes on to argue that "it is from the family tree transplanted by the Japanese Storm God (brother of the Sun Goddess) that sprouted Abraham, Moses, Aaron, Isaiah, and Jesus." (*Ibid.,* p. 68.)

We must now pass on to the second major variety of Shinto, regretfully ignoring the contributions of Confucianism to Shinto ceremonialism, the naturalistic influence of Taoism on an already naturalistic religion, the contributions of Zen to Bushido, to the Samurai, and to *kamikaze* practices, and the significance of *hari-kari* in relation to State Shinto.

Domestic Shinto

Religious services in the homes of private families center about a *kami-dana* or god-shelf. This serves as an altar upon which memorial items are placed. A mirror symbolizing the Sun Goddess, a wooden tablet recording the name of an honored family ancestor, a paper tablet containing the name of an important local deity, or a statue of some family or national hero or deity may rest side by side. A sacred rope hangs above the altar. Those who visit the shrine at Ise receive a token that naturally occupies a place on this shelf. The goddess of rice for farmers and the god of the sea for sailors are likely to have a place, as are statues of Confucius and *bodhisattvas* for those interested in scholarship, moral wisdom, future life, or forgiveness by grace. Conscientious Shintoists perform rites daily before the high shelf, sometimes in a simple manner much as some Westerners bow their heads in silence before a meal, though often there are prayers and token food offerings.

On anniversaries and holidays, or during a family crisis, a more elaborate ceremony may include the lighting of lamps or tapers, the offering of sacred rice wine, the placing of flowers or sacred twigs, or a display of some precious object or symbol of honor or grief. Home funeral services are held before this altar, unless the family also has a separate Buddhist altar in another room. Buddhist priests are commonly called upon to conduct death rites if the family considers itself also Buddhist. Domestic Shinto merges with State Shinto to the extent that the traditional deities and perhaps some symbol of the emperor receive attention during the family services. It may be purely private, however, and serve only personal needs. In addition to family souvenirs and to symbols providing hope and supporting morale, yea-saying suggestions may be associated with the *kami* altar, such as a calendar containing a good thought for each day of the month. For example: "Treat today's dawn as if it were the dawn of a new year. All day, live today as if it were New Year's Day. When the sun goes down, appreciate this evening as if it were New Year's Eve. And when dawn breaks tomorrow, again treat it as if it were a New Year's Day."

Sect Shinto

In addition to the pervasive influence of State Shinto, which Japanese tend to participate in as citizens of a nation, and to the variable private practices of Domestic Shinto, beliefs about the nature of life and how it ought to be lived have gathered people into groups, large and small, to support practices peculiar to these beliefs. All remain more or less consistent with State and Domestic Shinto. Some sects are excessively nationalistic and some sect saints occupy central positions in *kami-dàna*. Japanese culture seems to encourage new ways of conceiving and pursuing religious interests. Multitudes of sects have arisen and flourished, even if most of them eventually died out. No less than one hundred and forty were registered in 1900. Thirteen such sects receiving official recognition between 1876 and 1908 have attained a stability that promises their continuance for some time. In 1959, these thirteen sects averaged five hundred thousand members each, the two smallest having over fifty thousand and the two largest having over two million members each. They may be classified roughly into five groups, which we will call "Pure Shinto Sects," "Confucian Sects," "Mountain Sects," "Purification Sects," and "Faith-Healing Sects."

(1) The three PURE SHINTO SECTS maintain, in different ways, worship of ancient and contemporary national deities, insisting that Shintoism is a religion in spite of legal measures to make State Shinto a national, as distinct from a religious, institution. Each sect was established as an independent organization and is privately supported, in contrast with State Shinto, which receives financial support from the national government. The first of these, *Shinto Kyo* (Shinto Sect), emphasizes three creating deities, shows how Shinto embodies the Truth, the Good, and the Beautiful without having a creed to recite, and devotes itself to numerous social-welfare activities. The second, *Shinri Kyo* (Divine Reason Sect), believes in "the limitless miraculous power of all the gods that dwell in heaven, in the indivisibility of the physical and spiritual worlds, in the laws inherent in nature, in the attainment of inner tranquility, in the inspiration of the divine spirit, and in the

merging through sincerity of human and divine sympathy."
(*Discipline*, Quoted by D. C. Holtom in *The National Faith
of Japan*, London: Kegan Paul, Trench, Trubner and Co.,
Ltd., 1938, p. 197.) The third, *Taishu Kyo* (Great Shrine
Sect), functions primarily as a family or regional sect dear
to those on Idzumo who trace their ancestry to the "Great
Land Master," one of the deities mentioned early in the
Nihongi, and who attach great importance to the ritual cor-
rectness of birth, marriage, and death ceremonies. Membership records show 574,520, and 205,254, and 2,297,216
followers for each of these sects, respectively (See *Year-
book of Japanese Religions*, 1959), a great decline from
figures reported two decades earlier.

(2) Two CONFUCIAN SECTS, recognizing the debt that
Shinto worship ceremonies owe to Confucian teachings,
openly appreciate the virtues of Confucian doctrines in
stabilizing Japanese society. Although Confucius was a
foreigner in the Shinto scheme of things and thus rejected
by many extreme nationalists, these two sects see no inconsistency in recognizing Confucius as a great moral teacher
since he made no claim to divinity that a Shintoist could
find objectionable. Confucian ideals of "filial piety" and
"ancestor worship" were indeed followed by Shintoists and
his formulation of these ideals provided a precision that
proved useful when adopted in Japan. The first sect, *Shusei
Ha* (Improving and Consolidating Branch), highly reveres
the activities of Izanagi and Izanami, the male and female
creating deities who mold the habitable universe for our
benefit, and sees in such activities a divine example that
men should emulate in conducting the affairs of their families and societies. The Japanese words meaning "improving," "consolidating," "glorious," and "radiant," chanted
repetitiously, help to promote inner tranquility. The second
sect, *Taisei Kyo* (Great Achievement Sect), eclectically
embraces Shinto *kami*, Confucian ethics, Buddhist tranquility, contemporary science, industry, and business, and
royal ceremonial rituals. In 1959, Shusei had 54,080 and
Taisei had 59,900 members.

(3) MOUNTAIN SECTS make mountain climbing a part of
their devotions. They combine both healthful exercise, adventure, appreciation of the grandeur of nature, and fellowship in groups during ascents, on the one hand, with

worshipful remembrance that the gods first descended upon the mountains and that the mountains remain the home of the gods. Shrines constructed at the top of a mountain or at the bottom of an impressive waterfall provide places for special ceremonies. Many groups have been organized around specific mountains or mountain shrines, but three have become prominent enough to receive official recognition. Two of them, *Jikko Kyo* (Practical Conduct Sect) and *Fuso Kyo* (Sacred Guardian Sect), make Mount Fuji the central object of their worship. Not only do they climb it, but they adore it, write poems about it, paint it, and believe it to embody "the soul of the earth." Ideals of conserving natural resources combine with preserving the divine heritage enjoyed by the Japanese as a people. The third, *Ontake Kyo* or *Mitake Kyo* (Great Mountain Sect), makes Mount Ontake its venerated peak. Current membership: Jikko, 194,852; Fuso, 216,095; Ontake, 425,254.

(4) PURIFICATION SECTS believe that people, although naturally good, have become infected by physical and spiritual diseases that must be eradicated in order to regain health, happiness, and morale. Elimination requires specific attention to the problem and to both physical and mental activity. Appropriate rituals appealing for aid from the original Shinto deities are necessary. Two sects have attained prominence. The first, *Shinshu Kyo* (Divine Learning Sect), depends on the heritage of the Nakatomi family, appeals to departed emperors as well as to the originating deities, and prescribes both preventive techniques (food tabus, fasting for the body, and antistagnation efforts for the spirit) and expurgation techniques (fire-and-water ordeals for the body and recitational discipline for the spirit). Its fire-and-water rites will interest many. On April 9 and September 17 each year, a "fire-walking" or "fire-subdual" ceremony takes place; it involves controlling a hot fire so that it will not burn and enduring extreme heat on the feet. On June 30 and December 9 of each year, a hot-water ceremony occurs in which boiling water is sprinkled on the body as a means of eliminating evil. Cold water also is used for cleansing. The second, *Misogi Kyo* (Purification Sect), drawing upon traditions of the Shirakawa family, includes deep breathing among its cere-

monial methods. Recent statistics give Shinshu 559,108 members and Misogi 107,818 members.

(5) Three FAITH-HEALING SECTS, *Kurozumi Kyo, Konko Kyo,* and *Tenri Kyo,* report, respectively, 751,770; 619,126; and 2,047,720 members, thus constituting three of the four largest sects. *Kurozumi Kyo,* named after its founder, Kurozumi Munetada, priest of the Fujiwara family, who himself long sought to become a *kami,* subscribes to a kind of pantheism with the Sun Goddess as the supreme spirit of the universe. Munetada's personal experience of becoming a *kami,* not by ritual magic but by direct communication with an unseen power, shows the way for all to enjoy assurance of personal divinity, if they achieve moral excellence and mystical identity with the Sun Goddess. Not only man and God but man and man share immortality, so we may enjoy divine society as well as divine being. Maintenance of sincere attitudes and cultivation of feelings of joy are conducive to a mystical union with the ultimate, but methods may include incantations, massage, drinking and squirting holy water, use of written charms, and other animistic practices. However, social-welfare efforts, public lectures, and education have gradually replaced the more primitive methods.

Konko Kyo (Glorious Unity Sect), stems from the personal experiences of Kawate Bunjiro, an Okayama Prefecture peasant, whose healing experience led to a vision of the God who provides and sustains unity of heaven and earth. One hundred and eighty-two statements by this unlettered saint constitute the entire sacred literature of his sect. Sample: "God is the Great Parent of your real self. Faith is just like filial obedience to your parents. Free yourself from doubt. Open and behold the great broad Way of Truth. You will find your life quickened in the midst of the goodness of God. . . . God has no voice and his form is unseen. If you start to doubt then there is no end to doubt. . . . In all the world there is no such thing as a stranger." (Quoted in D. C. Holtom, *The National Faith of Japan,* London: Kegan Paul, Trench, Trubner and Co., Ltd., 1938, p. 262.) Although the term, *"Konko"* (variously translated as "Metallic Luster," "Golden Light," or "Glorious Unity"), does not appear on the original list of Shinto deities, its ideas do not conflict with, but maintain, even if in a modified and more unified form, the spirit of Shinto nature worship.

Tenri Kyo, which Westerners call "the Christian Science of Japan" because it was founded by Miki Nakayama, a woman born twenty-three years before the birth of Mary Baker Eddy, is the most vigorous of the faith-healing sects. On December 12, 1838, after an illness and prolonged trance, Miki felt the voice of God speaking through her: "I am the Creator, the true and real God. I have the Preordination for this Residence. At this time I have appeared in this world in person to save all mankind. I ask you to let Me have your Miki as My living Temple." (*The Short History of Tenrikyo,* Nara (Japan): The Headquarters of Tenrikyo Church, 1956, p. 3.) "To Me you are all My children; therefore I am burning with desire to help you." (*Ibid.,* p. 10.) "Though I help you, worship Me not by formulas, by kowtowing or by conjuring oracles as if I were a vain God." (*Ibid.,* p. 7.) But "I am going to initiate a 'service', the like of which has never been known since the Creation." (*Ibid.,* p. 10.) This service reenacts the creation of the world and men as an act of grace, which act serves as a model for all men to emulate. When people join in performing this service together, each one becoming joyous and merging with others within the divine heart of God, fear, antipathy, and disease disappear. Through Miki, God speaks of his "daily insistence that you should lead a joyous life." (*Ibid.,* p. 11.) So, "Let each day see you anxious to begin the service, since it will protect you from all sorts of calamities. Even a serious disease will certainly be cured by the sincere performance of it." (*Ibid.,* p. 12.)

part iii

Religions of Western Civilization

Chapter 11 Judaism

Western religions originated in animistic beliefs that received their earliest major developments in the Mesopotamian (Tigris and Euphrates) and Egyptian (Nile) valleys. Abraham (1900 B.C.?), the first significant person whose life prominently determined the course of events, once lived in Ur of the Chaldees near the mouth of the Euphrates River, and migrated to Haran near its headwaters, before wandering down the Mediterranean coast into Egypt. His nomadic life compelled him to move about from place to place in search of food. At each encampment he pitched his goatskin tents while he pastured his flocks. The exhaustion of food, water, or grass in one locality forced him to move on again. The sources of food and water necessary to life were regarded as powers highly valued or "worshipped" for their life-giving qualities. Thus springs and rivers were important, as were mountains, in which rivers usually originated.

One general name for these nature powers in Semitic languages is *"el"* (*"al," "il," "ol," "ul"*). Animistic powers may be referred to as "el," and both persons and places believed to be loci of powers were naturally called by the names of those powers. In fact the names of persons, then and now, derive from a person's being given the name of the place, and of its power, where he was born. One born in Dan, who takes the god of Dan as his own, becomes "Dan-i-el," meaning "Dan is my god" or "Dan is the source of my power." Similarly with Samuel, Manuel, Gabriel, Michael, Immanuel, Lemuel, Gamaliel, Ezekiel, Israel, Bethel, Jezebel. "El" may appear at the beginning of a name, as in Elizabeth, Elijah, Elias, Elihu, Elisha, Elam, etc. When names become compounded, "el" may appear in the middle, as in Jerusalem. "El" may persist in a name, such as "El Amarna" or "El Gizeh," to emphasize the importance of being aware of its existence as a distinct power. When the grammars for Romance languages were formulated, "el" became the definite article designating each power or entity.

Abraham

Abraham, while living in Haran, adopted the god of an impressive mountain, Mount Shaddai, hence called "El Shaddai," as his protecting deity. Looking for greener pastures, he went, even advised by El Shaddai, southward, settling on the outskirts of Canaan. When his wife, Sarah, bore him no child, he took an Egyptian handmaiden, thereby associating himself with Egyptian culture. Later, when he was a hundred years old, Sarah finally bore him a son, Isaac. When Isaac was old enough to marry, he sent back to Mesopotamia for a wife. Thus Abraham himself embodied in his own life the cultural influences from both ends of the "Fertile Crescent," the land between the Mesopotamian and Nile valleys. Egyptian influence was destined to increase, for when a terrible famine arose in Canaan, Abraham's descendants went into Egypt. They fared about as well as could be expected in a land where they had not been invited. Some (*e.g.,* Joseph, who had been sold by his brothers into Egyptian slavery) became officials in the Egyptian government. When Rameses II became Pharaoh, needing a large supply of free labor for his gigantic building program, he enslaved the Jews, forcing them to work under the lash. However, they must have prospered, for Pharaoh, becoming afraid of their growing numbers, commanded every male baby to be slain. During this period, Moses was born.

Enslavement of the Jews had theological significance. It meant that the Egyptians and their gods were more powerful than the Jews and their god or gods. El Shaddai, in whom Abraham had placed so much confidence, apparently either was no longer protecting the children of Abraham (how could he when the mountain where he dwelt was so far away?) or was not powerful enough to protect them here. The secret of success in those days was to gain an alliance with a more powerful deity. If you could get greater power on your side, or if you could get on the side of a greater power, your success was assured. Thus the superiority of the Pharaoh was regarded as evidence that he had a more powerful protecting deity than the Jews.

Moses

Moses, being born at a time when the Pharaoh decreed death to every Jewish male baby, survived because his mother, knowing he was to be killed, hid him among bulrushes along the river where the queen bathed. When the queen saw him, she was so taken with him that she kept him, even employing Moses' own mother to care for him. Moses obviously "had something" that other Jewish babies did not have. He was able to survive when they were slain. Even from birth, his followers could later say, he had superior mana, a power that circumvented the will of the powerful Pharaoh. Naturally, then, he was one who might well challenge the Pharaoh.

One day, after Moses had grown to manhood, he saw an Egyptian beating a Hebrew. Becoming enraged, he killed the Egyptian. Then, finding that his deed was known, he fled eastward beyond the Red Sea. He entered the land of Midian where he befriended and protected the daughters of Jethro, a Midianite priest, who finally gave him a daughter in marriage. Here Moses made acquaintance with the local deities as he adapted himself to the Midianite way of life. While Moses tended flocks about the base of Mount Sinai, he became impressed with the god of this mountain. Apparently it was a volcanic mountain, with flames belching forth from time to time. Its thundering voice shouted its tremendous power. As Moses grew to feel more at home with this mountain-fire god in whose shade he prospered, he began to wonder about the plight of his people in Egypt, and whether here might be a god who could overcome the god of the Pharaoh. Moses rose to the idea. But he was troubled by a little problem. His people in Egypt had never heard about, or had forgotten about, this mountain god, who apparently was called "Yahweh." ("Yahweh," translated into English via New Latin as "Jehovah," contains a stem, "Ya" or "Yah." This stem appears also as Ja, Jah, or Yo, Jo, Yu, Ju, Yi, Ji, Ye,

Je, which is common in Semitic and even Indo-European languages. It continues as a god-name in "John," "James," "Joseph," "Jesus," "Jude," "Judah, "Jacob," "Jonah." It is often combined with "el," as "Joel" or as "Elijah" or "Ysrael," *i.e.,* "Israel." It often occurs at the end of a name as "Iah," as in "Isaiah," "Jeremiah," or "Hezekiah.")

Moses was not even sure that this mountain god was Yahweh. So he asked the voice, "What is your name?" The answer recorded in ancient Hebrew apparently contains an ambiguity in tense that makes it possible to render it into English in several different ways. The King James version of the Bible reads: "I am that I am." I suspect that the Greek-influenced ideals of perfection, eternality, and timelessness had led to emphasizing the "isness" or being, as against the temporality, of God. Rabbi Max Leader of Albuquerque's B'nai Israel, in his television discussion "Rabbinic Judaism," translates Yahweh's self-description as "I shall be who I shall be," stressing future orientation as inherent in Yahweh's nature. I suspect that this interpretation more aptly captures both the common connotation of "Yah" as a stem signifying concern for an uncertain future and the spirit of urgency and ambition that has characterized the Jewish ethos throughout the centuries. Western civilization owes, I believe, much of its drive, optimism, and progressivism to its Jewish cultural ancestry.

Evidently Moses expected difficulty in converting the Jews to a new god. There was only one way to do this, namely, to prove that Yahweh was stronger than the god of the Pharaoh. Moses hurried to Egypt to win the Hebrews over to his plan. They were sceptical at first. Then he is supposed to have brought mysterious death to the firstborn of every Egyptian. This and other miracles gave the Jews confidence in him, and the Pharaoh, fearing his power, agreed to let them go. Moses led them safely across the Red Sea, out of bondage in Egypt, escaping a belated attack by Pharaoh's soldiers. This, and miraculous feeding in the desert wilderness, provided additional evidence that Moses had made a powerful alliance. He led his people to the foot of Mount Sinai, home of the god, which he climbed to talk things over with Yahweh. He had Yahweh announce to the people the conditions ("Ten Commandments") under which he would undertake to protect them. Then Moses went up again to obtain a contract ("The Covenant") carved in stone tablets and to hear many other laws that would be needed to guide the people, who were now on their own. According to this Covenant, which has played a most significant role in the history of Western religions, Yahweh was to protect the Hebrews and in return they were to serve him forever.

While Moses was up in the mountain conferring with Yahweh (for forty days and forty nights, according to the record), the people again became restless. Believing that both Moses and Yahweh had forgotten them, they called upon Aaron, their leader in Egypt, to make a golden calf, the symbol of nomadic prosperity and power, before they could proceed with confidence. Aaron gathered and melted enough bracelets and earrings to build a golden calf and prepared a festival to enkindle a spirit of power in it and a reverence for it. Just then Moses returned, rebuked them, destroyed the calf, restored confidence in Yahweh; but, in an initial tantrum, he dashed the tablets to pieces, saying the people were unworthy of such a Covenant if they could not keep it for even so short a time. Then Moses went back up into the mountain, apologized to Yahweh and came down again to lead his people in the direction of Canaan, "the promised land," which was part of the Covenant as the people understood it.

In a world where people were becoming increasingly agricultural, demand for land of one's own was great. The Jews had been nomads with no homeland of their own. They recalled that Abraham once lived on the outskirts of Canaan, but they remembered little of earlier history. Stories about Canaan were good; so they had hoped to return. Moses, in converting his people to Yahweh, obtained a pledge that Yahweh would help them to gain this land. Now it was quite a feat to wrest the land of Canaan from the Canaanites. The "promised land" was not to be a free gift. It had to be fought for; so, in effect, Yahweh promised to be a god of war, one who would lead his chosen people to victory over their enemies. As a god of war, he authorized the slaying of the enemy mercilessly.

This aspect has been dramatized by the battle of Jericho but there was also bloodless infiltration and intermarriage, to say nothing of earlier marriages of Abraham's offspring and progeny who never went to Egypt.

It is difficult for us in the twentieth century to grasp the nature of the agricultural ideas of the twelfth century B.C. Fertility depended upon powers capable of producing crops. Animistic thought conceives these powers as mana or, in Semitic terms, as els or baals. Each locality had its own host of local els, for obviously this plot of ground grows good wheat, but that plot does not. Some power, some el, causes the wheat to grow here, and some other, stronger el prevents it from growing there. Hence, if one is going to be a good farmer, he has to know where the crops will grow and where they will not. That is, he has to know what powers or els have control over this and that plot of ground. Now if the Canaanites knew where the crops would grow or how the baals functioned, then the Jews had to find out, if they were to be good farmers. The Jews had to placate them in just the same way that the Canaanites did. So, in inheriting the promised land, the Jews inherited the Canaanite baals. In conquering the promised land, the Jews and Yahweh conquered the Canaanite baals. In conquering them, they did not destroy them. They subordinated them. They put them to work for the Jews. All this was quite natural, and it worked well for a while. But as farmers devoted themselves more fully to their farming and their farm els, they progressively forgot about Yahweh, to whom they owed their release from bondage in Egypt, and about the terms of their Covenant with Yahweh.

When this fact was called to their attention, they were troubled. Or some of them were. Those who took the side of Yahweh were in a particularly dangerous position. In condemning the farm els, they were in effect condemning the very powers from which the farmers drew their food and clothing. They were, thus, disturbers of the peace. Their efforts, and apparent success at times, are dramatically symbolized by the story of Elijah on Mount Carmel. He challenged four hundred and fifty priests of baal to a contest in which each would try to demonstrate superior power for his deity by calling upon it to consume a bullock prepared for sacrifice. First to try were the priests of baal. They prayed and called to their god from morning until noon, but nothing happened. Then Elijah mocked them, suggesting that their gods were occupied elsewhere or were asleep and needed wakening. They cried louder and shouted still louder and danced about in frenzy, slashing themselves until blood gushed from their bodies, continuing this until evening, still without results. Then Elijah rebuilt the altar, prepared his bullock, poured water over the wood, and filled a trench about it. When Elijah prayed, flames burst forth and consumed the sodden wood and sacrifice and dried up the trench. The startled crowd, at Elijah's bidding, slew all the priests of baal. Again, Yahweh-worship was vindicated.

However, the farmers had to eat. If Yahweh could not provide them with food, they still had to deal with the baals in order to survive. The idea that Yahweh could provide food from the soil had to develop before Yahweh-worship was secure. Supporters of Yahweh were not willing to entertain this idea at first. This was not his function. This was not a part of his promise.

Nevertheless, the Jews prospered and eventually (a little before 1000 B.C.) established a kingdom controlling a vast territory. Kings Saul, David, and Solomon reigned independent during a period now called the "Golden Age" of Jewish history since, until very recently, it was practically the only time when the Jews had a land of their own. King Solomon, though not rich by contemporary standards, was very wealthy for his time. Yahweh had indeed fulfilled his promises. The promised land had been attained. Yahweh was indeed the god of the Jews.

Solomon's riches involved having many subject peoples under him. He owned many wives, a thousand, the record says. These were not all Jewish. Many were foreign, whether captives or gifts from other kings. He permitted many of these wives to worship their own gods. So the goddess Ashtoreth (Ishtar) of Sidon (formerly of Babylon), the god Chemoth of Moab, and Moloch were worshipped within his temple grounds. He contributed goods, which his wives sacrificed. He permitted images of these gods to be set up and their festivals to be celebrated. Hence we see henotheism, a tribal (Jewish) monotheism combined with recognition of many inferior and foreign gods. So firmly established was henotheism that we read in Micah the statement: "We will go in the name of our god and other nations in the names of their gods forever."

The fortunes of Yahweh suffered a setback at the hands of Rehoboam, son of Solomon, who, in order to magnify royal splendor, taxed the people heavily. When the people cried, "Your father's rule was heavy; lighten this crushing rule, and we will serve you," Rehoboam replied: "My father pressed you hard, but I will press you harder still; my father lashed you with scourges, but I will lash you with scorpions." Then the people revolted. When the king sent out his labor-gang boss, the people stoned him to death. Rehoboam fled. Then the people rallied about Jeroboam who had escaped to Egypt from Solomon's persecutions. Jeroboam was not a follower of Yahweh, but set up two golden calves for people to worship. The kingdom became divided into northern (Israel) and southern (Judah) parts. Their struggles with each other made them ripe for conquest. Heavy taxes reduced loyalty. In this moral and political mess, the fortunes of Yahweh dwindled considerably, while those of the various baals increased. It took the courageousness of the prophets to rescue Yahweh from oblivion. But they did much more than that, as we shall see.

The Prophets

Between the eighth and fourth centuries B.C., during the vassalages under Assyria, Babylonia, and Persia, a series of developments occurred that shaped the destiny of Western religion. Most of the numerous prophecies have been lost, for only those supporting Yahweh were preserved by Yahweh followers. All of these, on the one hand, proclaimed the same message: calling the people back to Yahweh. Repeatedly the people fell away. Most of them never did come back. On the other hand, the prophets lived at different times each with its peculiar problems and perspectives. Throughout the process, the ideas of the nature and functions of Yahweh became somewhat modified. A casual reader may not notice this. But once scholarship has pointed out the growth, anyone who reads can see it there.

This transition from henotheism to a universal ethical monotheism stands out as one of the most significant developments in Western religious history.

Elijah protested against regarding the ethical religion of Yahweh as just another variety of nature worship. Was Yahweh just another el, or baal, who happened to be stronger, or was he, as giver of the Decalogue, something more, something ethically superior? Of course, he was more powerful. The contest on Mount Carmel had demonstrated such power. But was this a temporary superiority? Many doubted. But Elijah's belief, which became recorded in scripture, had its long-range effect. His message was that Yahweh demanded not merely justice to Yahweh, but also that his followers treat each other justly. (Justice may not have been extended to enemies at this time; Yahweh was not always conceived as being just to enemies.) Another dramatic event emphasizes this demand. When King Ahab wanted Naboth's vineyard and Naboth refused to sell it to him, he became dejected. When Jezebel, his wife, saw this, she contrived to have Naboth killed. So Ahab got his vineyard. When Elijah heard of this crime, he presented Ahab with the facts in a clever fashion, giving as an illustration an unnamed man who had acted in this way. In the example, Ahab saw that the deed was wrong. When Elijah revealed that Ahab was himself this wrongdoer and that Yahweh's justice demands punishment for wrongdoing, Ahab was frightened into donning sackcloth and ashes. Why? Because Yahweh will bring his vengeance upon his people if they do not keep his commandments.

Amos, a country boy who came to the big city of Jerusalem and saw its ways, preached against laxity and corruption. He had visions foretelling another captivity and destruction of their cities. He detailed many ways in which Yahweh would send foes to punish Israel for their misdeeds. In the process, he implied that Yahweh had some power over the forces of nature as well as power over other nations. Yahweh is described as bringing a drouth, smiting fields with a blight of mildew, settling a cloud of locusts upon the land, slaying Jewish soldiers with an Egyptian plague, and sending a shattering earthquake. He even forms the mountains and creates the wind.

All this meant that Yahweh was much more than merely a tribal god of the Jews.

Hosea had married a woman who became unfaithful and left him. Yet, after years of infidelity, he took her back later in life. Hosea saw by analogy how Yahweh, who suffered from the unfaithfulness of his people, was still, in his mercy, willing to take them back. He makes Yahweh complain about Israel's lascivious whoring, describes Yahweh's patient scheming to buy her back when she becomes destitute and to allure her again as in her youthful days when she came out of Egypt's land. A remarkable twofold development occurs in the mind of Hosea about the nature and power of Yahweh. Through Hosea Yahweh says, "I will give her her vineyards from thence." Henceforth, Yahweh promises to provide the crops, grain, oil, and wine, so that no longer need Israel rely upon the baals. Even if the people did not immediately accept the view of a single prophet, embodiment of these ideas in Hosea's writings provided scriptural authority for later advances. The second development reemphasized unmistakably the conception of Yahweh as a god of love, a long-suffering, forgiving love. This view too played a more prominent role in later thinking.

Isaiah also preached a Day of Doom for Israel but believed that repeated purging was in the interest of spiritual betterment and that chastisement, punishment, and suffering were all part of a divine plan. Like Hosea, he believed that love and pity motivated Yahweh, not merely vengeance and justice. He promised that a remnant would remain faithful to Yahweh and that these would return to a condition of blessedness. He provided hope by predicting a messiah, thereby laying a basis in scripture for a new and powerful leader and for later Christian ideas of the coming, and second coming, of Christ as a messiah. Micah, who preached against the prophets of complacency who claim all is well as long as you have enough to eat, provided what some call a "spiritual definition of religion": "What does Yahweh demand of you but to be just and kind and to live in quiet fellowship with your God?" Or, perhaps more familiarly, "What does the Lord require of thee but to do justly and to love mercy and to walk humbly with thy God?" Like so many of the prophets, Micah was ahead of his time.

During a seventy-year silence of prophets after Micah, King Manassah led a movement back to a Canaanitish form of Yahweh-worship. As so often before and after, festivals, magical arts, household images, amulets, and sacrificial ceremonies had a strong pull on the people. Judah, a tribute-paying vassal of Assyria, found it expedient to erect shrines to Assyrian gods and goddesses. Manassah built altars to the sun and star gods of Babylon and Nineveh in the outer and inner courts of his temple. He supported altars to the various baals, and even sacrificed a son to Moloch in flames. Interest in Yahweh-worship almost died out again, and the preaching of the prophets seemed to have been in vain.

Then two things happened. First, the good King Josiah came to the throne. In repairing the temple, a high priest found a "previously unknown" book of the law. When Josiah heard its provisions, he called the people together and led them in a solemn oath to keep the statutes of its covenant. He then swept the temple clean of foreign gods and local baals. Yahweh-worship triumphed again. New ethical ideas were emphasized. Previously, ideals of strict justice—"an eye for an eye," "a tooth for a tooth," and "a son for a son"—had prevailed. Now, each should be put to death only for his own sin. If a son had not sinned, then the son should not die for his father's sin. Secondly, the prophets began to find their voices again.

Jeremiah foresaw the overthrow of the nation and preached against a futile war. He went, if not unheard, at least unheeded. He predicted slaughter, temple destruction, and captivity. Yet also, like Isaiah, he prophesied a return to better times. His most significant contribution was a new covenant to be made between Yahweh and each individual. Formerly, Yahweh's covenant was made by Moses with the Jewish people as a whole. Direct relationship between god and each person was largely missing. Jeremiah's Yahweh says: "I will put my law within them, and write it in their hearts." Although god-man relations were not worked out in detail, a start was made for a tendency that grew in magnitude later and that had far-reaching consequences.

As Yahweh became more directly related to each person, the significance of the temple as a place of group sacrifice and tribal worship declined. Also, the beginnings of a shift from a wholly external, vengeful, feared god toward an indwelling presence of a wholly compassionate divine spirit left scriptural traces that had tremendous effects upon later Jewish, Christian, and Moslem thought.

The destruction of Jerusalem came about because the Jews did not like paying tribute to Nebuchadnezzar. When they withheld taxes he crushed them again. After a third withholding, he decided to wipe them out completely. In 586 B.C., his armies destroyed the temple, ark, and city walls, and carried the upper classes off to Babylon. The Jewish empire was at an end. Yahweh-worship was ruined. Obviously the gods of Babylon were more powerful than the god of the Jews. This time Yahweh-worship should have disappeared forever.

But during the Babylonian exile, the captured Jews did not fare so badly. Nebuchadnezzar had no animosity for individual Jews but only against their organized nation. They were permitted to live together in a separate community with comparative freedom to follow their old ways of life and culture without disturbance. As a result, one of the most significant developments in Western religious history occurred: The synagogue was born. Since Christian churches grew out of synagogues, they too owe their origin to these Babylonian events. Jews gathered together in small groups on the Sabbath to read scriptures. Their interest in Yahweh was reawakened. But also Jewish scholarship received a great impetus. Whereas in Jerusalem people could participate in public temple ceremonies and sacrifices without being able to read, now they had to learn to read if they were to know about Yahweh. Scripture reading thus became a part of Sabbath religious services, a practice that obtains even today.

Still another significant effect of the Babylonian exile was the absorption of more Babylonian ideas. H. G. Wells, in his *Outline of History,* speaks for effect: "The Jews who returned, after an interval of more than two generations, to Jerusalem from Babylonia in the time of Cyrus were a very different people from the warring Baal worshippers and Jehovah worshippers, the sacrificers in the high places

and sacrificers at Jerusalem of the kingdoms of Israel and
Judah. The plain fact of the Bible narrative is that the
Jews went to Babylon barbarians and came back civilized.
They went a confused and divided multitude, with no sense
of national self-consciousness; they came back with an intense and exclusive national spirit. They went with no common literature generally known to them, for it was only
about forty years before the Captivity that King Josiah
is said to have discovered 'a book of the law' in the temple, and, besides that, there is not a hint in the record
of any reading óf books; and they returned with most of
their material for the Old Testament. It is manifest that,
relieved of their bickering and murderous kings, restrained
from politics, and in the intellectually stimulating atmosphere of that Babylonian world, the Jewish mind [and, I
might add, thus your mind and my mind] made a great
step forward during the Captivity. . . . The story of the Creation and the Flood, much of the story of Moses, much
of Samson, were probably incorporated from Babylonian
sources."

Charles Francis Potter, in another popular work *The
Story of Religion,* describes the debt of Judaism to Zoroaster: "A careful Bible student with any historical sense
is forced to recognize how very plainly the fact stands
out that the Hebrews borrowed the devil from the Zoroastrians. The Jews were taken into captivity in Babylon in
586 B.C., three years before Zoroaster's death. Before the
Captivity they had no devil in their theology. Fifty years
later Cyrus the Zoroastrian conquered the Babylonians
and restored the Jews to their homeland. For two centuries
they were ruled by Zoroastrian kings until the coming of
Alexander the Great. The theology of post-exilic Judaism
had a devil. Since the Zoroastrian religion of that time
strongly emphasized a chief among evil spirits called "The
Adversary," and since the post-exilic Jews called their
devil "Satan," which means "The Adversary," there can
be only one possible [?] inference. If anyone wishes to see
a literal verification of this, he has but to turn to the Bible
itself. In Second Samuel, the twenty-fourth chapter, written before the exile, you find the singular statement that
Jehovah moved David to number the people and then
punished the poor people for David's sin (!) by killing

seventy thousand of them with a pestilence. In First Chronicles, the twenty-first chapter, which is the later account of the same event written after their exile, it is Satan who suggests the census. Evidently the Jews had been somewhat troubled by the very obvious inconsistency of having Jehovah function as both the author of evil and its punisher, and welcomed the dualism of Zoroastrian theology which relieved Jehovah of such an embarrassing inconsistency."

Ezekiel, a prophet from a priestly family exiled in Babylon, dreamed of the return of the Jews and the restoration of their temple, and he so prohesied. He reminded the people of former days and stirred in them a desire to return. In doing so, however, he not only gave a new emphasis to individual responsibility in religious affairs but presented a more exalted conception of Yahweh as a sublimely transcendent and holy being, known to many nations.

Finally, Deutero-Isaiah brings prophetic evolution to its culmination. For Deutero-Isaiah, Yahweh is "the only God," "there is no other." His sphere of action is the whole world. He is everlasting and he alone created the heavens and earth, gave breath to peoples, controls all history, forms the light, produces the darkness, makes peace, and causes evil. He is the god of all mankind, gentiles as well as Jews, and he intends to save all. He needed a servant, someone to bear his message to all the people. Israel had been chosen, not to be recipients of unearned favors, but as servants of Yahweh. Their failure brought down his chastisement, but, being patient, he will try again. He will provide another messenger, or messiah, to lead his people.

The great significance of the Hebrew prophets for Western religions is their collective contribution to the development of Western monotheism. There is but one god, who is essentially an ethical being dealing ethically with men and expecting them to deal ethically with him. He also provides laws for men in their own interrelations and will reward or punish them for their virtues and transgressions. We fail to grasp the full import of the growth of Western monotheism if we neglect to realize how it also involved the evolution of ethical ideals. Four major early stages can be clearly outlined.

The first may be called THE ETHICS OF VENGEANCE. It

is illustrated by Lamech's boast (Genesis 4:23–24): "Adah and Zillah, hear my voice; ye wives of Lamech, hearken unto my speech; for I have slain a man for wounding me, and a young man for bruising me. If Cain shall be avenged sevenfold, truly Lamech seventy and sevenfold." The spirit of men in anger and of nations at war remains with us yet; but the ethics of vengeance prevailed unabated until some powerful parental law-giver could formulate and begin to enforce THE ETHICS OF JUSTICE. This second stage, embodied in the laws of Hammurabi and reflected in Hebrew ideas of Yahweh's demand for his people, may still seem crude by today's standards. Yet "an eye for an eye and a tooth for a tooth," demanding only one for one rather than seventy-seven for one, probably represents mankind's greatest forward step in ethics. This first step may well have been the hardest to take; indeed, not all of us have finished taking it. A third stage, idealizing JUSTICE TEMPERED WITH MERCY, replaces payment strictly in kind, *e.g.,* "a son for a son," with repayment in equivalent value, *e.g.,* "three cows for a son." Increase in wealth and the invention of coined money has facilitated the use of this kind of ethics. The fourth stage is THE ETHICS OF LOVE. Yahweh's own example of long-suffering love and his command (Leviticus 19:18), "Thou shalt love thy neighbor as thyself," illustrate this stage. Jesus, a Jew who "came to fulfil the Law and the prophets," repeats these ideals and extends them toward another extreme: forgive "seventy times seven." The ethics of love is not interested in justice but idealizes an obligation to give even when one does not receive.

These four stages receive expression in ideals of god-man relations also. At first, Yahweh was depicted as a god of vengeance. "Vengeance is mine, saith the Lord." In Samuel II, 24:15, Yahweh exacted not merely sevenfold or seventy-seven-fold but "seventy thousand men." Moses conceived Yahweh as just, as one who would protect his people if they would serve him according to their Covenant with him, and thus as one who would punish them if they failed, as well as help them when they continued to serve him. Hosea and Isaiah picture Yahweh as just but also as merciful, long-suffering, and forgiving, if man will but repent. Later, Jesus proclaimed that "God is love," and is one who, like a father, will forgive his children even when they do not ask to be forgiven. Furthermore, these stages may be found exemplified in man-God relations. In a spirit of vengeance, men sometimes curse God, and sometimes they say: "I'll be fair with God if God will be fair with me." Job (13:15) says of God: "Though he slay me, yet will I trust (love) him."

Rabbinic Judaism

The millenium from the fifth century B.C. to the fifth century A.D. seems to have been dominated by the rabbis or teachers. Ezra, the scribe, not only led more than a thousand Jews back to Jerusalem but also established a kind of theocratic system or priestly state. Sabbath observance, tithing, annual fasts and festivals, kosher dietary practices, and priestly enforcement of countless moral and religious laws became the rule, albeit with ups and downs. Scholarship prevailed and books were copied, revised, reorganized, and taught even in the villages. Whereas "The early Hebrews had created the Bible out of their lives; their descendants created their lives out of the Bible." (A. L. Sachar, *A History of the Jews,* N.Y.: Alfred Knopf, 1930, p. 88.)

When the Jews were dispersed from Jerusalem again, by the Romans in 70 A.D., rabbis fled elsewhere and continued their studies. Assembling from the Torah (written law, including the Pentateuch), Halakah (unwritten law), and Midrash (accumulated interpretations and opinions of rabbis) more than four thousand precepts applicable to current life, they organized an unbelievably complex and rambling literature into a manageable six-part Mishnah. Regulations for festivals, agricultural distribution, marriage, civil and criminal law, rituals and sacrifices, and purification procedures were spelled out in great detail. Meanwhile, Jews remaining in Babylon, enjoying a less hectic scholarly tradition, produced the Gemara, a combination of their own Halakah (studies of unwritten laws) and Haggadah (moral and religious lore). Later, the Palestinian Mishnah and the Babylonian Gemara were combined into the Talmud, a sixty-three–volume compendium brought to completion by the end of the fifth

century A.D. This has remained the core of Jewish interpretation ever since.

Jewish Philosophy

Although in a sense the Jews, like all men, have always
been philosophers, their primary preoccupation with practice has led to emphases upon moral, legal, and active religious philosophy. Rabbinic scholars tended to refrain
from metaphysical speculations about the nature of God
and the universe, even after proddings by Greek thinkers.
However, as early as 150 B.C. an attempt to harmonize
Jewish Biblical doctrines with ideals of Greek philosophers
was made by Aristobulus, a Jewish follower of Aristotle.
Philo (c.2 B.C.–50 A.D.), an Alexandrian Jew of a priestly
family, held that one and the same reason (Logos) inspired both Plato and the Prophets and, by allegorical
interpretations of the Jewish scriptures, "proved" that
Greek metaphysical principles and wisdom were already
implicit in what was meant by the stories of Adam, Eve,
Jacob, etc. Moses Maimonides (1135–1204) of Córdoba,
Spain, whence Jews had fled from Christian and Turkish
persecutions, profited from Arabic followers of Aristotle
and other Greek philosophers. Doubtless the greatest Jewish philosopher during the mediaeval period, Maimonides
not only influenced later Christian thinkers but bolstered
a tradition in Jewish thinking of respecting the wisdom of
philosophers.

Benedict Spinoza (1632–1677), a Dutch Jew, carried
rationalistic ideas originating in Greek thought further,
perhaps, than any other early modern philosopher, unless
it was Leibniz. Although a Jew, he was perhaps not "Jewish," since his philosophical ideas were so extremely rationalistic that he was expelled from his local synagogue as
"an atheist." Yet later historians eulogized him as "the
God-intoxicated man." God, Nature, Reason, and Substance were for him all identical, and the volitional side
of God and man, which played such an important role in
early Hebrew thought, seems completely subordinated to
the rational side. In my estimation, he "out-Greeked the
Greeks" in his idealization of reason. Thereby he ceased to
be "Jewish." The modern period has witnessed numerous

Jews who have pursued philosophy, but followers of Judaism will question whether they are giving expression to "Jewish philosophy."

Reform Judaism

However, within Judaism significant reforms have been under way. Although, in a sense, Jewish experience has always been involved in reform—whether the reforms of Moses or of the Prophets or of Ezra or of Zionism—partly because Jews have been subjected to so many varieties of cultural influence, the name "Reform Judaism" now applies to a recent and contemporary movement. Little more than a hundred years ago, when social upheavals were beginning to free Jews from ghetto life, within which orthodoxy prevailed, some rabbis sought to modify Jewish doctrines so as to adapt them to modern European conditions. Sabbath synagogue worship services were condensed, simplified, translated into the vernacular, and references to a coming Messiah, resurrection of the dead, restoration of a Jewish state, and ancient sacrificial ceremonies were omitted. An 1848 Declaration of German Jews boldly declared: "We recognize the possibility of unlimited development in the Mosaic religion. The collection of controversies, dissertations, and prescriptions commonly designated by the name Talmud possesses for us no authority either from the dogmatic or the practical standpoint. A Messiah who is to lead back the Israelites to the land of Palestine is neither expected nor desired by us; we know no fatherland except that to which we belong by birth or citizenship." (Quoted in David Philipson, *The Reform Movement in Judaism*, N.Y.: The Macmillan Co., 1931, p. 122.)

Although reform tendencies developed elsewhere in Europe, *e.g.*, England and Hungary, resistance and repression by Orthodox rabbis prevented great growth in the Reform movement until it took root in American soil. Rabbi Isaac M. Wise (1819–1900), great unifier and organizer, led developments through several conferences of American rabbis (*Ibid.*, Chapter XII) until, in 1872, the Union of American Hebrew Congregations was organized and, in 1875, was the Jewish Institute of Religion established in

Cincinnati. Reform synagogues dot the nation, with rabbis trained in the Reform college.

Rabbi David Shor of Albuquerque's Temple Albert has expressed the Reform attitude toward the Torah thus: "Reform Judaism looks upon it as a human document written by many men over a period of a thousand years. Orthodoxy itself has had to reinterpret it from time to time. Reform Judaism provides no blueprint for life after death. Belief in a specific Messiah who will lead Jews to dominance has been reinterpreted as hope for the coming of a Messianic age in which all men will enjoy peace and prosperity." Yet also, Rabbi Shor explained on another occasion, "A truly religious man can never know peace of mind in this world or the next. To be human is to be imperfect. Peace of mind (*i.e.*, perfect peace) is not possible for man. So the man who wants to be religious cannot have peace of mind, because social disturbances occur which demand his attention. He can be 'at peace,' but he cannot find 'peace of mind.' " We may observe here, as in early Judaism, an expectation, even an ideal, that is far removed from Hindu ideals of perfect peace. Jewish ideals may be more realistic than Hindu ideals so far as desires are concerned. Hindus idealize ultimate elimination of all desire, that source of all human evil, whereas Hebrews are concerned with a more desirable way of living. Hindu *Nirvana* is not pictured as a family affair, whereas Hebrew religious ideals remain essentially social, either familial, tribal, or universal. With the possible exception of Confucianism, no great religion has placed more emphasis upon the centrality of social life in its ultimate ideals than Judaism and its Christian and Moslem offshoots. The goal is to be "at peace" with others, including God, not "peace of mind" in which desires are eliminated and all problems have been permanently solved. Jews idealize life, not death. But Reform Judaism is not without its critics. (See Mordecai M. Kaplan's "Critique of the Reformist Version of Judaism" in his *Judaism as a Civilization,* N.Y.: Thomas Yoseloff, 1957.)

Jews in America today support three distinct religious organizations, though within each can be found members who lean in different directions. Orthodox Jews continue their ancient traditions only slightly modified by modern developments. Between Reform and Orthodox organizations is a group calling itself "Conservative." Orthodox Jews view Conservative Jews as pursuing a less radical variation of Reformism, whereas Reform Jews regard Conservatism as sticking too closely to now obsolete forms. But Conservative Judaism sees social and emotional values in retaining many of the traditional religious practices, values making for the solidarity, security, and persistence of the Jewish religion, which tend to become dissipated in more extreme Reformism.

We need not dwell here upon Zionism and the reestablishment of the state of Israel as a homeland of Jews. Facts about the struggles to establish it are widely known and it continues to remain near the center of the world political stage. Its rapid growth and promise of greater growth signify that the end of its struggles are not in sight. Not so well-known is the extent to which Orthodox ideas predominate in it and are being enforced with a strictness that appears tyrannical to moderates. American Jews continue to aid in its development and huge sums from private donations provide welcome support. More well-known in the United States, however, may be another aspect of Orthodoxy. A kind of left-wing Orthodoxy, called "Neo-Orthodoxy," has shaped up under the leadership of Martin Buber, Jewish Existentialist, whose writings include *I and Thou, Eclipse of God* and *Paths to Utopia.* The current popularity of Existentialism has led to curiosity about its varieties, and it may be that Buber's works now find more readers among non-Jews than among Jews. Whether such Neo-Orthodoxy is a permanent movement or a temporary fad remains to be seen. One Reform rabbi recently dismissed Jewish Existentialism as "the dying gasp of Neo-Orthodoxy."

Chapter 12 **Christianity**

The Teachings of Jesus

Christianity originated in the teachings of Jesus. His "Sermon on the Mount," "Lord's Prayer," and parables contain the essence of his wisdom. Many of the remarks attributed to him by various reporters, writing from memory or hearsay during the thirty to a hundred years after his death, continue to be a matter of debate. Some of his ideas seem intuitively clear to all. But many thoughts were expressed allegorically and so obscurely that even his immediate disciples could not comprehend their meaning until he explained it to them. Consequently, each expounder of the teachings of Jesus has tended to interpret them from his own perspective, and the interpretations of influential expounders have become a part of Christian doctrine. Each interpreter naturally attributes his view to Jesus. Those interpretations which were easier to comprehend or which better served the needs of listeners tended to gain prominence over those more difficult or less useful. Almost two millennia of such interpretation, some of it organized into institutionalized orthodoxy, leave most investigators lost in a jungle of views, unless their minds have been straitjacketed with a restricted literature. I propose to limit my remarks to quotations that appear to come most directly from the lips of Jesus and to point out three emphases in them that seem significant by way of contrast with other, including Oriental, views. These have to do with love, psychological principles, and concern with the present.

First we should note that, although Christianity originated, in a very fundamental sense, in the teachings of

Jesus, its orthodox versions involve, besides many later contributions, his Jewish heritage as well, as Jesus himself repeatedly asserted. How shall we treat the claim of some that he was so completely Jewish in his thinking that he expressed nothing that had not already been stated in earlier Hebrew scripture? He was born a Jew. Despite the report that he was conceived by a holy spirit, Matthew traces the lineage of his Jewish mother's husband, Joseph, back through the house of David to Adam. He was educated as a Jew and appeared early, at the age of twelve, to be something of a child prodigy in debating with temple priests in Jerusalem about the meaning of "the Law and the Prophets." He taught Jews almost exclusively, for his travels remained local and his hearers were limited to those who understood the Aramaic language. Once, when a Canaanite woman cried to him for help, "he answered and said, I am not sent but unto the lost sheep of the house of Israel." (Matthew 15:25.) He regarded himself as teaching a Jewish way of life, for repeatedly he remarked that he had come not to destroy, but to fulfill "the Law and the Prophets." His two-sentence summary of all the Commandments (Matthew 22:37–40), "Thou shalt love the Lord thy God with all thy heart, and with all thy soul, and with all thy mind" and "Thou shalt love thy neighbor as thyself," is a repetition of two sentences from the Torah (*i.e.,* Deuteronomy 6:5 and Leviticus 19:18). He accepted a kind of Messianic role to restore Jewish faith in God as he conceived him.

Yet something new, something fundamentally new, appeared in the teachings of Jesus. Granted, his ideas at first appear to differ only in degree from those of his Jewish predecessors, nevertheless sufficient difference in degree becomes, in effect, a difference in kind.

(1) The first difference centers in the concept of LOVE. The idea of Yahweh as a loving, forgiving, long-suffering father was not new. But Jesus "God *is* love" was new. The significance of the difference intended here may not be immediately obvious. Identification of God with love had the effect of tending to minimize, if not entirely exclude, two traits traditionally associated with the Hebrew Yahweh, namely, fear and justice. Earlier conceptions depict Yahweh as wrathful and vengeful—ideas, incidentally, re-

tained by Paul and carried on into orthodox Christian views. But in the mind of Jesus, "love casteth out fear," in men and in the nature of God. There is nothing in the nature of God as love that should cause us to fear God. Jesus commanded only that we "love God with all our heart, and soul, and mind." When we do, we have no room for fear. He spent most of his active ministry as a "healer of sick souls." By approaching those trembling with fear ("stricken with palsy") and managing to replace fear with confidence and love, he was able to restore them to sanity. By regaining faith in the power of love, they were "made whole again."

Demand for justice, also a traditional trait of Yahweh, disappears from Jesus' "Father." How did this happen? The ethics of love, which Jesus carried further than any other major religious leader, expressed itself in his advice to forgive "seventy times seven," to "turn the other cheek," to give, to him who asks for your coat, your cloak also, and to "love your enemies." Justice involves reciprocation, giving as you get and getting as you give. Moses' god was depicted as just, as one who would lead his people if they would serve him, but who would punish them if they failed to keep their Covenant with him. The prophets continued the idea that the sufferings of the Jews were the result of Yahweh's just punishment of them. But Jesus so magnified the power of love that justice was reduced to a subordinate role in God's nature. Whereas justice requires repayment of goods given, love gives without asking for anything in return.

The key image, available to everyone from his own personal experience (*i.e.,* that of parental love), may be examined for clues to the power of Jesus' thought and its practical success. A parent naturally loves his child. He tries to provide for his child's needs even when he knows that his child can never, and may never want to, give him anything in return. A mother who loves her child tends to forgive her child even when he hates her. Some say Jesus taught brotherly love. But brothers quarrel. Rather, he taught parental love. Parents love their children even when their children do not love them. The parable of the prodigal son illustrates how a father, first justly divided his wealth between two sons, one of whom took his share and squandered it while the other preserved and improved his family's wealth. When the wastrel returned, brotherly justice demanded his being cast out, but parental love welcomed him home with a feast and rejoicing. Luther A. Weigle (*The Training of Children in the Christian Family*, Philadelphia: The Pilgrim Press) cites a story (quoted in Ernest M. Ligon's excellent psychological study of the teachings of Jesus, *The Psychology of the Christian Personality*, N.Y.: The Macmillan Co., 1946, pp. 51–52) illustrating the power of parental love:

One morning when Bradley came down to breakfast he put on his mother's plate a little piece of paper neatly folded. His mother opened it. She could hardly believe it, but this is what Bradley had written:

Mother owes Bradley:

For running errands	$0.25
For being good	.10
For taking music lessons	.15
Extras	.05
Total	**$0.55**

His mother smiled, but did not say anything, and when lunch time came she placed the bill on Bradley's plate with fifty-five cents. Bradley's eyes fairly danced when he saw the money and thought his business ability had been quickly rewarded, but with the money there was another little bill, which read like this:

Bradley owes mother:

For being good	$0.00
For nursing him through his long illness with scarlet fever	.00
For clothes, shoes, gloves, playthings	.00
For all his meals and his beautiful room	.00
Total that Bradley owes mother	**$0.00**

Tears came into Bradley's eyes, and he put his arms around his mother's neck, put his little hand with the fifty-five cents in hers, and said, "Take the money all back, mamma, and let me love you and do things for nothing."

Love that gives everything without requiring anything is perfect love. "Be ye therefore perfect as your heavenly father is perfect" in love. Lest anyone should miss the idea that such love is parental, Jesus preferred the term "Heavenly Father" to "El" (God), "Adonoi" (Lord), or "Yahweh" (Jehovah). You may wonder why he did not prefer maternal to paternal love, since mothers usually seem more loving than fathers. The idea that god is masculine had already established itself in his patriarchal society and he accepted it. But distinctions between the sexes is of no consequence so far as conveying the idea that one who loves perfectly (expecting nothing in return) has lost interest in justice (expecting a fair return).

(2) Jesus, the psychiatrist ("healer of sick souls"), was concerned with "things of the spirit" and, no matter how much "those without ears could not hear" and interpreted what he said as having physical, metaphysical, and political reference, he nevertheless thought in terms of PSYCHOLOGICAL PRINCIPLES. These principles may all be found inherent in his ideal of parental love as having power to remove evil from the world. The Beatitudes, opening the Sermon on the Mount (Matthew 5:3–11), show how various ways of expressing love result in happiness: Those who remain humble even when their love is superior to that of others, mournful when they cannot give more to those whom they love, meek even in the face of angry attack, merciful even to those who deserve no mercy, peacemakers even when they have caused no trouble, all enjoy "the kingdom of heaven"—that spiritual realm in which love rules supreme.

The "kingdom of heaven" is neither a place in the sky nor a political empire, but an experience of bliss. "The kingdom of heaven is within you, and whoever shall know himself shall find it. Strive, therefore, to know yourselves and ye shall know that ye *are* the sons of the Father and ye shall know that ye *are in* the city of God and that *ye are* the city." (The Gospel of Thomas.) You do not have to compete with others for it. All that is needed to attain it is already within you. You do not have to wait until tomorrow, much less wait until a next life, in order to experience it. "The kingdom of heaven is at hand." (Matthew 10:7.) "Care not for the morrow." (Matthew 6:34.)

You do not attain it by making things or acquiring wealth. "Lay not up treasures upon earth..., but lay up for yourselves treasures in heaven." (Matthew 6:19–20.) But, if you do not already experience the happiness that comes from surrendering yourself to love (to the will of God who is love), then you must seek it. "Let not him who seeks cease till he find and when he finds, he shall be astonished; astonished he shall reach the kingdom, and having reached the kingdom, he shall find rest." (The Gospel of Thomas.)

(3) We have already expressed Jesus' emphasis upon APPRECIATION OF THE PRESENT rather than anxious concern for the future. The kingdom of heaven is already present unless we shut ourselves out of it by refusing to love. He rebuked those who thought they could attain happiness in the future only by acquiring wealth. "... take no thought for your life, what ye shall eat, or what ye shall drink; nor yet for your body, what ye shall put on. ...Who by taking thought can add one cubit to his stature?" (Matthew 6:25–27.) "Sufficient unto the day is the evil thereof." (Matthew 6:34.) When he was asked how to pray, Jesus did not speak either of future prosperity or of a future life. Rather, he took opportunity to stress the presence of life's ultimate values: "Give us *this day* our *daily bread.*" "For thine *is* the kingdom." Neither was Jesus greatly concerned about the past. The God of Abraham and of Moses, men now dead, was of little interest to him. "He is not the God of the dead, but of the living." (Matthew 22:32.) God is love and the power of such love in transforming our lives from tormenting fear into peace and confidence is something that can be directly experienced. One can be saved from the sins of hatred and fear by submitting willingly to the power of love, which will transform his life (give him a new birth) from hellish misery into heavenly bliss.

Jesus' religion is a religion of yea-saying, of saying "Yes" to love. God is love. So religion consists in saying "Yes" to God—not to a God of vengeance, not to a fearful God, not to a just God, one who demands justice, but to that God which is love and whose power is the power of love to overcome fear. His two commandments were: Love the lord thy God, or love Love, with all thy heart and mind and strength, and love thy neighbor (other lovers) as thyself. Whoever does this, his "*is* the kingdom of heaven." Whoever does this finds that he already has all other things needed to make him happy.

Jesus' message was simple, practical, workable for those willing to give it a fair trial, and unsurpassed in profundity of insight into human nature and its problems of how to overcome unhappiness. Yet, since desire, greed, pride, and fear also tend to dominate, and often succeed in dominating, human nature, we often remain blind to the nature and power of love. Those who marveled at his wisdom and his ability to cure psychological ills ("sick souls") found it easier to admire him as a miracle worker than as a teacher. Fear-oriented priests responded to reports of his miraculous feats with growing anxiety. Their natural reaction was to eliminate their fear by destroying his power through putting him to death. He appeared to be less concerned about them, however, than about his own disciples. For disciples he had sought unlettered men, "new bottles for his new wine": he had already given up trying to "pour new wine in old bottles." But when his own disciples seemed slow in grasping his message and embodying love (holy spirit) within themselves, as they needed to do if they were to become missionaries or "the light of the world," he suggested the analogy of a vine and its branches, conveying the idea that there was something continuous and unifying about love that dwells within each of us. To emphasize his ideals he spoke to them saying: "I [love] am the way and the truth and the life; no man cometh unto the Father [Love] but by me [love]." (John 14:6.) He was not particularly concerned about himself as a person, "the son of man," as he preferred to call himself. His messianic effort was directed toward helping us all to become sons of the Heavenly Father whose "kingdom of heaven" consists in all those whose lives embody that bliss which is mutual love.

If a lover willingly gives more than he gets, should the one loved be willing to receive more than he gives? Jesus was fully aware of the nature of the principle of reciprocity as something to be accepted. Indeed, he regarded it as almost synonymous with his two other commandments: "All things whatsoever you would that men should do to you,

do ye even so to them, for *this is* the law and the prophets."
(Matthew 7:12.) "Forgive us our debts as we forgive our
debtors." (Matthew 6:12.) Yet nowhere does he say that
we deserve love. We may receive love, but we should not
expect it as something deserved. "It is more blessed to give
than to receive." (Acts 20:35.) One is happier when he
loves than when he is loved. If "high" religion consists
in expecting no more than one deserves, is not Jesus' religion of love the highest when he views perfect love as a
willingness to give everything and receive nothing?

Paul

Paul was the "founder of Christianity," some say, for, although Christianity originated in the teachings of Jesus,
without Paul's tireless missionary efforts and extensive
travels the wisdom of Jesus might have passed into the
same oblivion that silenced the voices of multitudes of other
prophets. Furthermore, in the process, Paul's own ideas,
which differed somewhat from those of Jesus, became incorporated into scripture. More than one third of the New
Testament is devoted to the writings of Paul. Paul's teachings were often more influential that those of Jesus in shaping orthodox doctrine. The magnitude of Paul's contributions to Christian thought has suggested to some that it
might more appropriately be called "Paulianity" than
"Christianity."

Paul of Tarsus was not only a Jew of the "purest"
variety but also a Roman citizen. His birth in the "free"
(self-governing) city of Tarsus gave him rights to relatively unrestricted travel throughout the Roman empire in
a day of many enslavements and restrictions. Because
Tarsus was also a cosmopolitan center in which flourished
mystery religions and Stoic philosophy, Paul early became
acquainted with various notions of salvation and with the
Greek language, in which most of his letters were written.
He was well-educated, having studied in Jerusalem under
Gamaliel for fifteen years. He traveled widely, first as a
persecuter of Jesus' followers, and later as a missionary
spreading Jesus' ideals. Paul never met Jesus and appears
not to have been in Jerusalem during Jesus' lifetime. He

was converted during a trance while "on the road to Damascus."

Sources of Paul's ideas include Hebrew life and scriptures, the mystery cults, the teachings of Jesus, and his own personal experiences. Hebrew life he knew firsthand, at home, in Jerusalem, and in the Jewish communities to which he traveled. Having studied the scriptures for fifteen years, he was well acquainted with them. The mystery cults—such as those having Bacchus, Demeter, Orpheus, Cybele, and Attis, or Isis and Osiris, or Mythra as their deities—were widespread. Mythraism became Christianity's most serious competitor for a while; both included baptism, immortality, resurrections, a last judgment, a blissful heaven and a miserable hell, ethical rigor, a sacrificial person offered to god as atonement for sin; both organized into small secluded groups; and both observed Sundays and December 25 as great feast days. Paul employs the language of the mystery religions—"Washed in the blood of the lamb"—when interpreting the significance of Jesus to those familiar with mystery doctrines. Since he never met Jesus, his knowledge of his teachings was "second or third hand." His own experiences of the marvelous power flowing from Jesus' life and teachings were perhaps his most important sources. He realized that the followers of Jesus often acquired unusually great courage, which he himself witnessed, for example, at the stoning of Stephen. Resurrection stories testified to the persistence of Jesus' influence. Paul's own vision of Jesus on the road to Damascus and his own success in healing "in Jesus' name" produced his final convictions. His faith in the saving power of Jesus gave his life a new direction, a new significance, a new kind of influence that convinced him that he had found the true way.

Paul's ideals of God were typically Jewish, except for some modifications caused by the mystery cults and Jesus. God, creator of the world, is a person, loving and kind but also just, jealous, and wrathful, mysterious in his power and purposes and ways. God, having a stake in history, has intervened time after time. Finally, he sent Jesus as "the Messiah," not a political but a spiritual redeemer. Paul sometimes talks as if God created Christ and Christ created the world, and sometimes as if God were Christ or in Christ. Although Christ as the "Son of God" (Jesus referred to himself as the "son of man") is subordinate to God, yet Christ is most important because he personally sacrificed himself to save us, whereas God only sacrificed his Son as man. Although Jesus is a person, he is also more than human. He is the key figure in all history. Although absent, yet he is present, for "I live, and yet not I but Christ liveth in me." Paul did not always distinguish among God, Christ, and Spirit. Christ left us a comforter, a lesser divinity or divine power, which can guide us even if God or Christ is absent locally.

Man, created by God, fell by Adam's sin. The idea of "original sin," rejected by Jews and of no concern to Jesus, became a cardinal Christian doctrine due to Paul. Man, not merely each man, can be rescued from such original sin only by a tremendous act of grace by God, who, in sending his own Son as sacrifice, somehow propitiated his own demands that justice be done to recompense him for the injury to him because of man's sinning. Death on the Cross symbolized this sacrifice, proved God's grace, and paid the debt in full. "Jesus paid it all, now all to him I owe," explains a Paul-inspired hymn. All that any man needs in order to redeem himself is an act of faith and adoring service to Jesus. We too shall be resurrected and have immortal life, for if Christ cared enough for us to sacrifice himself on the Cross, he will not simply go off and let us perish. Did he not say "I go to prepare a place for you" and "I will come again"?

What will heaven be like? Paul's writings remain vague, except that in heaven we shall know each other and enjoy bliss. (Absence of any vivid description in Pauline scriptures led later to the addition of an independently written "Book of the Revelation of Saint John the Divine" depicting a city in the sky with golden streets and pearly gates.) Our immediate problem is to have faith in God's grace and power to redeem, to be zealous for a Second Coming of Christ, to pray without ceasing, to teach others, Jews first and then Greeks (circumcision becoming unnecessary to salvation). We should follow Jesus' commandments to love our neighbors as we do ourselves, shun idolatry, never to be conceited, never revenge ourselves. We should have "faith, hope and love, and the greatest of these is love." While waiting for the Second Coming, which Paul expected momentarily, we should distinguish between spirit and body and not yield to fleshly temptations. The celibate life is best, but it is better to marry than to burn. Women should have a subordinate place. We should obey governments because they are ordained by God. We should submit to persecution, but keep our courage up: "If God be for us, who can be against us?"

Although Paul believed that he voiced Jesus' teachings, careful study will reveal some differences, which have been minimized and, in effect, denied in the framing of orthodox Christian doctrines. (1) Jesus emphasized love as against fear, a love that destroys fear, whereas Paul appealed to both love and fear: Beware lest ye be not ready for the second coming. We continue "to stand in danger every hour." (I Corinthians 15:30.) He quotes with approval the warning: "Vengeance is mine, saith the Lord." For Jesus, "God is love," a perfect love in which no taint of vengefulness remains. (2) Jesus emphasized love as against justice: forgive seventy times seven. Paul retained both love and justice as traits of God: God also punishes. (3) Jesus taught self-confidence: "Thy faith hath made thee whole." Paul taught faith in "Christ and him crucified." (I Corinthians 2:2.) "And if there is no resurrection of the dead, then Christ also has not risen; and if Christ is not risen, then our preaching is in vain, and your faith is also in vain." (I Corinthians 15:13–14.) (4) Jesus taught that people are not really sinful, if their hearts are pure. Paul saw people as steeped in original sin, whether aware of it or not, and unworthy to be saved, and saved only by the grace of God, mysteriously and magically. (5) For Jesus, rebirth of self-confidence is possible only by love. For Paul, conversion requires conviction of sin, so fear is necessary to bring it about. (6) For Jesus, "the kingdom of heaven is within you." For Paul, "Behold, I tell you a mystery; we shall not all die, but we shall all be changed. In a moment, in the twinkling of an eye, at the last trumpet; for the trumpet shall sound, and the dead shall be raised incorruptible, and we shall be changed." (I Corinthians 15:51–52.)

The Patristics

The spread of Christianity and the founding of Christian churches in various cities around the eastern end of the Mediterranean Sea, including Corinth, Ephesus, Alexandria, and Rome, resulted in the formulation of the Nicene Creed at the Council of Nicaea in 325 A.D. During this period of three centuries, the early Church Fathers, called "Patristics" after the Latin term *pater* (father), faced many problems that had to be settled before Christianity became firmly established. We select from the rich record only three kinds of problems.

(1) When an essentially Jewish message was brought to Greeks, Romans, and Egyptians, ideas couched in Aramaic and Hebrew had to be translated into languages (*e.g.*, Greek, Latin, Arabic) formed around foreign ideologies. Paul wrote in Greek, thus easing the transition. But when the idea of Yahweh as creator of the world from nothing by an act of will was translated into the Greek as "Demiurgos," a subordinate deity who molded eternally existing matter after an eternally existing plan, transformations took place that created intellectual as well as scriptural problems. When John tried to express ideas about the divinity of Jesus by saying, "In the beginning was the Word, and the Word was with God, and the Word was God," he used the Greek term "Logos" (related to our English word "logic"), which hardly conveys much about Jesus' notion of himself and God as love. Consequently, conceptions quite different from what Jesus had in mind grew and became established in foreign churches as "Christianity." Once these foreign terms became part of the scriptures and were used in expounding Christian doctrine, then problems arose as to how to explain these new terms to Hebrew-speaking Christians. Greek philosophical concepts seeped into formulations of Christian doctrine that led, later, to pre-Christian Aristotle's being accepted by the Church as "the Philosopher" who provided a metaphysics lacking in Jewish-Christian history. "As Gentiles became Christian, Christianity became Gentile." (E. G. Bewkes and others, *Experience, Reason and Faith: A*

Survey in Philosophy and Religion, N.Y.: Harper and Brothers, 1940, p. 327.)

(2) Early Christians were persecuted as radicals, disturbers of the peace, and dangerous to the status quo. They were imprisoned, fed to lions in amphitheatres, forced to fight for their lives with gladiators. They hid in catacombs, traveled by night, and suffered from starvation when they escaped torture. However, the Emperor Constantine (274–337), fearing defeat in a crucial battle, promised he would be converted if the Christian God would bring him victory. He won, and after that Christians became political favorites, a fortune that, through the centuries, they magnified into an expansive Holy Roman Empire. However, sects developed in the different cities and provinces of the Empire and quarrels between them weakened it. Constantine, needing political solidarity in order to maintain his empire, demanded that the bishops leading the various sects get together to settle their differences. Thus issues concerning relations between Church and State contributed to the problem of attaining doctrinal uniformity. In the process of discussing doctrinal questions in councils of bishops, those ideas which were defeated were declared heresies, while those which won approval in the voting came to constitute orthodoxy.

(3) Of the many questions that had to be settled before Christian doctrine received its final shaping, we can here examine only a few. The records of these doctrinal debates constitute some of the most fascinating and enlightening literature in the history of Christendom. Unfortunately, little popular awareness of them exists. Nevertheless, many of the questions recur in the minds of each individual Christian, and, although we shall present views in relation to their Patristic defenders, most readers will already be familiar with the issues.

(a) When disagreements arose about the true doctrine, they could be settled convincingly only if there could first be agreement about reliable sources of knowledge about God, Christ, the Holy Spirit, and what these had said. Jesus, Paul, and many others experiencing redemptive grace had been inspired. Was the source of divine knowledge inner (revealed to each person by the

Holy Spirit in a mystical experience) or outer (revealed in scriptures that could be examined objectively and reasoned about)? The Christian experience, according to Paul, was essentially mystical. He himself had been converted in a trance. A redeemed person felt himself identical with Christ, or at least with the Holy Spirit. In experiencing such mystical identity, one had ideas, feelings, hopes, urges to express, insights to state. In this condition, one seems to have direct insight into the truth. But different mystics had different insights to report. Their disagreements produced conflict instead of peace. When converts sought insight, first from one and then from another, they received conflicting replies. This was confusing. Some were given to "speaking with tongues," an occurrence so common that Paul himself had admonished people not to do so in public. Do so privately, in small groups, so you will not appear ridiculous. Either explain what you are saying, or have someone else explain for you, or keep still. Although mystical experience, in which one intuitively apprehends a divine being, was essential to orthodoxy, mysticism (the use of mystical experience to learn true doctrine) was not. Such mysticism was declared heretical.

Thus orthodoxy leaned toward reason, especially in dealing with the Greeks, as against nonreason. But, despite this tendency, both the mystical experience of each Christian and the metaphysical doctrine of "The Trinity," which was declared "a mystery," prevented the Church from becoming completely rationalistic. In fact, the later rationalism of the Enlightenment was feared as an enemy of the Church. Thus, the orthodox view became one that rejected both mysticism and rationalism as adequate means to a knowledge of the divine.

(b) As time passed and more varieties of speculations on the nature of God, Christ, man, and the universe entered the minds of professing Christians, the issue of how to decide among them became more pressing. Christian Gnostics elaborated magnificent systems that went beyond scriptural warrant. This raised the issue of which scriptures can be relied upon. Marcion (c. 110–165), claiming Jesus had brought a new law, rejected Yahweh the old law-giver and all ancient Jewish scriptures, keeping only the gospel of Luke and the letters of Paul. Justin Martyr (c. 105–165) and other Apologists, on the other hand, approved Greek ideals, including the tenets of Socrates and Plato, as well as those of Moses and Isaiah. Irenaeus (c. 130–200), Bishop of Lyons, proposed a principle that finally won general acceptance. Those teachings which are in agreement with those of the Twelve Apostles should be accepted. Using this principle, the early Fathers were thus moved to adopt those scriptures which now constitute the Old and New Testaments of the Bible. Disputes did not end entirely, but major conflicts about which scriptures would be orthodox were largely quieted. Another result was agreement upon "The Apostle's Creed."

(c) However, given authoritative scriptures, conflicting interpretations of their meaning arose and continued, not merely during the first few centuries but throughout later history, contributing to schisms within the Church and to the proliferation of Protestant sects. Shall each individual reader or bishop be free to interpret as he chooses, or shall a proper reading be decided upon by a council of bishops? Council approval became orthodox, although then serious problems arose as to who were qualified to serve as council members and what to do in cases of close voting. Breaks between Greek and Roman Churches created two competing sets of councils. However, adoption of the council system did reduce disunity and established the principle that the council, which had decided upon which scriptures were to be included in the Bible in the first place, continued to be superior to those scriptures so far as deciding upon an authoritative doctrinal interpretation is concerned. The Papal announcement (November, 1950) of belief in the bodily ascent of Mary into heaven is a recent example of the continuing operation of this policy.

(d) One particularly troublesome set of doctrinal problems centered about questions of the sameness or difference, and equality or inequality, of God, Christ, and the Holy Spirit. Jesus had conceived God as a Heavenly Father and as love, but he left no metaphysics or theology. Paul had conceived God as creator, just, lov-

ing, and fearful, and as a Father; he conceived Christ as his Son; and he mentioned a Comforter or Holy Spirit. All were divine. But Paul, too, left no metaphysics or theology, no clear-cut definitions of relations among God, Christ, and the Holy Spirit. Increasingly people wanted to know, especially after becoming acquainted with theories of such relations in Greek thought. Was Jesus God? If so, did God die on the Cross? How could God die? Did God become incarnate in man? Only once or many times (as Hindus believe)? If Jesus was not God, how did he differ from God? Were there two Gods, God and Jesus? Were the two Gods equal, or was one subordinate? Jesus was the Son; God was the Father. Is the Son inferior to the Father? Is the Son separate from the Father? How closely are they related?

Arius (c. 256–336), a theologian in the Church in Alexandria, pursued monotheistic ideas in the tradition of Deutero-Isaiah, Jesus, and Paul. There is only one God. He could not have died on a cross. Hence, Jesus who died on the Cross was different from God, less perfect than God, created by God. Christ was the Logos of God that entered into the body of Jesus at his creation. Jesus did not exist before creation, but God did. Jesus was divine, however, because God's Logos was embodied in him. Yet, since Paul had held that Jesus is a savior God who is resurrected and with whom real union may take place when we are redeemed, Arius was condemned as a heretic for these views, though as a person he was readmitted into the Church.

But this did not settle the matter. If Jesus is God, in what sense is he God? Reason says that either you have one or two but not both one and two. Sabellius (fl. at end of 2nd century) proposed to solve the problem by conceiving God and Christ as consisting of a single substance with two coequal natures or "essences." But this view was regarded as heretical; how can a Son be coequal with his Father? The view that God was one substance with two unequal aspects or manifestations— God the Father as superior to God the Son—was passed over in favor of the view that God was one substance, superior to its two manifestations—namely, as Father and as Son—which were coequal.

How did the Holy Spirit fare in the foregoing controversies? Some regarded God, Christ, and the Holy Spirit as three different substances but debated whether they were equal in importance (a kind of tritheism) or unequal, with Christ subordinate to God and with the Holy Spirit subordinate to Christ, as in Arianism. Some preferred Sabellius' single substance with God, Christ, and the Holy Spirit as three coequal natures of the same substance; some accepted the idea of a single substance with three natures but saw the Christ-nature subordinate to the God-nature and the Holy-Spirit–nature subordinate to the Christ-nature. The view that finally won out was that held by Athanasius (c. 298–373). God is a single substance that has three manifestations or *hypostases*, a Greek term that was translated into Latin as *"personae"* and later into English as "persons." These are "God the Father," "God the Son," and "God the Holy Spirit." These three are equal, rather than the Holy Spirit's being subordinate to the Son and the Son to the Father. But all three are subordinate to "God." Hence, the final view, now called "Trinitarianism," retained both the coequality of the Father, Son, and Holy Spirit and the superiority of God to all three. But Trinitarianism was unreasonable. How can we have one God and three Gods at the same time? (Judaism and Islam have continued to reject Trinitarianism as pseudo monotheism.) The Church declared the doctrine of the Trinity a "mystery," true whether reasonable or not, and known through revelation in the scriptures already accepted as orthodox.

(e) Is God omnipotent and omniscient? If so, then is man free? Here is a problem that plagued not only the early Fathers but that still perplexes every Christian and every theist. Pelagius, a British monk who lived in Rome, accepted the common claim that God is absolutely perfect in power, knowledge, and goodness. If so, then God caused everything, including evil and sin. Hence, man is not to blame for sin, but God is. At least this conclusion seemed to follow logically from the assumptions. Such a God would have to be unjust, for he both causes man to sin and then punishes him for his sin. Pelagius rejected the conclusion that God caused

man to sin. Instead, he claimed that, since God is perfectly good, whatever he causes is good, so man is really good. Man has free will, and each man's sin is his own. But Pelagius' view was declared heretical because it contradicted the scriptural (Pauline) view of original sin. The orthodox view became one incorporating several doctrines: both that each man inherits original sin and that each man is responsible for his own sin; and both that God caused all and that God did not cause sin. Here again is a view not wholly clear to reason.

(f) Does the Devil share divine power? Reason was employed in trying to solve the problem of the existence of evil in the world in another way. If God is perfectly good, perhaps he is not perfect in power. Scriptures mention the Adversary, Satan, or Devil, who does have power. How powerful is he? Manichaeism, a Christian movement influenced by the Zoroastrian dualistic theology having a God of Light (and good) and a God of Darkness (and evil), pictured the world as consisting of two spheres of action and influence, the spiritual and the fleshly or material. The two Gods thus divide the world between them, the all-good God promoting spiritual welfare and the evil Devil ensnaring all he can in vice. Indeed, if the Battle of Armageddon, described in the book of The Revelation of St. John the Divine (16:16–21), is not a mere sham battle but a genuine violent encounter between the forces of good and evil, in which the forces of evil really threaten to win, then the scriptures themselves testify to the presence of a tremendous evil power that challenges the power of God. But since Manichaeism would have resulted in another kind of duotheism (not of God and Jesus, but of God and the Devil) and since it denied the accepted doctrine of the omnipotence of God, it too was declared heretical. The conclusion resulting from this debate established in the Christian doctrine still another paradox: God is all-powerful; the Devil limits that power.

(g) How is God related to the world and to men? Here arose another set of knotty problems as bothersome as those encountered in relating God, Christ, Holy Spirit, and Devil. The views of Origen (185–253), the most influential Christian philosopher before Augustine,

contributed much to the orthodox conclusion. Accepting Trinitarianism, in which Jesus and the Holy Spirit were conceived as coeternal with the Father in God, and thus as existing prior to the beginning of time, Origen concluded that the world and human souls also are coeternal with God because, if God is both creator and eternal, *i.e.*, eternally a creator, and if being a creator implies the being of a creation, then that which is eternally created is as necessary as that which is eternally a creator. Here Greek logic was at work, and the influence of Platonism exerted its full force. The problems involved here almost resulted in another scandal, which later received treatment in terms of the Aristotelian distinction between "potency" and "act." Souls, for Origen as for Plato, are eternal, existing before the beginning as well as after the end of time. They too are divine, even if having a lesser divinity than Father, Son, and Holy Spirit. The orthodox solution was reached by differentiating degrees of emanation in God: The Son is "begotten," not "made." The Holy Spirit "proceeds," but is not "begotten" and not "made." Souls are "made," but are not "begotten" and do not "proceed" from God.

The Nicene Creed, agreed upon by a majority at the Council of Nicaea in 325, fixed for some time the official Church views. It consists of only two sentences. But one needs to have some insight into the complex controversies preceding it in order to begin to comprehend its significance. "We believe in one God, Father Almighty, maker of all things visible and invisible; and in one Lord Jesus Christ the Son of God, begotten of the Father, only-begotten, that is from the substance of the Father, God from God, Light from Light, true God from true God, begotten, not made, of one substance with the Father, through whom all things were made, both the things in heaven and the things on earth; who for us men and for our salvation came down and was made flesh, was made man, suffered, and rose again on the third day, ascended into heaven, and cometh to judge the quick and the dead; and in the Holy Spirit. But those who say, 'There was once when he was not,' and 'Before his generation he was not,' and 'He was made out of nothing,' or pretend that the Son of God is of another subsistence or substance, or created or alterable or mutable, the Catholic Church anathematizes."

At the Council of Chalcedon in 451, six other phrases or sentences were added, to make official other items by then agreed upon. "[1] Christ is fully God, and fully man, of the same nature with God, both in his humanity and in his divinity; [2] He is divine, begotten of God; he is human, born of the virgin Mary; [3] He was begotten before all ages, and in these later times, for man's salvation; [4] He is like men, save that he alone is sinless; [5] He is to be acknowledged in two natures, distinct, yet indivisible, inseparable, and not to be confused or changed; [6] Mary as his mother is the 'Mother of God.' "

Augustine

Augustine (354–430), "the formulator of Christian theology," was the most influential theologian in the history of Christendom. His ingenious integration of opposing traditions stands as one of the greatest intellectual achievements of all time. His synthesis of Hebraic and Greek ideals, built upon the accepted Biblical scriptures and upon orthodox creeds adopted by earlier Councils of Church Fathers, is responsible for the most characteristic theological views predominating in Western thought. In order to appreciate the magnitude of his genius and the full significance of his synthetic achievement, we should do two things: The first consists in summarizing and comparing the outstanding differences between typical Hebrew and Greek ideals that became ingredients in Christian thought; the second consists in showing how these contrasting ideals became integrated into a single view in Augustine's synthesis.

(1) The key ideals of Hebraic and Greek thought may be represented summarily by two terms, "Will" and "Reason," respectively, *provided* these terms be interpreted broadly enough. Since Greeks "will" and Jews "reason," these terms must be understood as standing for *emphases* rather than as exclusive differences, as characterizing typical cultural ideals rather than as necessarily descriptive of any person. "Will," in the broad sense intended here, includes

that which is common to a rich cluster of meanings expressed in such words as: "desire," "love," "fear," "hate," "trust," "hope," "reverence," "favor," "forgiveness," "will," and "will not." "Reason," as used here, finds expression in such words as "rational," "form," "law," "inference," "mathematical," and "theoretical." Although both of these general terms, "Reason" and "Will," refer to aspects of human nature, cultural ideals expand them into cosmic principles.

Once the general notions of Will and Reason have become clear, certain other contrasting characteristics of these generalized ideals can be observed. *(a)* Since Will may be frustrated, the outcome of willing is uncertain. But since Reason is determined, the outcome is sure, predictable. (A mathematical problem, when worked correctly, always yields the same answer.) *(b)* Will is personal. Reason is impersonal. *(c)* Will arouses emotion. Reason stays unemotional. When Will becomes intensified, it may cause greater effort and influence the outcome. But Reason remains uninfluenced by emotion; crying will not change the answer to a mathematical problem. *(d)* Will is unique and particular in the sense that each act of will, each desire, each fear, love, or hate occurs at a particular time and place. Reason is common and universal in the sense that its laws remain true at all times and in all places. *(e)* Will is free; it can choose, it can change, and free choices make differences in consequences. Reason is determined; its nature cannot change, so one must conform to it. Will may be whimsical, but not Reason. *(f)* Since Will can affect the outcome, the future is important to its fulfillment, and since Will acts in time, time continues to be significant. But since Reason stays fixed and unchanging, true regardless of time, time has little importance for it. Will is essentially temporal. Reason remains essentially timeless. *(g)* Since the outcome of Willing may be in doubt, a believer suffers anxiety, concern, restlessness, worry. Since the outcome of Reasoning can be certain, a believer should remain calm and undisturbed. (Having deduced what is necessary, his conclusion is final; hence conviction or dogmatism becomes justified.)

Consequences of the different emphases of Hebrew and

Greek conceptions of the nature of God, the world, man, and values may now be noted, allowing for some oversimplification for purposes of clarity.

(a) God (Yahweh) as conceived by the Hebrews was a Lord (Adonoi) who wills, loves, hates, hopes, and fears. God (Logos) as derived from Greek sources was an impersonal principle of order, regularity, or rationality. God (Yahweh) is free to do as he wishes; he can change his mind if he wants to do so and may be arbitrary or whimsical. God (Logos) is a fixed pattern of possibilities that remains eternally unalterable; God's nature is perfect, completely determined, hence not free to change. God (Yahweh) decides order by his will. God (Logos) stands as an order that limits what can be willed. When God (Yahweh) is idealized as perfect, nothing limits his will; "God" equals "unlimited will." When God (Logos) is idealized as perfect, no will (not even God's) can disturb the eternal order; "God" equals "eternal order."

(b) The Hebraic world was conceived as populated by animate powers or wills, called "els." Such a world continues as a battleground of wills in which struggle makes a difference; the history of conquests by Egyptians, Babylonians, etc., and of the Canaanites, etc., serves as a constant reminder. The Greek mind conceives its world as a system of natural law, operating constantly in the same way regardless of men's desires to change it; one must accept (submit his will to) the laws of nature if he would use, benefit from, or enjoy them (as in science and engineering). The Hebraic world appears as an historical process, a cosmic drama, in which each life and circumstance occur uniquely and unrepeatably. The Greek world manifests cyclical processes in which (like day and night or the seasons of the year) each kind of thing recurs regularly in accordance with its own fixed nature.

How is God related to the world? God (Yahweh) created the world from nothing by an act of will (fiat): "Let there be light, and there was light." The Greek world was never created but existed eternally; "nothing from nothing comes"; God (Logos) also existed eternally as its internal ordering principle. God (Yahweh) has a real stake in history and favors those who favor him, even taking sides in battle. God (Logos), like the laws of mathematics, can favor no one; what happens in history makes no difference to God since God remains eternally (timelessly) perfect. God (Yahweh) can destroy mankind if he chooses. (He did once by a flood, saving Noah.) But mankind, having its own eternal nature (logos), must be as indestructible as God (Logos). God (Yahweh) punishes disloyalty ("Sin" is disobedience to God's will), though he can be merciful and may be influenced by our prayers, entreaties, and sacrifices to him. God (Logos) requires no feeling of loyalty and cannot be influenced by prayers, since the laws of nature or of mathematics cannot be changed by coaxing.

(c) Each man (H)* consists basically in a personal will, a collocation of desires or wants. (The first thing a baby does when he is born is to let out a yell to let you know he is alive.) Each man (G) exists as a rational animal, a bit of cosmic reason come alive. (A baby has to learn that he cannot have everything he wants; the law of gravitation is one of his first teachers.) Will (H) is free, and each man's will acts as an unmoved mover. Reason (G) is determined and consists of unchanging laws that cause our choices. Each man is free (H) to reason or not to reason, as he chooses; freedom is obedience to desire or impulse. Freedom (G) consists in conformity to one's own nature or in obedience to reason; impulse (will) is irrational and hence unnatural and evil. Man (H) is primarily a doer or actor; hence he should seek to manage, to be a ruler, to become interested in the practical. Man (G) is primarily a thinker; hence he should seek to understand, to be a scientist, and to devote interest to the theoretical. Since Will (H) is temporal, man's interests focus mainly in his temporal being: birth, life, death, and in his parents, children, grandparents, and grandchildren, who have importance for him. Since Reason (G) endures eternally and the laws of logic remain changeless, man merely embodies or exemplifies them temporarily; ra-

*The letters "H" and "G" stand for "Hebrew" and "Greek" and are used here to indicate their contrasting views.

tionality (rather than children) is most important; children become' important because they embody Reason. (Hence one should treat all children, *i.e.*, reasoners, alike rather than favoring some, even one's own, over others.) Family life is good because everyone wants (H) to have a family (or because God wills one to have a family: "Be ye fruitful, multiply and replenish the earth"). Family life is good because it is man's nature (G) as a social animal to have a family; but the individual person is more important than the family.

Although highly developed ideals about an afterlife were not a part of either the Hebraic or Greek spirit as summarized here, certain implications of each can be drawn out. The ideal life (H) is everlasting or is one whose time never stops. The ideal life (G) must be eternal (timeless), since the rational soul is by nature nontemporal. Man (H) should not be conceived as dual, *i.e.*, as having a soul that can be separated from his body; man's soul (Will) dies with his body. Man (G) is dual in the sense that his body is inferior to his soul, for his soul (Reason) is eternal, whereas his body is merely a temporary embodiment of it.

(d) What is the ultimate nature of values? Will (H) acts as the source of both good and evil. "Good" consists in the satisfaction of desire; "evil" consists in frustration of desire. Reason (G) serves as the source or goal or standard for both good and evil. "Goodness" is the (proper) source of will, is "that at which all things aim," is "self-realization" of one's own nature; "evil" consists in disharmony, ignorance of the good, or irrationality (*e.g.*, willfulness). Rightness or oughtness (H) consists in acting in such a way that you will get what you want (or what God wants). Rightness or oughtness (G) consists in acting in accordance with principles inherent in your own nature or in the nature of the universe (*i.e.*, acting reasonably). Salvation (H), where we have man's will to go against the Will of God (sin) upon whom he depends for perpetuity, requires repentance: a surrender of his will to the Will of God. Wisdom (G), which consists in "knowing thyself" as a rational soul and in acting accordingly, fulfills itself

best through contemplative appreciation of the "eternal verities" as ultimate goods.

(2) Augustine's synthesis incorporated each of the foregoing pairs of opposing ideals, and many more. Furthermore, it tried, and in large measure succeeded, in doing so in ways that remained in agreement with additional insights of Jesus, Paul, and others as recorded in scriptures, as well as with the orthodox conclusions of the Christian Councils up to his time. His synthesis has so thoroughly dominated Christian theology that many readers familiar with that theology will be surprised to discover its composite nature and will perforce admire the marvelous ingenuity involved. To "H" and "G" we now add "C" to designate ideas which seem to be peculiarly or primarily contributions of earlier Christian thought.

(a) God, for Augustine, is both a Lord (Adonoi) (H) who wills and Logos (G). He remains perfectly rational (G) and wills everything (H). In him, Reason and Will are identical. God's Will is perfectly free (H) because determined completely by his own rational nature (G). God never whimsically wills what is unreasonable, because, as perfectly rational, he cannot. Having been influenced greatly by Plotinus, the Neoplatonist, Augustine conceived God as an absolute unity (G). Not only is there one God (H), but God is One (G). God, as perfect, remains absolutely superior to all else (G); all else must be less than perfect (G). He is the only absolutely prime mover or uncaused cause (G, H).

God is all-knowing in the sense of having Platonic "Ideas" (eternal Forms) eternally present in his mind (G). His mind contains universals or essences *and* ideas of particular things (G). These "Ideas" equal "The Truth" (G). But God appears also like the Hebrew Yahweh in being a person whose will is all-powerful, whose justice requires punishment for sin, whose freedom of will persists unlimited except by his own justice, goodness, grace, and promises, whose majestic Lordship is perfectly awesome, and whose unselfish grace is utterly magnificent (H). And God is also like Jesus' "Heavenly Father" in being "Love," like Paul's God who graciously sacrificed his "only begotten Son" for our sins, and like Athanasius' "Trinity" in being three-in-One rather than one of the three (C).

(b) The world was created by God out of nothing (H). God willed the universe (H). Yet God proceeded rationally in creating the world, and everything in it owes its form to God (G). Although form and matter in particular things were created together, all forms preexisted eternally in the mind of God (G). The world had a beginning in time and can perish (H). The world was not created in time and space, but time and space were created by God as part of the world (G). Continued existence of the world depends upon God's will (H); however since Reason and Will are identical in God, he will will its continuance as long as necessary (G). The created world is good (G, H), both because God's love and benevolence (H) wants what is good, and because his nature, as perfect, implies or necessitates the good (G). Yet evil arises in the world, because man wills to disobey God (H) because his imperfect nature makes it impossible for him to reason (and thus to will) perfectly (G).

(c) Man is a union of soul and body. Although his soul begins in time, and thus did not preexist (H, C), it does not die, *i.e.,* is eternal (G) or everlasting (C). But since its existence was foreknown in God's mind, its essence is really eternal, and thus it had an eternal nature prior to its coming into existence (G). Man's body also begins in time (in fact, soul and body begin together), but their separation at death does not end their being (C), for later all bodies will be resurrected and re-united with their souls (C). The soul is a simple immaterial or spiritual substance (G) entirely distinct from its body (G). The soul is the only part really worth saving (G) and salvation can easily be explained as the soul gaining its freedom from bondage to its body (G, C). But, also, the body is not evil; it is not a prison house of the soul (H). Death, or separation of soul from body, should not be considered a desirable thing (H). Resurrection (*i.e.,* living again) requires a body (G, H, C), but life with God is eternal, and so requires no body (G).

Man (*i.e.,* both soul and body) can be nothing apart

from God (G). That is, his nature exists as wholly determined (G). Yet he is also free to choose (H). Man
is like God in this, for God is both wholly determined
by his own rational nature (as all-good, all-knowing,
all-powerful, eternal, etc.) (G) and yet wholly free
(H); in fact, God is determined by his nature to be
wholly free (G). Man, in being free (H) but not all-
knowing (G, H), naturally mistakes his freedom for
independence. Such a mistake flows naturally from his
ignorance (G), but his mistake is his own, not God's
(H, C), for it is due not so much to his likeness to God
(both God and man are free to will) (H), but to his
difference from God (man is completely dependent
and imperfect, God is completely independent and
perfect) (G). So God, being just (H, G), must necessarily (G) punish (H) man for man's mistake (G) or
sin (H). God made man perfect (*i.e.,* an imperfect copy
of a perfect pattern) (G), for a perfect God could not
do otherwise. But in Adam (H) man freely chose to
"fall" (H, C), and Adam's "original sin" has been inherited by all men since (C). In sinning (H, C), man,
became unworthy (G) and freely chose to turn away
from God (H), who is man's source of perfection (G);
man thus willingly surrendered his birthright (H).

(d) God, although all-good and all-knowing (G), is
powerless to prevent man from following his own imperfect nature (G) and from suffering the consequences
(H, G). God so loves his creatures (H, C) that he
chooses to save some anyway (H, C). Whom shall he
choose? How God decides the answer to this question
may be, from man's limited point of view, a mystery
(C), but he can be sure that God is just (H, G), and
thus God's choice must be perfect (G). God, being all-
knowing, foreknew whom he would have to choose (G),
but this in no way forced man's will (H), for each
man's will is his own (H), even though determined by
his own imperfect nature (G). Thus man is predestined,
both by God's perfect nature and his own imperfect
nature (G) to choose freely to sin (H). Man cannot
do otherwise (G) than to choose to sin (H), since it is
his nature to do so (G). God cannot do otherwise (G)
than to choose to punish sinners for sinning (H), since

it is his nature, as just, to do so (H, G). Yet also, God, as love (H, C), cannot do otherwise (G) than save all whom he can (G). God is gracious (H, C). But God cannot be gracious unless he sheds grace (G), *i.e.,* unless he saves some who are unworthy to be saved. Once God's grace has saved men from themselves (*i.e.,* from their own ignorance), they will be so amazed at his generosity (H, C) in bestowing this eternal gift (G) upon them who are inherently unworthy of being saved that they will glorify him forever. Those eternally damned also testify to God's glory (G) even if not willingly (H), because they will recognize their punishment as flowing necessarily (G) from his justice (H, G).

Even though God, creation, man, and salvation are ultimately rational (G), man, due to his imperfection, is irrational (G). Being irrational, he cannot wholly understand the truth (G). So, if he is to know more of the truth than, by nature, he has any right to know (G, H), he must obtain this knowledge through some irrational means, *i.e.,* through revelation (H, C). Although he cannot knowingly believe the unreasonable (for man as God's creature is inherently rational) (G), nevertheless he cannot wholly understand (G, H) what is reasonable. He naturally mistakes imperfect reasons for perfect ones (G). So, the only way to perfect knowledge (G) is for man to trust in God's revelations even though he cannot fully understand them (H, C). Since Reason (G) and revelation (H, C) have their ultimate source in God, they cannot be contradictory (G), even though our imperfect minds cannot understand why. Actually, the saint (one who willingly does God's Will) and the philosopher (lover of wisdom, *i.e.,* of Reason, or the Logos, or God) should be the same, for in God, Will and Reason remain identical. Although one has a duty to understand what he believes (G), he also has a duty to believe what he does not fully understand (H, C). Fortunately, the Church has been established to aid men both in understanding and belief (C).

Theocracy (government by God) flows naturally from the fact that government by wisdom (Logos) (G) and government by the Will of the Lord (Adonoi) (H) are the same. Eternally, God is the Ruler (*i.e.*, both the Lord [H] and the Standard of Perfection [G]) of the "City of God." His rule in this world must be imperfectly administered by men. His authority can be embodied in the Church (C), infallibly to the extent that it actually expresses his perfection, fallibly to the extent that it expresses his perfection imperfectly (G). This is just like a soul being "saved" to the extent that its will and reason attain conformity with each other and thus with God's Will and Reason, and "damned" to the extent that its will refuses to follow or remains ignorant of Reason.

Man depends upon God's grace for help in achieving his goal. God has provided specific means (C). Scriptures revealing the Will of God (H, C) enable man through faith to transcend his weakness (C). The Visible Church has been provided (C) to interpret the scriptures (C), explain their reasonableness, and to offer aids to faith (C). Only the ignorant, the foolish, and the sinful will refuse to make use of them (C). Since devotion to things of this world over which men have power tends to distract their attention from the fact that they remain ultimately powerless, monastic separation from worldly distractions becomes desirable and the Church should assist in providing such monastic aids (C).

Yea-saying for Augustine involves a synthesis of Hebrew, Greek, and earlier Christian ideals and a Church established to provide aids for men who cannot otherwise believe. The idea of God as perfectly just requires men to expect no more than they deserve, thus exemplifying "high" religion. Yet men whose imperfect minds cannot quite believe God can be so perfectly just, often do expect more than they deserve, thus exemplifying "low" religion. Should those who, recognizing the justice of their punishment for their imperfection (by being condemned to Hell) give up all hope? No. Why? Because God is also perfect in grace. This does not mean he will save all, but only enough to demonstrate his grace, even as he must punish some to demonstrate justice. And because the Church has been established to help him overcome his imperfection. But do not these two reasons then lead men to hope for more than they deserve? Yes. Then does not the establishment of a Church for this purpose constitute "low" religion?

Although Augustine's ingenious synthesis provides for both intellectual and volitional assent, thus having the advantages of both the Hebraic and Greek traditions without all of the disadvantages of either, the opposites did not remain synthesized. Opposites are actually different as well as ideally identical in God. The differences of opposing ideals reassert themselves from time to time and thus constitute ingredients in Christian thinking that give it an unstable character. They provide the bases for the recurrent emergence of conflicting issues—such as those between Thomists and Scotists, Calvinists and Lutherans, and Rationalism and Romanticism—that wracked Christian harmony in later times. The numerous paradoxes inherent in Christian theology and embodied in Augustine's synthesis remain a source of intellectual indigestion that constantly causes revulsion and new brands of heresy. Although Augustine's synthesis solved many problems in ways pleasing to orthodoxy, orthodoxy itself embodied other problems that produce schisms, protests, and reforms, to say nothing of those who rejected the churchly scheme altogether.

Roman Catholicism

Rome gradually became the primary center of Catholic thought and control until, during the Middle Ages, its intellectual structure dominated the European mind and its political power prevailed widely. Chief intellectual architect of "the Mediaeval Mind" was Thomas Aquinas (1227–74) whose preferences for Aristotelian philosophy, as against the earlier Platonic philosophy, helped make the pre-Christian Aristotle (384–322 B.C.) "The Philosopher" of the Catholic Church. Thomas' teachings, as a professor or schoolman, were, and still are, called "Scholasticism." They picture God as a "First Cause" or "Prime Mover" that remains eternally unmoved. God is "Pure Act," whose being is perfected without any action other than its "act" of being. God is omnipotent in the sense of functioning as an uncaused cause of all, as a formal principle of causality, and thus as "creator" of all. But God is impotent in the sense that it is powerless to change itself in any way or to be changed by anything else. (Our prayers cannot influence God.) God is also the "Final Cause" or goal of all creation, which, being imperfect, must recognize as its ultimate goal that perfection of being which alone an eternally inactive being can be. God is "man's last end"; for whatever other purposes a man may have, they remain less than ultimate, less than the best, less than perfect. A man can perfect his own ends only in proportion to his approach to that "last end," God, which alone remains completely perfect.

For Thomas, the structure of the universe may be summarized under three headings: God, Man, and God-Man. Not only is God pure act, absolute simplicity, absolute perfection, absolute intelligence, including absolute consciousness and absolute will, but as creator functions as Father, who begot an only Son (Logos) who became man, and through them and the Holy Spirit manifests itself as "The Blessed Trinity." The revealed doctrine of the Trinity is a supernatural mystery, which the mind cannot discover for itself or comprehend fully even after hearing about it. Creation involves God going outside of himself and producing the world from nothing. Creation is of three kinds: (1) Pure spirits or "angels" (each being a unique species, in contrast with men who are all of one species). (2) Pure matter or the cosmos, which involved a beginning of time and development of the world through seven periods. (3) Man, who is a mixture of spirit and matter, or soul and body.

Each man, though composed of both soul and body, is by nature a single substance. But he is dual in another sense. He has both a natural and a supernatural character. God first endowed man with both "preternatural gifts" (freedom from suffering, ignorance, labor, and concupiscence) and "supernatural gifts" (sanctifying grace and gifts of the Holy Spirit; "beatitude" or immediate knowledge of God), as well as free will to appreciate God's supremacy or not as he chose. In Adam, the first man, human pride chose to refuse to admit God's superior being. By this act, all men inherit "original sin" as part of their nature. The "fall of man" resulted in his being deprived of "preternatural gifts," which have never been restored, and of "supernatural gifts," which may be restored through Christ's atonement and through the sacraments. The goal of man's life is happiness, but true happiness can be achieved only in the beatific vision or immediate apprehension of God. Thus the goal of life is a supernatural, not a natural, goal; and it cannot be attained in this life. Man's soul is by nature eternal and its goal is eternal happiness. But, having sinned and turned away from God, a soul must look forward to eternal damnation unless it freely chooses to turn to God during this present life after which it will be too late. Fortunately, the Church has been established to help it return. But to understand the Church, we must first understand Christ, "the God-man," who established it.

Christ is one person having two distinct natures. Christ is God the Son, the second "Person" of the Blessed Trinity. Christ is a man, Jesus of Nazareth, born of the Virgin Mary, "Mother of God." His mission on earth was to bring about the redemption of man whereby man might be brought back to God. He provided a way and revealed that way to all men through his disciples, who must "go forth and baptize in the name of the Father, Son, and Holy Spirit." After three years of active ministry, he was crucified, died, and was buried, and on the third day he rose from the dead and ascended into heaven. But before he died he established his Church, with the disciple Peter as its head. Peter and his successors, the Roman Popes, possess a guiding power that amounts to a divine certitude so that transmission will be assured. Thus the power of Christ to redeeem men continues to be embodied in the Church. During his earthly lifetime, Christ was physically present; now he is physically present continuously in the Sacrament of the Eucharist. He taught with divine authority; this continuing authority of the Church in matters of faith and morals is called "infallibility." He worked out redemptive sacrifice by his death on the Cross; this redemptive act is represented sacramentally in the celebration of the "Mass" (Eucharist). Christ forgave sins; power to forgive sins was conferred through the apostolic succession and holy orders, and may be exercised by priests upon appropriate confession and penance. Christ brought "new life," a way to be "born again"; the Church may provide such new life through the Sacrament of Baptism, initially, and later through other sacraments. The "Seven Sacraments" are BAPTISM, which initiates birth into supernatural life; CONFIRMATION, which signifies sufficient growth toward maturity to have assented to the way voluntarily; EUCHARIST, a receipt of nourishment for further growth by eating the body and the blood of Christ transubstantiated in bread and wine by priestly blessing; PENANCE or CONFESSION, which assists in the restoration of health to one's supernatural life; EXTREME UNCTION, which may aid in restoring supernatural health at the end of life; HOLY ORDERS, which provide a person with priestly power to rule and exercise public acts; and MATRIMONY, which sanctifies a union aimed at preservation through propagation.

The Church is in Heaven, where it is called "the Church Triumphant," in Purgatory, where it is "the Church Suffering," and on earth, where it is "the Church Militant." All its members, whether on earth, in Heaven, or in Purgatory, continue in a holy fellowship through their union in the one body of Christ. Purgatory is a condition after death for those whose good works have saved them from Hell but whose evil thoughts and deeds prevent them from meriting the joy of Heaven immediately. Purgatory is a place wherein one may become purged of his VENIAL SIN, a pardonable sin for which he has not fully paid his debt of temporal punishment. Those in Purgatory may be "loosed from their sins" by our prayers and good works in their behalf. A MORTAL SIN or DEADLY SIN, in contrast with "original sin" and "venial sin," kills a soul's supernatural life by depriving it of sanctifying grace; the soul of one who dies in a state of mortal sin falls straight into the flames of Hell, where its body joins it on "the Last Day." Each soul receives a PARTICULAR JUDGMENT immediately after death that determines its individual future. But on "the Last Day," all will share in the GENERAL JUDGMENT, when the sentence passed on each shall be made known to all, and when, at the sound of the Archangel's trumpet, all men will rise from their graves with the same bodies they had in life, to enjoy everlasting life or to suffer everlasting punishment, as each deserves. Those who have said "Yea" to the supernatural power and glory of God and to the justice and grace of His plan of redemption for man will be blessed eternally, whereas those who have refused to say "Yea" to God in this life will have to recognize their mistake eternally; they will suffer in never beholding God's glory and will be eternal witnesses to the truth of such yea-saying by their awareness of the justification for their suffering.

In addition to the TEN COMMANDMENTS OF GOD, Roman Catholics should obey the COMMANDMENTS OF THE CHURCH. In a Paulist Press pamphlet, *What Catholics Believe*, Mother Mary Loyola interprets these commandments somewhat as follows. "By the First Commandment we are commanded to worship the one true and living God, by Faith, Hope, Charity, and Religion. The sins against Faith are—false religions, willful doubt, disbelief, or denial of any article of Faith, and also culpable ignorance of the doctrines of the Church. We expose ourselves to the danger of losing our Faith by neglecting our spiritual duties— the Sacraments, Mass, morning and night prayers, daily examination of conscience, grace at meals, etc., by reading bad books, by going to non-Catholic schools, and taking part in the services of a false religion. . . ." The Second Commandment "requires us to speak with reverence of God and all holy persons and things, to keep our lawful oaths and vows. . . ." The Third Commandment "requires us to keep Sunday holy. The Church tells us this is to be done by hearing Mass and resting from servile works. . . ." The Fourth Commandment: "The love of our neighbor proves our love of God. . . . Children are bound to obey their parents in all that is not sin. . . . We are commanded to obey, not our parents only, but also our Bishops and pastors, the civil authorities, and our lawful superiors. . . . Wives are commanded to be subject to their husbands. Servants are bound to respect, obedience, and fidelity to those whose service they have entered. . . . By the Fourth Commandment parents are bound to provide for their children, to instruct and correct them, to give them good example, and a good Catholic education." The Fifth Commandment: ". . . forbids all willful murder. Except in a just war, in self-defense, or in the name of the law, we may not take the life of another. Neither may we take our own, either by direct suicide or by such vices as shorten life. The drunkard sins against this Commandment." The Sixth and Ninth "Commandments forbid whatever is contrary to holy purity in thoughts, words, or actions. With regard to thoughts, it is important to remember that what is not willful is not sinful. A thought may haunt us for days, but as long as we would gladly be rid of it, and try to turn our minds away from it, there is no sin. Immodest plays and dances are forbidden by the Sixth Commandment. . . . And we must avoid idleness and curiosity." The Seventh and Tenth Commandments "forbid all covetous thoughts and unjust desires for our neighbor's goods and profits, and all unjust taking or keeping what belongs to another. . . ." The Eighth Commandment "guards our neighbor's good name. It forbids all false testimony, rash judgment, and lies."

"There are six chief Commandments of the Church. The First Commandment of the Church is to keep the Sundays and Holydays of Obligation holy by hearing Mass and resting from servile works." These are "Christmas Day, Circumcision, Ascension Thursday, the Assumption of Our Lady, and All Saints. . . . The Second . . . is to keep the days of fasting and abstinence appointed by the Church, so that we may mortify the flesh and satisfy God for our sins. . . . The Third Commandment . . . is to go to confession at least once a year. . . . The Fourth . . . is to receive the Blessed Sacrament at least once a year. . . . The Fifth . . . is to contribute to the support of our pastors. . . . The Sixth . . . is not to marry within certain degrees of kindred, nor to solemnize marriage at forbidden times, that is, from the first Sunday in Advent till the day after Christmas and from Ash Wednesday till the day after Easter Sunday. . . ."

Politically, Roman Catholicism is organized as an episcopal system (*i.e.*, governed by bishops) with a complex hierarchy headed by a Pope in Rome. Although Roman Catholicism idealizes theocracy, or government by God, it accepts in practice a doctrine of "the two swords," one spiritual and one political, wherein the Church and its members "render unto Caesar" political obedience when and as necessary. However, the Church maintains a small politically independent territory surrounding its Vatican headquarters in Rome and sends and receives ambassadors to and from numerous national states, thereby acting as a political state. Various functions of the Catholic system are carried out through many organizations, some of which are called "Orders." Outstanding Orders include the Benedictines, the Franciscans, and the Dominicans, each emphasizing some facet of life, such as devotional prayer, scriptural study, daily labor, assistance to the poor, and propagation of the faith. Far more than half of all Christians in the world adhere to Roman Catholicism. Although they constitute about one-third of the religious population in the United States today, their numbers continue to grow faster than most others.

Eastern Orthodoxy

Until 1054, the Christian church was organized into five major Bishoprics, namely, those with headquarters in Alexandria, Antioch, Constantinople, Jerusalem, and Rome. On July 16 of that year, a legate from the Roman Bishop (Father, Papa, or Pope) presented the Bishop (Father, Pater, or Patriarch) of Constantinople with a statement of anathema or excommunication. On July 24, the latter excommunicated the former. Although we cannot here go into the political and doctrinal causes of long-standing (*i.e.,* since about 587) schismatic tendencies, we must note that this rift has been a serious handicap to the growth of Catholicism. Recurrent attempts to heal the breach persist even today. The four Eastern Bishops continue their association, with the Archbishop or Patriarch at Constantinople being regarded as "the first among equals." Predominance of the Greek Language (in which the New Testament was written) in the Eastern Churches has resulted in their being called the "Greek Orthodox" Churches, in contrast to the Roman Catholic Church, which not only has its headquarters in Rome but uses Latin as its main official instrument of communication.

In most doctrinal matters, the two branches remain the same. Some differences, however, prove to be interesting. The Eastern Churches have held no general or ecumenical councils for further clarifying points of doctrine but retain unchanged those agreements held prior to the schism. The Roman Catholic Church, on the other hand, has continued to make official pronouncements clarifying matters of faith and morals. The Greek Church does not accept such doctrines as the Immaculate Conception, the bodily ascent of Mary, credit for merits or indulgences, purgatory, celibacy of all priests, and the infallibility of the Roman Pope. Greeks continue to use leavened bread for their Eucharist ceremonies, prefer "transformation" to "transubstantiation" of the blood and body of Christ, elaborate their liturgy into a long and complex devotional ritual, celebrate only one Mass per day, prefer symbolic icons to sculptured statues for representing Christ, Mary, and other saints, and emphasize appreciation of Saints Basil, Chrysostom, Sophia, and George in contrast with purely Roman saints such as Thomas Aquinas. Perhaps the best known schismatic difference centers about a seemingly trivial doctrinal issue as to whether the Holy Spirit proceeds from the "Father and the Son" or from "the Father through the Son."

For a while, after 1453 when Constantinople fell to the Turks, leadership among the Eastern Churches passed to the Slavic Orthodox Churches, especially the Russian Orthodox Church. Moscow was regarded by the Russian Patriarch as "The Third Rome" (captured Constantinople having been "The Second"). The continuing prominence of the Russian Church, at least until the Communist revolution, has led many Eastern Orthodox thinkers to regard Moscow as replacing Rome among "the five" main Bishoprics constituting the Eastern Church. Mention should be made of the fact that many relatively independent branches exist within and cooperate with numerous other national states, such as Poland and Lithuania, and that others persist independent of state support or sanction in India, Turkey, and Canada, for example. In the United States, the more than two million followers of Eastern Orthodoxy tend to cooperate and participate in local churches despite their diverse national and linguistic origins.

Lutheranism

Although attempts to reform the Roman Church were not new (the names of Eckhart, Tauler, Suso, Wyclif, Hus, Savonarola, and Erasmus stand out among earlier critics), the Protestant Reformation did not attain serious proportions until the revolt of Martin Luther (1483–1546). Luther was a devout, studious priest of the Augustinian Order, who taught theology at the University of Wittenberg. His soul-searching and scripture-searching spirit rebelled against the crass way in which John Tetzel "sold indulgences." Catholic doctrine permits authorized priests to grant a reduction of time served in purgatory in turn for a good deed, a gift of money to the Church being considered such a good deed. A "Treasury of Merit" from surpluses of good deeds by Christ and the saints was said to be stored in Rome for dispensation for this purpose. Pope Leo X, who wanted money to finish a new basilica at Rome, had commissioned priests to gather money for this project. Tetzel enjoyed serving as a particularly high-pressure salesman, apparently, for reports of his rhymed jingles and boasting techniques have yielded some classic phrases: "As soon as the coin in the coffer rings, a soul from purgatory springs" and "I have saved more souls by my sale of indulgences than have the saints by all their sermons." Luther, provoked by such crude bartering, posted ninety-five critical theses on the door of his cathedral in Wittenberg for public discussion. He intended no break with the Roman Church but merely to restrain or eliminate what he considered un-Christian beliefs and practices. Yet his public pronouncements in effect challenged the authority of the Pope, who asked him to recant. He felt that he could not. Excommunication followed. Fortunately, political conditions were such that he obtained protection under the ruler of Saxony who found it expedient to attain additional political independence from Roman power.

Luther continued to accept most of the Roman views. His differences from them, however, yielded significant influences as time went on. He believed that the Church hierarchy had failed because priestly intermediaries tended to separate man from God; Luther believed that men could have direct communion with God through prayer. Luther believed that the holy scriptures proclaimed salvation "by faith alone," rather than through "works," including "penances"; he rejected the idea that priests can perform magical acts through the sacraments, though he kept baptism and eucharist as spiritual aids. His rejection of the need for Church and priestly intervention led naturally to a "Back to the Bible" emphasis, whereby each individual would read the Word of God for himself. He translated the Bible into German and the recent invention of the printing press enabled widespread adoption of Bible reading. He proclaimed a "universal priesthood of all believers" in place of an ordained clergy as a special class. His doctrine has been summarized in three *"solas"* (onlys): "Scripture alone, Grace alone, Faith alone" are needed for men's salvation.

Lutheranism prospered but its emphasis upon individual interpretation of scriptures ("As God gives us to see the light") led to further differences of opinion and contributed to the multiplication of denominations. Among the several varieties of Lutherans independently organized in the United States today, three stand out, each comprising about a third of their eight million members. Most conservative, perhaps, is the "Lutheran Church, Missouri Synod." "The American Lutheran Church" was formed through a merger of several Lutheran groups in 1960. "The Lutheran Church of America" represents another merger of Lutheran synods that is still in process, the largest body involved being "The United Lutheran Church." Lutheranism remains strong and growing, for it claims some eighty million adherents which constitute about one-third of all the Protestants in the world today.

Calvin and the Presbyterians

John Calvin (1509–64), student of theology, law, and Greek in Paris, Orléans, and Bruges, developed a rationalistic outlook that led him to challenge Roman doctrines, flee to Switzerland, and aid in the establishment of the first major Protestant theocracy. His rigorous deductions from traditional assumptions about the perfect "sovereignty" of God led to a completely deterministic, or "pre-destinarian," interpretation of Christian doctrine. Since only God is perfect, as Augustine had already asserted, all creatures, no matter how good, remain necessarily imperfect. If a man could but recognize the fact of his imperfection and the glorious perfection of God implied therein, he would thereby behold the glory of God and accept his own inglorious state as logical and just. But, being imperfect, a man naturally mistakes his imperfect being as more independent, free, and perfect than it is. Thereby he sins, sin being his willingness to see God as less perfect than God is. Being imperfect, man deserves, and should expect and want, to reap the consequences of his imperfect nature. But his very imperfection prevents him from being willing to accept its consequences. Hence, he justly deserves the punishment that is in store for him.

But God, being perfect in both justice and grace, of necessity "sends" to Hell precisely that number which his perfection in justice implies, and "saves" precisely that number which his perfection in grace implies. Logically, no imperfect creature has the power to resist the perfect power of God to damn those justly deserving damnation or to save those whom his perfect grace has "elected" for salvation. A man must be as powerless to resist God's grace as he is to resist God's justice. Hence, neither goodwill nor good works on the part of any man can save him if he is not already "elect," and neither evil deeds nor evil desires can condemn him if he is "elect." A man does not do good works so that he will become saved but because he is already saved by God's election. Hence, the services that the Church claims for its sacraments and the whole hierarchical system are a gross mistake of imperfect men who scheme to influence and overcome the already perfect power, wisdom, justice, and grace of God. Thus the teachings of the Roman Church are really sinful.

How can one know whether or not he is "elect"? The test is quite simple. Ask yourself the question: "Are you willing to suffer eternal damnation for the glory of God?" If so, then you are elect. If not, then you are damned, for you refuse to recognize the perfection of the perfect being and to be willing to accept the just consequences of your own imperfect being. Whereas Lutherans search their souls to see whether they have and maintain sufficient "faith" (involving an act of individual will), Calvinists search their souls to see whether they have been endowed with sufficient grace by God to be willing to suffer the eternal damnation implicit in their imperfection. To question the perfection of God's wisdom in "deciding" whom to save and whom to condemn is itself a mark of imperfection and sin.

Perhaps, in the foregoing, I have taken the liberty to emphasize a logic implicit in Calvin's thought more precisely and succinctly than Calvin himself did in his *Institutes of the Christian Religion*. But, given both traditional assumptions about God's perfection and logical deductions, certain consequences do follow necessarily—consequences that men, because incompetent, naturally tend to overlook. Presbyterian and other followers of Calvin have tended progressively to soften the rigor of his logic and language, thereby gradually reembodying in Protestant teaching and practice some of the very mistakes that Calvin revolted against in Roman Catholicism. Despite doctrinal allegiance to predestination, many Calvinists now tend to stress, much as Lutherans and Catholics do, the need for personal effort in shaping the will to do good so that one will be rewarded for his goodwill and deeds.

Although, theoretically, Calvin propounded a theocracy, practically, political decisions and their enactment had to be made and carried out by men. Democratic ideals, inherent in the implication that God's grace is bestowed equally upon those elected by God to receive it, permitted no man to be superior to another in political power. Yet, since children, even though elect, have immature views, control naturally gravitates to the elders ("presbyters") and the resulting system of electing representatives to bear responsibility for governing and teaching functions came to be called "Presbyterianism." No ordination of ministers was necessary. Geneva, Switzerland, being freed from Papal control, became a haven for liberal thinkers of many sorts, but some of these were condemned by Calvinists. Michael Servetus, for example, was burned at the stake for his heretical Unitarian views. Calvinism in turn influenced events in other countries. Calvinists in France came to be known as Huguenots, in Holland as the Dutch Reformed Churches, in Scotland, under the leadership of John Knox, Covenanters and finally as Presbyterians. The "Westminster Confession" summarizes their essential doctrines. Localization of government permits diversity, and the more than forty million followers of Calvinism in the world today have been organized into about one hundred and twenty-five sects. Some four million Presbyterians in the United States divide themselves into eleven different denominations.

Anglicanism

In England, the most outstanding form of the Reformation came to a head when King Henry VIII, rankled because the Catholic clergy refused to annul his marriage, persuaded Parliament to declare that the "bishop of Rome" had no jurisdiction in England. Other doctrines remained virtually unchanged, though issues having to do with permitting clergy to marry, having copies of the English Bible in churches, removal of images from churches to prevent idol worship, and allowing alternative forms of communion brought some minor modifications in belief. The results of these changes were embodied in *The Book of Common Prayer,* established for uniform usage by an act of Parliament in 1559, and in a creedal statement called "The Thirty-Nine Articles of the Church of England." The Anglican or "Episcopal" Church, as it is often called, became incorporated in the United States as "The Protestant Episcopal Church in the United States of America" and claims about two million adherents. Other independent churches that share sympathies with the Church of England are the Church of Wales, the Church of Ireland, the Episcopal Church of Scotland, the Anglican Church of Canada, the Church of India, Pakistan, Burma, and Ceylon, the Church of England in Australia and Tasmania, the Church of the Province of New Zealand, the Church of the Province of South Africa, the Church of the Province of West Africa, the Church of the Province of West Indies, the Nippon Sei Ko Qwai, and the Chung Hua Sheng Kung Hui.

Congregationalism

Englishmen dissatisfied with Anglican episcopal control and prevented by law from meeting openly as a separate congregation, sought freedom of worship first in Holland, in 1609, and then in the New World in 1620. Sailing from Plymouth, England, in the Mayflower, one hundred and two brave adventurers before they landed drew up "The Mayflower Compact," which served as a model charter for a government of the people and by the people. The Pilgrims were followed by others, known as "Puritans." Biblical and Puritanic ideals predominated in the minds of these and other New England colonists; so much so that when congregational legislation occurred, Puritanic ideals were enacted into law—including the Sunday "Blue Laws," as they were called later, some of which remain in effect today, two hundred years later. Dominance of the clergy in political affairs may be guessed from a now-famous saying that "what Hooker preached on Sunday was made law on Monday." Public taxation to support township churches established Congregationalism as "the churches of the standing order."

Five distinctive emphases of Congregationalism may be noted. (1) EDUCATION OF CHILDREN became compulsory early and extended to colleges for the training of ministers. Harvard College was founded by Congregationalists, as were about fifty others, including Amherst, Beloit, Bowdoin, Carleton, Dartmouth, Dillard, Fisk, Grinnell, Howard, Knox, Oberlin, Pomona, Smith, Wellesley, Williams, and Yale. A striking feature of these colleges now is that none of them is, in any strict sense, denominational; they have become independent, private institutions, neither controlled nor supported by denominational funds. (2) CONGREGATIONAL FORM OF CHURCH GOVERNMENT means that the ultimate source of control rests with the members of each congregation themselves, not with any clerical hierarchy either of the episcopal (government by bishops) or presbyterian (government by elected representatives) type. Each church calls its own minister and no minister beloved of his people can be removed by external power. Each local congregation draws up its own articles of faith and its own charter and bylaws, and modifies them at will. (3) CREEDAL FREEDOM follows from the foregoing governmental system. One Congregational Church, for example, admits persons to membership in three ways: by "Affirmation of Faith, acknowledging Jesus as Lord and Master of one's life," by "presentation of a letter of transfer from any Protestant Church" or "by signifying one's sympathy with the general purposes of the church." This third criterion of eligibility is about as liberal as can be found anywhere.

(4) HUMANITARIAN REFORM, including antislavery and world-peace efforts, often characterizes Congregational interests. (5) COOPERATION WITH OTHER DENOMINATIONS has been so common that Congregationalists have been referred to as "the interdenominational denomination." They have already participated in about ten unions with other groups and support ecumenical movements through city and state councils of churches, through the National Council of Churches of Christ in America, and through the World Council of Churches. The most recent merger is that in which the "Congregational Christian Churches" (resulting from an earlier union) joined with the "Evangelical and Reformed Church" (also the result of a recent union) to form "The United Church of Christ" in 1961. This new United Church of Christ not only has organized itself to promote social reform through its "Council for Christian Action" but also stands ready to reform itself, if need be, at any time.

Methodism

John Wesley (1703–91), an Anglican student at Oxford, wearied of the coldly intellectual discourses accompanying formal reading of *The Book of Common Prayer* at Sunday rituals. He longed for an emotional experience of the presence of God and His loving and saving grace. Together with his hymn-writing brother, Charles, and George Whitfield, he formed a little group for methodical study of the scriptures and regular prayer in their rooms. Derisively, they were called the "Holy Club" and "Methodists" because of the earnestness and regularity of their practices. Rural immigrants into industrial cities, who were rootless and ill-prepared to profit from intellectual formalism, hungered for inspiration and significance in their meaningless and sordid lives. Preaching by the Wesleys, seeking to stimulate their fellow Christians within the Church of England, led them to hold services in the streets and fields, with such tremendous success that new chapels were constructed for conducting their services, and the "stewards" serving to facilitate these meetings gradually evolved an organization that became the basis of a new denomination. "Circuit riding," the name given to ministers' traveling to bring services to small groups, grew in significance and spread to the United States, especially under the missionary activity of Whitfield, Peter Cartwright, and Thomas Coke, and westward across the Alleghenies by Francis Asbury.

Doctrinal emphases of the early Methodists centered about the importance of attaining experiences of personal assurance of the presence and saving power of Christ working within one's own life. In order to aid the growth in conviction of such experiences, three stages came to be distinguished. The first was CONVERSION, in which one became "convicted of sin," accepting intellectually the truth of Christian doctrine and its plan of salvation, repentant for one's sins, both original and personal, and willing to try to learn more about the way and become seriously devoted to it. The second was CONSECRATION, in which the willingness to learn and to strive toward experiencing perfection of Christian love was affirmed as complete and wholehearted. The third, SANCTIFICATION (or "entire sanctification" or being "sanctified holy"), occurred when one attained that experience in which he became fully aware of "being saved" because he embodied within himself both perfect assurance of God's love for him and his own love for God and his fellow men. Although backsliding was possible in any of these stages, restoration could be achieved through recurrent prayer, privately in one's "inner closet" and at frequent prayer meetings, and, when needed, additional trips to the "mourner's bench." The person experiencing perfection of love not only automatically devoted himself to the welfare of others, whether through ministering to their spiritual or their physical needs, but did so fearlessly.

Increase in membership brought more formal organization and, although semiannual "revival" services and summer "camp meetings" continue in many places, the early literal fundamentalism that dominated preaching has gradually given way to a much more liberalized outlook, especially as the population has become urbanized and ministers have received more college and seminary training. Midweek prayer meetings have tended to evolve into social fellowship programs, and then, as church organization became complex enough to require several educational specialists, desire to make full use of the "church plant" has subdivided both Sunday and weekly meetings into specialized group meetings, including Cub Scouts, hobby clubs, ping-pong games, and social dancing.

Although wide ranges of conservative-versus-liberal views prevail among members and ministers, various tendencies toward more liberal views seem to be increasing. In addition to those who continue to prefer relatively simple and unsophisticated Bible messages selected to provide spiritual uplift and social harmony, several varieties of philosophical subtleties have taken root and flourish in the Wesleyan colleges supported by the Methodist Church. Among these, the "Personalists" have been most prominent for many decades, especially under the leadership of Borden Parker Bowne, A. C. Knudsen, and E. S. Brightman at Boston University and R. T. Flewelling, longtime editor of *The Personalist,* at the University of Southern California. But two other philosophical schools have grown in prominence: The first is "Neo-Orthodoxy," which gives allegorical, highly subjective, and somewhat existentialist interpretations to the doctrines of "total depravity" and "original sin"; the second is "Humanism," which rejects doctrines of depravity and sin and supernatural deity while accepting the teachings of Jesus, who called himself the "son of man," as a supreme example of human wisdom; men are essentially good, and the use of Biblical myths and parables to inspire better living makes church participation worthwhile.

Regardless of differing doctrinal interpretations and philosophical leanings, Methodists tend to unite in promoting the "social gospel," or in implementing Christian love through social service. Monastic ideals of early and mediaeval Christianity have completely disappeared and support of "charity" and "missionary activity," which still continues, is beginning to be replaced by support of public welfare and social security programs and efforts toward church union. Rifts in Methodism, in 1828 and 1844, were healed, in 1939, with the formation of The Methodist Church. Serious efforts to unite organizationally with other Protestant denominations are under way. "The Social Creed of the Methodist Church," often revised annually, spells out areas of common concern, including those of threats to family life, economic welfare, world peace, civil liberties, and delinquency and crime. Whereas "skid-row" rescue missions are still sponsored by the independent Salvation Army, Methodist support of the Women's Christian Temperance Union has modulated in favor of Alcoholics Anonymous, boy's clubs, welfare homes, adoption agencies, CARE, and UNESCO. There are still about twenty different denominational organizations among the more than twelve million Methodists in the United States, and even others among the more than thirty million Methodists in the world. But growing desire for reunion with other Christians, illustrated in the establishment of the United Church of Canada in 1925, foreshadows the probable eventual disappearance of the name "Methodist" from the title of major Christian institutions.

The Quakers

George Fox (1624–91), after a profound conversion experience, believed that the true Christian life is to be found not in subscribing to any set of doctrines, belonging to any church organization, or participating in any Sunday or other sacramental rituals, but in constant or recurrent direct communication with God through awareness of his presence within and in devoting oneself to "concerns" for his fellowmen under the guidance of such awareness. God speaks directly to and through whomever he will whenever such a person is willing to listen and act. Awareness of the divine presence was spoken of as "the inner light," which manifested itself through one's genuine goodwill and conscientious effort to help others. Two kinds of consequence flow from such a view.

The first is that direct inspiration and revelation by God makes the Bible not the only source of the "Word of God," since God continuously reveals his will to every man who will listen to his own inner voice. There is no need for sacraments or rituals of any sort, for these tend to focus attention on objects outside the self rather than upon the inner light. They tend to stand between God and man as mediators that diminish the recognition of God's immediacy within the self. There is no need for either a priesthood or a professional ministry, for when one can hear God directly he has no need of another human interpreter no matter how well-trained. There is no need for payment of tithes to support such a ministry. But there is need for silent meditation (without music and without books) in which one intently seeks to know the will of God relative to matters of present concern. Meetings may be held at any time, though convenience and custom have resulted in holding them weekly, monthly, and yearly.

At a meeting, the members assemble and sit in silence for some time. When anyone feels that he is moved to speak about any matter that he believes should become a group concern, he breaks the silence and speaks, presenting a problem, called a "quiry," for common consideration. Others may respond with silence while meditating upon the problem and seeking inner light for its solution. Whoever then is moved to speak about the problem in terms of the light that he has received has his say. If all receive the same light, then a general consensus of the group expresses itself gradually and the asker of the question may then be encouraged to act upon his personal problem or the problem may become one for group concern requiring others to accept responsibility for action. When members receive different insights and convictions from their inner light, discussion and gentle persuasion may follow. If the "sense of the meeting" fails to become unanimous, action involving the group is postponed for further consideration at a later meeting. No formal rules of parliamentary procedure are followed, since the unanimity sought is a spiritual affair, not a mechanical nose-counting numerical majority. Although meetings may remain entirely unguided, a clerk of the monthly meeting is selected by consensus to record decisions. Meetings may be called to consider specific issues, including those in which a couple proposes marriage. Feasibility of a marriage of members within a group may become a group concern and, after the match has been generally approved, a meeting is arranged during which the couple appear and sit in silence separately, and, without any minister or any other individual officiating, after a suitable period of silence, the two stand and present themselves before the group to announce their intentions and pledge their faithfulness to each other.

The second consequence is that Quakers tend to become particularly conscientious about their personal and social interests. Honesty in business and courtesy, reliability, and responsibility in social relations characterize the Quakers. Early social reformers have made lasting contributions, such as Elizabeth Fry in prison reform, Dorothea Dix in mental hospitals, and Susan B. Anthony and Lucretia Mott in woman suffrage. William Penn established Pennsylvania and Philadelphia ("the City of Brotherly Love") as a "holy experiment" in guaranteeing complete religious freedom and considerable political responsibility. Although God may move a Quaker to fight, Quakers tend to be pacifists, opponents of capital punishment, and supporters of world peace movements. Although "The Religious Society of Friends," as they call themselves, may decide to raise money to support some political cause, their relatively small numbers (about 180,000 in the world, most of them in the United States) and personal involvement in social concerns has led to participation in person-to-person assistance activities, such as work camps, boys' clubs, aiding integration of minorities, and adult education programs. The American Friends Service Committee has become such an outstanding example of effective aid in promoting peace and goodwill in needy areas that the United States Peace Corps movement has adopted many of its methods in promoting international goodwill. Quakers have been generous in their founding and support of colleges, including Bryn Mawr, Earlham, Friends, George Fox, Guilford, Haverford, Swarthmore, Whittier, William Penn, and Wilmington, and have persistently advocated nonviolent methods in educational practices.

The Unitarians

The words "unity," "unitary," and "unitarian," when applied to the nature of God, may signify either (1) any monotheism, such as that held by Jews and Moslems, where God is regarded as having a single being and nature, (2) any anti-Trinitarian Christian doctrine or movement, such as those advocated by Arius, Socinus or Deists, or (3), more specifically, the views of those anti-Trinitarian Christians who have associated themselves together under the name "Unitarian," usually regarding Jesus not as God but as a man of great prophetic wisdom. Unitarians trace their theological origins to Jewish ideals expressed in the Old Testament, regard Jesus as teaching a unitary conception of God, point to historical facts that Christianity was officially neither Trinitarian nor Unitarian during the first two or three centuries A.D., and cite myriad examples to support the claim that the spirit of Unitarianism continued through the centuries as an unorganized but dynamic religious ideal. Erasmus, famous Renaissance humanist, omitted the famous "proof-text" for Trinitarianism from his New Testament because he regarded it as a later interpolation. Michael Servetus, a Spanish physician who discovered blood circulation through the lungs and who wrote a book *On the Errors of the Trinity,* was burned at the stake at Calvin's request.

The oldest Unitarian church in the world, still holding services, is said to be in Kolozsvár, Transylvania; its congregation was reported converted to the Unitarian position in 1568, about fifty years after the Lutheran reformation began. The name "Unitarian" appeared in written records about 1600. Faustus Socinus (1539–1604), an Italian theologian, fled to Poland in 1579 to escape persecution for his anti-Trinitarian views. Joseph Priestley, discoverer of oxygen, founded the first churches in North America using the name "Unitarian" in 1794 and 1796. Other great names in Unitarian history include Ralph Waldo Emerson, Thomas Jefferson, John Adams and John Quincy Adams, Dorothea Dix, Oliver Wendell Holmes, William Cullen Bryant, Nathaniel Hawthorne, Henry W. Longfellow, James Russell Lowell, Julia Ward Howe, Susan B. Anthony, Horace Mann, Daniel Webster, and, more recently, Albert Schweitzer. The Unitarians founded two theological seminaries, one at Harvard in 1819 and one at Chicago in 1844; the latter, the Meadville Theological School, functions as a member of the Federated Faculty of the theological schools associated with the University of Chicago.

Despite extremely broad bases for membership, such as "making a positive commitment to the righteous life," certain controversies have troubled the Unitarian movement. During the twenty-year period 1830–1850, German Idealism influenced Emerson and other Transcendentalists, some of whom quit the Unitarian ministry. After the Civil War, disputes arose as to whether pastors should remain in their parishes or whether some should "go West and grow up with the country." Between 1920 and 1940, there arose the Humanist controversy over whether Unitarians need to believe in God at all in order to be religious. Although Unitarians continue to be divided somewhat on this latter issue, eastern Unitarians tend to be more theistic and western Unitarians less so, their differences do not seem sharp enough to be very troublesome. The most recent controversy has to do with whether or not Unitarians should be regarded as Christians. Since Unitarians regard the Bible as a thoroughly human book, serving to inspire men's religious sentiments if one selects the right parts of it, and since they regard not only later Western writings but also scriptures of Oriental religions and philosophies as inspirational, some of the more freethinking Unitarians believe they have gone beyond the confines of Christian traditions and should no longer have to bear the Christian label. Unitarians generally regard creeds as divisive, so try to avoid formulating one that will be required of all members. They also support, through their Unitarian Service Committee, social welfare projects in Nigeria, Cambodia, Greece, Korea, and Gallup, New Mexico, though many of them prefer to emphasize municipal, national, and UNESCO methods of providing solutions for social needs.

The Universalists, originating as a distinguishable movement as early as 1770 in the United States, pay tribute especially to the efforts of John Murray and Hosea Ballou, and recognize three "professions": the "Winchester Profession" (1803), the "Boston Profession" (1899), and the "Washington Profession" (1935), each more liberal than its predecessor. A salient feature of their doctrine is the view that all men eventually will be saved from sin and there will be no endless punishment. Although originally Trinitarian, Universalist clergymen had largely adopted Unitarian doctrines by 1850. Now the main difference between Universalists and Unitarians seems to be that, for the former, God is believed to be too good to damn men while, for the latter, men are believed to be too good to be damned by God. The new Unitarian Universalist Association claims more than a thousand religious societies, including 679 churches and 359 fellowships, and its adherents and associates number approximately two hundred thousand persons.

The Baptists

When Baptists are called "Protestants," many of them protest, saying Baptist doctrines were held long before the Protestant Reformation and have been held continuously since the time of Jesus and of John the Baptist, who baptized Jesus. Absence of historical documentation supporting this claim need not deter one from recognizing similarities between immersion in the Jordan River (where sprinkling cups were probably not handy anyway) and immersion in a baptizing tank behind a church pulpit. Also, the symbolism of washing away the sinful life appears to be more genuine when immersion is complete; sprinkling or a damp pat on the head does not carry with it quite the feeling of completeness that total submersion can. Furthermore, an infant cannot willingly commit his life to abstain from sinning, so infant baptism must be useless for this purpose. A person must have reached adulthood or at least the age of accountability (usually regarded as eight years or older) before he can decide for himself to commit his life and will to the service of God. Therefore, neither infant baptism nor sprinkling seems sufficient to assure the required commitment.

Just when the Baptists had their beginnings continues to be a matter for discussion. The Anabaptists or "rebaptizers," so-called by their enemies because they refused to recognize the value of infant baptism, opposed not only the Roman Church but also Zwingli in Zurich in 1528. Conrad Grebel, the first Anabaptist martyr, was executed by drowning in 1627 by Zwingli's Zurich council. English Baptists trace their origins to John Smyth's baptizing himself and followers in 1608 and to Thomas Helwy's establishing the first Baptist church in England in 1612. These men were "General Baptists," believing that Christ died to save all men, *i.e.*, that all men would actually be saved, in contrast with the "Particular Baptists" who, Calvinistically, believed that Christ died to save only the "elect." Roger Williams founded the first Baptist Church in America in 1639. Baptist insistence upon separation of church and state contributed to the First Amendment to the Constitution of the United States, guaranteeing religious liberty. Division of Baptists into Northern and Southern groups in 1845 over Civil War issues has never been healed and some twenty-six different Baptist denominations exist in the United States today. Of the forty million Baptists in the world, something less than half of them live in the United States. The Southern Baptists claim more than ten million members, the American Baptists (formerly Northern Baptists) about two million, and two large Negro groups about seven million.

Christian Science

Mary Baker Eddy (1821–1910), one of the few women accredited with founding a religion or denomination, experienced a remarkable healing of body and confidence of mind during her fortieth year, after a life of illness, sorrow, and uncertainty. Drawing upon her New Hampshire Congregationalist background, she discovered abiding satisfaction from interpreting the Bible as revealing not only the goodness of God but the unreality of evil. After extensive study of the scriptures, she published a volume, *Science and Health with a Key to the Scriptures* (1857), expounding the view that God is Spirit, and that all ideas of Matter are illusory or unreal. Sin and suffering are the result of permitting ideas of evil to occupy the mind, so the way to freedom from illness and disease, as well as from fear and hate, is to pray devotedly that the everpresent goodness of

God, who is himself the life we live, help us to overcome our submission to evil thoughts. Our confidence that we have been healed of illness or fear signifies our attaining or regaining full trust in the goodness of God.

As Mrs. Eddy's followers grew in numbers, they organized a church in 1892 and built "The Mother Church" in Boston in 1906. Now more than three thousand branches exist in forty-five countries. The Church of Jesus Christ, Scientist, to use its official name, has no paid ministers, does not perform any of the sacramental rituals (which, being "material," must thus be evil or illusory) for it believes externalized activity tends to degrade purely spiritual affairs, conducts Sunday services from printed lessons drawn from both the Bible and *Science and Health* so that the same lesson can be read in all churches in the world on the same Sunday, and authorizes teachers and healers (Christian Science Practitioners) to serve both spiritual and physical needs in preference to priests and physicians. At each Sunday service, two readers, one man and one woman, read, alternately, selected portions of the Bible and of *Science and Health* giving Mrs. Eddy's interpretation. A Christian Scientist may call a physician or use drugs if he chooses, but he will call upon God as a first, not as a last, resort. About twelve thousand full-time practitioners have become available to serve Christian Scientists who may need help in praying their way back to fully-healed, healthy, wholesome living. Christian Scientists do not believe in resurrection of the body after death, because the body, like all matter, is unreal; and full self-realization of one's truly spiritual nature will bring one to the recognition of an eternal spiritual life entirely freed from all evil and thus from all concern for the body.

The Mormons

The Church of Jesus Christ of the Latter Day Saints, organized on April 6, 1830, attributes its recent origin to Joseph Smith, who, as a child of fourteen, had visions of God and Christ telling him not to join any of the Methodist, Presbyterian, Baptist, and other churches in his Palmyra, New York, neighborhood, of the angel Moroni's telling him about buried golden plates bearing additional holy scriptures, and of messengers conferring upon him and others both an Aaronic and a Melchizedek Priesthood. The *Book of Mormon,* being a translation of these plates, relates the story of three main peoples who came to the American continent, one soon after the dispersion from the Tower of Babel and two about six centuries B.C., and how they too were taught Israelitish and Christian ideals. The Mormons, as they have come to be called, believe that God provides continuing revelation, both directly to individuals and through the Bible and *Book of Mormon.* Since those in other churches have drifted away from God's teachings, his restoration of his priesthood constitutes the Mormon Church as the only true one now.

Mormons regard God, Christ, and the Holy Spirit as three distinct persons. Hence they reject Trinitarianism. They believe that human souls precede birth in mortal bodies and expect all persons to become "exalted" in one of the "Three Degrees of Glory" after death. There are not two places, heaven and hell, but three: The Telestial Kingdom, for those who neither accept Jesus nor deny the Holy Spirit; the Terrestrial Kingdom, for those followers of Jesus who have not been valiant in their testimony for him; and the Celestial Kingdom, for those valiant in testimony. Men are essentially good, not totally depraved; they can progress and become better, both during this mortal life and after. Those now living may assist the dead through prayers and posthumous baptism in one of several Mormon temples, where genealogical files assist in keeping the records straight. God, our Father, had a father who had a father, etc., and we, if we attain the Celestial Kingdom, may beget our own spiritual children and guide them through mortality on a celestial body (star) of our own. Thus divine progeneration did not begin with some absolute first cause and will not stagnate in some timeless heaven, but the cosmic order enjoys progressive creation and progressive spiritual development for all who freely choose to make themselves worthy of Celestial "exaltation" and who work honestly, assiduously, and soberly to do so. Mormons have become noted for their honesty, hard work, cooperation, sobriety (abstaining from coffee as well as alcoholic drinks), and many children (and, as an early expedient, many wives).

Persecutions that drove Mormons to Pennsylvania, Ohio, Missouri, Illinois, and finally to Utah resulted in Utah's becoming a predominantly Mormon state. Church headquarters have been established in Salt Lake City, with its famous Mormon Temple and Tabernacle. Brigham Young University stands as the leading Mormon university, but the state University of Utah also has a large number of Mormon students and faculty. Except for top officials, Mormons support no paid ministers, but each able male youth serves a two-year period as missionary before undertaking his life's work. Each male may serve not only as an "Elder" but also as a "High Priest," "Bishop," "Patriarch," or "Apostle," preaching, baptizing, or otherwise filling responsible offices in the Church. Tithes and Church-owned farms, industries, and banking enterprises keep the Church prosperous, and Church relief societies and welfare programs keep their members secure. Mormons number about a million and a half (most of whom live in the United States, though missions have been established in about thirty countries), not including persons belonging to The Reorganized Church of Latter-Day Saints with headquarters in Independence, Missouri.

Christian Existentialism

Existentialism is a recent variety of Romanticism that rebels against reducing religion to reason, required beliefs (affirmation of faith in obsolete creeds), and rituals (fixed forms of worship). It protests against fixed universal statements true of all men, which ignore the unique personal encounter that each must experience for himself in order to be authentically religious. It asserts that truth is subjective, not objective, particular, not general, and involves emotional commitment, not merely intellectual assent and behavioral indifference. Blaise Pascal (1623–62), French mathematician and physicist, early bemoaned the failure of reason to settle our doubts and satisfy our deepest interests: "The heart has reasons which the reason does not know." Soren Kierkegaard (1813–55), the first significant modern Christian existentialist, rebelled against the formalism of his Danish church and Hegel's grandiose rationalistic scheme by locating the core of religion in the heart of each individual faced with a particular encounter requiring choice and decision, irrevocably risking and committing his very existence therein. His *Either/Or, Fear and Trembling, Sickness Unto Death, Attack on Christendom,* and other works remain classic expressions of the view that truth is subjective, particular, unique, momentary, and always a decisive assertion of a will to believe and to act in the face of uncertainty and even of absurdity. Whether or not a God exists externally to one's vision, one's own subjective insistence on believing that an eternal deity exists is sufficient reason for believing and acting.

Religious experience is "authentic" only as one continues to encounter uncertainties and decides courageously and responsibly to see and act in one's own way. Creedal assurance and church regulations that provide feelings of permanent security in an eternally guaranteed system destroy the very heart of authentic religion. Churches and creeds kill religion, destroy God, deaden men. Attempts to reason one's way out of doubts end in failure; for the rationalist must himself irrationally affirm the very premises he uses to silence the demands of his will, which forever refuses to be permanently entombed in syllogisms or embalmed in conclusions.

Germans, such as Karl Barth and Rudolph Bultmann, Americans such as Paul Tillich and Reinhold Niebuhr, French Catholics such as Jacques Maritain and Gabriel Marcel, Russian Orthodox such as Nicholas Berdyaev, and Jews such as Martin Buber, all, in varying ways, express the spirit of Christian or theistic Existentialism. The more one penetrates to the core of Christian Existentialism, the more he realizes that its emphasis upon anxiety, concrete uniqueness of individual encounters with reality and unreality ("nonbeing"), perpetual spiritual crises, and voluntary commitment to risks and the courageous affirmation of those risks, as the ultimate constituents of life and the universe, the more he realizes the lack of significant difference between theistic and atheistic varieties of Existentialism. Existentialism, in calling attention to an essential aspect of human existence, emphasizes a significant dimension in human thinking and acting; but, as with every good idea, men inspired by it tend to carry it to extremes, reducing the whole man to some essential part of him that others have ignored or denied. Man needs to say "Yea" to his own worth *and* unworthiness in the face of fearful uncertainties; but to create continuing crises, idealizing anxiety, and perpetuating despair beyond actual need may signify morbidity as truly as can creedal dogmatism or blind optimism. It is true that man is not *just* a thing, object, or instance of a rational or mechanical law; but man is *also* a thing, an object, and a particular embodying many universals. Does not sanity in religion and life require willingness to say "Yea" to both, or, indeed, to all of the truths about man?

Ecumenical Movements

Repeated schisms have divided Christianity into multitudes of sects. Although this multiplicity testifies to the richness in variety of forms that it may take, the schisms have grown to such proportions that many Christians regard too much diversity as a serious evil. Reform resulting in further splintering is now being countered by reform aimed at reunion. Although organizational divisiveness has always been regretted, recent trends in world development have magnified the evils to a point where many believe that unnecessary division threatens the very existence of Christianity itself. Some of these evils are spiritual, some economic, and some defensive.

(1) Christianity has persistently claimed to be a universal religion, one proclaiming love for all mankind and idealizing a "City of God" as one large happy family. When doctrinal and organizational differences produce antagonisms among Christians, the failure to achieve its objective is obvious. When Christianity causes distrust instead of love and trust, it must accuse itself of being unchristian. In an age when Christianity faces attacks from so many external sources, it can hardly afford the luxury of internal inconsistencies that substantially weaken it.

These divisive ills plague Christians at all levels. Children, youth, and young people contemplating marriage become disturbed about the seeming unreasonableness of differences that separate them unnecessarily. Adults, finding themselves fenced off from their Christian neighbors, fellow workers, and fellow citizens in religious affairs tend to wonder whether the inconveniences are worthwhile. If they conclude that their differences do not matter significantly even when the doctrines assert that they do, they begin to doubt whether the doctrines themselves matter significantly. Ministers, finding need for cooperation in combatting community ills, are embarrassed by their differences and by their competitive duplication of functions. But especially in mission work, where conflicting claims bewilder and repel prospective converts, missionaries find it both expedient and spiritually uplifting to join in a common cause that their warring denominations back home have difficulty in comprehending. When denominational leaders seek to establish chairs for religious instruction in state colleges, they find their efforts rebuffed, not because they cannot provide well-qualified instructors but because each of several denominations insists upon giving its own separate course in the "Life of Christ," for example.

(2) Denominational differences result in economic inefficiency from duplication of services instead of profiting by division of labor. Costs of building and maintaining a church plant, of training and supporting qualified ministers, and of administration have soared and promise to become more complex and expensive. Empty pews and empty pulpits, chronic in many places, have become acute in others. Underpaid ministers leave the ministry while small or partly-filled churches suffer because they do not join forces and facilities with other nearby churches having a similar doctrine. As people become increasingly mobile and fail to find precisely the right denomination in their new neighborhoods, they are inclined to drift away rather than join a denomination that they had previously learned to distrust. People of wealth who will money to support Christian endeavor often draw back from endowing sectarian movements engaged in squabbles when public or other nonsectarian agencies apply their charitable efforts more impartially and efficiently. Competition among marginal churches is not just a sin; it is tending to become suicidal.

(3) Ecumenical movements are being spurred also by the need for additional strength to meet attacks upon

Protestants (to say nothing about Christendom as a whole) by *(a)* Roman Catholics, *(b)* intellectuals, and *(c)* other religions.

(a) The size, solidarity, political and economic power, and rate of growth, as well as superiority in clerical training of Roman Catholicism not only place Protestantism at a considerable disadvantage in competition but also promote fear of its being overwhelmed and eventually driven out. The record of the treatment of Protestants in Catholic-dominated countries presents a frightful picture. Increasing awareness among Protestants that internal conflicts may so weaken them that they can no longer compete with Catholics has persuaded many of them of the practical necessity of ecumenical efforts.

(b) Attacks by "intellectualism," both inside and outside the churches, muster increasingly challenging evidence against both the truth and the adequacy of Christian doctrines and practices. Critical scholarship, much of it supported by churches seeking the truth about their own history and foundations, have raised additional doubts about the absoluteness and exclusiveness of Christian and sectarian claims. Materialism, romanticism, socialism, emergentism, humanism, pragmatism, existentialism, positivism, Zen, and many other philosophies have arisen to provoke thought and to provide alternatives to traditional Christianity. Increasing education, communication, and travel produce a great many ideas that both compete with and depreciate Christian ideas and values. Modern science and technology have become the respected sources of wisdom rather than ancient scriptures. Secularism, or the devotion of self more fully to the myriads of necessary and appealing activities outside the church, has become overwhelming. Secularism, many cry, is the chief enemy of religion.

(c) Other religions, such as Islam, Buddhism, Confucianism, and Communism, have become more aggressive and, as the world grows smaller, confront us more frequently. The progressive lack of success by missionaries in accomplishing doctrinal conversion has become widely known. Warnings by sociologists that missionaries often produce cultural conflicts that do more harm

than good by disrupting established moral patterns give us further pause for thought. Rising nations resent foreign interference and increase restrictions that exclude sectarian propagandists. But an even more serious threat to the luxury of Christian sectarianism appears as we become aware of the growing numbers of Christians who have been enticed into other religions. When Christians live in comparative isolation, foreign religions may easily be regarded as false and fearful. But as Christians become personally acquainted with confident Moslems, saintly Buddhists, and wise, urbane, and happy Confucians, and receive informed and appreciative answers to their queries about other religions, they not only learn to respect them but, if they have been misled by their own Christian teachers, they may wonder, at least, whether Christianity must depend for its maintenance upon misrepresentations of those religions. Also, a growing awareness of the ancientness, insight, inspiration, tolerance, and effectiveness of the scriptures and institutions of other religions produces appreciations that may be accompanied by deep doubts about the truth and the advisability of doctrinal exclusiveness characterizing Christian orthodoxy.

How did ecumenical movements begin and how have they progressed? Two sorts of reunions should be distinguished. The first consists of mergers of two or more sectarian organizations into one new agency. The second consists of interdenominational cooperation through a federal organization that leaves the participating denominations intact and independent. A third kind of movement that establishes an independent transdenominational organization, such as the YMCA and YWCA, expresses the ecumenical spirit and provides practical opportunities for interreligious living, but does not in itself function as an agency for uniting denominational organizations. Its example, and its influence upon persons, does provide continuing impetus for sects to consider possibilities for further cooperation.

The first sort of reunion has already made amazing progress. We have already mentioned some of these mergers: the American Lutheran Church formed from several Lutheran groups in 1960; the Lutheran Church in America resulted from a union of the United Lutheran Church with the Augustana, the American Evangelical, and the Finnish Evangelical Lutheran Churches in 1962; the United Church of Christ formed in 1961 by the joining of the Congregational Christian Churches with the Evangelical and Reformed Church, both of which were products of recent unions; the Methodist Church united the Methodist Protestant Church, the Methodist Episcopal Church, and the Southern Methodist Church in 1961.

Serious discussions now under way are exploring possibilities for a huge merger of the Methodist Church, the Protestant Episcopal Church, the United Church of Christ, and the United Presbyterian Church. Together, these four groups have more than eighteen million members in the United States. Despite the air of hopefulness prevailing during the 1962 discussions held in Washington, D.C., the United States exhibits a tardy effort in this direction, in light of the interdenominational mergers already accomplished in other countries. The United Church of Canada brought Methodists, Congregationalists, and Presbyterians together in 1925. The Reformed Church of France resulted from integrating the Evangelical Methodist Church of France, the Reformed Evangelical Church of France, the Reformed Church of France, and a union of Evangelical free churches in 1938. The Church of Christ in Japan coalesced fifteen denominations in 1941. The Dutch Reformed Church absorbed other Reformed Churches in the Netherlands in 1946. The Church of South India grew from a union of Presbyterians and Congregationalists in 1908, which added the Methodists in 1925 and the Anglicans in 1947. The Evangelical Church in Germany federally joined twenty-seven independent regional churches in 1948.

Our second·sort of reunion, joining independent denominations in federated action, attained a major landmark in the United States with the formation of the Federal Council of Churches of Christ in America in 1908. This became the National Council of Churches of Christ in America in 1950. The World Council of Churches held its first assembly at Amsterdam in 1948, its second in Evanston during 1954, and its third in New Delhi in 1961. The Russian Orthodox Church participated in the New Delhi meeting and the Roman Catholic Church sent an official observer. Talks between the heads of the Anglican and Roman Catholic Churches recently and between the Roman Catholic and Greek Orthodox branches reveal additional stirrings. Pope John XXIII promises to go down in history as famous for calling the First and Second Vatican Councils in 1962 and 1963 to prepare the way for greater Christian unity. How far these movements will go can only be guessed at present, but certainly powerful forces are at work.

No summary of interdenominational cooperation is complete without some mention of the roles of student movements. The Student Christian Movement, guided by John R. Mott, as early as 1886 set a pace for enthusiasm in world youth missions. Student YMCAs. organized on college campuses continued to spark reflective thinking and social conscience as well as awareness of needs for church reunion. In 1895 they promoted the far-reaching World Student Christian Federation, which now joins student Christian movements in seventy-seven countries. Most college campuses in the United States today, excepting those supported by narrow sects, enjoy interdenominational fellowship.

In concluding this chapter on Christianity, I am tempted to apologize for neglecting so many other significant sects, such as the Brethren, the Churches of Christ and Disciples of Christ, the Churches of God, the Church of the Nazarene, the Churches of the New Jerusalem (Swedenborgian), the Foursquare Gospel, Jehovah's Witnesses, the Mennonites (with fourteen denominations in the United States), the Moravians, the Pentecostal Churches (nine varieties), the Salvation Army, the Seventh-Day Adventists and many others. But the limitation of space make such omissions necessary.

Why did Islam arise? Most of our great religions began in the sixth century B.C. or earlier, but Islam started during the sixth century A.D., about a millennium later. Were there not enough religions in the world already? Why did Islam spread so rapidly and so far? It claims more followers today than any other religion except Christianity. Why does it continue to appeal and to compete successfully with Hinduism, Christianity, Buddhism, Taoism, Confucianism, Shintoism, and Judaism? As we shall see, its message is simple, direct, only mildly demanding; yet it inspires confidence and provides assurance. It arose in a place where the time was ripe, and it grew, as have so many religions, through the fortunes of political alliances and successful military conquests. It combines a spirit of brotherhood and social conformity with a lofty, yet practicable, theology and a simple creedal behavior. Permeating a society, it becomes a way of life and, indeed, a civilization.

Mohammed

An Arabian camel-caravan manager of the Quraysh tribe dominating Mecca's Kaaba (sacred black stone) concessions, Mohammed learned from pilgrims and traveling merchants about Jewish and Christian ideas of God. Dissatisfied with the sometimes cruel animistic practices prevailing among his kinsmen and neighboring tribes, he wondered about, admired, sought after, and meditated upon ideas of a single almighty God. After marriage to a rich widow, he found time to pursue his thoughts in earnest, in a cave on Mount Hira outside the city of Mecca. Here the archangel Gabriel, a messenger from God, appeared to him, requesting him to recite. Reluctant at first, this supposedly illiterate doubter responded to his promptings, after encouragement by his relatives, with greater faith and confidence. His sayings, reported as revelations from God through Gabriel, were recorded by others and eventually gathered together, in the order of their length, as the *"Qur'an"* or "Koran." Although sayings of Mohammed, other than those attributed to Gabriel, were gathered into various *"Hadiths"* (statements), together constituting the *"Sunna"* (traditions), the Koran remains the sole book containing revelations of God (Allah) to Mohammed.

When Mohammed appeared in front of the sacred Kaaba to preach his new message, he was scoffed and jeered, yet tolerated at first. Then, as his one-God teachings interfered with profits from animistic worshippers, he came to be treated more rudely. Protected by a powerful uncle and vendetta law, he continued preaching for awhile, until his wife and uncle died. Then he fled from persecutions. By good fortune he was invited to establish control at Medina, three hundred miles north of Mecca, where feuding tribes needed a strong neutral ruler. His escape from Meccan attacks and flight to Medina in 622, called the *"Hegira,"* was of such momentous significance that Moslems use it to mark the year One of their own calendar.

In Medina, Mohammed built the first mosque and established public worship. To gain arms and other supplies for his followers, he led a small band that robbed a Meccan caravan. War followed, with Mohammed first stronger, then weaker, then stronger than his Meccan enemies. In capturing Mecca in 630, he became the chief ruler, conquering opposing tribes and uniting all of Arabia under his own theocratic rule. After his sudden death in 632, Abu-Bakr, a leading devotee, became his successor (caliph), followed after a year by Omar, who captured Damascus and Syria from the Christians. Jerusalem, Palestine, Egypt, North Africa, Spain, and Persia all fell to Moslem conquest. Later, armies went into Turkey, Mongolia, India, and Africa, and large populations were converted as far east as Indonesia and the Philippines. India, when freed from British rule, was split into two separate countries at Moslem insistence, Pakistan becoming a new Moslem nation. Politically, Moslem countries remain a potent force to be reckoned with in any world-shaping decisions. Islam, still growing and spreading, is a religion that more Christians, as well as Hindus, Humanists, Buddhists, and Communists must meet and deal with in vigorous competition.

Islamic Doctrine

The teachings of the Koran may be presented rather simply. Its central ideas consist in the following:

(1) ONE GOD. "There is no God but Allah," though, as elaborated later, he may be called by as many as the ninety-nine names. The "foremost attribute is Rabb, which means provider, sustainer and cherisher." (Khalifa Abdul Hakim, *Islamic Ideology,* Lahore: Publishers United, Ltd. 1951, p. 54.) He is creator, maintainer, and dissolver of the world. He is omnipotent, omniscient, absolute. He is eternal and yet dynamic. He is unchangeable and yet compassionate and merciful. Being the cause of causes, immanent as well as transcendent, his functions are endless for he acts everywhere. However, a careful student of the Koran will observe the evolution of concepts about the nature of Allah as Mohammed's thoughts develop. In *Sura* IV: 20, we notice that "God is easily turned." The earlier *suras* (sayings, or sections, of the Koran) view God as governing men loosely, whereas later *suras* depict him as more rigorous. At first, Mohammed was not so sure of himself and his conceptions of God. Later, his conviction became firmer; then he spoke of God as the inscrutable determiner of every man's destiny.

(2) MANY PROPHETS. "We must believe in all the messengers of Allah ... from Noah to Muhammad." (Mahumd Shaltout in *Islam—The Straight Path,* Edited by Kenneth Morgan, N.Y.: Ronald Press, 1958, p. 91.) Moses, the Hebrew Prophets, and Jesus are included. Even those not mentioned in the Koran must be accepted. But the last and mightiest is Mohammed. After him we need no more, although God will not leave any age or time without some messenger. All scriptures recording God's revealed messages, including the Jewish Pentateuch and the Christian New Testament, should be respected; but the pinnacle of revelation occurs in the Koran by comparison with which all others pale into relative insignificance.

(3) ANGELS. Since Allah has no visible form and thus

should never be depicted by any image, he must appear to men through messengers. Gabriel, messenger to Mohammed, is only one of a host of servants who descend with his decrees, observe and keep a record of men's thoughts and conduct for the Last Judgment, assist Moslems in battle, and guard the gates of Hell. *Iblis* (*Diablos,* or the Devil) or *Shaitin* (Satan), a fallen angel, rules Hell and tempts men on earth into it.

(4) THE LAST DAY. A Day of Judgment, foreknowable through signs and portents, quaking earth and crumbling mountains, announced by a last trumpet, will see a rising of all from the dead and a reading of the records of each man's deeds, with consequent consignment to eternal Heaven or Hell.

(5) HEAVEN AND HELL. The lucky ones who go to Heaven will dwell "in gardens of pleasure," surrounded by "eternal youths with goblets . . . of flowing wine" but "no headache shall they feel therefrom, nor shall their wits be dimmed." They will be rewarded with "fruits such as they deem the best, the flesh of fowl as they desire, and bright and large-eyed maids. . . ." The unlucky ones will squirm "in hot blasts and boiling water, and a shade of pitchy smoke." (*Sura* LVI. Translated by E. H. Palmer, 1900, reprinted in *The Koran,* London: Oxford University Press, 1933, pp. 466–67.)

Islamic doctrine, although simple, aims to be adequate for all needs. Hence, there are endless commentary, interpretation, and application by those who study it and live by it. As we shall see, numerous schools of thought have arisen to provide more adequate theories where the Koran itself remains vague. Islamic teaching includes also certain religious duties, summarized as "The Five Pillars," that have been interpreted extensively, and ethical and legal precepts for guiding daily life. As Moslems moved into other countries, they needed to debate the philosophies and religions therein; consequently they developed their own accounts of how Islam deals better with human problems than these do.

The Five Pillars

Five specific kinds of religious acts are expected of all able Moslems.

(1) REPETITION OF THE "WORD OF WITNESS." "I witness that there is no God but Allah and that Mohammed is his Prophet." Repetition is intended to be no mere recital of words but a reaffirmation of wholehearted conviction in Islam and its doctrine.

(2) PRAYER. Reverence, not petition, is the purpose of prayer. Feelings of reverence become more fully embodied through a fixed form of physical prostration involving seven movements. The first consists in standing facing Mecca, proclaiming "God is the Most Great." Then one recites the opening *sura* of the Koran: "Praise belongs to God, the Lord of the worlds, the merciful, the compassionate, the ruler of the Day of Judgment! Thee we serve and Thee we ask for aid. Guide us in the right path, the path of those to whom Thou art gracious; not of those with whom Thou art angry, nor of those who go astray." Recitation of another *sura* or passage from the Koran may accompany this first. Then, keeping his back straight, the worshipper bows from his hips until his back assumes a horizontal line; his hands then rest on his knees while he says "Great God." Then he straightens up, saying "God is Most Great." Next, he kneels and touches his head to the floor, saying "God the Highest" as he descends. Then he raises himself and sits on his heels, saying "God is Most Great." Finally, he touches his head to the ground a second time. When this seven-act bowing or *rak'ah* is repeated immediately, the first step is omitted. Conclusion of a series of *rak'ahs* brings forth again the Word of Witness: "There is no God but Allah and Mohammed is his Prophet."

Prayers occur five times each day, with two *rak'ahs* at daybreak, four at noon, four in midafternoon, three after sunset, and four early in the night. One may pray wherever he happens to be, but, when possible, prayer should occur congregationally in a mosque. Upon entering a mosque, one should remove his shoes and wash himself in a pool, provided at the entrance, to help in purifying himself physically and spiritually. No seats, statues, pictures, or pulpit exist in a mosque. No music, not even singing, occurs in mosques. One may bring a prayer rug. Men line themselves up in rows and enact the ritual uniformly under the direction of an appointed leader. Moslems have no priests or ministers. An *imam,* who announces the time of assembly by shouting from a minaret (now through loudspeakers), directs the ritual by enacting it himself. A reading from the scriptures or a short sermon may accompany the service. Friday is especially recognized as a holy day when all should attend a mosque service. Such prayers take place also at funeral services and at two annual feasts, Ramadan and al-Qurban.

(3) FASTING. A second physical form of worship takes place during the month of Ramadan. This consists in refraining from eating, drinking, and sexual intercourse from before sunrise until after sunset during the month. Although the Ramadan period memorializes God's granting revelation to Mohammed during the month of Ramadan, its continuing purpose is also to promote spiritual testing, awareness of experiences that the poor have when hungry, and deliberate discipline of the will so as to keep it sensitive to proper duties.

(4) RELIGIOUS TAX. *Zakat* is a voluntary gift to the poor, to educational and health institutions, to debtors, to collection officers, and to police or military persons defending the faith and fighting against unbelievers. Various formulas have been worked out, such as one-tenth of one's income from land watered by rain and one-twentieth from irrigated land, and two and a half percent of savings. Additonal gifts by the prosperous are expected.

(5) PILGRIMAGE. Still another physical or overt expression of worship consists in a journey to Mecca at least once in a lifetime for all who are able. Annually, during the sacred month of *Dhu'l-Hijja,* thousands of pilgrims gather from all directions, and from various countries, castes, and occupations, in an atmosphere of brotherhood and holiness in and around Mecca. Ceremonial traditions include wearing a seamless white robe, fasting as during Ramadan, refraining from harming any living creature, and even shaving one's head. Three major stages in the public ceremonies occupy all who have strength to do so. The first consists in running three times and then walking four times around the Kaaba, stopping each time to kiss the black stone at its southeast corner, except when crowded conditions do not permit. The second, the Lesser Pilgrimage, involves running seven times between two hills, imitating

Hagar's frantic search for water for her crying son. The third, the Great Pilgrimage, finds the large multitude assembling on the plain of Arafat several miles east ("a day's foot journey") of Mecca, from which rises the small Mount Arafat on which Mohammed preached his farewell sermon. From noon till sunset people walk about in a worshipful attitude, sharing each other's mood and an atmosphere of holiness. Sunset climaxes this disciplined pilgrimage (*hajj* or *hadj*). Having finished this ceremony, all then shout as loud as they can, or use noisemakers, while they journey through the night back toward Mecca. At sunrise each pilgrim casts seven pebbles down a hill at Muna, crying "In the name of God! Allah is almighty," at every throw. A "Great Festival" includes the slaughtering of sheep or camels and feeding those who may not have brought sacrifice with them. After three days of merrymaking, a return to Mecca for a final circuit of the Kaaba terminates the ceremonies.

Although *Jihad* or a holy war, to repel attackers and destroy disbelievers, is neither one of the "pillars" nor advocated by those Moslems seeking in earnest to make Islam a peaceful religion, the Koran itself commands: "Fight in God's way with those who fight with you; but do not start a fight." "Kill them wherever ye find them, and drive them out of whence they drive you out; for sedition is worse than slaughter." (*Sura* II: 186, 187.) "Fight those who believe not in God and in the last day, and who forbid not what God and His Apostle have forbidden, and who do not practice the religion of truth from amongst those to whom the Book has been brought, until they pay the tribute by their hands and be as little ones." (*Sura* IX: 29.) Even Jews and Christians have been singled out in *Sura* IX: 30: "God fight them! How they lie!" Immediate transfer to Paradise is promised those who die in holy battle.

Four Wives?

Moral precepts given by Mohammed are very much like those of other ethical systems. Kindness to parents, avoidance of adultery, cheating, and lying, refraining from stealing from orphans, and the like, are admonished in some detail. Condemnation of superstitious practices prevailing among the animists against whom Mohammed fought helped raise moral standards. Some injunctions which seem striking today include those against drinking intoxicating wines, eating pork, gambling, and usury. Slavery was accepted in his time, but it has been discouraged since. Perhaps most astonishing to many non-Moslems is Mohammed's permission for men to marry "by twos, or threes, or fours." (*Sura* IV: 2.) Monogamy is commonly practiced; a plurality of wives was intended apparently only for cases such as "if you fear that you cannot do justice between orphans." Islamic law and practice continue to authorize a man to marry a second wife where the initial objectives of marriage, such as begetting children, fail to be fulfilled. A story appeared recently of a Moslem wife who, overburdened with work, requested her husband to marry a second wife; when he refused, she took her case to court and won.

Moslem Sects

The prevalence of controversy, both during Mohammed's lifetime and ever since, mars the peace idealized by Islam. Tradition has it that even Mohammed himself predicted that his followers would form no less than seventy-three divergent groups, surpassing in number the sectarian divisions among both Jews and Christians. Most of the contentiousness has faded into forgotten history, but those quarrels which continue to divide the sects must be acknowledged when we try to comprehend the varieties of views bearing the name "Islam."

Two main groups of sects have been distinguished as Sunnites and Shiites. The Sunnites, so named because they accept as authoritative the *Sunna* or traditions embodied in the *Hadith,* are regarded as the more orthodox or conservative branch and have the largest numbers of followers. They consider their leaders as mere men who devote themselves perhaps more than others to doing good deeds. The Shiites, who claim to be the true legitimists, believe their leaders, or *imams,* to be divinely inspired, thereby embodying both the authority and wisdom needed to deal with new issues as they arise. Shiites have proved more adaptable and pliable in the face of changing circumstances; hence they commonly act in ways that introduce new precedents. Thus the Sunnites tend to follow a more rigorously orthodox policy based on appeals to the authority of tradition whereas the Shiites believe that divine inspiration continues to express itself through contemporary leaders in such a way that newer revelations may appear to deal with new situations. These two broad divisions among Moslems have sufficient significance and complexity to deserve individual attention.

The Sunnites

Orthodoxy accepts the teachings of Mohammed as revealed in both the Koran and the *Hadith* (sayings attributed to him, with interpretations by his immediate followers). When questions arise, they can be settled by appeal to his sayings. However, even within this broad policy, perplexing differences exist. The first sect developed when Ali, the fourth caliph, promising to be rigorous, suddenly compromised with Ommiad competitors; reportedly twelve thousand disgusted warriors deserted him to become *Kharijites* (secessionists). When the Ommiad tribesmen gained control, moving the capital to Damascus, the *Kharijites,* believing the Ommiads to be Moslems for economic and political reasons rather than true followers of the Prophet of Allah, fought them fiercely. However, they were outnumbered and wiped out, except for a few, whose views still prevail in Zanzibar and Algeria.

Another group, believing that not men, but only Allah, can judge a man's true intentions, refuses to condemn men who appear to be sinners. They believe that judgment upon disbelievers and other evildoers remains God's province and beyond the wisdom of imperfect men. Consequently, they hold that final judgment upon any man should be postponed until God himself becomes ready. Called "Postponers" *(Murjites),* they tolerated Ommiads as well as Christians and Jews, who appeared to be something less than wholehearted in their acceptance of Islamic doctrine and rule.

By the end of the first century of Islamic control, there arose, in opposition to both the more fanatical *Kharijites* and the lax *Murjites,* a group that emphasized those Koranic passages locating responsibility in human choices. The leaders of this group, known as *Mutazilites,* at first represented more puritanic, orthodox, and missionary tendencies. Later, as their contacts with Zoroastrians, Christians, and Greeks increased, they responded by becoming more rationalistic. They adopted the view that nothing can be true that is contrary to reason. Allah himself must be completely rational. Issues regarding the freedom or necessity of God's will, which plagued Jewish and Christian theologians, recurred within the context of Moslem orthodoxy. Divisions resulted in four main schools of thought, which, curiously, prevailed in different geographical areas.

The first of these four, the *Hanafi* school, founded in Iraq by a Persian who adapted the teachings of Mohammed to conditions in his own country, prevails chiefly in India and China and countries once occupied by the Ottoman Turks. The second, the *Maliki* school, founded in Medina, accepted not only the Koran and *Hadiths* but also took into consideration effects upon public welfare when making decisions. This school flourishes mostly in North Africa and upper Egypt. The third, the *Shafi'i* school, which prefers the *Hadith* to the Koran when differences between them arise because developed traditions represent an advance in the growth of Moslem civilization over its primitive forms, prevails in Indonesia, southern Arabia, lower Egypt, and parts of Syria. The fourth, the *Hanbali* school, most conservative of the four, which proclaims the eternality of the Koran and demands literal conformity to its teachings, remains influential throughout Saudi Arabia today.

The Shiites

A minority group (of about twenty million adherents) believes Mohammed intended that his own direct descendants, rather than elected leaders, should serve as authoritative heads of the Moslem religion. Ali, his cousin and son-in-law, and Ali's two sons, Hasan and Husein, who ruled as caliphs briefly, are regarded as the legitimate heirs of a semidivine authority whereas the elected caliphs, Abu-Bakr, Omar, and Othman, are held to be usurpers and still cursed in Friday prayers. After the twelfth legitimate caliph disappeared in a cave in 878, infallible and sinless authority has remained hidden but is expected to reappear as a *Mahdi,* or divinely guided leader, who will restore the true religion, conquer the world for Islam, and reign for a glorious millennium. Many sects developed, of which three or four remain today. The followers of Kaisani believe that Ali's third son by a *Hanafite* girl was Ali's true successor. The followers of Zaid accept the first four legitimate caliphs but regard Zaid as the fifth and have their own series of successors thereafter. The followers of Ismail, who died before his father, the sixth legitimate caliph, still claim the descendants of Ismail as the true line of authority. They generated the Carmanthian revolutionary movement, the Fatimid Caliphate in Egypt (969–1171) and the Assassins ("hashish eaters") headed, until recently, by the fabulous playboy Agha Khan. The main group, sometimes called the *Imami* sect, accept all twelve of the legitimate caliphs and so are known as "The Twelvers."

Moslem history reads so much like a story of perpetual family quarrels that one wonders whom it can serve as an inspiring religion. Yet disputes about legitimacy of succession have not produced great disagreement about the basic teachings of Mohammed himself. The Shiites tend to take a middle position regarding the crucial issue of free will, differing from both those who advocate determinism and those who advocate free will by holding that will is neither completely determined nor completely free. Consequently much personal responsibility for intelligent application of revealed doctrine exists.

We cannot here take time to pursue the views and practices of the Dervishes, the Druses, the Wahhabis, or the numerous varieties of trends in different countries. But everyone should know something about the distinctive views and practices of the Sufis.

The Sufis

Moslem mystics, now grouped into hundreds of orders and numbering many millions of adherents, emerged gradually out of Moslem orthodoxy, possibly somewhat influenced

by Christian and Hindu mystics. Not only is God one and
infinite and everywhere, as Mohammed had said, but we
are, or can be, identified with God, by means of a beatific
vision through which we become absorbed in God. Although Moslem mysticism has had a long and intricate
history (See A. J. Arberry, *Sufism*, 1950) that cannot be
summarized easily, we select a few sentences that sample
its general spirit. The mystic feels himself identified with
the being, goodness, wisdom, and enjoyment that are God's
or, rather, that are God. Although we are not God, neither
are we other than God. "Love is the mood of the Sufi,
gnosis his aim, ecstasy his supreme experience." (Gustav
E. von Grunebaum, *Mediaeval Islam. A Study in Cultural
Orientation*, 1946, p. 133.) Since the experience of the
identity of self with God is intuitive and sure, neither scriptural revelation, orthodox traditions, rational arguments,
nor social sanctions are needed for assurance of truth.

At first most Sufis (wool-wearers) were ascetics who isolated themselves from social issues. But as others followed
their example, they influenced the thought and practice of
Moslems in organized societies, many of whom accepted
Sufi ideals even when they themselves could not practice
them wholeheartedly. Although Baghdad remains as much
a center of Sufiism as any place, Sufiism has spread through
Iraq, Arabia, Syria, Egypt, Turkey, and India and, indeed,
may be found as a strain of thought in almost every large
Moslem community. If Islam can meet with other religions
on any common ground, it may come closest to doing so in
the area of mysticism. Persian Sufi poetry has become
world-famous for its grandeur; almost everyone has heard
portions of *The Rubáiyát of* Omar Khayyám in Edward
FitzGerald's translation: "Take the cash and let the credit
go." From Lebanon, Kahlil Gibran has affected many
through his famous little book, *The Prophet*.

Islamic Philosophy

The profundity and significance of Moslem thinkers for
Western philosophy and religion have escaped popular
attention for too long. Influenced by Aristotle and Neo-
platonism, al-Kindi (d. 873), al-Farabi (d. 950), ibn-Sina
(Avicenna) (d. 1037), and ibn-Rushd (Averroës) (d.

1198) developed rationalistic interpretations of the nature of the universe and God. Building upon the Mutazilite doctrine that nothing could be true if contrary to reason, they explored metaphysical problems concerning the nature of universals and particulars, the first cause, matter, eternity, souls and God, and how true knowledge originates. Whereas al-Kindi and Avicenna were Persians, the great synthesizer of rationalistic and voluntaristic traditions in Moslem thought was the Spaniard Averroës. He awakened Christian mediaeval philosophers to the true Aristotle, making the history of Christian philosophy and theology highly indebted to Moslem thinkers as transmitters of Greek thought. Al-Ghazzali (1058–1111), a Sufi mystic, irritated by the success and extreme rationalism of Moslem philosophers, damned them in a telling book, *The Destruction of Philosophy*. For him, the world does not emanate from God, but is a manifestation of God who permeates everything. Averroës replied to al-Ghazzali with a volume, *The Destruction of the Destruction*, providing a doctrine of "the twofold truth" (reason and revelation) that served as a pattern for mediaeval Christian thinkers.

The Sikhs

Nanak (1469–1538), born a Hindu under Moslem rule in India, proclaimed, after his own revelatory vision, "There is no Hindu and no Muslim." Like his predecessor, Kabir, he opposed formalism and believed that devotion to the one God who transcended all religions surpasses devotion to God in any of his particular guises, whether as Vishnu or Allah. The teachings of Nanak and of many of his forerunners and followers, together with hymns, verses, and devotional readings, have been gathered together in the *Granth*, sacred scriptures of the Sikhs. The largely peaceful development of Sikhism took a military turn when Gobind Singh became the tenth *guru* (teacher) (1666–1708). The murder of his father led Singh (lion) to organize his followers into a military theocracy. Initiation into his society by baptism and communion, *i.e.*, sprinkling and sipping, was attained with sugar stirred in water by a two-edged dagger. Initiates adopt the five *k*'s: *kesh,* uncut hair wound into a topknot; *kangha,* a comb; *kara,* a steel bracelet; *kachch,* shorts; and *kirpan,* a double-edged dagger. Sikhs, making good soldiers and reliable policemen, are now in demand where persistent rigor in maintaining public order is needed.

With more than five million adherents today, Sikhism continues as an independent religious tradition. Its leader recently started a fast to induce the government of India to grant it a separate state; but after a Hindu started a counterfast, he gave up, much to the annoyance of his followers, who made him shine shoes in public as a punishment for his failure. In a world in which the sharpest dividing line between East and West, *i.e.,* India (Hindus) and Pakistan (Moslems) exists, Sikhism, a product of both and a challenge to the intolerance of both, stands out as a significant example of success in reconciling the two.

Baha'i

Conflicts, cruel persecutions, and murders form the background of still another world religion seeking peace through devotion to one God. In 1863, on the banks of the Tigris river at Baghdad, Husayn Ali Baha Ullah announced publicly his divine mission to reveal again God's will for a unified humanity and a oneness for all religions. Preceded by the Bab who, on May 23, 1844, had declared himself the forerunner of a new religion, he had suffered imprisonment and torture along with some twenty thousand Babis who were martyred in two decades. After the Bab was shot in 1850, Baha Ullah's lands near Teheran were confiscated and he was exiled, first to Baghdad, then to Constantinople, then Adrianople, and finally to Acre near Haifa on the Palestinian coast, where, on Mount Carmel, the international headquarters of the movement have since been established. Upon his death in 1892, his son, Abdul Baha, assumed leadership of the group, to be succeeded in 1921 by Shoghi Effendi, "Guardian of the Faith," who died in 1957. A majority of the Baha'is regard continuation of a "Hereditary Guardianship" irrelevant to their movement, but one persistent group proclaims Charles Mason Remy "The Second Guardian," thus constituting a split in a religion opposed to disunity among religions.

However, Baha'i teachings have a wide appeal, especially

when viewed as pervasive principles and considered apart from the historical particulars of the movement. Twelve ideals are upheld as basic: "(1) The oneness of mankind. (2) Independent investigation of truth. (3) The foundation of all religions is one. (4) Religion must be the cause of unity. (5) Religion must be in accord with science and reason. (6) Equality between men and women. (7) Prejudice of all kinds must be forgotten. (8) Universal peace. (9) Universal education. (10) Spiritual solution of the economic problem. (11) A universal language. (12) An international tribunal." Who can fail to join in praising all or most of these ideals? "They imply establishment of a world commonwealth in which all nations, races, creeds and classes will be closely and permanently united, in which the autonomy of its state members and the personal freedom and initiative of individuals that compose them are definitely and completely safeguarded. This commonwealth must . . . consist of a world legislature, whose members will, as trustees of the whole of mankind, ultimately control the entire resources of all component nations, and will enact such laws as will be required to regulate the life, satisfy the needs and adjust the relationships of all races and peoples." (Shoghi Effendi, excerpt from a letter dated March 11, 1936.) Focal center of some ten thousand Baha'is in the United States is the Baha'i Temple erected in Wilmette, Illinois, by the National Spiritual Assembly of the Baha'is of the United States and Canada. In 1962 Baha'is claimed their teachings had already taken root in two hundred and sixty countries.

Chapter 14 **Humanism**

What Is Humanism?

Humanism is a religion. Some Humanists claim that it is not only the major religion of Western civilization but of all mankind, since human beings are naturally humanistic. In fact, these Humanists contend all other religions are Humanistic also either by revealing and serving human ends or by giving human reasons that men can and should find their goals in superhuman ends. The failure, until recently, of Humanists to institutionalize their doctrines and their refusal to organize specifically ecclesiastical agencies whose members can be counted has given a false impression that Humanism is not a great religion, is not a widespread religion, even is not a religion at all. Except for a few scattered examples, such as Auguste Comte's "religion of humanity," some left-wing Unitarians, and a few branches of the American Humanist Association and the International Humanist and Ethical League, Humanism is not essentially a "church" religion. Many Humanists believe that it would be foolish to organize a separate and specialized institution for the purpose of saying, and appreciating the fact, that man is man, man is good, man is an end in himself, when all, or almost all, of his other institutions are designed for this purpose, even when not so clearly stated. About the only reason for a specifically Humanistic religious society is to protest against those who say that man is not good or an end in himself. For men naturally pursue human goods whenever their normal instincts have not been warped and misdirected by mistaken ideologies. Man is naturally religious and his natural religion is Humanism.

But what is "religion"? Those who have been nourished in Judaic, Christian, or Islamic traditions, with their limiting perspectives, have tended to define religion as "belief in God" or "belief in gods" or "spirits" or "superhuman beings." But anyone acquainted with the numbers and varieties of atheistic religions must recognize the inadequacy of this commonly accepted definition of religion. Religion is a complex of beliefs and practices finding its culmination in confident living. Two aspects need distinguishing: beliefs and practices. These beliefs pertain to the nature of the universe, man and values. Values are of two kinds: *intrinsic,* or ends in themselves, and *instrumental,* or means to ends. Being religious, a person needs to know whether life has a goal and what it is, or where life's ultimate values exist and in what they consist. Once his conceptions of the nature and locus of ultimate intrinsic value have been formulated, then whatever will help him to attain that goal is an instrumental value. Evils, things that prevent him from achieving the goal, should be avoided. Goods, things that promote its attainment, should be sought. But surely, in order to be religious, one cannot always be just seeking that which he has not yet found; for he will tend to give up hope if he cannot begin to realize the end he seeks. Life has two characteristics, namely, those aspects of existence which can be changed and those which cannot. To those which cannot be changed, one needs to learn to say "Yea," for they are in fact a part of what is ultimate in life and in the universe. Practices, the second aspect of religion, consist in whatever man does in order to attain his ultimate goal and to help him to accept it for what it is when he arrives at it.

Is, then, Humanism a religion? Are there any beliefs common to the doctrines of all those who call themselves "Humanists"? First, regarding the universe, Humanists are naturalistic. The universe is natural. It acts in accordance with its own nature and is not influenced by anything outside it. The universe includes everything, so there can be nothing external to it to influence it. It is self-contained, self-sufficient, and self-caused in the sense that it needs nothing outside itself to cause it. However, having said that the Humanistic view of the universe is naturalistic, we cannot say much more about that nature, since Humanists do disagree about it. Some regard it primarily as materialistic, some as mentalistic, some as organicistic, for example. Some regard it as permanent, some as changing, some as both permanent and changing. Some think of it as completely determined, some as completely free, and some as both. These disagreements about the ultimate constitution of the universe, which result in irreconcilable splits among Humanists, do not constitute disagreements about the more general belief that the universe is essentially naturalistic.

Secondly, regarding the nature of man, Humanists are also naturalistic. That is, man is a product of nature *and* has a nature of his own. Furthermore, Humanists agree that man is good, or that it is good to be a man, and that it is better for a man to be than not to be. Humanists recognize the existence of evil, but evil consists in whatever prevents a man from continuing to exist and to enjoy life. Where possibilities exist for improving men and their joys, one is obligated to seek such improvement, for obligation *consists* in the power that a greater good has over a lesser good in compelling our choices. However, to say that human nature is natural still does not say very much about how that nature is constituted. Humanists differ in their beliefs as to whether man is primarily rational or volitional, static or evolving, individual or social, improving or degenerating, simple or complex, determined or free, wise or stupid, the same everywhere or widely differing in quality and kind. But despite all these differences, Humanists agree that, however man's nature is conceived, there is something ultimate and irreducible about it. A man may have been caused and he may perish, but while he exists there is something unique and substantial about him. Not only mankind, but each man, is something that cannot be reduced to, or explained completely away in terms of, anything else. For example, man is neither merely a "dance of atoms," as reductionistic materialists claim, nor a puppet of some cosmic deity, as some supernaturalists insist. Each man has a nature that remains uniquely his own, no matter how much it shares in common with other men or other things in the universe. In some fundamental sense, each man is a unique being having an irreducible ultimate value.

Thirdly, regarding values, Humanists are likewise naturalistic. Each man is an end in himself, and being an end in himself is part of his own nature, and thus is natural. The ultimate goal of man is to be found, first, inside of the universe and not outside of it, secondly, inside mankind and not outside of it, and finally, inside each man and not outside of him. Humanists may disagree regarding whether man is essentially selfish or altruistic, individualistic or socialistic, hedonistic or idealistic, and how he may best attain and enjoy his ultimate values. But these disagreements do not prevent Humanists from sharing in common the belief that, however man's ultimate value may be conceived, it can be reduced neither to some nonvalue aspect of the universe nor to some nonhuman value. Each man's intrinsic value (end in itself) is his own. He does not borrow that value from some other being (*e.g.,* God or gods), even though his own nature and value may have been caused by other beings and may be heightened through sharing values with other beings. Other intrinsic values (*e.g.,* God, other persons or animals as ends in themselves) there may be, and observation of them may indeed improve the quality of his own enjoyment. But they function as added riches to his world, rather than constitute the only intrinsic values that he may enjoy. Each man is an end in himself, not merely a means to some other end or merely an enjoyer of ends that are not genuinely his own.

Finally, regarding conceptions of instrumental values and their embodiment in practice, Humanists may differ so widely that search for common commitments may prove futile. Of course, regarding such needs as food and health, pride and security, and the principles discoverable by investigation through the sciences, such as physics, biology, economics, and psychology, Humanists may all tend to agree, but even here some Humanists remain antiscientific and may be lured by whim or fancy into odd and generally untenable beliefs and practices without ceasing to be Humanistic. Bad Humanists are still Humanists, just as bad Christians are still Christians. No matter how fine a dream of utopia a Humanist may prepare, some other Humanist will find a flaw in it for his own Humanistic reasons. Humanists generally appreciate the values of family, community, state, and world societies, and both public and private social agencies for producing and maintaining that which is worthwhile. Yet some Humanists are antisocial, as well as antisocialistic. Many Humanists participate in traditional church services as the most conveniently available means for improving the appreciation of human values. Other Humanists have become so antitraditional that they regard anything called "religious" as antihumanistic. But such divergences do not prevent Humanists from practices that are alike in attempting to attain their goals within life and not outside it.

History of Humanism

Humanism has been with us since Greek times, and the Renaissance, with its revival of Greek learning, stands out as a well-known period in Western civilization when Humanistic interests became widespread. But too little is known about primitive and modern varieties of Humanism, Western and Oriental.

Humanists may trace their origins back to the beginnings of man. Not only was man always naturally Humanistic, but the varieties of primitive practices that Western anthropologists have come to call "religious" may be best understood as Humanistic efforts of men to understand and realize themselves. When primitive man wondered about himself, he observed two things: similarities and differences between himself and other things. Hence, seeking insight, he either interpreted himself in terms of other things (man is like a monkey, a fox, a bird, etc.—totemism) or interpreted other things in terms of himself (monkey, fox, bird, etc., is like a man—personification). Anthropomorphic thinking (conceiving nonhuman things to have human characteristics) is naturalistic and Humanistic thinking. The whole history of theology, primitive and modern, may be conceived as a story of man's attempts to understand himself through projecting his ideals into some perfect form that he must emulate. All Gods are anthropomorphic, "made in the image of man." Shallow Humanists who damn "all religion as superstition" eliminate valuable opportunities for gaining knowledge of how human nature operates in framing its dreams of a better world. Studies in the psychology of primitive mentality can yield great insight into how Humanistic thinking began and how it continues today.

Greek philosophy served as a major source of Western civilization. Rationalistic science, which has led to deterministic materialism, perfectionistic theology, which has led to doctrines of the imperfection (even total depravity) of man, and Humanistic ethics, which have led to ideals of individual self-realization, owe something to Greek thought. Socrates' quest for understanding the nature of the good life, Aristotle's doctrine of the golden mean, Epicurus' ideals of enlightened self-interest, and the Sophists' proclamation that "man is the measure of all things," illustrate Greek Humanism. "Knowledge is virtue," says Socrates, for "no man does wrong voluntarily." Happiness is the end of man. It is true that Greek philosophy also contained antihumanistic elements. The kind of naturalism illustrated by Thales' generalization, "All is Water," reduces man to water. Socrates' Humanistic "know thyself" represents a rebellion against subordinating man to other things. I am indebted to my colleague, Hubert G. Alexander, for the insight that, historically, in each age Humanism stands against reducing man to some nonhuman category, hence has a negative quality about it. Yet Humanism is essentially positive, not negative, in its basic tenets. Its basic claim is that "man is good, ultimately and irreducibly good." Humanist doctrine becomes negative whenever it meets other doctrines that seek to negate it. The shape of its negativism may vary from age to age, but the core of its positive doctrine remains the same throughout history.

The prevalence of the Humanistic spirit during the Middle Ages, when the mediaeval mind of Roman Catholicism had its heyday, is defended by John Herman Randall, Jr., (*Making of the Modern Mind,* Boston: Houghton Mifflin Co., 1940, Chapter VI.): "The troubadours of gay Provence ... turned Christian chivalry into the glorification of human love. ... In sober Aquinas there is already the blend between this sense of the worthwhileness and dignity of all that is specifically human, and the antique humanism of Aristotle. Thomas has hardly a trace of asceticism; his whole treatment of the flesh and its impulses is inspired by the Aristotelian principle of maintaining the supremacy of the most characteristically human part of man, his reason. Though the head of scholasticism reached to heaven, its feet were firmly planted on the solid ground of a humanistic appreciation of man's life as an organic union of soul with body." (P. 117.) One need only recall such great names as Chaucer, Boccaccio, Rabelais, Petrarch, Shakespeare, Voltaire, Christopher Marlowe, Francis Bacon, Rembrandt, and Erasmus to realize the extent of Humanistic reactions against subordinating living man to a God conceived as an "unmoved mover." Even mediaeval popes became Humanistic: Pope Alexander (a Borgia) left legends of reveling in luxurious halls in the Vatican. Pope Julius II appears to have said: "If we are not ourselves pious, why should we prevent other people from being so?" And Pope Leo X: "Let us enjoy the Papacy, now that God has given it to us."

Renaissance Humanism, too well-known to need reviewing here, accompanied a "Revival of Learning" that reawakened man's interest in the virtues and values of human affairs, after being somewhat clouded during the Dark Ages and strictly subordinated to the "Supreme Science," *i.e.,* perfectionistic theology, during the mediaeval period. Michelangelo exemplified, perhaps as well as anyone, the Renaissance ideal of the well-rounded man, as expressed in Castiglione's *Book of the Courtier* (*i.e.,* Gentleman). The ideal man was one well-versed in all of the arts, music, painting, poetry, letters, and sciences, as well as in practical affairs and love. And the period of the Protestant Reformation was not without its leading Humanists, such as Beza, a contemporary of Calvin.

Early modern Humanism prospered through The Enlightenment. Not only during the Age of Reason, when men believed they could attain utopia here on earth if only they would become completely reasonable, but during the Age of Romanticism, when men believed the world's original paradise could be regained if only men would throw off the "chains of reason" enslaving free spontaneous wills in systems sanctioning moral, political, and theological laws, Humanistic ideals prevailed. Empiricism declared that all knowledge originates in sensory experience and hence is relative to human nature and human experience. Deism rejected revelation and supernaturalism, making natural religion supreme. David Hume refuted belief in miracles. J. S. Mill provided methods for acquiring inductive generalizations and supported Utilitarianism, which propounded "the greatest happiness for the greatest number of people." The idea of Progress captured the human imagination and men worked hard, devoting themselves to exploring, conquering, and improving the world. Immanuel Kant's "Copernican revolution" located the source of science and human assurance within the mind, not in external revelation. His "categorical imperative" expressed a rational law of human nature: "Treat mankind, whether in yourself or in others, always as an end, never as a means merely." Auguste Comte's "religion of humanity" even developed a *Catechism of the Positive Religion* and worshipped Man in Positivistic Churches, a movement having considerable influence in South America. The democratic ideals of Thomas Jefferson and other signers of the American Constitution accepted Humanistic ideals and hopes and embodied them by declaring as inalienable the rights to life, liberty, and the pursuit of happiness. The American Constitution is a major Humanistic document, and the Government of the United States stands as a supreme example of a Humanistic institution.

Evolutionism, sparked by Charles Darwin's *Origin of Species,* not only established beliefs in the "struggle for existence" and "survival of the fit," but social Darwinism, the view that human superiority is due in part to the evolution of morality, which enabled men cooperating in highly developed ethical systems to surpass brutal "tooth and claw" survival techniques. Herbert Spencer expanded evolutionism to include psychology and even astronomy. When it became obvious that the evidence for geological, biological, sociological, and moral evolution supported the idea of Progress, its spread and general acceptance became inevitable, even causing theologians, such as John Fiske, to argue that God's plan for the world was essentially evolutionary. An early reluctance of theists to admit evolution gave way eventually to evolutionary arguments for the existence of God. American Pragmatists, such as William James and John Dewey, extended the evolutionary viewpoint to explain the nature of truth, logic, and science as well as theology. "True ideas are those which survive," says James. Logic is but an instrument of biological adaptation, says Dewey. Ideals are not fixed goals that enslave men, but expressions of human needs growing out of unsolved problems. Education consists not in memorizing but in training to adapt. Other evolutionists, such as the Emergentists C. Lloyd Morgan, S. Alexander, and R. W. Sellars, the Creationist J. E. Boodin, and the Romanticist Henri Bergson, made additional contributions. Even the half-converted Whitehead demonstrated in some detail how God, too, evolves. But popularization of evolutionary Humanism owes perhaps more to poets than to philosophers. Who has not heard W. H. Carruth's "Each in His Own Tongue":

> A fire-mist and a planet,
> A crystal and a cell,
> A jellyfish and a saurian,
> And caves where cavemen dwell;
> Then a sense of law and beauty,
> And a face turned from the clod—
> Some call it Evolution,
> And others call it God. (1909)

Contemporary Humanism

Pragmatists have played a leading role in American Humanist movements. The many works of William James, such as *Pragmatism, A New Name for Some Old Ways of Thinking* and *The Varieties of Religious Experience*, and of John Dewey, such as *Reconstruction in Philosophy* and *A Common Faith*, remain classic sourcebooks. George Herbert Mead's *Mind, Self and Society,* demonstrating how a person's ideas of himself have social origins, has been scarcely less influential. Some works by a host of followers include: Max Otto's *The Human Enterprise;* T. V. Smith's *Live Without Fear;* Baker Brownell's *Earth is Enough;* Harry A. Overstreet's *We Move in New Directions;* John Herman Randall's *The Making of the Modern Mind;* Corliss Lamont's *Humanism as a Philosophy;* and Horace Kallan's *Secularism Is the Will of God.*

But other naturalists who distrust Pragmatism may express a more materialistic emphasis, such as Roy Wood Sellars' *Religion Coming of Age,* or Gardner Williams'

Humanistic Ethics. Some Humanists prefer idealistic outlooks, as in Durant Drake's *The New Morality,* Oliver L. Reiser's *The Promise of Scientific Humanism,* and Hartley Burr Alexander's *Nature and Human Nature.* Humanism has been expressed by other independent minds, in Arthur E. Burtt's *Types of Religious Philosophy,* Harold A. Larrabee's *Reliable Knowledge,* and G. P. Conger's *The Ideologies of Religion.*

American theological schools have supported notable Humanist professors, such as Harvard's J. A. C. F. Auer *(Humanism States Its Case)* and Chicago's A. E. Hayden *(The Quest of the Ages)* and Henry N. Wieman *(The Source of Human Good).* But professors in many fields are Humanists, such as chemist Linus Pauling, physicist Leo Szilard, historian Harry Elmer Barnes, anthropologist Clyde Kluckhohn, psychologist J. H. Leuba, zoologist Herman J. Muller, physiologist Maurice Visscher, Literature Professor Llewellyn Jones, and educators John L. Childs and George Axtelle.

We should not ignore prominent Britishers who have been influential in the United States, such as Julian Huxley *(Religion without Revelation),* Bertrand Russell *(Why I Am Not a Christian),* H. J. Blackham *(Living as a Humanist)* and F. C. S. Schiller *(Studies in Humanism).* Continental Humanism, to say nothing of South American and African movements, must await some other time.

Unitarian ministers, such as John H. Deitrich, James Luther Adams, Edwin T. Buehrer, Harold Buschman, and Elmo Robinson preach Humanism. Curtis W. Reese has published *Humanist Religion;* Charles Francis Potter, *Humanism—A New Religion;* and A. Powell Davies, *The Ten Commandments.* Ethical Culture Societies, led by Felix Adler and organized into the American Ethical Union, publish *The Ethical Outlook* and have established branches in at least ten cities. But the chief organized movement speaking for Humanism in the United States is the American Humanist Association.

Instigated in 1927 at the University of Chicago, and later organized as the Humanist Press Association, publishing *The New Humanist,* a group composed largely of Unitarian ministers and professors from several universities prepared "A Humanist Manifesto," signed by thirty-four of them and published in May, 1933. Its preamble asserts: "Religions have always been means for realizing the highest values of life." But "There is a great danger of . . . identification of the word *religion* with doctrines and methods which have lost their significance and which are powerless to solve the problem of human living in the Twentieth Century." "Today man's larger understanding of the universe, his scientific achievements, and his deeper appreciation of brotherhood, have created a situation which requires a new statement of the means and purposes of religion." Its fifteen affirmations include beliefs that "the universe is self-existing," "man is a part of nature," "the traditional dualism of mind and body must be rejected," "man's religious culture . . . is a product of gradual development," "religion must formulate its hopes . . . in light of the scientific spirit and method," "religion consists in those actions, purposes and experiences which are humanly significant," and "complete realization of human personality is the end of life," which should be sought "here and now." Asserting also that "the time has passed for theism, deism, modernism" and discouraging "belief in the supernatural" and "wishful thinking," it "affirms life" and "endeavors to establish conditions of a satisfactory life for all, not merely for a few."

Attached to the Manifesto was a note saying that "the individuals whose signatures appear would, had they been writing individual statements, have stated the propositions in differing terms." Many Humanists have been critical of the wording and the Association itself considers the Manifesto "a dated document representing a sounding of views taken at a particular time" and expects that debate among Humanists about "What is Humanism?" doubtless will continue for a long time.

Although Professors John Dewey and Roy Wood Sellars were prominent among the framers of the Manifesto, Edwin A. Wilson, Unitarian minister, has been chiefly responsible for the success of the organization because he has given lifelong full-time devotion to it. He edited *The New Humanist* and its successor *The Humanist,* and the *Bulletin* and now its successor *The Free Mind,* and has served as Executive Director of the association from its beginning. His own views can be sampled in a booklet, *The Fourth*

Faith (Protestantism, Catholicism, and Judaism being the other three): Humanism "has no church to embody it." "Most Humanists do not know they are Humanists" and many of them "may not even know they are religious. . . . Theirs is a secular faith." The Humanist "is more concerned for people than for anything else, . . . recognizes no master race or class, . . . accepts the findings, the methods, and the world-view of modern science, . . . has faith that together men possess the intelligence, the skills and the will to end war and build security in a free and just world." "Freedom of thought and action are necessary to his way of life."

The American Humanist Association has established headquarters in Yellow Springs, Ohio, with seventy chapters in the United States. It has adopted a symbol, which may become as representative of Humanism as the cross has become of Christianity, based on Edwin Markham's poem (from *Shoes of Happiness,* N.Y.: Doubleday & Co., 1922):

> He drew a circle that shut me out
> Heretic, rebel, a thing to flout;
> But Love and I had the wit to win:
> We drew a circle that took him in.

Oriental Humanism

Chinese civilization has been generally more humanistic than either Hindu or Western civilization. The Humanism of Confucius is well-known. The Naturalism (Taoism) of Lao-tzu is thoroughly humanistic. Even Mahayana Buddhism imported from India became transformed into

Humanistic Zen. Western theists, failing to recognize that Chinese Humanism is religious, report popular superstitious beliefs and practices as evidence of the low status of religion, whereas Chinese culture is the sanest, most humanistic of the world's three major civilizations.

Hindu civilization, in spite of its traditional emphases upon a combination of polytheism and the ultimacy of spiritual unity, has manifested more Humanistic thinking than most Westerners realize. First of all, two of India's greatest religious philosophies, Jainism and Sankhya-Yoga, are not only explicitly atheistic, but regard each individual soul as inherently eternal and equal, in its perfected form, to a god, not unlike the Christian God in being eternal, all-knowing, all-powerful, all-good, and perfectly free from all imperfection. Although not naturalistic in the Western sense, these philosophies do believe each individual to be an irreducible, unique, ultimate end in himself. Hindu religions are typically self-help religions whereby each individual is almost solely responsible for realizing his own goal, the popular polytheisms being regarded as means to this end.

Gotama, the Buddha, was one of the world's great Humanists (See my *Philosophy of the Buddha*, N.Y.: Harper and Brothers, 1959, and N.Y.: Collier Books, 1962), in spite of some antihumanistic developments in both Theravada and Mahayana Buddhism. Ranjee Shahani, writing on "The Great Humanists of India" (*The Humanist*, January-February, 1960), includes not only Mahavira (the Jain) and Buddha, but also Kabir (Hindu poet), Nanak (founder of Sikhism), Gandhi, and Nehru. Two Humanist societies active in India today are the Indian Radical Humanist Movement, with its own publishing house (Renaissance Publishers) and weekly organ (*The Radical Humanist*), and the Humanist Union, with headquarters at Naini Tal, U. P.

International Humanism

The International Humanist and Ethical Union, organized in Amsterdam in 1952, held its Third International Congress in Oslo in 1962. Its constituent members include the American Ethical Union, the American Humanist Association, the British Ethical Union, the Humanist League of Belgium, the Dutch Humanist League, and the Indian Radical Humanist Movement. Associated with it also are the French Humanist Federation, the Austrian Society for Ethical Culture, the Indian Humanist Union, the Nigerian Humanist Association, the New South Wales Humanist Society, the Japanese Humanist Society, the Israeli Spinozaeum, the German Monist Union, the Humanist Ethical League of Norway, the Humanist League of Denmark, the Korean Humanist Association, the Dutch Humanitas, and the Rationalist Press Association of England. It publishes a quarterly, *International Humanism.*

Varieties of Humanism

How much can Humanists disagree and still remain Humanists? Humanist explanations of the nature of the universe, man, and values have taken many forms. Humanism holds that humanity is natural, but it does not, as a general doctrine, place limits upon how the nature of man shall be explained. Materialistic, spiritualistic, and organicistic Humanists give different accounts of the universe and man. Rationalistic Humanists insist that man is essentially a rational animal who attains his goal by being reasonable and restraining his irrational impulses, whereas Romanticistic Humanists believe human impulse vitalizes the enjoyment of being and ought not be crushed into mathematical molds. Empiricistic, rationalistic, positivistic, agnostic, realistic, intuitionistic, and pragmatic Humanists differ regarding the source of knowledge of nature and values. Ethically, Humanists may dispute whether men are basically selfish or altruistic, whether men should be optimistic or pessimistic, and whether or not universal moral principles can be discovered and formulated. Politically, some Humanists seem more socialistically inclined while others remain individualistic in their ideals.

All these varieties of interpretation "are Humanistic or antihumanistic depending upon their unwillingness to sacrifice the ultimately human to something nonhuman, or to something less than human or more than human, which somehow appears as more ultimate. Humanism is committed unconditionally neither to acceptance nor rejection

of theism or atheism, capitalism or communism, spiritual-
ism or materialism, etc., so long as these can be experienced
as expressions of man's nature rather than as a mere ad-
dendum to it." ("Varieties of Humanism," *The Standard,*
April, 1951, p. 335.) The materialism that freed nature
from supernatural puppetry was Humanistic in rescuing
man from being reduced to a mere creature of God's self-
realization, but it became antihumanistic when it concluded
that, therefore, man could be reduced to a material
mechanism. "Marxism begins by expressing Humanistic
motives in seeking to free men from the inhumanities of
'capitalistic slavery,' but ends by admitting that men are
pawns in a dialectic of history which demands a quota of
human sacrifice to the necessities of violent revolution."
(*Ibid.,* p. 334.)

Furthermore, each science or other area of specialty
that discovers something essential to the nature of man
may then try to reduce the significance of other essentials
to its own. A chemist may picture man as merely a quantity of atomic particles. A physicist may explain him as
primarily a complicated electrical mechanism. A biologist
may claim him as solely a creature of evolution. A physiologist may view him as entirely a product of his organs,
glands, diet, diseases, and their development. An anthropologist may depict him as only a product of his culture.
A social psychologist may describe him as a victim of his
social environment. A linguist may believe him to be completely molded by his language. An artist or musician may
see man as primarily an aesthetic animal. Each of these
specialists has a Humanistic contribution to make to man's
understanding of himself. But whenever a specialist of any
kind tries to reduce the whole of man to any one part of
him, he thereby becomes somewhat antihumanistic.

"Two more ideas seem necessary for understanding Humanism. First, being Humanistic is also a matter of degree,
for both those who acknowledge and those who repudiate
Humanism are more Humanistic in their spirit and outlook at some times than at others." (One difference between a Humanistic theist and a theistic Humanist consists
in whether one believes that man is good because he is
good for god or whether he believes that belief in god is
good because it is good for man.) "Secondly, Humanism

as a movement flows on with new varieties to be expected in the future." (*Ibid.*, p. 337.) Humanism is to be found within many other religions. Some Methodists, for example, regard Jesus as a Humanist. Theologian Ralph W. Nelson (Disciples of Christ) wrote *The Experimental Logic of Jesus*. Reform Judaism advocates Humanism. The social ideals formally adopted by the National Council of Churches from time to time continue to be saturated with Humanistic thinking. Hence, American Humanists remain divided regarding whether the interests of Humanism can best be promoted by opposing established denominational organizations or by participating in and encouraging the progressively Humanistic tendencies operating within the more liberal denominations.

Conclusion

Chapter 15 World Religions and World Religion

Most religions are world religions. At least the great living religions surveyed in the present volume regard themselves as world religions. Judaism and Shintoism might be considered exceptions, but earlier racial or nationalistic tendencies have given way to broader outlooks and Reform Judaism and Neo-Shintoism now conceive their message as universal in intent. One might point out that Judaism, Christianity, and Islam are Western religions, that Hinduism, Jainism, and Buddhism are Indian religions and that Taoism and Confucianism are Chinese religions. But now there are Christians all over the globe. Islam has spread through India, the Philippines, and Indonesia. Buddhism has permeated China and Japan. It is true that we can trace the origins of religions to particular places and show how their development occurred primarily in certain geographical, racial, cultural, and even political traditions. But when we examine their doctrines and aims, we find they all tend toward the view that their beliefs and practices are good for all mankind. The more exclusive a doctrine is, in the sense that it claims to be the only true one, the more its adherents insist that all men ought to believe it; hence it is good for, intended for, and available to all. In fact, the followers of each religion usually claim that one mark of its own superiority over other religions is its universality.

Yet mankind lacks a world religion in the sense that it is in fact the only one or only true one and in the sense that it is superior to others because it embodies within itself the virtues of all other religions. The spokesmen for each religion may claim either that it alone is true or that it alone is superior. But so long as adherents of other religions make similar claims, the issue can hardly be settled without appeal to a superior principle in terms of which conflicting claims can be evaluated objectively. Although it is possible that one existing religion might ally itself with a world dictator who would forcibly impose it and eliminate all others, if men's minds remained free, this would be but a temporary condition. Although the possibility exists that a new religious genius may yet arise to announce a religion that will surpass all other religions in virtue and appeal, this seems unlikely. Two other possibilities, which may indeed reenforce each other, appear more probable avenues for mankind to take. One of these is to pursue syncretistic tendencies already under way. The other is to pursue comparative studies scientifically to demonstrate more fully the ultimate nature of religion, what is required to fill man's needs, and the ways that best serve those needs.

Syncretistic Tendencies

Before examining unifying movements, let us observe a reason, inherent in the nature of religion, that each religion naturally seeks to become universal and that (and the reason is the same) world religions will tend toward one world religion. The goal of religion is confident living. Confident living reaches its pinnacle in minds completely freed from doubt. Awareness of the presence of conflicting views causes doubt. Thus one cannot expect to attain the goal so long as awareness of opposing beliefs continues. One might, of course, hide from the alternatives; but one who does this consciously also knows that he deceives himself and thereby comes to doubt his own intellectual honesty. Once the human mind has been opened to genuine alternatives, it cannot expect to attain confidence by deliberately shutting its eyes to them. At this time in history, when rapid intermingling of the world's great cultures opens new vistas of genuine ways to the goal, we can attain confidence only by facing the alternatives, not by running away from them. Political, economic, scientific, educational, communicational, and population-mobility factors combine to confront more and more of us with awareness of the choices. Since we seek assurance that ours is the true view, we need increasingly to have these alternatives examined and evaluated in ways that we can trust. Unless

we happen to have been prejudiced by childhood identification with some movement, we are likely to regard the *ipse
dixit* argument of every religion as rather hollow. We now
require demonstration of superiority in fair competition, so
those religions which remain unwilling to risk this con-
frontation thereby betray an inherent doubt.

Syncretism has indeed been taking place. Let us glance
at factors conducive to unity in each of the three great
civilizations.

Hindu philosophical development has been one toward
ever-increasing unity, as shown in Chapters III and VI.
Scholars reasoned that, if each of many different gods was
praised as supreme in scriptures, they must really all be the
same god. The great gods Vishnu, Shiva, and Brahma became merged into the trinity *(trimurti)* with the three subordinated to the one ultimate unity, Brahman, which either
is perfectly purified of parts (as in Advaita Vedanta) or
incorporates all its infinite parts without disunity (as in
Visistadvaita Vedanta). The doctrine of reincarnation
was employed to unify multiplicities of gods as *avators,*
incarnations, of Vishnu, even including Buddha and Christ.
The four paths *(Yogas)* are but different ways to the same
goal and, indeed, intermingle whether one realizes this or
not. The message of many modern Hindu seers, such as
Rabindranath Tagore and Sri Aurobindo, proclaims the
virtues of enjoying the unity of all mankind as well as of
the gods, and reveals all the religions as varieties of expressions of one underlying source and ultimate value. Swami
Nityaswarupananda has devoted much of his life to promoting "the felt unity of mankind."

Chinese culture appears to have retained a sense of
naturalness in which differences never became dichotomies.
Confucianism extended the concept of Nature (Tao) to
society and government. Mo Ti and the Legalists differed
in their methods, but the disputes among philosophers seem
seldom to have produced sectarian conflicts among the
people. The "Three Truths" of China, which include the
foreign Buddhism, appear to many as supplementary
rather than divisive. Japanese Shintoism not only incorporated Confucian and Taoistic ideas, but also, eventually,
Buddhist doctrines by recognizing Shinto deities as *bodhisattvas.*

Western civilization finds unity in the acceptance of early Hebrew ideas and scriptures by both Christianity and Islam. Jesus, the Jew, announced "other sheep have I which are not of this fold," giving rise to the belief that he referred to people professing other religions. The Hebrew scriptures incorporated into the Christian Bible as its "Old Testament" constitute its largest part. Followers of Mohammed were admonished to respect believers in "the Book," as well as to accept Moses and Christ as speaking for Allah. Islam's "ninety-nine names of God" include names used in other religions. Sufi poets assert the oneness of all being. We need not review the ecumenical movements within Christianity, including many mergers of Protestant churches, formation of the National Council of Churches of Christ in America, ecumenical gestures between Roman Catholics and Greek and Protestant groups. The Baha'is list among the first principles the oneness of mankind and the single source of religions. The Unitarians have become so inclusive in their appreciations of other religions that some question whether they can any longer be called "Christians." Conferences of Protestants, Catholics, and Jews illustrate continuing interreligious cooperation in Western civilization.

But in addition to indications of reunion within each civilization, we may observe synthesizing trends among these three. Incorporation of Buddhism as one of the "Three Truths" of China is a major example. Ryubo Shinto, identifying Shinto deities with Buddhist *bodhisattvas,* is another. But some Neo-Shintoists have gone even further, believing that the original Shinto deities were Jews dwelling first in the original paradise, the Garden of Eden. Sikhism, merging the Hindu and Moslem traditions—still among the most bitterly antagonistic in the world—into a single religion, avers "there is no Moslem and no Hindu." Sri Ramakrishna actively joined and devotedly pursued several religions, proving for himself that all lead to the same goal. Western religions have tended to be exclusive and slower to amalgamate, yet we do have the example of the Christian Yoga Church in California. Zen and Yoga have gained followers in the United States.

Finally, we should notice the feeble but genuine efforts of representatives of various religions to meet in a congress to discuss matters. The first World's Parliament of Religions was held in Chicago in 1893. Half a century later, again in Chicago, the first World Fellowship of Faiths assembled. Progress, as compared with the first congress, included (1) invitations not only to major religions but to all faiths and (2) all were challenged to focus their attention upon the solution of man's problems rather than engaging in a parade of rival religions. Not all reached the heights of ecstatic fellow feeling expressed by Frank L. Riley in advocating a "Bible of Bibles" or "One religion with sixty scriptures." Robert Ballou's *Bible of the World* (N.Y.: Viking Press, 1939) is a significant gesture in this direction. The World Congress of Faiths holds annual meetings in London and other lectures under its auspices from time to time.

Comparative Studies

In addition to the practical efforts to cooperate and unite, scholarly inquiries into the histories and common nature of all religions have been under way for a long time. Historians in all cultures have investigated religion, but today the history of religions has also become a field for specialists. Already in 1900 the International Congress for the History of Religions held its first meeting in Paris. Its tenth congress met in 1960 in Marburg, Germany. *History of Religions, An International Journal for Comparative Historical Studies,* was launched at the University of Chicago in 1961, and the *Journal for the Scientific Study of Religion,* published by the Society for the Scientific Study of Religion at Yale University, also appeared in 1961. Among privately endowed agencies, the Blaisdell Institute for Advanced Study in World Cultures and Religions, Claremont, California, directed by Herbert Schneider, Professor Emeritus of Philosophy of Columbia University, supports university research, especially at the graduate level. The Union for the Study of the Great Religions, headed by K. D. D. Henderson, General Secretary of the Spaulding Foundation, Oxford, England, has branches in Canada, India, Pakistan, the Near East, West Africa, and the United States. The United Nations Educational, Scientific, and Cultural Organization includes an International Council for Philosophy and Humanistic Studies, which subsidizes the International Congress of the History of Religions and sponsors publication of the *International Bibliography of the History of Religions.* An astounding amount of research is taking place, especially when we remember the research institutes supported by the various religions themselves, the scholarly efforts of teachers of religion in colleges, universities and theological schools, to say nothing of the religious investigations by sociologists, anthropologists, psychologists, and social psychologists.

Some studies have such a detached air about them that their factual results may best be stored away in books, perhaps to be forgotten. But the awareness of a need for genuine and prolonged encounters between competent scholars nurtured in different religions has led to practical experiments in interreligious study. In addition to the international houses at numerous universities where students from different nations intermingle in daily life, institutions designed for extended contact between advanced scholars representing various religions have been established. A notable example is the Center for the Study of World Religions at Harvard University, headed by Robert Slater. Kenneth Morgan, Director of the Fund for the Study of the Great Religions, entertains guests at the Chapel House, Colgate University. Charles A. Moore, editor of *Philosophy East and West,* has worked tirelessly to establish an East-West Center at the University of Hawaii where both faculty and students come from several cultures. This is now flourishing as a center for both cultural and technical interchange under a grant from the U. S. Department of State.

In addition to these historical studies and personal encounters by resident scholars, we should be aware of conclusions announced by scholars. One of the most competent and most recent studies is that guided by P. T. Raju, formerly Head of the Department of Philosophy in the University of Rajasthan, who has served as visiting professor in several American and European universities. Raju presents two noteworthy theses. The first contends that the time has come to establish comparative philosophy as a distinct discipline because we now live in a *world,* not just in a nation or in a civilization, and we need to understand ourselves as world citizens. This need is so significant that we ought to recognize it by developing undergraduate and graduate (doctoral) curricula in Comparative Philosophy. Raju was joined by John Wild of Harvard University, A. J. Heschel of the Jewish Theological Seminary, and W. T. Chan of Dartmouth College in a study of Greek, Hebrew, Chinese, and Hindu ideals. He then drew a conclusion from this comparative study. His cautious second thesis is that, despite all their differences, religions have something in common, namely, man. What man is continues to be a problem, but with this problem in common a beginning of mutual understanding can be made. This collective effort to establish a new dimension in philosophical and religious scholarship may do just that.

The prospect for developing this new dimension serves as a hopeful note upon which to close this section on World Religion and this volume on *The World's Living Religions.*

Reading Suggestions

INTRODUCTION

Chapter 1. WHAT IS RELIGION?

Abernathy, G. L., and T. A. Langford, *Philosophy of Religion; A Book of Readings,* N.Y.: The Macmillan Company, 1962.

Bahm, Archie J., *Philosophy, An Introduction,* Bombay and New York: Asia Publishing House, (1953) 1964. Chapters I, XXV.

Bronstein, D. J., and H. M. Schulweis, *Approaches to Philosophy of Religion,* N.Y.: Prentice-Hall Inc., 1954.

Houf, Horace T., *What Religion Is and Does,* N.Y.: Harper and Brothers, 1945.

Widgery, Alban G., *What is Religion?* N.Y.: Harper and Brothers, 1953.

Chapter 2. PRIMITIVE RELIGION

Cornford, Francis M., *From Religion to Philosophy,* London: Longmans, Green and Co., 1958.

*Lowie, Robert H., *Primitive Religions,* London: Routledge, 1925, 1958.

*Radin, Paul, *Primitive Man as Philosopher,* N.Y.: D. Appleton and Co., 1927, 1957.

*Radin, Paul, *Primitive Religion,* N.Y.: D. Appleton and Co., 1927, 1957.

*Radin, Paul, *The World of Primitive Man,* N.Y.: Abelard-Schuman, Ltd., 1953, 1960.

Part I. RELIGIONS OF INDIA

Chapter 3. HINDUISM

*Bahm, Archie J., *The Wisdom of Krishna, Bhagavad Gita,* in preparation.

*Asterisk indicates paperback edition also available. Last date pertains to appearance in paperback.

Chatterjee, S. C., *Fundamentals of Hinduism*, Calcutta: Das Gupta & Co. Ltd., 1950.

Dasgupta, Surendranath, *Hindu Mysticism*, N.Y.: Frederick Ungar Publishing Co., 1961.

Morgan, Kenneth, *The Religion of the Hindus*, N.Y.: Ronald Press, 1953.

Nikhilananda, Swami, *The Upanishads*, 4 vols., N.Y.: Harper and Brothers, 1949–59.

*Prabhavananda, Swami, and Christopher Isherwood, *The Song of the Lord, Bhagavad-Gita*, N.Y.: New American Library, 1944, 1954.

*Prabhavananda, Swami, and Frederick Manchester, *The Upanishads: Breath of the Eternal*, Hollywood: Vedanta Society of Southern California, 1948, 1957.

*Zimmer, Heinrich, *Philosophies of India*, N.Y.: Bollingen Foundation, Inc., 1951, 1956.

Chapter 4. JAINISM

Chakravarti, A., *The Religion of Ahimsa*, Bombay: Ratanchand Hirachand, 1957.

Jain, J. P., *Jainism, The Oldest Religion*, Banaras: Banaras Hindu University Press, 1951.

Mehta, Mohan Lal, *Outlines of Jaina Philosophy*, Bangalore: Jain Mission Society, 1954.

Rampuria, Chand, *Jainism as a Faith and a Religion*, Calcutta: Sri Jain Swetamber Terapanthi Mahasabha, 1946.

Rampuria, Chand, *The Cult of Ahimsa*, Calcutta: Sri Swetamber Terapanthi Mahasabha, 1947.

Tatia, Nathmal, *Studies in Jaina Philosophy*, Banaras: Jain Cultural Research Society, 1951.

Chapter 5. BUDDHISM

*Bahm, Archie J., *Philosophy of the Buddha*, N.Y.: Harper and Brothers, 1958, 1962.

Grimm, George, *The Doctrine of the Buddha*, Berlin: Akademie-Verlag, 1958.

Morgan, Kenneth, *The Path of the Buddha*, N.Y.: Ronald Press, 1956.

Pratt, James B., *The Pilgrimage of Buddhism*, N.Y.: The Macmillan Co., 1928.

Saunders, Kenneth J., *Gotama Buddha, A Biography*, N.Y.: The Association Press, 1920.

Chapter 6. VEDANTISM AND YOGA

*Bahm, Archie J., *Yoga, Union with the Ultimate*, N.Y.: Frederick Ungar Publishing Co., 1961.

Bahm, Archie J., *Yoga for Business Executives and Professional People*, N.Y.: Citadel Press, 1965.

Chatterjee, S. C., and D. M. Datta, *Introduction to Indian Philosophy*, Calcutta: University of Calcutta, 1960.

Dasgupta, Surendranath, *A History of Indian Philosophy*, 5 vols., London: Cambridge University Press, 1922–55.

Hiriyanna, Mysore, *Outlines of Indian Philosophy*, London: George Allen and Unwin, 1951.

Nikhilananda, Swami, *Vivekananda: The Yogas and Other Works*, N.Y.: Ramakrishna-Vivekananda Center, 1953.

Radhakrishnan, S., *Indian Philosophy*, 2 vols., London: George Allen and Unwin, 1927.

Radhakrishnan, S., and Charles A. Moore, *A Sourcebook in Indian Philosophy*, Princeton: Princeton University Press, 1957.

Sinha, Jadunath, *History of Indian Philosophy*, 2 vols., Calcutta: Sinha Publishing House, Vol. I, 1956; Vol. II, 1952.

Part II. RELIGIONS OF CHINA AND JAPAN

Chapter 7. TAOISM

*Bahm, Archie J., *Tao Teh King by Lao Tzu*, N.Y.: Frederick Ungar Publishing Co., 1958.

*Day, Clarence, *The Philosophers of China*, N.Y.: Citadel Press, 1962.

Fang, Thomé H., *The Chinese View of Life*, Kowloon: Union Printing Co., 1957.

*Fung, Yu-lan, *A Short History of Chinese Philosophy*, N.Y.: The Macmillan Company, 1948, 1962.

Lin Yutang, *My Country and My People*, N.Y.: John Day and Co., 1935, 1959.

Lin Yutang, *The Importance of Living*, N.Y.: John Day and Co., 1937.

Siu, Ralph Gun Hoy, *The Tao of Science: An Essay on Western Science and Eastern Wisdom*, Boston: The Technology Press, Massachusetts Institute of Technology, 1957.

Sung, Z. D., *The Symbols of the Yi King*, Shanghai: The China Modern Education Co., 1934.

Welch, Holmes, *The Parting of the Way*, Boston: The Beacon Press, 1957.

Chapter 8. CONFUCIANISM

Chang, Chia-sen, *The Development of Neo-Confucian Thought*, N.Y.: Bookman Associates, 1957.

33 *Reading Suggestions*

*Creel, H. G., *Chinese Thought from Confucius to Mao Tse-Tung,* University of Chicago Press, Chicago, 1953, 1960.

Creel, H. G., *Confucius, The Man and the Myth,* N.Y.: John Day & Co., 1949.

Dubs, Homer H., *Hsuntse: The Moulder of Ancient Confucianism,* London: A. Probsthain, 1927.

Hughes, E. R., *The Great Learning and the Mean-in-Action,* N.Y.: E. P. Dutton and Co., 1943.

Legge, James, *The Four Books,* 1893, various editions.

Liu, Wu-chi, *A Short History of Confucian Philosophy,* Harmondsworth: Penquin Books Ltd., 1955.

Mei, Y. P., *Motse, The Neglected Rival of Confucius,* London: A. Probsthain, 1934.

*Ware, James R., *The Sayings of Confucius,* N.Y.: New American Library, 1955.

*Ware, James R., *The Sayings of Mencius,* N.Y.: New American Library, 1960.

Chapter 9. BUDDHISM

*Burtt, Edwin A., *The Teachings of the Compassionate Buddha,* N.Y.: The New American Library, 1955.

Conze, Edward, *Buddhist Texts Through the Ages,* N.Y.: Philosophical Library, 1954.

Eliot, Charles, *Japanese Buddhism,* London: Longmans, Green and Co., 1935; N.Y.: Barnes and Noble, 1959.

Lee, Shao Chang, *Popular Buddhism in China,* Shanghai: The Commercial Press, Ltd., 1940.

Morgan, Kenneth, *The Path of the Buddha,* N.Y.: Ronald Press, 1956.

Murti, T. R. V., *The Central Philosophy of Buddhism,* London: George Allen and Unwin, Ltd., 1955.

Takakusu, Junjiro, *The Essentials of Buddhist Philosophy,* Honolulu: University of Hawaii Press, 1947.

Zen Buddhism

Herrigel, Eugen, *Zen in the Art of Archery,* N.Y.: Pantheon Books, 1953.

Herrigel, G. L., *Zen in the Art of Flower Arrangement,* London: Routledge, and Kegan Paul, 1958.

Kakuzo, Okakura, *The Book of Tea,* Rutland (Vt.) and Tokyo. Charles E. Tuttle Company, 1956.

*Ogata, Sohaku, *Zen for the West,* N.Y.: Dial Press, 1962.

Suzuki, Daisetz T., *The Essentials of Zen Buddhism,* London: Rider and Co., 1962.

Suzuki, Daisetz T., *Zen and Japanese Culture*, Tokyo and Rutland (Vt.): C. E. Tuttle Co., 1958.

Shin Buddhism

Tsunoda, Shodo, *Buddhism and Jodo-shinshu*, San Francisco: Buddhist Churches of America, 1955.

Chapter 10. SHINTOISM

Anesaki, Masaharu, *History of Japanese Religion*, London: Kegan Paul, Trench, Trubner and Co., Ltd., 1930.

Benedict, Ruth, *The Chrysanthemum and the Sword*, Boston: Houghton Mifflin Co., 1946.

Ballou, Robert O., *Shinto: The Unconquered Enemy*, N.Y.: The Viking Press, 1945.

Gunsalus, Helen C., *Gods and Heroes of Japan*, Chicago: Field Museum of Natural History, 1924.

Holtom, Daniel C., *Modern Japan and Shinto Nationalism*, Chicago: The University of Chicago Press, 1943.

Part III. RELIGIONS OF WESTERN CIVILIZATION

Chapter 11. JUDAISM

Browne, Lewis, *Stranger Than Fiction*, N.Y.: The Macmillan Co., 1925, 1933.

*Browne, Lewis, *The Wisdom of Israel*, N.Y.: Modern Library, 1945.

*Davies, A. Powell, *The Ten Commandments*, N.Y.: New American Library, 1956.

Dinin, Samuel, *Judaism in a Changing Civilization*, N.Y.: Columbia University Press, 1933.

Goldman, Solomon, *A Rabbi Takes Stock*, N.Y.: Harper and Brothers, 1931.

Herberg, Will, *Judaism and Modern Man*, N.Y.: Farrar, Straus and Young, 1951.

Kaplan, Mordecai, *Judaism as a Civilization*, N.Y.: Thomas Yoseloff Inc., 1934, 1957.

Philipson, David, *The Reform Movement in Judaism*, N.Y.: The Macmillan Co., 1931.

Schwartz, Charles and Bertie, *Faith Through Reason: A Modern Interpretation of Judaism*, N.Y.: The Macmillan Co., 1946.

Chapter XII. CHRISTIANITY
Jesus

*Branscomb, Bennett H., *The Message of Jesus*, Nashville (Tenn.): Cokesbury Press, 1926, 1960.

*Craig, Clarence T., *The Beginning of Christianity*, N.Y.: Abingdon-Cokesbury Press, 1943.

*Daniel-Rops, Henry, *Jesus and His Times*, N.Y.: E. P. Dutton and Co., Inc., 1947, 1954, 1958.

*Enslin, Morton S., *Christian Beginnings*, N.Y.: Harper and Brothers, 1948, 1956.

*Goguel, Maurice, *Jesus and the Origins of Christianity*, 2 vols., N.Y.: The Macmillan Co., 1933, 1960.

Ligon, Ernest M., *The Psychology of the Christian Personality*, N.Y.: The Macmillan Co., 1946.

*Schweitzer, Albert, *The Quest of the Historical Jesus*, N.Y.: The Macmillan Co., 1961.

Paul

*Davies, A. Powell, *The First Christian*, N.Y.: Farrar, Straus and Cudahy, 1957.

*Deissmann, Gustav A., *Paul, A Study in Social and Religious History*, N.Y.: Hodder and Stoughton, 1912, 1957.

*Dodd, Charles H., *The Meaning of Paul for Today*, London: The Swarthmore Press, 1920, 1957.

*Goodspeed, Edgar J., *Paul*, Chicago: University of Chicago Press, 1922, 1959.

The Patristics

Carrington, Philip, *The Early Christian Church*, London: Cambridge University Press, 1957.

Goodspeed, Edgar J., *Apostolic Fathers*, N.Y.: Harper and Brothers, 1950.

Grant, Frederick C., *The Early Days of Christianity*, N.Y.: The Abingdon Press, 1922.

*Workman, Herbert B., *Persecution in the Early Church*, London: C. H. Kelley, 1906, 1961.

Augustine

*Cochrane, Charles N., *Christianity and Classical Culture*, N.Y.: Oxford University Press, 1940, 1957.

*Hatch, Edwin, *The Influence of Greek Ideas on Christianity*, London: Williams and Norgate, 1890, 1957.

*Harnack, Adolf, *The Mission and Expansion of Christianity in the First Three Centuries*, N.Y.: G. P. Putnam's Sons, (1904–05) 1908, 1962.

Oates, Whitney J., *Basic Writings of St. Augustine*, N.Y.: Random House, 1948.

*Przywara, Erich, *Augustine: An Augustine Synthesis*, N.Y.: Harper and Brothers, 1958.

Roman Catholicism

*Bainton, Roland H., *Reformation in the Sixteenth Century*, Boston: Beacon Press, 1952.

*Farrow, John, *Pageant of the Popes*, N.Y.: Sheed and Ward, 1942.

*Gilson, Etienne H., *Reason and Revelation in the Middle Ages*, N.Y.: Charles Scribner's Sons, 1938.

*Hughes, Philip, *Popular History of the Catholic Church*, London: Burns, Oates and Washburn, Ltd., 1940.

Eastern Orthodoxy

*Benz, Ernst, *The Eastern Orthodox Church: Its Thought and Life*, Garden City (N.Y.): Doubleday and Co., 1963.

Stanley, Arthur P., *History of the Eastern Church*, N.Y.: Charles Scribner's Sons, 1884.

Lutheranism

*Bainton, Roland H., *Here I Stand: A Life of Martin Luther*, N.Y.: Abingdon-Cokesbury Press, 1950, 1959.

*Belloc, Hilaire, *How the Reformation Happened*, N.Y.: R. M. McBride and Co., 1928, 1961.

*Boehmer, Heinrich, *Martin Luther: Road to Reformation*, Philadelphia: Muhlenberg Press, 1946, 1957.

*Schram, W. E., *What Lutherans Believe*, Minneapolis (Minn.): Augsburg Publishing House, 1946.

Calvinism

*Harkness, Georgia, *John Calvin: The Man and His Ethics*, N.Y.: Henry Holt and Co., 1931, 1958.

*Lingle, Walter L., *Presbyterians: Their History and Beliefs*, Richmond (Va.): John Knox Press, 1928, 1960.

Anglicanism

*Dawley, Powell M., *Episcopal Church and Its Work*, Greenwich (Conn.): The Seabury Press, 1955, 1961.

*Neill, Stephen C., *Anglicanism*, Harmondsworth (England): Penguin Books.

Congregationalism

An Adventure in Liberty, Boston: Pilgrim Press, 1961.

Walker, Williston, *A History of the Christian Church*, N.Y.: Charles Scribner's Sons, 1934.

Methodism

*McConnell, Frances J., *John Wesley*, N.Y.: Abingdon Press, 1939, 1961.

*Rauschenbusch, Walter, *A Theology for the Social Gospel*, N.Y.: The Macmillan Co., 1917, 1961.

The Baptists

Sweet, William W., *The Baptists*, N.Y.: Henry Holt and Co., 1931.

Torbet, Robert G., *A History of the Baptists*, Philadelphia: Judson Press, 1950.

The Quakers

*Brinton, Howard H., *How They Became Friends*, Wallingford (Pa.): Pendle Hill Press, 1961.

*Van Etten, Henry, *George Fox and the Quakers*, N.Y.: Harper and Brothers, 1959.

Unitarianism

*Bainton, Roland H., *Hunted Heretic: The Life and Death of Michael Servetus*, Boston: Beacon Press, 1960.

*Parke, David L., *Epic of Unitarianism*, Boston: Beacon Press, 1957, 1960.

Christian Science

Bates, Ernest S., *Mary Baker Eddy: The Truth and the Tradition*, N.Y.: A. A. Knopf, 1932.

Braden, Charles S., *Christian Science Today*, Dallas (Tex.): Southern Methodist University Press, 1958.

The Mormons

Bennett, Wallace F., *Why I Am A Mormon*, N.Y.: Thomas Nelson and Sons, 1958.

Howells, Rulon S., *The Mormon Story*, Salt Lake City (Utah): Bookcraft, 1957.

Christian Existentialism

Cochrane, Arthur C., *Existentialists and God*, Philadelphia: Westminster Press, 1959.

*Herberg, Will, *Four Existentialist Theologians*, Garden City (N.Y.): Doubleday and Co., 1958.

Macquarrie, John, *Existentialist Theology*, N.Y.: The Macmillan Co., 1955.

Ecumenical Christianity

Goodall, N., *The Ecumenical Movement*, London: Oxford University Press, 1961.

Lee, Robert, *The Social Sources of Church Unity*, N.Y.: Abingdon-Cokesbury Press, 1960.

*Tavard, George H., *Two Centuries of Ecumenism*, Notre Dame (Ind.) Fides Publishers Association, 1960, 1962.

Chapter 13. ISLAM

*Andrae, Tor, *Mohommed: The Man and His Faith*, N.Y.: Charles Scribner's Sons, 1936, 1960.

Cragg, Kenneth, *The Call of the Minaret*, N.Y.: Oxford University Press, 1956.

*Guillaume, Alfred, *Islam*, Harmondsworth (England): Penguin Books, 1954.

Hakim, Abdul, *Islamic Ideology*, Lahore: Publishers United, Ltd., 1961.

Iqbal, Muhammad, *The Reconstruction of Religious Thought in Islam*, London: Oxford University Press, 1934.

Morgan, Kenneth, *Islam—The Straight Path*, N.Y.: Ronald Press, 1959.

*Von Grunebaum, Gustav E., *Medieval Islam: A Study in Cultural Orientation*, Chicago: University of Chicago Press, 1946, 1954, 1961.

Sufism

Arberry, A. J., *Sufism*, N.Y.: The Macmillan Co., 1950.

Sikhism

Archer, John C., *The Sikhs in Relation to Hindus, Moslems, Christians and Ahmadiyyas*, Princeton: Princeton University Press, 1946.

Bahaism

*Esslemont, J. E., *Bahaulah and the New Era*, Wilmette (Ill.): Baha'i' Publishing Trust, 1928, 1950.

*Ferraby, John, *All Things Made New*, Wilmette (Ill.): Baha'i' Publishing Trust, 1960.

Chapter 14. Humanism

Auer, J. A. C. F., *Humanism States Its Case*, Boston: Beacon Press, 1933.

Brownell, Baker, *Earth is Enough*, N.Y.: Harper and Brothers, 1933.

*Dewey, John, *Reconstruction in Philosophy*, N.Y.: Henry Holt and Co., 1920, 1948, 1950.

*Dewey, John, *A Common Faith*, New Haven: Yale University Press, 1934, 1960.

Huxley, Julian S., *The Humanist Frame*, N.Y.: Harper and Brothers, 1962.

*Huxley, Julian S., *Religion Without Revelation*, N.Y.: New American Library, (1927) 1959.

Kallan, Horace, *Secularism is the Will of God*, N.Y.: Twayne Publishers, 1955.

*Lamont, Corliss, *Humanism as a Philosophy (The Philosophy of Humanism)*, N.Y.: The Philosophical Library, 1949, 1957.

Morain, Lloyd and Mary, *Humanism as the Next Step*, Boston: Beacon Press, 1954.

*Otto, Max, *Science and the Moral Life*, N.Y.: New American Library, 1949.

*Smith, Thomas V., *Live Without Fear*, N.Y.: New American Library, 1956.

CONCLUSION

Chapter 15. WORLD RELIGIONS AND WORLD RELIGION

Barrows, John H., *World Parliament of Religions*, Chicago, 1893.

Cranston, Ruth, *World Faiths: The Study of the Religions of the United Nations*, N.Y.: Harper and Brothers, 1949.

Northrop, F. S. C., *Ideological Differences and World Order*, New Haven: Yale University Press, 1946.

*Northrop, F. S. C., *The Meeting of East and West*, N.Y.: The Macmillan Co., 1946, 1960.

Northrop, F. S. C., *The Taming of the Nations*, N.Y.: The Macmillan Co., 1952.

Raju, P. T., and S. Radhakrishnan, *The Concept of Man, A Study in Comparative Philosophy*, London: George Allen and Unwin, Lincoln (Neb.): Johnson Publishing Co., 1960.

Raju, P. T., *Introduction to Comparative Philosophy*, Lincoln: University of Nebraska Press, 1962.

World Fellowship of Faiths, N.Y.: Liveright Publishing Corporation, 1935.

Index